Word Become Flesh

Dimensions of Christology

Brian O. McDermott, S.J.

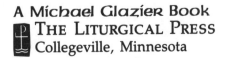

A Michael Glazier Book
THE LITURGICAL PRESS
Collegeville, Minnesota

NEW THEOLOGY STUDIES

General Editor: Peter C. Phan

*

Editorial Consultants:
Monika Hellwig
Robert Imbelli
Robert Schreiter

*

Volume 9: Word Become Flesh: Dimensions of Christology

A Michael Glazier Book published by The Liturgical Press

Cover design by David Manahan, O.S.B.

6	7	8	9

Library of Congress Cataloging-in-Publication Data

McDermott, Brian O.
    Word become flesh : dimensions of Christology / Brian O. McDermott.
      p.   cm. — (New theology studies : v. 9)
    "A Michael Glazier book."
    Includes bibliographical references and index.
    ISBN 0-8146-5015-5
    1. Catholic Church—Doctrines.   2. Jesus Christ—Person and offices.
I. Title. II. Series.
BT202.M39434   1993
232'.8—dc20

                                      92-34915
                                          CIP

In grateful remembrance of my three parents:
Alice, Jack, and Noël

Contents

Editor's Preface

This series entitled *New Theology Studies*, composed of eight volumes, is an attempt to answer the need felt by professors and students alike for scholarly yet readable books dealing with certain Catholic beliefs traditionally associated with dogmatic theology. The volumes treat of fundamental theology (revelation, the nature and method of theology, the credibility of the Christian faith), trinitarian theology, christology, ecclesiology, anthropology, and eschatology.

There has been, of course, no lack of books, published singly or in series, both in this continent and elsewhere, which are concerned with these central truths of Christianity. Nevertheless, there is room, we believe, for yet another series of texts on systematic theology, not because these offer entirely novel insights into the aforementioned teachings, but because it is incumbent upon Christians of every age to reflect upon their faith in light of their cultural and religious experiences and to articulate their understanding in terms accessible to their contemporaries.

Theology is traditionally described as faith in search of understanding, *fides quaerens intellectum*. The faith to which the contributors to this series are committed is the Christian faith as lived and taught by the (Roman) Catholic Church. It is, however, a faith that is ecumenically sensitive, open to ways of living and thinking practiced by other Christian communities and other religions. The understanding which the series seeks to foster goes beyond an accumulation of information, however interesting, on the Christian past to retrieve and renew, by means of the analogical imagination, the Christian Tradition embodied in its various classics. In this way, it is hoped, one can understand afresh both the meaning and the truth of the Christian beliefs and their multiple interconnections. Lastly, the contributors are convinced that theology is a never-ending quest for insights into faith, a *cogitatio fidei.* Its ultimate purpose is not to provide definite and definitive answers to every conceivable problem posed by faith, but to gain an understanding, which will always be imperfect and fragmentary, of its subject, God the incomprehensible Mystery. Thus, theology remains an essentially unfinished business, to be taken up over and again in light of and in confrontation with the challenges found in every age. And our age is no exception, when, to cite only two examples, massive poverty and injustice structured into the present economic order, and the unprecedented meeting of religious faiths in new contexts of dialogue, have impelled theologians to reconceptualize the Christian faith in radical terms.

Contrary to some recent series of textbooks, *New Theology Studies* does not intend to advocate and advance a uniform or even unified viewpoint. Contributors are left free to present their own understanding and approach to the subject matter assigned to them. They are only requested to treat their themes in an integrating manner by situating them in the context of Tradition (highlighting their biblical, patristic, medieval, and modern developments), by expounding their theological meaning and function in light of current pronouncements of the Magisterium, by exploring their implications for Christian living, and by indicating possible different contemporary conceptualizations for these doctrines. The goal is to achieve some measure of comprehensiveness and balance by taking into account all the important issues of the subject matter under discussion and at the same time exhibit some thematic unity by means of a consistent method and a unifying perspective.

The eight volumes are intended primarily as resource books, "launching and landing bases," for upper-division theology courses in Catholic colleges and seminaries, but it is hoped that they will be useful also to people—priests, permanent deacons, religious, and educated laity, inside and outside of the Roman Catholic communion—interested in understanding the Christian faith in contemporary cultural and ecclesial contexts. We hope that these volumes will make a contribution, however modest, to the intellectual and spiritual life of the Christian Church as it prepares to enter its third millennium.

Peter C. Phan
The Catholic University of America

Preface

Christology never stands still. Even the most cursory view of its history discloses as much. But the last twenty-five years have witnessed a mushrooming of interest in, and writing about, the topic that is nothing short of extraordinary. It is not that specialists have narrowed down the areas of exploration and used their skills to engage in Christological "piecework." Rather, the most fundamental questions are at issue: the divinity of Jesus; his relationship to Judaism; his significance in the light of Christians' encounter with other world religions; the challenge from feminists; Jesus' (and Christianity's) capacity to do justice to the cry of the poor and the oppressed, particularly in the Third World. The challenges are immense, and they show up in Christology because they are nothing less than the impact of the struggles and concerns of our times and cultures on those reflective Christian believers called theologians.

This particular exploration of Christology is the fruit of several intersecting currents: seventeen years of teaching Christology at Weston School of Theology; a year-long sabbatical after leaving office as religious superior of the Weston Jesuit Community; and finally, a providentially-timed invitation from Mr. Michael Glazier to write the Christology volume for this *New Theology Studies*. One more book in Christology can be justified if it addresses the needs of a sufficient audience. Time will tell if such is the case.

Basically, the book seeks to achieve some of the major objectives of a basic course in Christology: to orient the student in the area of theology by tracing the principal developments in the New Testament and in later Church tradition, and by giving attention to some of the principal concerns of contemporary culture and the way some of the present-day types of Christology try to respond to those concerns. Thus I decided to offer

13

a range of contemporary Christological proposals rather than one to the exclusion of others. I sought as well to give more attention to soteriology than often happens in traditional Christology; the separation of consideration of Christ's "person" from that of his "work" was a most unfortunate divorce, and certainly foreign to the New Testament.

A major challenge to North American theology is the call to develop a liberationist theology and spirituality that does not simply mimic other varieties of liberationist thought but that stays close to the peculiarities of our own scene. One of the possible avenues that intrigues me is the development of a dynamic notion of representation (a notion that, as I suggest later on, is central to Christology) in connection with contemporary research on how groups and institutions function on both the conscious and unconscious level. This line of thought would concern itself with the Church but also to the public (social, political, and economic) dimensions of life in North America in their relationship to other parts of the globe. But that is a project that moves beyond the modest intentions of this present work.

I want to thank all my students at Weston, in the other schools of the Boston Theological Institute, and at various summer schools and workshops over the years who have challenged me and taught me. I want to thank James Crampsey, S.J., of Heythrop College, London, for his critical reading of the New Testament material, and Ms. Liza Burr for her careful editorial help. I wish to acknowledge as well the Lilly Endowment for helping to make that editorial help possible, and the Maryland Province of the Society of Jesus for offering me the opportunity of a sabbatical leave during the 1988–89 academic year.

1

Introducing Christology

Christian life takes its name from Jesus Christ. If there is anything distinctive about Christian identity, or anything specific about Christian thought and activity, it is the relationship to that person of two thousand years ago whom his followers confess as alive and powerfully active in our time as the Risen Lord.

Christology is the word about Jesus, the Word of God: orderly speech (*logos*) about the Christ or "anointed One" of God. Of all the areas of Christian theology, Christology considers what is most specific and distinctive about Christianity: its appeal to Jesus Christ as the way to the depths of God and to the most authentic and hope-filled relationships with other human beings and with our planet earth.

There are, to be sure, many words addressed to and spoken about him. The Eucharist, as the Church's central act of worship, has a primacy here. Every Sunday in churches around the globe Christ is praised and thanked and worshiped to the glory of God, from a *favela* in Rio de Janeiro to Saint Peter's in Vatican City. In Eucharistic celebration the community of believers lets itself be gathered by the proclaimed Word, the Word that is filled with the life and light of Christ's Spirit. Then that community lets itself become a self-offering to God, included within the self-offering of Christ on the cross which, thanks to the resurrection, continues in the heavenly liturgy in which the pilgrim Church participates. The Church's obedience to the injunction "Do this in memory of me" from Christ's Last Supper with his disciples becomes, in the gracious power of the Holy Spirit, the Eucharistic commemorative act that spans the centuries and the cultures of this world. The Eucharist has been celebrated in times of famine and plenty, in the presence of tyrants and saints, in hope of liberation or as false balm on guilty consciences. All kinds of circumstances and needs have occasioned, all possible respect and disrespect has colored, its celebration. Placed in the hands of sinners and saints, the Eucharist is essentially Christ's action in the world, with room enough for all sinners and all saints, for every time and season, for every mood of hope or despair. Whenever the Word who is Christ touches that saint, that sinner, that season, that mood or need, there exists the chance that they may be lured into the flow of his relation to God, the fount of all life, in the action of the persuasive Spirit.

The presence of Christ is in no wise restricted. Thanks to the resurrection, Christ relates to the world in a boundless way. As Vatican II also taught, the aspirations and hopes of all humankind for genuine security, for lasting peace, for the protection and fostering of human dignity and rights, for genuine community among peoples, for proper use of and respect for the environment, are all signs of the action of Christ's Holy Spirit in our world.[1] Nothing human is foreign to Christ and to his Spirit. All efforts to serve humankind without making of it an idol, all struggles to bring about authentic justice and peace, all strategies of liberation and emancipation that truly intend the good of humankind, however provisional and revisable they may be, all bear for Christians the sign of Christ, a word about Christ and a word or appeal from Christ. Unlike the Eucharistic action, these struggles and efforts are very often not explicit words about Christ or words addressed to him. Indeed, the struggle may be against a destructive collusion between certain Church leaders and political leaders who are oppressing the people, and the protest against such collusion may take the form of an attack on Christ or Christianity: Christ against "Christ." Vatican II made the point that certain forms of atheism, when they do not fall into idolatry, i.e., the absolutizing of a finite, relative reality, can be bearers of grace insofar as they are protesting against false gods entertained by "religious" people. Just as Isaiah called the pagan king Cyrus "God's anointed" because he freed the people of Judah from their captivity to the Babylonians (Isa 45:1), so too atheists may perform this work of purification that serves God's humanizing reign.

The Word addressed to believers by Christ, the words addressed by them to him are, therefore, many: from the most ecclesial to the most profane, the most sacramental to the most implicit, the most conciliatory to the most conflictual and controversial.

Among all these words, Christology offers its own. Although the word of worship spoken to Christ and the word of loving service that speaks of Christ are the primary words—living Christology, if you will—there

---

1. *Gaudium et spes,* "Pastoral Constitution on the Church in the Modern World," in W. M. Abbott and J. Gallagher, *The Documents of Vatican II* (New York: American Press, 1967), chs. 2 and 3, 222–38.

is also that word, that orderly sequence of words, which again and again attempts to "give an account of the hope that is in us" Christians (1 Pet 3:15).[2]

Christology is the reasoned account of Christians' faith in Jesus of Nazareth as the Christ of God. Using the famous words of Anselm of Canterbury (d. 1109), Christology seeks to serve faith by seeking to understand it (*fides quaerens intellectum*: faith seeking understanding), so that by understanding their faith more and more Christians might enter into it more deeply and more responsibly, increasing their ability to relate it to more and more dimensions of their lives: the personal, interpersonal and societal, cultural, and political.

Christology is about Jesus as the Christ. Thus it focuses on a particular individual who lived a quite restricted life in Palestine two thousand years ago. Not human nature as such, or a people as such, but first of all a singular *who*, a someone named Jesus from a small town in Galilee, is the object of its interest.

But Christology views Jesus in his context, too. He is of the Jewish people and embedded in their history of covenant and betrayal, joy and suffering, longing and memories. In fact, Christians proclaim him the Christ—which means "anointed one," one who has been appointed to a public function or role. Christians therefore view Jesus against the horizon of expectation in Judaism, asserting that he is the fulfillment of that expectation; thus a particular people with its history and its traditions forms part of Christology. Efforts to separate Jesus from his Jewishness, efforts that scholars have attempted time and again by portraying him as the fulfillment of Jewish hopes but not really belonging to the Judaism contemporary with him, are really at best ahistorical and at worst anti-Semitic treatments of this man from Nazareth.

But there is more. Christology explores the meaning of Jesus of Nazareth as the Christ *of God*. And so Jesus the single individual relates not only to a particular people's hopes and longings but to all of reality and to the ultimate ground of that reality, the living God, source of all and the power over and through all. Christology thus has to do with the meaning of all of life, of all peoples, of all individuals, because Christianity affirms that Jesus is related to, indeed identified with, God and the divine purpose in all of nature and history. There will be room in Christology for both narrative and philosophy, for (detailed) story and (ultimate) structures, for the unrepeatable event and the recurrent pattern. Both story (of Jesus' life and death, of the people of Israel, of the Church's life in Christ's Spirit) and philosophy (of being, of person, of natures, of knowledge and freedom) are meant to serve, as all theology must serve, the pri-

---

2. All scriptural quotations are from the Revised Standard Version.

mary words addressed to and about Christ, the word that is worship and the word that is loving service of one's brothers and sisters in Christ's name.

Types of Theology

There have been many kinds of Christology in the life of the Church, for there have been many kinds of theology, and the previous section already touches on several of them. It would be helpful early on in our exploration to consider three of the principal types of theology available today in terms of their dominant concern and principal (but not necessarily exclusive) starting-point and source of nourishment.

The first type approaches matters in a manner that is primarily *academic* and *intellectual*, and school, as the place in which scholars and clergy are educated, shapes its concerns and starting-point and sources of nourishment. This theology deals with texts primarily, whether they be the texts of the Scripture, the texts of the dogmatic tradition of the Church, and/or the texts of earlier or contemporary theologians. The primary purpose of this kind of Christology is the discovery or further exploration of the *truth* of what is believed by the Church and individual Christian believers. The scholastic (i.e., school-oriented) theologies of the High Middle Ages, such as Thomas Aquinas', would be an excellent example of this type of theology and Christology. The nineteenth and twentieth century neo-scholastic theologies would be recent Catholic versions of this same kind of theology and Christology.[3] In the latter instance seminary education provided the context for the particular kind of theology offered. On the contemporary scene an example of this kind of theology would be that of Wolfhart Pannenberg, a German thinker whose background is Lutheran but who is developing a more post-denominational kind of theology.[4] In many ways Pannenberg is addressing the university with his theology, seeking to show how the understandings opened up by healthy, critical theology can helpfully connect with the deeper concerns of the natural and human sciences. Intellectual coherence is a very compelling value and goal for a theologian such as this Munich professor.

A second type of theology finds its starting point in the Church's *worship* and in the many forms in which Christians directly engage the mystery of God and Christ in their public and personal lives. Theology in this form is mystagogical in purpose, that is, it seeks to lead the student into

3. G. A. McCool, *Catholic Theology in the Nineteenth Century: A Search for a Unitary Method* (New York: Seabury, 1977).

4. W. Pannenberg, *Theology and the Philosophy of Science*, trans. F. McDonagh (Philadelphia: Westminster, 1976).

the living mystery of God and its transforming power. Truth is deeply cherished here, but transforming love is valued and pursued even more, and love here is, first and last, love of God, in which love of neighbor is the essential implication or corollary. The patristic tradition (i.e., the Church Fathers and Mothers who wrote in the first six centuries) were intent on leading people into the gracious Mystery, even while they were eager to engage in polemics with other theologians or Church leaders if they felt that orthodoxy was threatened.[5] The monastic tradition, from the Desert Fathers and Mothers and the Benedictine family down to our own century, consistently develop theology (and Christology) as a *lectio* (reading of texts) that leads to *meditatio* (meditation on the meaning of the text) and then to the goal of *oratio* (prayer) in which heart speaks to Heart.[6] The Reformers in the sixteenth century (Martin Luther being a prime example) wrote a theology that was meant to be preached, so that believers would be challenged by God's Word to choose God's justification of them and to surrender their own self-justifying efforts.[7] In our day theologians such as Karl Rahner and Frans Jozef van Beeck manifest a mystagogical concern and continually remind the reader that the full point of theology and Christology comes to expression only in the act of worship and surrender, however much we might want to substitute something less "all-consuming" as the final norm of theological validity.[8]

In addition to school-oriented theology intent on discovery of academically expressed truth and theology grounded in worship and seeking transformation by love we encounter a third kind of theology, one which gives pride of place to praxis, or, in other words, a combination of action-influenced theory and informed practice bent on the transformation of oppressive social structures. Transforming love and critical theory are held together in this approach, but horizontal love—love of neighbor—is the way knowledge and love of God is authenticated and manifested in history. Academic theology and Christian worship can function in these theologians as objects of suspicion at least as much as sources of inspiration. This kind of theology did not begin in the late twentieth century. The patristic period included many writers who criticized the social injustice of their

5. P. Phan, *Message of the Fathers of the Church* 15: *Grace and the Human Condition* (Wilmington, Del.: Michael Glazier, 1988).

6. J. Leclercq, *The Love of Learning and the Desire for God: A Study of Monastic Culture*, trans. C. Misrahi (New York: Fordham University Press, 1961).

7. J. Wicks, *Luther and His Spiritual Legacy* (Wilmington, Del.: Michael Glazier, 1983); L. Richard, *The Spirituality of John Calvin* (Atlanta: John Knox, 1974).

8. J. J. Bacik, *Apologetics and the Eclipse of Mystery: Mystagogy According to Karl Rahner* (Notre Dame, Ind., and London: University of Notre Dame Press, 1980); F. J. van Beeck, *Christ Proclaimed: Christology as Rhetoric* (New York: Ramsey and Toronto, 1979). See also G. Wainwright, *Doxology: The Praise of God in Worship, Doctrine, and Life: A Systematic Theology* (New York: Oxford University Press, 1980).

time, using the forms of knowledge and theory available to them at the time. With the differentiations of consciousness represented by the social sciences our contemporaries are able to bring to theology a level of social analysis impossible in an earlier age. Thus the political theology of a Johann Baptist Metz and the Latin American liberation theology of a Gustavo Gutiérrez represent a way of theologizing that concerns itself with change of structures through critical theory and transforming praxis.[9] Theologians such as these eschew ideas for their own sake or worship that is not tested by deeds of love on behalf of the marginated, the "other," in one's midst.

After this brief survey of types of theology a word of caution is in order. Such an overview can only treat some "family" traits and does not do justice to the concrete theologies that might fall within one type or other. Truth, the transforming love of God, and love of neighbor through change of social structures do not exclude each other; indeed, they require each other. Any Christian theology worthy of the name will concern itself with each dimension. But the differing needs of regional churches and "signs of the times" (Vatican II) will dictate that the center of gravity and nourishing sources of a specific theology will be more academic, more worship-oriented, or more geared to institutional reforms.

The Jesus of History and the Christ of Faith

No matter what type of modern Christology one is studying, it will be shaped by concerns proper to modernity, and in particular the modern sensitivity to history. The Enlightenment developed this sensitivity by reclaiming human rationality as a critical function with respect to all inherited traditions, whether religious or political and cultural. The new humanism, which was part of the Enlightenment's genius, saw the human as the measure of all things. At the same time there arose the beginnings of modern historical science, a concern to determine the true nature of the past so that its claims on the present could be adjudicated.

A critical passage into theological modernity was made when Gotthold Ephraim Lessing (d. 1781) published some writings of Hermann Samuel Reimarus (d. 1768), a professor of oriental languages at the University of Hamburg. Reimarus had written a critical study of the New Testament which, because of its controversial nature, he had attributed pseudonymously to a certain Wolfenbüttel; thus the writings became known as the "Wolfenbüttel Fragments."[10] Reimarus began the fateful separation of

---

9. J. B. Metz, *Faith in History and Society: Toward a Practical Fundamental Theology*, trans. D. Smith (New York: Seabury, 1980); G. Gutiérrez, *Theology of Liberation*, trans. and ed. C. Inda and J. Eagleson (Maryknoll, New York: Orbis, 1988).

10. *Reimarus: Fragments*, ed. C. H. Talbert, trans. R. S. Fraser (Philadelphia: Fortress, 1970).

the historical Jesus and the Christ of the Church. Jesus was a moral teacher not given to mysterious matters of faith. He was completely this-worldly in his intentions, preaching a kingdom of God that was political, public and historical. Because this kingdom failed to materialize, the apostles, to save matters, developed the doctrine of a spiritual kingdom that was not of this world.

Once they were published, Reimarus' views stirred up many of his German theological colleagues. Some argued that Jesus and the apostles did not really differ in their basic doctrines, but that the this-worldly and the other-worldly ways of speaking about God's kingdom were different ways of expressing the doctrine of salvation to different audiences, the Jewish and the Gentile.

In the wake of Georg Wilhelm Friedrich Hegel's idealistic philosophy, David Friedrich Strauss published an extensive life of Jesus.[11] Strauss posited an authentic historical core to Jesus' teaching in affirming that Jesus was clear about being the Christ and openly taught that fact. But around the historical core there developed what Strauss called myth, an idealizing portrait of the Messiah figure which was the product of human reason in its quest for wholeness and totality. Thus Strauss introduced a split between Jesus as we can know him through publicly verifiable means (arriving at the "historical core"), and Christ as the product of human reason or cultural ideals or interior faith-conviction. Jesus as known by history was true but not meaningful, while the Christ-myth was profoundly meaningful though rationally, not historically, grounded.

Friedrich Schleiermacher sought to root Christian faith in human consciousness. Unlike Strauss, however, he did not root it in human reason as an idealizing faculty, but in human consciousness in its immediate awareness (*Gefühl*: "feeling") of absolute dependence. Jesus is known as the Christ through Christians' recognition of the effect of Christ on conscious life.[12]

Other theologians sought to ground faith in Jesus in terms of his inner psychological states. Since the New Testament communicates very little about them, these authors were forced to project onto Jesus those states of mind and emotion which were considered the most exalted and worthy by the Western European world of the nineteenth century. In the famous image of the great historiographer of that period, Albert Schweitzer: they looked down the well and saw the reflection of their own mind.[13] For

11. D. F. Strauss, *The Christ of Faith and the Jesus of History: A Critique of Schleiermacher's Life of Jesus*, ed. L. Keck (Philadelphia: Fortress, 1977).

12. F. Schleiermacher, *The Christian Faith*, ed. H. R. MacIntosh and J. S. Stewart (New York: Harper and Row, 1963).

13. A. Schweitzer, *The Quest of the Historical Jesus: A Critical Study of its Progress from Reimarus to Wrede*, trans. W. Montgomery (New York: Macmillan, 1964).

Schweitzer himself, Jesus was a thoroughly alien figure of two thousand years ago who preached an impending final cataclysm—the eschatological woes—through which God's reign would be inaugurated. Jesus taught at best an interim ethic for the brief period preceding the end of the age, but he was in no way a liberal, moralizing teacher who would fit comfortably into the nineteenth-century scheme of things. The reign of God would come about by God's powerful act and not the cumulative efforts of well-meaning human beings. In the famous conclusion to *The Quest of the Historical Jesus*, Schweitzer summarized:

> The study of the Life of Jesus has had a curious history. It set out in quest of the historical Jesus, believing that when it had found Him it could bring Him straight into our time as a Teacher and Savior. It loosed the bands by which He had been riveted for centuries to the stony rocks of ecclesiastical doctrine, and rejoiced to see life and movement coming into the figure once more, and the historical Jesus advancing, as it seemed, to meet it. But He does not stay; He passes by our time and returns to His own.[14]

In 1892 Martin Kähler published *The So-Called Historical Jesus and the Historic, Biblical Christ*.[15] By his distinction between *historisch* (historical) and *geschichtlich* (historic) Kähler sought to rescue Christ from the toils of empirical, historical research and restore him to the preaching of the Church where alone, he believed, the authentic, historic, Christ could be encountered in a saving way. The historicity (*Geschichtlichkeit*) of Christ consisted in his availability for encounter in faith, and the reconstruction of a Jesus of history did not create a personal presence who could do anyone any good, certainly not for everlasting life.

Johannes Weiss (d. 1914) argued that eschatology (i.e., awareness of, and concern about, the end of history) pervades the New Testament writings and that this eschatology is completely futuristic or "consistent," a proposal which had the effect for him and many of his contemporaries of making those writings very alien documents, and certainly contributed to the demise of liberal Protestant theology.[16] Wilhelm Wrede (d. 1906) proposed the famous "messianic secret" as a way of understanding Mark and the other Gospels as well. According to Wrede, Jesus never claimed to be the Messiah and his disciples did not think he was such during his earthly ministry. To square this state of affairs with the early Church's faith in Jesus as Messiah, Mark, followed by the other evangelists, por-

---

14. Ibid., 399.

15. M. Kähler, *The So-Called Historical Jesus and the Historic, Biblical Christ*, trans. C. Braatan (Philadelphia: Fortress, 1964).

16. J. Weiss, *Jesus' Proclamation of the Kingdom of God*, ed. R. H. Hiers and D. L. Holland (Philadelphia: Fortress, 1971).

trayed Jesus as regularly commanding his disciples to silence about his true identity during his earthly ministry.[17]

In his great work *Church Dogmatics*, Karl Barth refused to base faith on human reason or human experiences.[18] Faith alone is saving, and faith is the work of Jesus Christ in the Spirit in the hearts of those to be justified, i.e., those who will share in Christ's righteousness. Barth's work represents a profoundly Christocentric theology.

Rudolf Bultmann, a major twentieth-century historian of early Christianity, made use of the early philosophical writings of Martin Heidegger to develop an existentialist understanding of Christian faith.[19] While Bultmann as an historian was able to say some substantial things about the earthly Jesus, as a theologian he considered the historical Jesus to be part of Jewish religious history. The preached Christ of the cross is to be distinguished from the historical Jesus, since the former alone is the one who is full of saving power for those who are obedient in faith to him. The preached Word draws its hearers into authentic existence, liberated from the false past of idols and deceitful securities and opened up to God's future. Bultmann urged a full-scale program of demythologization of the good news, so that the true scandal of the preached Cross would not be obscured by the preaching of an outmoded conception of the world of the first century after Christ. Although Bultmann and Barth disagreed strongly about a number of issues, they both agreed that seeking to base faith on historical research was just another form of works righteousness, the effort to save oneself by one's own means rather than seeking salvation through faith in the grace of God's Word alone: *sola fide, sola gratia, solus Christus* (by faith alone and grace alone, Christ alone saves us).

Rudolf Bultmann's influence on contemporary theology has taken many forms. One of these has been the reaction of some of his students to his conviction that historical-Jesus research was not theologically relevant. In 1953 a former student of Bultmann, Ernst Käsemann, gave an inaugural lecture at the University of Marburg entitled "The Problem of the Historical Jesus."[20] In this lecture he argued that the historical Jesus was indeed significant, and that on several counts. First of all, the kerygma (or faith-proclamation of the New Testament) contains internal reference to the pre-Easter Jesus as the one who stands at the center of the once-and-for-all eschatological event of salvation, and thus historical research into that

17. W. Wrede, *The Messianic Secret*, trans. J. Greig (Cambridge: J. Clarke, 1971).

18. K. Barth, *Church Dogmatics vol. 1: The Doctrine of the Word of God, Part 2*, ed. G. W. Bromiley and T. F. Torrance (Edinburgh: T. and T. Clarke, 1975) 187–227.

19. R. Bultmann, *Existence and Faith: Shorter Writings of Rudolf Bultmann*, ed. S. Ogden (Cleveland: World, 1968).

20. E. Käsemann, "The Problem of the Historical Jesus," *Essays in New Testament Themes* (Philadelphia: Fortress, 1982) 15–47.

figure is required by the nature of the kerygma itself. Second, a principal way by which the Church can protect itself against the recurrent temptation to docetism (i.e, the view that Christ only "seemed" to be human) is to anchor its preaching in the life and ministry of the pre-Easter Jesus insofar as he is recoverable by historical-critical means. The Church's affirmation of the identity of the Easter Christ with the pre-Easter Jesus means that the universal has occurred in the particularities of the past, and we know the past through historical science. Third, by not exploring what we can indeed know about the Jesus of then, we allow Christ to become a kind of blank screen onto which Christians and others can project their own desires and attitudes and values, without any "objective" challenge from that figure of the past who was not every kind of person with every kind of intention but rather a single individual who did and said specific things with specific intentions within a particular and unrepeatable historical era.

Käsemann's programmatic lecture spawned a host of efforts to reclaim historical Jesus research for theology. The general view, shared by him, has been that such research cannot have the function of legitimating the kerygma or the Church's faith, but that it can protect the Church's proclamation from distortion; moreover, the inclusion of historical data in the theological study of Jesus Christ bears witness in its own way to the particularity of Christ and Christianity and to the fact, all-important for Christian faith, that God's salvation has come and does come to history through history.

Historical research deals with a range of probabilities. It is essentially dependent on testimony, principally in the form of written records, but includes archeological evidence as well: artifacts, architecture, and so forth. Absolute certainty is never the result of historical research, for in principle the testimony is different from the reality testified to, and one comes to know the past only through its own history of interpretations as they are recovered by historians and other scholars dealing with the past. Through such research one builds up an image of the past, to some extent like a hypothesis, letting details fill in or challenge the larger picture and allowing the larger picture to help make sense of the details. This interpretive mutual dependence of the part on the whole and the whole on the part is intrinsic to all human understanding, but never more so than in the historical reconstruction of the past.

Contemporary theory of interpretation (or hermeneutics) has made it quite clear that no return to the past is made without prejudice, that is, without prejudgments. Rudolf Bultmann spoke of the hermeneutical circle in which we go to a text of the past with our own questions and concerns and "subject" the text to what we bring to it, seeking thereby to shed light on it. Completing the circle, we must go to the text with as clear an awareness of these prejudgments as possible so that we can listen to the text as "other" than our questions and concerns, as capable of addressing us and shedding light on our situation. Hans-Georg Gadamer has explored the positive role of bias or prejudgement, and contributed the insight that interpretation involves a critically conscious melding of the horizons of text and interpreter.[21]

The main concern of the interpreter, writes Paul Ricoeur, is not to discover the intention of the author hidden behind the text. Rather, the interpreter needs to become sensitively attuned to the world opened up in front of the text as a set of patterns of being-in-the-world which he or she is invited critically and compassionately to experiment with. Interpretation is like a conversation that involves give-and-take between text and interpreter, each contribution of a partner affecting both the other partner and the conversation as such.[22]

Recently certain exegetes and theologians, both Catholic and Protestant, have proposed that the historical Jesus, the pre-Easter Jesus, was and is *in principle* capable of grounding Christian faith. They do not mean by this that the reconstructions of historical research themselves do have this grounding function, but that the person Jesus was in his earthly life is sufficient warrant for faith. They leave room for the possibility that the resurrection may have been psychologically required for the arousal of faith, given the disciples' state of mind at the time of Jesus' execution. These scholars are reacting to a view which sees the resurrection as compensating for a purported revelational deficiency in the pre-Easter Jesus.[23]

Edward Schillebeeckx in his important work *Jesus: An Experiment in Christology* makes historical research an integral part of the Christological task, and does so with impressive detail. Historical study cannot prove the truth of the faith; on this point he is very clear. But he stresses the claim of the pre-Easter Jesus, his manner of life and ministry, as that to which the disciples return in memory, after Jesus' death, under the impulse of grace and the experience of forgiveness. There is the strongest desire on this theologian's part to rob nothing from the historical Jesus in favor of a revelatory event after his life and ministry which would allegedly supply what was hitherto missing, namely, revelation and its convincing power.[24]

21. H.-G. Gadamer, *Truth and Method*, trans. and ed. G. Barden and J. Cumming (New York: Crossroad, 1986) 267–74.

22. See D. Tracy, *The Analogical Imagination: Christian Theology and the Culture of Pluralism* (New York: Crossroad, 1981); idem., *Plurality and Ambiguity: Hermeneutics, Religion, Hope* (San Francisco: Harper and Row, 1987).

23. See J. Galvin, "The Origin of Faith in the Resurrection of Jesus: Two Recent Perspectives" *Theological Studies* 49 (1988) 25–44.

24. E. Schillebeeckx, *Jesus: An Experiment in Christology*, trans. H. Hoskins (New York: Seabury, 1979).

Wolfhart Pannenberg stands out as a major contemporary Protestant theologian who has given history a privileged role in his Christology. Not only does he incorporate the results of historical criticism into his portrayal of Christ, particularly with regard to Jesus' claims and implicit self-understanding, but he develops a philosophy of history and hermeneutics that sees historians as anticipating an all-inclusive totality within which the details make sense. This anticipated totality must be historical but must also embrace all history. Moreover, the full meaning of history can only be derived from its end or goal. Yet this end is still outstanding, and so history's full meaning is in no wise disclosed. Pannenberg maintains that the end of history and its anticipated totality have occurred as an event that is both within history and beyond, therefore embracing, history. This event was the resurrection of Jesus of Nazareth, an event which occurred within the apocalyptic horizon of understanding and which was the pre-happening of the end of history in a way that was already and not yet.[25]

Thus, according to Pannenberg, historians ought to be open to the claims of Christianity because the anticipatory structure of dynamic historical reason finds its fulfillment in the resurrection of Jesus. Pannenberg would admit that the historians who would be most likely to see this congruence between Christianity and the dynamism of historical reason would be Christian historians or, better, Christian philosophers of history. But he is not asserting, as some have thought, that one can prove the resur-[...] empirical way; his argument is more nuanced. Only within [...] of the hermeneutical and philosophical perspectives on the [...] rical reason does his presentation of the "historicity" of [...] n attain, for him, its meaningfulness and its truth as that context which historical reason seeks in all its explorations.

Many of these attempts to do justice to historical questions and findings in Christology have been summarized as efforts to develop a "Christology from below" or "ascent-Christology" as distinct from a "Christology from above" or "descent-Christology." The former begins with the historical Jesus of the ministry and traces the growth of faith in him through his life, death and resurrection. The latter takes John 1:14 as its guiding text and makes the central focus God's initiative in sending the Word incarnate among us for our salvation. "Christology from above" is often associated, as well, with the doctrine of the immanent Trinity, that is, the inner life of God as Father, Word and Spirit, which becomes "economic" in the divine self-communication to creation. For this writer

---

25. W. Pannenberg, "The Revelation of God in Jesus of Nazareth," *Theology as History*, ed. J. Robinson and J. Cobb (New York: Harper and Row, 1967). Apocalyptic literature was a Jewish form of protest literature. It gave expression to a longing for God's final act of salvation which would bring the "present evil age" to a close and inaugurate a totally "new age" in which the just would be vindicated and the oppressors punished.

the choice to be made is not for one of these approaches to the exclusion of the other, but the choice of the rightful way of relating the concerns appropriate to historical critical reason to the conviction that arises from Christian worship and service that in the ministry, death, and resurrection of Jesus we encounter the wondrously generous initiatives of a loving God on behalf of a broken world.

Let us step back for a moment from this review and consider the situation of the ordinary Christian in relation to the problem of faith and history.

As Christians grow up in the Church, they form a mental image of Christ. Their image may be very indistinct and, one hopes, undergoes many changes as they mature. It is a mixture, comprising pieces of the gospel accounts, things said or written about Christ by others, and their own experiences of Christ in their own lives, as well as their ideas about what it would be like to be the "authentic human being" and the Son of God incarnate. This image may well contain historical reminiscences of the pre-Easter Jesus insofar as the pieces of gospel accounts that enter into it reflect authentic Jesus-material.[26]

Now the relationship of ordinary Christians (or even extraordinary Christians, for that matter!) to Christ is not reducible to that mental image, however true or untrue to Jesus-as-he-was it may be. Christians are bonded to Christ by the Holy Spirit at work in their hearts, and this relationship is imageless; it is, as the tradition puts it, *apophatic*. What is the connection between these two dimensions of the Christian's relationship to Christ?

On the one hand, we have to say that Christians are not saved by virtue of the Christ-image present in their minds. They are saved on the basis of their faithfulness to grace in their lives as that grace is lived out in loving service to their neighbor and in surrender to the living God. On the other hand, the Christ-image can have an immense impact on the way Christians live out their lives as disciples of Christ. It matters immensely which Christ they are following. For example, is he a Christ who reaches out to those who are different from himself with genuine hospitality, or does he remain with his own kind? Is he someone who was miraculously born among Jews but was not a Jew himself, so that allegiance to him can be used to warrant persecution of Jews, as has happened time and again in the history of Christianity? Is he a Jesus who had time for everything and everyone, thus making more finite Christians feel perpetually guilty because they must be selective in their loves and commitments, or is he someone who had to focus his attention on some at the expense of others, thus showing us that the commandment of universal love must

---

26. V. Harvey, *The Historian and the Believer: The Morality of Historical Knowledge and Christian Belief* (New York: Macmillan, 1966).

be lived out in very particular ways with only a finite amount of energy and resources?[27]

One of the great temptations, regarding our relationship to Christ, is to make of him simply a symbol for certain values deemed most important by a group or individual at a given moment in history. Such values, like love for one's country, or sexual emancipation, or political revolution, or obedience to the prevailing authority, can become the idol, the all-consuming reality, with Christ's role being relegated to that of the mere carrier of them. But the historical Jesus did not espouse every value, nor did he incarnate every political conviction or every cultural ideal. For Christians who believe he is the Son of God incarnate, Christ embodied a pattern of life which completely respected the limitations of his own time. He related to contemporary social structures as a charismatic healer and preacher of God's reign would relate to them in the first century c.e., not as someone with the differentiated human consciousness of the twentieth century which understands the dynamics of society as a cultural, political, and economic system. Although what historical science tells us about Jesus of Nazareth is hardly extensive, it is nonetheless precious. This is so because Christians want to know whatever they can not only about the one whom they are trying to follow, but also about the nature of his pattern of life, for that pattern of life leads to resurrection and to the increase of God's reign, which is the flourishing of humanity.

We do not learn about Jesus' earthly life to imitate it. None of us, even if we tried, could become another Jesus of Nazareth. We are each called to live our own life in community within the limits and opportunities of our own talents, time and place. Nor are we called to follow the pattern of Jesus' life in all respects. Few of us are called to become itinerant preachers and healers. Jesus made a whole set of decisions that were his own; they involved spending his finite, human energy on some people and not others (he became the master and teacher of the Twelve, but he did not seek out non-Jewish people), on some causes and not others (he preached God's reign but did not try to rescue John the Baptist or overthrow the Roman occupying forces).

Another point is more philosophical. We know history, we know the past events of our world insofar as they are recoverable in a "scientific way," through the critical labors of the historian. As graced response to divine revelation, faith as such does not generate the historian's kind of knowledge of past events, but it does give the believer knowledge of them, for example, through learning the creed or hearing the gospel proclaimed in liturgy. Christian faith has everything to do with history and with facts ("states of affairs the affirmation of which is true"), although these two

---

27. See J. L. Segundo, *The Liberation of Theology*, trans. J. Drury (Maryknoll, New York: Orbis, 1976) 162–65.

are not synonymous. Faith puts historical facts into a perspective, namely, the perspective opened up by relationship with the self-revealing and self-communicating God.[28] By participating in the community of interpretation which is the Church, the Christian learns to perceive historical occurrences in relation to the God disclosed in the Old and New Testaments. Unlike deists, Christians recognize that certain events in history reveal and communicate God and divine salvation more focally or definitively than others, and that the understanding of those events in faith aids in the interpretation and appreciation of other events, indeed, of all human history.

It is as true in theology as elsewhere that events and their significance, events and their interpretation, cannot be separated, although they can and must be distinguished again and again. Every named event involves selection from a field of intermeshed events, and stands out from that field of events in relation to a particular standpoint. Our knowledge of events is always perspectival. Discussion of events reveals and implies a certain interest on the part of the one who selects the event. No events would "arise" in a world of total disinterest. But the intermeshing of event and interpretation does not mean their simple identification, as common sense recognizes. For some interpretations of an event are simply wrong, and every interpretation of an event is limited and can be recognized as perspectival. That very recognition reveals already a certain transcendence of event and interpretation to a second level of interpretation: the interpretation of all interpretations as limited.

Earlier I mentioned that the careful and critical study of the historical sources regarding Jesus of Nazareth keeps us from making a kind of "Everyperson" or abstract ideal out of him, because he was a particular individual and no other. It also keeps him from being identified with each and every cause so that he is only significant in relation to causes.

But there is another major dimension here. The Jesus Christ we Christians pray to, commit our lives to, act in the name of, and follow as disciples is not an image reconstructed from history but the living Jesus Christ who is present in the Church and in the world in the power of the Holy Spirit. This full presence is expressed and experienced in direct encounter, embodied not in theology, nor the study of history, nor the writing of moral theology books, but in the concrete Christian activities of worship (public and private) and service to the Body of Christ and of the larger world. This activity, this performative living in response to the Risen Christ in the world, is the all-embracing context for theology and for the Christian's study of theology and history.

Christology as a discipline of theology cannot and must not protect one from either personal relationship with Christ in prayer or the rigors of

28. G. O'Collins, *Fundamental Theology* (New York and Ramsey: Paulist, 1981) 156–60.

discipleship in living out the Christian message. The knowledge of who Jesus Christ is comes not first and last from study about him but from active engagement with him in prayer and action, in prayerful action, i.e., action which is rooted in increasing dependence on Christ as the ultimate Savior and Liberator of all peoples and all history, and prayer which leads one again and again to the neighbor in need, the neighbor oppressed, the neighbor hungry and homeless or lying wounded in the street.[29]

Any Christology which neglects worship and prayer on the one hand, or the path of discipleship in relating, after the pattern of Jesus, to people and the social structures which can benefit or oppress them on the other, is a deficient Christology. To be sure, prayer and liturgy sometimes serve as a "cop-out" for people. One goes to Mass on Sunday and fulfills a modicum of one's ecclesiastical obligations, thus using religion consciously or unconsciously to remain embedded in one's prejudices or denial-systems or conspiracy with unjust social structures. But, as an old adage has it, *abusus non tollit usum*: The misuse of something, in this case liturgical worship, does not invalidate its proper role and use. The dynamism and content of good liturgy are such as to transform the imagination, school the affections and draw one into a movement which is Christ's self-offering to the Father in the revelation of the Holy Spirit; good liturgy leads one, as well, into sharing in Christ's self-offering to the world in solidarity and service.[30] Good liturgy, liturgy which serves its true purpose, directs one's whole self again and again to the real God and the real world. The daily life of discipleship, with its choices made according to the mind of Christ (Phil 2:5) is what liturgy expresses in a very explicit and concentrated way. It is equally what Christology seeks to study, critically appropriate, and foster by relating the values, struggles, and issues of one's own culture to the Church's and the individual Christian's living relationship with Christ.

The Sources of Christology

In a way we have already entered into the discussion of Christology's sources. The primary source of Christology, as of all Christian theology, is the revelation of God through Jesus Christ in the power of the Holy Spirit. That revelation finds its primary witness in Scripture and tradition. Since this is not the place to explore in detail the nature of Scripture

29. The adage of Ignatius of Loyola is apt here: "Pray as though everything depended on you, and act as though everything depended on God." See J. W. Padberg, *Studies in the Spirituality of Jesuits* X, n. 5 (November 1978) 320.

30. D. Saliers, *The Soul in Paraphrase: Prayer and the Religious Affections* (New York: Seabury, 1980); P. Palmer, *A Company of Strangers: Christians and the Renewal of American Public Life* (New York: Crossroad, 1981).

and tradition and the relationship between them, let it suffice to say that Scripture provides the privileged witness to the life, death, and resurrection of Jesus Christ and to the decisive beginnings of the Church's faith. Indeed, in the New Testament we come to know Jesus Christ in and through the expression of the faith of the early Church. And that scriptural expression of the Church's faith is the normative beginning of tradition. As Vatican II taught, Scripture and tradition are not two sources of revelation, and thus two sources of theology as it seeks to understand revelation, but a unitary yet differentiated process of mediating God's saving truth. As Vatican II expressed it:

> . . . there exist a close connection and communication between sacred tradition and sacred Scripture. For both of them, flowing from the same divine wellspring, in a certain way merge into a unity and tend toward the same end. For sacred Scripture is the word of God inasmuch as it is consigned to writing under the inspiration of the divine Spirit. To the successors of the apostles, sacred tradition hands on in its full purity God's word, which was entrusted to the apostles by Christ the Lord and the Holy Spirit. Thus, led by the light of the Spirit of truth, these successors can in their preaching preserve this word of God faithfully, explain it, and make it more widely known. Consequently, it is not from sacred Scripture alone that the Church draws her certainty about everything which has been revealed.[31]

Tradition is thus the living process of transmission of God's self-revelation in the life, liturgy, prayer, action, thought, and writing of the Church down through the centuries, as that life is guided by the Holy Spirit. The Spirit guarantees that the Church will be, at root, a faithful recipient of that revelation. Tradition must be faithful to Scripture and must always unfold, in different times and cultures, the one self-revelation of God in Christ and the Spirit which received its original witness in the inspired Holy Scriptures. God shares the divine life with the Church (and through the Church, with the whole world) down through the centuries in a way which takes history most seriously. In and through the responses of various individuals and communities, further expression is given to God's self-communication, new aspects of it are brought to light, some truths highlighted, others recognized or treated as less central. We do not know God's self-revelation apart from its reception by human beings, both as communities and as individuals, down through history. Objectivity (in the sense of the offer of God's life and light) and subjectivity (in the sense of the reception of what is offered) are intertwined. Catholics believe that

---

31. *Dei Verbum*, "Dogmatic Constitution on Divine Revelation," in W. M. Abbot, *The Documents of Vatican II* (New York: America Press, 1967) 117n.; on the magisterium see F. A. Sullivan, *Magisterium: Teaching Authority in the Catholic Church* (New York and Ramsey: Paulist, 1983).

the Holy Spirit preserves the Church from error with regard to the most important truths which bear on our salvation. The Spirit is able to work through human limitations, weakness, and sinfulness and to maintain the Church in the truth, i.e., in its unity with the self-revealing God in Christ through the Spirit.

Christology, in seeking to understand Jesus Christ and the implications for human living of relationship to him in worship and discipleship, is thus led to examine Scripture and tradition as a unitary and pluriform witness to the presence and action of Christ in the Church and in the world. This examination will be a critical one, that is, it will refer to historical-critical and literary studies of the New Testament and historical study of the development of the Church's dogma, or official doctrine, as well as the contributions of philosophy and systematic theology (as critical conversations with culture) in determining the meaning of Christ in relation to the gifts and needs of particular times and cultures.

For Catholic Christology, the official magisterium of the Church provides a principal source as well as norm and guideline. Both the solemn definitions of general councils and the ordinary magisterium have their respective roles to play here. Many of the Church's doctrinal definitions occurred in the early centuries of the Church's life, and they have exercised a profound effect on subsequent Christological reflection. Catholic theologians approach the statements of the magisterium with the same kind of critical interpretive perspective as that with which the magisterium urges scholars to approach the human expression of God's Word in the Old and New Testaments. They seek to determine the context of the statements made in the great councils, for example, their prehistory, and the history of their reception, all for the sake of determining the doctrinal intent of the council.[32]

Who is the Christ studied by Christology? the historical Jesus of Nazareth as reconstructed by historians? the Christ present in the liturgy? the Christ witnessed to in magisterial documents of the Church? the Christ of theologians down through the ages? the Christ of art? the Christ witnessed to by saints and martyrs and those who struggle in his name for just social structures? the Christ of personal devotion? the Christ discussed by followers of other religions (like Martin Buber and Mahatma Gandhi) or by atheists (like Milan Machovec)?[33]

---

32. On the scholarly approach to Christ in the New Testment, see the Biblical Commission's instruction of 1964 on the historical truth of the Gospels (*Acta Apostolicae Sedis* 56 [1964] 712–18); for ET and commentary see J. Fitzmyer, *A Christological Catechism: New Testament Answers* (New York and Ramsey: Paulist, 1982). On the relationship of theologians to the magisterium see Sullivan, *Magisterium*.

33. On Martin Buber see H. Urs von Balthasar, *Martin Buber and Christianity: A Dialogue between Israel and the Church* (London: Harvill, 1961). For Gandhi's view of Christ, see *Gandhi's Autobiography: The Story of His Experiment with Truth*, trans. M. Desai (Washington, D.C.:

The answer is, first of all, all of the above. Christ gives himself to be known and related to in multiple ways, and by definition one cannot restrict the ways in which Christ may reveal himself, both within and outside the Church. Those who engage in Christology can learn from everyone and everywhere: from the simplest peasant in a barrio of Sao Paulo, an anchorite of fourteenth-century England such as Dame Julian of Norwich, Pope Leo the Great of the fifth century, the great Council of Chalcedon and the Gospel of Luke, a friend's struggle with addiction, the prayer overheard on the lips of one's young daughter, Rouault's paintings of Christ as a clown, and the theologian seeking to make sense of Christ in view of the horrendous darkness of Auschwitz.

But to say that the potential sources of Christology are immense, indeed are as wide and deep as our graced and sinful humanity, does not help us in a methodological way.

Where should one begin one's Christology and how should one proceed?

The Method of Christology

This book will pursue the development of Christology beginning with Jesus of Nazareth in his public ministry until his death insofar as responsible late-twentieth-century scholarship permits us to come to some firm knowledge about his message, his words and actions and, indirectly through them, his understanding and intentions. It will also consider in at least an initial way the New Testament's theological expressions of his ministry and death, developed in the light of the communities' memories of Jesus and faith in his resurrection as well as their own experiences of the Spirit. It will then examine the resurrection from a historical point of view and in hermeneutical perspective. Next we will consider the Christological conceptions which, on the basis of the Easter event, arose as identifications of Jesus in the early Church. I will seek to show that there is genuine continuity between the Jesus of the ministry and the Jesus Christ who comes to be witnessed to in the New Testament as it reflects the proclamation, worship, and discipleship of the communities of the early Church. As we continue, we shall examine the basic conciliar statements about Christ, and explore traditional and contemporary understandings of his humanity, his saving work, and his unity with God.

Public Affairs Press, 1960). A Marxist interpretation of Christ is offered by M. Machovec, *A Marxist Looks at Jesus* (Philadelphia: Fortress, 1976). On art and Christology see, e.g., J. Pelikan, *Jesus Through the Centuries: His Place in the History of Culture* (New Haven: Yale University Press, 1985). On the witness of Christians in present-day Latin America see W. O'Malley, *The Voice of Blood: Five Christian Martyrs for Our Time* (Maryknoll, New York: Orbis, 1980) and R. J. Schreiter, *In Water and In Blood: A Spirituality of Solidarity and Hope* (New York: Crossroad, 1988).

The starting point of Christology is not the reconstructed Jesus of historical record however; theology does not simply translate into faith-language the material recovered by historians, in all its fragmentariness and probability. As precious as that material is, Christians do not relate to Jesus as a historian would, although they can surely be aided and challenged by the historian's discoveries. The theologian begins Christology within the framework of faith, as one who shares in the Church's faith in the God of Jesus Christ and in Christ as the definitive self-revelation of God through the inspiration of the Holy Spirit. The whole, unrestricted Jesus Christ is the Christ present in the Church's worship and discipleship, and mediated in Scripture and tradition. The Christ of then, the Christ of now, and the Christ who is to come thus constitute the full "object" of Christology.

The truth of Christology is in its unfolding, but this unfolding must be critically appraised: Not everything that Christians have said about Christ is true or, if true, significant.

One norm of Christology must be the most responsible account of the pre-Easter Jesus that can be obtained. This is a historical norm but, for the reasons given above, an important one.

A second norm is the New Testament's witness to Jesus Christ. As the Spirit's work, Scripture expresses the unity running through the diversity of experiences and formulations of the earliest communities which constituted the early Church.

Another norm of Christology must be the authentic teaching of the Church as it has been expressed in the councils (principally the first seven general councils) and in Church teachings interpreted according to their various degrees of authority.

A final norm of Christology must be the needs, aspirations, and values of one's own culture and time as they are brought into critical correlation with Christian faith and its symbols. In this encounter both the culture and the faith are tested. Will the faith (in the persons of believers) be able to extend genuine hospitality to those needs, aspirations, and values, no matter how challenging they may appear to be? And will (at least some) people living in the culture be open to the challenge of bringing those dimensions of their culture into relationship with Christ, to find out what good news (amidst critical sifting) lies in store for the life of that culture?

Thus Christology has a set of norms, working in mutual reciprocity. Christology is an interpretive enterprise which seeks to interpret the faith-experience of the Church and to assess critically the interpretations of that faith-experience. At each stage of its development, Christology has needed to listen to culture and to notice Christ's presence in and for that culture, as well as to bring together Christ and culture in a way that involves, again and again, a threefold process of acceptance (incarnation), critical transformation (Cross), and eschatological hope (resurrection).[34] The bringing together of culture and Christ in this threefold way does not happen simply in the mind of the Christologist. He or she is not the Church, the human faith-experience, and the critical interpreter all rolled into one. The Christologist is a student of the Church's faith-experience, a student of culture, and a student of the multiple ways in which they meet: in prayer, in collaborative activity aimed at maintaining the good and changing the evil structures of society, in suffering and joy and expectation.

The basic aim of this book, then, is to provide an orientation to Christology and to soteriology (the doctrine of salvation) as part of Christology. On the one hand, the level on which this text is written is not that of an elementary introduction. On the other hand, the result does not claim to be original. This orientation is offered to the reader with the hope that he or she will be enticed to study yet further the principal traditional and contemporary authors referred to in the course of the discussion. A second aim, and indeed hope, is that the reader will find in these pages some resources which will prompt a deeper understanding and appropriation of his or her own relationship to Christ, "the pioneer and perfecter of faith" (Heb 12:2).

34. See F. J. van Beeck, *Christ Proclaimed: Christology as Rhetoric.*

2

The Ministry of Jesus of Nazareth

The Jesus Christ in whom Christians believe, and in whose name they gather to pray and struggle for justice in a broken world, was a human being who lived a quite particular earthly life in Palestine almost two thousand years ago and who is alive and effective in today's world as the Risen One. In order to come to some understanding of his identity, therefore, we shall have to examine both what historical inquiry can tell us about him in his pre-Easter existence, and the ways in which the believing community over the centuries has confessed him as the Risen Lord.

The historical inquiry into the life of the pre-Easter Jesus is complicated by the fact that the principal sources of information about him are the writings of the New Testament, which—whether they be the Gospels, or the Acts of the Apostles, or the Epistles, or the Book of Revelation—are confessional documents expressing the faith-experience of the authors and of the local churches which produced the various writings.[1] As nineteenth- and twentieth-century New Testament scholars developed textual criticism (to establish the most reliable ancient texts) and source criticism (thereby tracing the lines of dependency in the development of the written traditions), followed by form criticism (to determine the oral stages of the texts) and redaction criticism (to learn the contribution of the evangelists as final redactors or editors), it became increasingly apparent that the New Testament authors and communities were not interested in communicating bald, factual reports about Jesus' words and activities, but that they felt free to refashion inherited traditions about Jesus in ways which would allow him to address their own issues and concerns.

---

1. Contemporary pagan references to Jesus were very few indeed. For a convenient summary of them see J. A. Fitzmyer, *A Christological Catechism: New Testament Answers* (New York and Ramsey: Paulist, 1982) 11–12.

The New Testament writings are, therefore, the fruit of memories of Jesus (*anamnesis*) combined with the earliest communities' experience of life in his Spirit (*pneuma*). The diversity of the New Testament writings is very great because of the diversity of memories, Spirit-experiences, and issues and concerns facing the different communities. One of the basic differences among the writings has to do with the amount and kind of attention given to the life and ministry of the pre-Easter Jesus. To begin with there are, of course, four narrative accounts of Jesus' earthly activity, his death, and the events surrounding his resurrection, each with its own particular theological themes and emphases despite the intricate pattern of interrelationships among the first three gospels. Other New Testament writings do not offer many details of the story of the earthly Jesus but are content to summarize Jesus' life and identity. Paul, for example, says very little about the historical course of Jesus' life, preferring summary formulas referring to Jesus' obedience to his Father, his expiatory death, and his saving resurrection. The New Testament's diversity extends as well to all important aspects of Christian faith, such as Church life, ministry, and the sacraments.

A recent, thorough study of the unity and diversity of the New Testament concluded that the unity of its witness consists in the pervasive conviction that the risen and exalted Jesus Christ is one and the same as Jesus of Nazareth, who ministered and was crucified in Palestine.[2] This focal unity does not derive simply from the occasional binary kerygmatic formula of identity such as we find in 1 Corinthians 12:3: "No one can say '*Jesus is Lord*' except by the Holy Spirit." Rather, it is a fundamental identification, which constitutes the leitmotif appearing throughout the New Testament in many forms. Consider, for example, Jesus' predictions regarding his passion and resurrection (Mark 8:31 par.) which, in their present form, are due to Church formation. Recall, as well, the narrative of the risen Jesus showing his hands and side to the skeptical disciples (John 20:20). Peter's speeches in Acts also identify the Jesus whom the leaders of the Jews crucified with the exalted Lord (e.g., Acts 2:14-36). As a final example we may cite Paul's use of an early confessional fragment: "the gospel concerning his Son, who was descended from David according to the flesh and designated Son of God in power according to the Spirit of holiness by his resurrection from the dead, Jesus Christ our Lord" (Rom 1:3-4).

The situation which the New Testament presents to us can be expressed in another way. Here we encounter one Jesus and many Christologies, or, if that last word sounds too systematic, one Jesus and many confes-

---

2. J. D. G. Dunn, *The Unity and Diversity of the New Testament: An Enquiry into the Character of Earliest Christianity*; see also P. Perkins, "Theological Implications of New Testament Pluralism," *Catholic Biblical Quarterly* 50 (1988) 5-23.

sions (*kerygmata*) of faith about him and his meaning for humanity. Indeed, our cognitive way to Jesus runs through these many confessions of faith, for we cannot meet Jesus in his historical uniqueness except through the testimonies of the New Testament authors. Testimony provides the avenue of approach to any historical figure, to be sure. But in the case of Jesus, the testimony in question is that of committed disciples who wrote out of the conviction that the Jesus of memory was identical with the Jesus with whom they were united in faith, worship, discipleship, and ministry.

In the previous chapter we dealt with the question why we should concern ourselves with the Jesus of two thousand years ago. At this juncture we would do well to recognize several cautions regarding the historical approach to the pre-Easter Jesus.

Historians do not operate in a value-free zone, as it were. Scholars, and so too the methods they employ, are influenced by a web of presuppositions about reality which can remain quite implicit as they carry on their work. These presuppositions may prevent a historian from paying attention to an original feature of the past that does not "square" with a contemporary sense of how things are. One's bias about what kind of event could have happened in the past often derives from a conventional way of viewing things which is itself laden with unacknowledged metaphysical presuppositions about the nature of reality. Indeed, biases of every kind can play their role in the historical approach to Jesus. Thus, for example, form criticism as developed in nineteenth-century Germany contained certain assumptions about the relationship of oral traditions to written ones which now appear to be incorrect. Some form-critical scholars maintained that the most original form of tradition enshrined in the New Testament had to be the kerygma, or proclamation, regarding Jesus, and that the narrative units and catechetical traditions evolved from these simpler forms.[3] We now realize that there can be no clear chronological sequence in the emergence of kerygma (proclamation), narrative and catechesis.

Another caution is fairly obvious. The actual Jesus who lived two thousand years ago remains richer than any historical portrait of him and so even as a historical figure, will always transcend what historians write about him. This remark applies, of course, to any human being who is the subject of historical research. The historical portrait—or better, fragmentary picture—of Jesus must remain partial. It will always be revisable and at best probable in the certainty it offers. The actual, unique Jesus of the past is, as a person, incommunicably himself and not reproducible in his actuality and uniqueness. Thus when one uses the phrase "the historical

---

3. For a critique of form criticism see E. Güttgemanns, *Candid Questions Concerning Gospel Form Criticism: A Methodological Sketch of the Fundamental Problematics of Form and Redaction Criticism*, trans. W. G. Doty, 2nd, cor. ed. (Pittsburgh: Pickwick Press, 1979).

Jesus," one should mean by it the partial portrait of Jesus obtained, with varying degrees of probability and possibility, by historical-critical scholarship, and prefer terms such as the "actual" Jesus or the "earthly" Jesus to designate the individual who lived two thousand years ago.

But how are we to decide which material in the New Testament can rightfully contribute to the delineation of the historical Jesus? In other words, how can scholars decide which sayings and actions attributed to Jesus by the New Testament writers constitute authentic Jesus-material? Over the years exegetes have developed various criteria, and in the course of time a number of exegetes and theologians have agreed on three principal ones.[4]

The first is the criterion of dissimilarity. Rudolf Bultmann, a principal member of the form-critical school, developed this criterion. According to it, any saying or deed attributed to Jesus in the New Testament whose parallel cannot be found either in the Old Testament or the Judaism of Jesus' time on the one hand, or in the thought and life of the early Church on the other, can be ascribed to him. For example, Jesus' habit of eating with notorious public sinners has no parallel either in Judaism before or during Jesus' time or in the early Church, which imposed conditions on table fellowship in the community. This dissimilarity argues strongly, therefore, that Jesus actually did eat with public sinners.

This criterion needs, of course, to be employed with care and nuance. Use of it must not trap one into thinking that Jesus said and did only unique things, that he was not deeply rooted in his own Jewish tradition, or that there was no continuity between what he said and did and the teaching and activities of the early Church. In addition, our knowledge of Judaism at the time of Jesus and of the early Church is constantly being revised and increased. Nevertheless, applied in conjunction with other criteria, the criterion of dissimilarity can help the scholar identify authentic Jesus-material.

The second criterion is that of multiple attestation. There are in the gospel narratives sayings and deeds attributed to Jesus that show up in many independent literary *sources* such as the Q-source (the postulated source, principally of sayings, which accounts for much material common to Matthew and Luke but not found in Mark), Mark, M or L (the material peculiar to Matthew or Luke), and John; these sayings and deeds appear as well in a number of different *types* of tradition such as parables, acts of healing, sayings, and pronouncement stories. For example, Jesus' references to God's kingdom are found in all of the sources and all of the prophetic types, as Rudolf Bultmann has catalogued them: visions, preaching of salvation, woes and threats, warnings and exhortations, and

---

4. On the question of criteria see, for example, N. Perrin, *Rediscovering the Teaching of Jesus* (New York: Harper and Row, 1976) and E. Schillebeeckx, *Jesus: An Experiment in Christology*, 88–100.

apocalyptic predictions; they are also present in wisdom-*logia* (sayings) and "I-sayings."[5] Again, this criterion needs to be used with care, first, because our understanding of the inter-relationship of the earliest traditions is still evolving and, second, because we cannot conclude that sayings and deeds of Jesus attested by only one source or one type of tradition are for that reason not authentic. This criterion cannot be employed negatively or exclusively any more than the first one.

The third criterion that comes into play when seeking to determine authentic Jesus-material in the New Testament is called the criterion of coherence. As one's picture of the historical Jesus builds up detail by detail, one can begin to accept as authentic other traditions that cohere or correspond to the authenticated material, even when those traditions are attested by only one source or one kind of source. An example of this would be the parable of the Good Samaritan, which we find only in Luke's Gospel. The parable itself (Luke 10:30-35) fits perfectly the pattern of Jesus' storytelling, and also coheres with his attitude toward outcasts such as Samaritans.

With an awareness of the kind of criteria employed by exegetes, we shall now proceed to consider the ministry of the pre-Easter Jesus in a summary way, not arguing for each element of the portrait but drawing on the research of established exegetes for a basically reliable, if fragmentary, portrait.

Jesus' Ministry of Word and Deed in the Spirit

In a very summary historical reconstruction of Jesus' life, we can say that he was a native of Nazareth in Galilee and son of Mary. He was raised in a pious Jewish family in the usual way, and throughout his public life he lived the religious life of a pious adult Jew, praying regularly each day and participating in the religious events associated with the Temple and synagogue.[6] At around the age of thirty, Jesus was baptized by John in the Jordan and subsequently began a mission to Israel as a charismatic preacher and healer. His ministry centered principally in Galilee but he also preached in Judea, with one or more trips to the capital city, Jerusa-

5. J. Riches, *Jesus and the Transformation of Judaism* (New York: Seabury, 1982) 87-90.

6. See G. Vermes, *Jesus the Jew: A Historian's Reading of the Gospel* (New York: Macmillan, 1974) and his *The Gospel of Jesus the Jew* (Newcastle-on-Tyne: University of Newcastle-on-Tyne Press, 1981); D. Flusser, *Jesus*, trans. R. Walls (New York: Herder and Herder, 1969); D. A. Hagner, *The Jewish Reclamation of Jesus: An Analysis and Critique of the Modern Jewish Study of Jesus* (Grand Rapids, Mich.: Zondervan, 1984); and J. H. Charlesworth, *Jesus Within Judaism: New Light from Exciting Archeological Discoveries* (Garden City, New York: Doubleday, 1988).

lem. It appears that his mission was restricted to the Jews, but he did engage openly with Gentiles when circumstances led to such encounters. During the course of his ministry, he assembled a group of disciples called the Twelve, a term charged with symbolic significance. Toward the end of his life, he entered Jerusalem amid acclamation by his followers. He proceeded to perform a prophetic act by overturning the tables of the moneychangers in the Temple, which led to his being denounced by the Sadducees to the Romans. Betrayed by Judas, one of the Twelve, Jesus was crucified by the Romans under Pontius Pilate as a messianic pretender, this charge being expressed by the title affixed to his cross, "King of the Jews."

Such a general picture does not do justice to Jesus, his message, or his ministry, but it can provide an initial orientation. Thanks to New Testament scholarship, it is possible to offer more details which, although fragmentary when compared to a modern biography, are precious nonetheless.

The three foci of attention and critical inquiry in the quest for historical information about the pre-Easter Jesus are the sayings tradition, the activities tradition, and Jesus' execution by the Romans. This last focus we shall reserve for the next chapter.

One of the difficulties under which inquiry into the sayings tradition labors is that often we cannot presume that the context given by the evangelist or his source for a saying is the historically authentic one. Yet one of the important ways of determining the meaning of a statement is by considering its context. A second difficulty was alluded to earlier: it is the fact that the early Church felt quite free to admit as "sayings of the Lord" utterances of Spirit-inspired prophets who, in the name of Christ, addressed the concerns of their community.

Jesus, Abba, and God's Reign in the Sayings Tradition

Even though God does not appear in Jesus' life (or ours, for that matter) as a particular being alongside other beings (because God is not a finite, particular "anything"), Jesus both named God and spoke about the Holy One of Israel; without a doubt the God of Israel stood at the center of his existence and concern. God, and God's concerns, were the "plot" of Jesus' life.

Jesus addressed God as "Abba," praying with that name on his lips. An Aramaic word, "Abba" was originally a lalling sound ("baby-talk") which then evolved into a term of address used first by children and later by adults to address their father. The name expressed both reverence and familial closeness. Joachim Jeremias, who highlighted this aspect of the historical Jesus, went too far when he asserted that Jesus was unique in adopting this term of filial intimacy, yet his use of the word was extraordinary at the time and certainly characteristic of his way of relating to God.[7] We do not know much about the domestic prayer of Jews at that time, but their public prayer communicated a sense that God was the transcendent one, who was to be approached only in the most reverent and solemn way. Indeed, many Jews saw the Roman occupation of their country as a sign of God's displeasure with them because of their sinfulness, which led to an even deeper sense of distance from the all-just and all-holy one. In the context of his proclamation and ministry Jesus' use of "Abba" could have suggested (to those who believed him to be of God and not of Satan) that this man from Nazareth's experience of the God of Israel had been marked by extraordinary intimacy. Jesus' sense of God was a profoundly personal one, but it was not simply private, because it colored his understanding of what God wanted for all those open to his message. While Jesus invoked God in nearness with a masculine name, as was customary in his time, the distinctive note that is special to him is the utter nearness of God. In a land marked for many by a sense of God's remoteness, Jesus spoke in a new way about the living God.

The Abba-experience of Jesus constitutes a most significant dimension of his relational identity, expressed in terms of the one to whom he was responding: the God of Israel.

Another equally important aspect of Jesus' sayings about God was his proclamation of the reign (or kingdom) of God. While the metaphor of God's reign figures in the Old Testament, it does not have the frequency of use that one finds with Jesus. It is attributed to Jesus some sixty-three times in the Gospels and, though a number of these instances are due to the evangelists' editing, the phrase still remains a key element of the pre-Easter Jesus' message.

The concept or symbol of God's kingdom is deeply embedded in ancient Near Eastern religious thought.[8] In Israel's history the reference is primarily to God's acting as king on behalf of God's people, blessing them, granting them well-being, protecting them, and conquering their enemies. Since this kingship was not a condition or state of God apart from the condition of God's people, God's kingship was to some extent a future eventuality, for Israel needed again and again to contend with enemies stronger than itself who often triumphed.

7. There is no record in the Old Testament of individuals addressing God directly as "my father." Nor is there any record of such usage in Palestine in Jesus' time, according to J. Jeremias, *New Testament Theology, vol. 1: The Proclamation of Jesus*, trans. J. Bowden (New York: Scribner's, 1971) 61–68. This represents a modification of his earlier view; see Schillebeeckx, *Jesus*, 256–69.

8. On the symbol of God's kingdom, see N. Perrin, *The Kingdom of God in the Teaching of Jesus* (Philadelphia: Westminster, 1963) and his *Jesus and the Language of the Kingdom: Symbol and Metaphor in New Testament Interpretation* (Philadelphia: Fortress, 1976).

9. E. P. Sanders, *Jesus and Judaism* (Philadelphia: Fortress, 1985) 141–50.

In the sayings attributed to Jesus, E. P. Sanders counts six different meanings that the term "kingdom of God" can have: (1) "kingdom" in the sense of covenant, e.g., "It is hard for the rich to enter the kingdom of heaven" (Matt 19:23; Mark 10:23; Luke 18:24); (2) the kingdom as still to be fully established: "Thy kingdom come!" (Matt 6:10); (3) the kingdom as a future, otherworldly, unexpected event in which the righteous will be separated from the wicked (Matt 13:40-42); (4) the kingdom as a decisive future event which will result in a recognizable social order involving Jesus' disciples and presumably Jesus himself (Matt 19:28; Luke 22:28-30); (5) the kingdom as present in the words and deeds of Jesus (Matt 12:28; Luke 11:20); and (6) the kingdom as a reality whose character can be narrated, (e.g., Matt 20:1-16).[9] Scholars have given most of their attention to the difference and connection between the present and future meanings of the kingdom. In this regard Sanders expresses salutary caution:

> [Jesus] used the word "kingdom" an overwhelming number of times in comparison with other terms, and it was forced to carry a very wide range of meaning. We have no sayings which allow us to come to the clarity which we can achieve with Paul, thanks to our having such passages as Rom 8.23. "Future" and "present" in the teaching of Jesus have constituted a worrisome problem because we cannot say clearly what is present—nor even precisely what he thought of as future, whether a new order or a cosmic cataclysm. He may well have thought that "the kingdom" in the sense of the "power of God" was at work in the world, but that the time would come when all opposing power would be eliminated, and the kingdom of God in a somewhat different sense would "come"—be ushered in. The surviving sayings material does not allow us to offer this as being definitely Jesus' view, but it seems the most probable supposition.[10]

John Riches sees in Jesus' use of the kingdom symbol a prime example of his transformation of traditional Jewish material.[11] Whereas traditionally God's kingdom was associated with the destruction of God's enemies, Jesus removed this motif from the core of his teaching. In addition, he de-emphasized the holiness of God insofar as that implied strict boundaries of "pure" and "impure" and "ins" and "outs." Forgiveness and mercy are the primary themes of the kingdom as Jesus spoke of it.[12] This shift within the horizon of Jewish conceptuality is striking, and yet possible

10. Ibid., 152.

11. J. Riches, *Jesus and the Transformation of Judaism*, 102-11.

12. Ibid., 100.

and plausible in the context of a creative reworking of the tradition. More-over, as we shall see, the kingdom is associated with spontaneous festive meals and with close contact with outcasts, the poor, the sick, and the oppressed.

To the extent that the metaphor referred to an event, it evoked the power of God whose definitive rule would spell salvation for Israel and the end of the "present age." This divine rule would be personal, social, and public in its effects. God's kingdom called for decision on the part of those to whom its coming was proclaimed; they must be open to the grace and favor being offered them. For those who were closed to its proclamation, the kingdom would spell judgment rather than salvation. Jesus preached God's reign with the utmost urgency and in sending the Twelve out to preach and heal as he did, showed that he wanted them to proceed with the greatest haste, for the end-time was drawing nigh. This atmosphere of supreme eschatological urgency is very difficult for us to enter into, but it is a reminder of how different the situation of Jesus' ministry was from that of our own time. Jesus was telling people that God had turned toward them with unconditional love and that they should let themselves be overtaken, overwhelmed by that love. The news was completely good, rooted in the unlimited goodness of God. But it was utterly serious as well, in that one's eternal life or destruction hinged on whether one was open to the gift contained in the message. The proclamation of life, if rejected, would necessarily become a judgment of death. Because of the grave consequences of Jesus' message, he tried many tactics to win people over to the goodness of his news, from partying with sinners to speaking in world-transforming parables.

Both Jesus' Abba-experience and the central role of God's reign in his preaching indicate the Godwardness of this individual. Modern scholar-ship has made it abundantly clear that Jesus' identity and activity entailed the God of Israel. If you want to have anything to do with Jesus, you must reckon with Jesus' God, the God of the Jewish covenant. God, and God's rule in human affairs, was what Jesus was all about.

This Godwardness suffusing his Abba-experience and his preaching of God's reign involved an experience of the Spirit of God as well. In certain prophetic traditions of the Old Testament, God's consummation of human history would mean the full outpouring of the Spirit on the elect, the chosen ones destined for salvation (e.g., Joel 2:28-29). Jesus' free-dom with God-Abba and his prophetic sense of the imminent arrival of the kingdom had much to do with the prophetic bestowal of the Spirit in the end-time, which ancient traditions also associated with John's bap-tism of Jesus in the Jordan. After his prophetic anointing, Jesus appeared on the scene in Galilee as a charismatic, prophetic teacher and healer, that is, as one filled with the Spirit of God, energized and led by the Spirit, and able to share that Spirit with the Twelve as he sent them out on mission to Israel (Mark 6:7).[13]

The Godwardness of Jesus, along with his relation to Abba, to God's reign, and to the Spirit of the end-time, translates into definite ways of behaving toward people and definite content in his teaching.

Jesus' Powerful Deeds in the Activities Tradition

Jesus presented himself to people as a charismatic exorcist and healer, that is, as one endowed by the Spirit of God with the power to cast out evil spirits and to heal the sick.

No matter how one wishes to explain the exorcisms in contemporary terms, there is little question among biblical exegetes and historians of the New Testament that Jesus saw himself as locked in combat with the Evil One, Satan or the Devil (Mark 1:32-34). In the Synoptic traditions we find possibly fifteen healings and five exorcisms, and in the Johannine tradition three healings. The fact that we have multiple independent attestation, in a number of different kinds of sources, to healings and exorcisms performed by Jesus argues strongly for a core of authentic material in this regard, and for the view that the early Church considered these deeds of Jesus to be as important as his words.

In the thinking of Jesus' day, serious illness and the influence of the Evil One were related, so that there can be no strict demarcation of healings from exorcisms. Nonetheless, some of the exorcisms are clearly portrayed as such (e.g., Mark 1:23-27). These stories depict Jesus as fully the match and more of the evil spirits he encountered, and able by the power of his word to expel them. This pattern of conflict and incursion into enemy territory, as it were, represents a salient feature of Jesus' ministry. In some respects he acted like those Jewish rabbis of the time who were empowered by the Spirit of God to exorcise.[14] The difference between them and Jesus lies in the context within which he performed his exorcisms and did his preaching: the inbreaking reign of God to which his words and deeds gave decisive expression. "But if it is by the finger of God that I cast out demons, then the Kingdom of God has come upon you" (Matt 12:28 and Luke 11:20).[15] In this way Jesus indicated that the reign of God involved liberation from the radically alienating power of the Evil One and the restoration of possessed persons to *self*-possession

13. On Jesus and his relationship to the Spirit, see J. D. G. Dunn, *Jesus and the Spirit: A Study of the Religious and Charismatic Experience of Jesus and the First Christians as Reflected in the New Testament* (Philadelphia: Westminster, 1975).

14. For example, Hanina ben Dosa, a first-century C.E. Galilean healer and exorcist; see Vermes, *Jesus the Jew*, 72-78.

15. On the authenticity of this saying see J. D. G. Dunn, *Jesus and the Spirit*, 44-49.

within the community. The anticipation of the arrival of God's kingdom meant wellness in one's body and psyche and social being. Those thus liberated were not necessarily invited into close discipleship with Jesus, but they had to reckon individually with the person and the word whose power had freed them, and with the arrival of that God for whom Jesus spoke and acted.

In present-day terms we would understand at least some of Jesus' exorcisms to be healings of illnesses that could be naturally intelligible. For example, the boy "freed" in Mark 9:14-29 was no doubt an epileptic, but Jesus as a child of his time apparently interpreted the boy's condition as possession. While the New Testament cannot answer all our contemporary questions about the existence of demons and evil spirits, it is clear that its authors fully believed that Jesus was in mortal combat with forces far more powerful than personal sin or fatal physical illness.

Jesus not only freed people from the power of the Evil One but also healed many people of their actual sicknesses. A firm core of authentic "healing" material presents itself to the critical student of the New Testament which, like the material dealing with the exorcisms, must be taken seriously. Again, Jesus' healings are part and parcel of his proclamation of God's profound good will toward people, especially those broken in body and spirit, a good will that seeks human well-being through the arrival of God's full reign as the consummation of human history. Of course, Jesus did not heal every ill person in Israel at the time; indeed he had no "program" of healing at all. The pattern suggested by the Gospels consists in afflicted people, or their relatives and friends, approaching Jesus and asking for help. The unsystematic character of the healings reminds us that Jesus was not intent on a gradual amelioration of the outer situation through his efforts and those of his disciples, but rather was proclaiming the imminent consummation of history in the coming reign of God, a reign which was given powerful anticipatory, if transitory, expression in these healings.

In the Synoptic traditions Jesus' exorcisms and healings are generally called *dynameis* ("deeds of power"). In John's Gospel they are termed *erga* ("works") or *semeia* ("signs"), the latter usage telling us also that the accent falls not on the miraculous character of these deeds but on their revelatory role with regard to Jesus and the salvation he brought. "Miracle" or "wonder" are not the preferred terms for the exorcisms and healings in the New Testament, and the absence of their use does seem to be deliberate.

One of the compelling reasons for accepting the authenticity of the core of *dynameis* stories is the fact that Mark, on whose Gospel Matthew and Luke depended in various ways, sought in the first part of his Gospel to prevent a false understanding of Jesus' messiahship, i.e., as conceivable apart from his Cross. That Mark's Gospel contains so many stories of Jesus' "deeds of power" gives eloquent testimony to their firm rootedness in authentic Jesus-tradition, even though Mark realized that they were open to serious misinterpretation.

What are we to make of such mighty deeds today? The question of miracles has produced a whole library of books and articles in modern times because of the problems raised by the Enlightenment's critique of such "unscientific" events. Only a few reflections are possible here.[16]

1) There are four distinguishable types of mighty acts or signs found in the New Testament: exorcisms, healings, resuscitations, and so-called nature wonders such as the feeding of the five thousand (Mark 6:34-44 and Matt 14:22-32; John 6:1-13) and Jesus' walking on the water (Mark 6:45-52; John 6:16-21). A literary-critical analysis of the material shows that certain traditions have undergone amplification, as when we read, for example, that one blind man is healed in Mark 10:46 and two in Matthew 20:30; four thousand are fed in Mark 8:9 and five thousand in Mark 6:44. Some of the stories may derive from a linguistic misunderstanding, for example, the report of Jesus' appearance to the disciples on the sea (Mark 6:48-49), when the Greek word could also mean "on the seashore" (John 6:19). Again, Jesus' cursing of the fig tree (Mark 11:12-14, 20), which strikes us as an arbitrary use of power reminiscent of the apocryphal gospels, might well rest on a mistranslation of the Aramaic which, as Joachim Jeremias has suggested, could have the meaning: "No one will ever eat fruit from you again [i.e., because the end will come before your time of ripeness]."[17] There are also folkloric accretions in some of the stories. Joseph Fitzmyer has called the account of the Gerasene demoniac and swine (Mark 5:1-20) the most fantastic of the miracle stories. The exaggeration involved, depending on the location envisaged by the story—the swine would have had to race from six to thirty miles to arrive at a cliff—shows similarities to fantastic stories collected in apocryphal gospel traditions about Jesus.[18] Finally, some stories may originally have been resurrection narratives, for example, the miraculous draft of fish in Luke 5:3-6.[19] Even if we make allowances for amplifications, transpositions,

---

16. On miracles see R. H. Fuller, *Interpreting the Miracles* (London: SCM, 1963); R. Latourelle, *The Miracles of Jesus and the Theology of Miracles* (New York and Mahwah: Paulist, 1988); F. Mussner, *The Miracles of Jesus: An Introduction*, trans. A. Wimmer (Notre Dame: University of Notre Dame Press, 1968); L. Sabourin, *The Divine Miracles Discussed and Defended* (Rome: Catholic Book Agency, 1977); H. C. Kee, *Miracle in the Early Christian World* (New Haven: Yale University Press, 1983); X. Léon-Dufour, ed., *Les miracles de Jésus selon le Nouveau Testament* (Paris: Editions du Seuil, 1977).

17. Jeremias, *New Testament Theology*, 87.

18. Fitzmyer, *A Christological Catechism*, 35-36.

19. R. E. Brown, *The Gospel According to John XIII-XXI* (Garden City, New York: Doubleday, 1966) 1091.

and linguistic misunderstandings, there remains a firm core of material which asserts that Jesus exorcised demons and healed the sick.

2) There is a consistent atmosphere evoked by the narratives that is simple, direct, and lacking in "spectacle," whether or not Jesus' refusal to offer a sign to the Pharisees when they ask for one is historical. The mighty acts partake of the mystery of the kingdom's arrival, and cannot be appreciated for their real "point" by neutral or belligerent spectators.

3) Jesus often commends recipients of healing for their faith which has made them well. The early Church understood by this that the person's relationship to Jesus, or better, to God in and through Jesus, was the reason for his or her being healed; Jesus was not simply commending the healed person for some inner psychological disposition such as trust, independent of the object of that trust.[20] The person participated in the event of healing through openness to God's being at work in Jesus.

4) It is noteworthy that usually the healing *dynameis* are performed on behalf of those whom Jesus encounters for the first time. There is a different sort of *dynamis* reported by the evangelists which has to do with mighty acts of Jesus performed in relation to those who already have faith in God through Jesus, namely, the disciples. Jesus' rebuke and calming of the sea (Mark 4:35-41 par.), the feeding of the multitude (Mark 6:34-44), and Jesus' walking on the water with Peter (Mark 6:45-52 par.) challenge the disciples to stronger faith in God as working in and through Jesus; strictly speaking, they are not part of the public ministry in the Synoptics. Moreover, there are no nature miracles in the recorded sayings of Jesus. Many scholars argue that the disciple-oriented wonders are constructions of the early Church based on a linguistic misunderstanding (for example, the report of Jesus' walking on water which was discussed above) or on an incident in Jesus' life that is historically irretrievable (for example, the feeding of the thousands). It is striking that, except in the Gospel of John, the narrative of the feeding of the multitude does not mention the actual wonder being witnessed by the crowd; only the disciples seem to see it. This omission may signal the meaning (and limits of meaning) of the narrative. The evangelists' challenging the Church to deeper faith in the midst of crisis is probably the setting which best interprets these stories.

5) Performance of these mighty deeds on Jesus' part presented an ambiguous profile to people of his day. In their world-view "miracles" were quite possible and by no means unheard-of. The question which arose for them was not, "Can such things occur?" but rather, "If such a thing has happened, by whose power was it done, God's or the Evil One's?" Mighty deeds such as healings did not signify that an individual was divine, as many modern Christian apologists have taught. (Indeed, the very term

20. Fuller, *Interpreting the Miracles*, 42–45.

"divine" admitted much broader attribution in ancient than in modern times.) They suggested rather that the wonder-worker belonged to and drew energy from a higher power, one whose long-term objectives could be either beneficent or malevolent toward humanity.

On those occasions when Jesus could not heal people, the reason lay in their lack of faith, that is, their attribution of his power to the Evil One, not their refusal to admit that he could do such deeds. Jesus could evoke two contradictory responses and interpretations.

6) A number of scholars, and in an extensive way Edward Schillebeeckx, have summarized Jesus' behavior in his pre-Easter ministry as that of the eschatological prophet, the spokesperson of God in the last days when God is on the verge of bringing about full salvation for those destined to enjoy it. According to the Old Testament, this prophet, anointed by the Spirit, gives sight to the blind (Isa 35:5-6, 8), hearing to the deaf (Isa 42:18), comfort to those who mourn; he preaches good news to the poor, and frees the imprisoned (Isa 61:1-3). Both Matthew (11:4-5; Luke 7:22) and Luke (4:16-21), under the influence of "Q," describe Jesus' activity in terms of the eschatological prophet.[21] It is reasonable to suppose that Jesus' performance of certain deeds of power (such as healings) contributed to his being recognized as the eschatological prophet. This recognition, confirmed and deepened by the Easter experiences, then allowed early Christians to ascribe to him other deeds or events traditionally attributed to the eschatological age, such as the rising of the dead (Isa 26:19; see Luke 7:11-17). Jewish interpretation of Second and Third Isaiah and of the Wisdom literature concerning the kingly wisdom figure Solomon ("Son of David"), the wise teacher and healer, provided much material for early Christian reflection on the full significance of Jesus' powerful acts. Because of this freedom on the part of the early Church to attribute to Jesus plenipotentiary powers on the basis of his exaltation at Easter, it will not be possible to unravel with anything like complete certainty the core of authentic mighty deeds that go back to the historical Jesus from the larger traditions that have accumulated in amplification of that core.

Jesus and the Forgiveness of Sins

Jesus exorcised people and cured their illnesses. Did he forgive them their sins as well? We find only two places where Jesus explicitly might be thought to have done such a thing (Mark 2:1-12 and Luke 7:36-50). The striking yet thoroughly Jewish thing which Jesus is reported to have said in each of these passages is that the individual's sins were forgiven, which no doubt involved the so-called theological passive, that is, the use of the passive voice so as to avoid writing God's name. God forgave the

---

21. Schillebeeckx, *Jesus*, 441-49.

paralytic's sins and the woman's sins. For Jews—including Jesus—only God could forgive sins. Yet Jesus' declaration of God's forgiveness of sinners might have conveyed such a sense of intimacy with, and authorization from, God that it would have been viewed as a provocative act even by those well disposed toward him.

But the provocative character of Jesus' declaration of God's forgiveness did not end there. It has been argued that historically Jesus differed in one striking respect from his Jewish contemporaries with regard to the forgiveness of sins. In Jesus' day it was universally expected that those who sinned in a serious way against their neighbor would make restitution to the offended party and would demonstrate their repentance with a sacrifice in the Temple; lesser offenses could be atoned for simply by repentance and the sacrifice, which gave an outward sign of repentance.[22] What is striking about Jesus is that he is never portrayed as requiring this process of the sinners he encountered. E. P. Sanders writes: "[Jesus] may have offered [sinners] inclusion in the kingdom not only *while they were still sinners* but also *without* requiring repentance as normally understood, and therefore he could have been accused of being a friend of people who indefinitely *remained* sinners."[23] For example, Jesus does not ask Zacchaeus to make restitution; the tax collector volunteers to do so (Luke 19:1-10). Jesus' sense that the reign of God was imminent might have been the reason for this suspension of normal procedure, in addition to his view that the days of the present Temple were numbered (see below). If such was Jesus' attitude and behavior, it would have offended not only the Pharisees and Sadducees but ordinary pious Jews as well.

Deserving of special attention in this connection is Jesus' custom of eating and drinking at table with all sorts of people, rich and poor, the "righteous" and public sinners.

This table fellowship constituted an eloquent statement on Jesus' part, given that—and here lies the crucial key—Jesus was preaching the imminent arrival of God's salvation under the symbol of the kingdom. This orientation made such a public and recurrent deed "loaded" with religious significance for those who had eyes to see and ears to hear. In the ancient world, and certainly among the Jews of the first century C.E., to invite another to break bread together at table meant to share life with him or her and to enter into a relationship of mutual trust. That Jesus showed eagerness to break bread with sinners, those who had disobeyed the law, was not lost on his adversaries. As one who apparently saw himself as offering God's salvation in an unconditional way, Jesus effectively said to sinners: "Dine with me, enter into a trusting relationship with me,

---

22. Sanders, *Jesus and Judaism*, 206.
23. Ibid. His emphasis.

share life with me, and in that dining with me you will know and receive God's accepting love, which will mean the forgiveness of your sins. No need to go through the rituals prescribed by the Law for returning to God's good graces. Simply be open to the gift which God offers you through me.''

The basis in Jesus' pre-Easter ministry for the early Church's recognition of the risen Jesus as source of the forgiveness of sins, and not simply as one empowered to declare God's forgiveness of them (Col 1:14) and to commit to the Church the ability to forgive and retain sins (John 20:23), would seem to be primarily his practice of offering table fellowship to notorious sinners. An additional basis can be found in his exorcisms and healings considered as liberative incursions into the territory of the Evil One. The early Church, in light of the eschatological event of Easter, interpreted the risen Jesus as the eschatological Son of Man endowed with all authority and with all cosmic powers subject to him (e.g., Matt 28:18). But there is a basis in the ministry of Jesus for that post-Easter development.

Jesus confronted people with an implicit claim, which could create followers or denouncers: the claim, implied in his activity as preacher, healer, and table host, that he was able to declare people forgiven by God, without any need for Temple, sacrifice, or the customary restitution. Even the best-intentioned could take offense at him for this. With good reason the saying "Blessed is he who takes no offense at me" (Luke 7:23) is attributed to Jesus.

Jesus' Teaching

Jesus traveled about Galilee and Judea preaching the kingdom of God and teaching with authority. Unlike the scribes of his day, who went to school for many years and were then ordained as instructors in the Law, Jesus taught without any human accreditation, and even more striking, without appealing to the written or oral tradition as warrant for his teaching. In all the scholarly discussion about authentic material in the teaching attributed to Jesus, this feature seems to be agreed on by a large cross-section of students of the New Testament.[24] It was this feature which made his teaching an occasion for scandal and fascination, even when he was offering instruction which resembled other currents of reformist Judaism. We have already seen how God's reign, as an event which is imminent with regard to its full arrival but already dawning in Jesus' ministry, provides the pervasive matrix or center which illuminates his more particular teachings. In addition, his deeds of healing and exorcism, as acts of

---

24. Typical is the view of Georg Strecker, *The Sermon on the Mount: An Exegetical Commentary*, trans. O. C. Dean (Nashville: Abingdon, 1988) 62.

liberative forgiveness, illuminate some of the burden of his teaching. At this point we shall consider some of the principal elements of the teaching ascribed to him, which may well go back to the Jesus of the pre-Easter ministry, remembering all the while that critical scholarship on the sayings tradition is an area of continuing discussion and dispute.

The Parables.   While storytelling was an intricate part of Jesus' culture, as it is of all "oral" societies, Jesus' use of the parable seems to have been unique to him, affording striking access to his imagination in the service of God's reign.[25] As employed by Jesus, the parable was neither an illustration of a moral teaching, nor an allegory, nor a teaching that could be faithfully and adequately translated into non-parabolic truth. In most cases his parables tell about ordinary human life, with God and God's reign forming the plot of the story rather than a particular component of it. An element of excess or surprise springs forth from the story, provoking or shocking the listener by turning his or her world askew or upside down, and thereby challenging the listener to be open to the gift that the teller is offering. The story of the vineyard owner who gives the same pay to each worker irrespective of the length of time he has worked prods the listeners' sense of justice and fair play. Their response to the parable reveals who they are: either people who demand strict justice (God help them!) or people who are open to a world founded on generosity "beyond all reason" (Matt 20:1-16). The God who refuses to follow our rules draws near in Jesus the parable teller.

When his audience hears the story of the good Samaritan, they are invited to identify with the man in the ditch as the priest and Levite pass by, ignoring him. Then they are confronted with a quandary. The half-breed Samaritan approaches and touches the wounded man, and they remind themselves of the rabbinical teaching that the Messiah's coming could be delayed if faithful Jews allowed someone like a Samaritan to touch them. Their world is mortally challenged, for here the Samaritan approaches with compassion the man lying in the ditch. The world "feels" like this when the reign of God shows up in human relations. Can these listeners allow the Samaritan to be the compassionate neighbor beyond all stereotypes and prejudices? Can they, in turn, permit themselves to give up the observance of a religious duty and to respond to the appeal of a stranger in need, thus turning him or her into a neighbor?

In the story of the prodigal son (or better, prodigal or extravagant fa-

25. J. Jeremias, *The Parables of Jesus*, trans. S. H. Hooke, 2nd rev. ed. (New York: Scribner, . Linnemann, *Jesus of the Parables: Introduction and Exposition*, trans. J. Sturdy (New larper and Row, 1967); D. O. Via, *The Parables: Their Literary and Existential Dimen- hiladelphia: Fortress, 1967); B. McDermott, "Power and Parable in Jesus' Ministry," larke, ed., *Above Every Name: The Lordship of Christ and Social Systems* (New York msey: Paulist, 1980) 83–104.

ther) the father's going out of the house to wait eagerly for the wasteful son's return, and his forgiveness and lavish welcome of that son, are contrasted with both the elder brother's narrowness of heart and the returning son's preoccupation with his own unworthiness and the new form adversity has given to his selfishness. The father's behavior refuses to correspond to either the guilt-riddenness and self-centeredness of the one son or the rigidity and lack of love of the other. His welcome and acceptance of the errant son is defined by neither the younger son's shame and remorse nor the elder son's "good" behavior. It is the father's own choice to be lavish in love.

The New Testament sees Jesus as the primary parable of God's reign not only in what he said during his ministry, but in who he was and what he did. Indeed, the parable is the gospel in miniature.[26] There are two sides to Jesus' parable telling. First, he showed what God was like in his own dealings with people, in his "excessive" yet human way of acting. He revealed God as infinitely merciful and compassionate, wholly intent on the flourishing of human beings, the all-holy challenge to all complacency and mediocrity. God's nearness and the coming rule of God in its fullness are manifested through Jesus; he is the disclosure of God for all humankind, the disclosure which does not remove God's inexhaustible mystery but does bring that mystery near to all that is human. Second, Jesus shows what the human looks like when God is allowed to reign in human affairs. God's reign is mysterious, hidden, but nonetheless effective, as the mustard seed and leaven work in secret but with hugely disproportionate results. A divine excess shows up in human relations, a certain kind of excess which marks the authentically human.

Both the parables as living, provocative word and the teller of the parables raise the fundamental question, Who is this person?

The Beatitudes. The Beatitudes are found in Matthew's Sermon on the Mount (Matt 5:3-11), addressed to the disciples, and in Luke's Sermon on the Plain, addressed to the disciples and the crowd (Luke 6:20b-26). A case can be made that three of the four beatitudes found in Q are attributable to the historical Jesus: Those addressed to the poor, the hungry, and those who mourn.[27] Of the poor, Jesus says that they are blessed because the reign of God is theirs. Of the hungry and those who mourn, he says that they are blessed because they will be satisfied and comforted. Each of these statements is addressed to a group of people existing in some form of misery and oppression; it declares that they will experience a future reversal and compensation because God will act on their behalf (the

26. J. R. Donahue, *The Gospel in Parable: Metaphor, Narrative, and Theology in the Synoptic Gospels* (Philadelphia: Fortress, 1988).

27. For examination of the issues involved see J. Lambrecht, *The Sermon on the Mount: Proclamation and Exhortation* (Wilmington, Del.: Michael Glazier, 1985) 45-58.

theological passive) through the arrival of the divine reign.[28] The Lukan version of the Beatitudes matches the Q-source in all but one blessing. Matthew shifts the accent to interior attitude: The phrases or terms "of spirit" and "of heart," "those who thirst for righteousness," the "meek" and "merciful" refer not to a social group and its plight but to spiritual disposition.[29] Luke stresses the reality that "now," in the time of messianic fulfillment by Christ, the poor, the hungry, and those who mourn are blessed. Moreover, he adds woes addressed to the rich in keeping with his view, perceptible throughout his Gospel, that the rich are *ipso facto* people in great trouble because of the enslaving power of possessions.

In both Matthew and Luke the Beatitudes receive special notice and a certain pride of place in the Sermon, while the Sermon itself appears at an early stage in each gospel. We find additions by the early Church to both the number of beatitudes and the reversal statements. But the oldest formulas, in their simplicity and directness, share in the liberating power of Jesus' emergence in Israel as preacher of radical good news to those who feel most the absence of God's kingdom of justice and well-being.

The sense of each declaration depended essentially on the situation of the hearers who received this word from Jesus. God's advent to the poor through Jesus renders them blessed now. The distinction between the blessing and reign of God belonging to the poor now, and their satisfaction and laughter in the near future, reflects the already/not-yet tension of the kingdom's arrival. The blessing arrives in the form of Jesus and begins to become actual in the welcome by the poor of Jesus as God's offer of salvation. The prophets' call for a return to the just rule of Yahweh and for the overcoming of social injustice and corruption, which made life utterly unjust for the powerless, becomes in Jesus' declaration an implicit statement of (beginning) fulfillment. Jesus comes to those who have no recourse in human history and declares that God, who works through him, not only stands on their side and will suffice for them, but also will come to them soon in all fullness and reveal that sufficiency for all to see. In the changed situation of post-Easter Christianity, the Beatitudes suggest that in the ongoing life of the community of disciples there is blessing for those who remain companions of Jesus and walk a path modeled on his.

Jesus and the Law. Jesus of Nazareth was an Aramaic-speaking Jew living in Galilee at a time when the influence of Hellenistic and Roman culture was widespread and several currents of reform were in motion. Contemporary biblical scholarship has come to appreciate the complexity of the religious and cultural composition of Palestinian Jewry. No easy and clear distinction can be made between a Palestinian Jewry relatively

28. Ibid., 52.
29. Ibid., 63.

untouched by Greek culture, and a Greek-influenced Judaism contemporary either with Jesus or with the composition of the New Testament writings.[30] The various reform movements, such as the lay group of Pharisees and the sectarian community of the Essenes, when contrasted with the priestly, conservative Sadducees, provide further necessary background for understanding Jesus' appearance on the scene as a teacher.

When one seeks to perceive, through the complex lens of the gospel traditions, the attitude of the pre-Easter Jesus to the Law, the various strands of Jewish thought come into play.

For the Pharisees of Jesus' time, the Law or Torah consisted in both the written Torah as they understood it, namely, the Pentateuch (the five books attributed to Moses) plus the Prophets and the Writings, and the oral Torah or traditions of the fathers, the Halakah, or "fence around the Law." For the scribes, all of this was from God and revelatory of God's will, obedience to which meant salvation.

Other Jews, such as the Sadducees, took a more conservative approach, restricting the Torah or Law of God to the Pentateuch, and viewing the rest of the written Scriptures as inspired and of God but added because of Israel's sinfulness. For them, the Halakah was of human origin and not inspired by God. Thus in Palestine at the time of Jesus there was conflict between groups of Jews regarding the status and interpretation of the Torah, in a broad or narrow sense.

Furthermore, in the early Church there were deep and painful divisions about the relation of Christians to the Law, divisions which are particularly evident in the letters of Paul and the Gospel of Matthew. These divisions have shaped the Jesus-tradition.

Many of Jesus' criticisms of the Law and its observance, as ascribed to him in the New Testament, resemble the conservative line of thinking in that he felt free to criticize and indeed ignore the oral tradition of the Law. For example, with regard to the Sabbath, he declared that one might act to help a neighbor even if the situation was not life-threatening (Mark 3:1-6 par.). When he defended his disciples for rubbing together ears of corn on the Sabbath (Mark 2:23-28 par.), his basic appeal was to God's intention in creating the Sabbath: The Sabbath signified blessing and freedom for human beings, not their enslavement through entanglement in false casuistry (Mark 2:27).

Recently a number of scholars have cautioned against a too facile acceptance of the authenticity of the descriptions of disputes between Jesus and the Pharisees as we find them in the Gospels. They argue that many of these disputes actually occurred among early Christians in the Gentile

30. See M. Hengel, *Judaism and Hellenism: Studies in Their Encounter in Palestine in the Early Hellenistic Period*, trans. J. Bowden (Philadelphia: Fortress, 1974); S. Freyne, *Galilee from Alexander the Great to Hadrian 323 B.C.E. to 135 C.E.* (Wilmington, Del.: Michael Glazier, 1980).

mission, and between Christians and Jews during the period of definitive separation from Judaism. The evangelists and the sources they employed retrojected these controversies into Jesus' ministry.[31] This does not mean that there was no conflict at all between Jesus and the Pharisees, but it did not have the centrality suggested by the Gospels. Historians of first-century Judaism remind us that the Pharisees of Jesus' time did not demand that other Jews follow their religious practice of extending to daily life the laws of purity demanded of all in relation to the Temple cult. Thus if Jesus did not follow their practice, they would not have been likely to attack and criticize him. The prominence given to conflict between Jesus and the Pharisees in the Gospels reflects the historical situation after 70 C.E. and the Roman destruction of the Temple, when the Pharisees became the dominant group in Judaism and so the primary force with which Jewish Christians had to contend as they began to separate from Judaism.[32]

In the Sermon on the Mount, Jesus is pictured as speaking in antitheses ("You have heard that it was said . . . but I say to you," e.g., Matt 5:21-22). It is not certain that this way of speaking, which was employed by some of the scribes, goes back to Jesus. Among the antitheses in the Sermon of the Mount, two do appear to originate with the pre-Easter Jesus: the prohibition of divorce and the commandment to love one's enemies. Not Matthew's version, but rather Jesus' strict prohibition of divorce as recorded in Q and reflected in Luke, seems to be authentic. Jesus reiterated God's original will regarding marriage from the creation account: "Everyone who divorces his wife and marries another commits adultery, and he who marries a woman divorced from her husband commits adultery" (Luke 16:18). This teaching is paralleled among the Essenes of Qumran.[33] Also authentic is the *logion* "Love your enemies" (Matt 5:44, and possibly 5:48 as well).[34] With this commandment Jesus called people to love without boundaries and therefore to love, rather than hate, the sinner, the one person whom some ancient traditions allowed to be hated. This particular teaching does not appear to be unique to Jesus in its content but, according to all the evidence we have, nothing so simple, direct, and personally warranted (as distinct from authentication by appeal to the Torah) was taught by any other Jews before Jesus or contemporary with him.[35] As John Riches comments:

31. See, for example, W. D. Davies, *The Setting of the Sermon on the Mount* (Cambridge: Cambridge University Press, 1964).

32. See A. Saldarini, *Pharisees, Scribes, Sadducees in Palestinian Judaism* (Wilmington, Del.: Michael Glazier, 1988).

33. J. A. Fitzmyer, *The Gospel According to Luke X–XXIV* (Garden City, New York: Doubleday, 1985) 1120.

34. Ibid., 219.

35. On this point see ibid., 219–20; V. P. Furniss, *The Love Command in the New Testament* (Nashville: Abingdon, 1972) and J. Piper, *"Love Your Enemies": Jesus' Love Command in the*

The love which is demanded is something more than an extension of the love of the brotherhood to those outside, because it demands a reorientation of the love of the brotherhood. Love is no longer primarily a quality of relationships within the fold, within the walls which hold the dark and threatening powers at a distance; it is something which must prove itself in the engagement with that which is inimical and threatening.[36]

Another area in which we have evidence of Jesus' teaching is that of laws of purity. By his activity Jesus taught that certain traditional lines of division, indeed segregation, between clean and unclean were irrelevant. He consorted and ate with public sinners, with a freedom which shocked many and no doubt delighted and intrigued others (Luke 5:30). The reign of God, he taught, is like the most hospitable of hosts who sends out an invitation that is downright indiscriminate and desires only that the invitation be accepted with joy and alacrity (Matt 22:1-10 par.). God's reign has everything to do with forgiveness and mercy and nothing to do with making human categories of the "pure" and "impure" into absolutes.[37] Furthermore, Jesus declared that it is not what goes into people that makes them unclean, but what comes out of them, i.e., out of their mouths and hearts (Mark 7:18-23 par.). What pollutes is human opposition to the divine power of forgiveness and love.[38]

The closer one draws to the pre-Easter Jesus and his attitude toward the Law, the more apparent it becomes that his attitude was neither anti-Law nor anti-Jewish nor anti-tradition. There are distinctive elements in his teaching, yet his overall views were of a piece with some of the best contemporary Jewish thinking regarding the Law and its purpose in human life.[39]

The authority implied in Jesus' critique of certain understandings of the Law became an explicit Christological theme in the post-Easter communities. Jesus as the exalted Son of Man had been given all power and sovereignty (Mark 2:28 par.; cf. Dan 7:14) and thus was Lord of the Sabbath. Indeed, for Paul Jesus became *the* mediator between God and humans, replacing the Law in that function, because in his view the blessings of salvation were mediated to Christians in and through the risen Jesus in the community, no longer in and through the Jewish Torah (Rom 3:21; cf. 1 Tim 2:5). The pre-Easter Jesus acted as the end-time prophet from God. In taking liberties with the Law and calling people to a more pro-

Synoptic Gospels and the Early Christian Paraenesis (Cambridge and New York: Cambridge University Press, 1979).

36. J. Riches, *Jesus and the Transformation*, 135.

37. Ibid., 100.

38. Ibid., 140.

39. See n. 6.

found observance of its spirit, he allied himself with certain strands of reformist Judaism. Yet his sense of authorization found no parallels in the Judaism of his day. He did not appeal to tradition for his teaching, and this dimension of his teaching stands out, even if a number of his particular teachings were paralleled among his fellow Jews.

It may well be true, as some have argued, that Jesus' attitude toward the Law would not, of itself, have constituted sufficient legal grounds for leaders of the Jews to instigate his execution.[40] But this does not mean that his way of relating to the Law, when viewed in conjunction with all of his teaching and action, might not have implied an extraordinary claim about his relationship with the divine originator of that Law, a claim which would become all the more dangerous when the enthusiasm of the crowd for him swelled and he challenged the Temple by word and deed.

The Calling of Disciples. Among the assured results of research into the pre-Easter Jesus is his calling of disciples. While many men and women were affected by Jesus' teaching and healing touch, only a few became disciples, and even fewer became members of his intimate circle, those disciples who were called the "Twelve." The name had a symbolic function, possibly referring to God's intention—communicated through Jesus—to restore the "completed" Israel, with the Twelve as its regents, when the new age arrived. Unlike the rabbis, who accepted into their circle students who petitioned to join them, Jesus himself called disciples to "come after him" and to participate in his mission. "And he went up into the hills, and called to him those whom he desired; and they came to him. And he appointed twelve, to be with him, and to be sent out to preach and have authority to cast out demons" (Mark 3:13-15). This text reflects both Jesus' initiative in calling the Twelve and the fact that they were to do as he did. Just as Jesus was being sent by God to preach the reign of God and cast out demons, so they were being sent by Jesus to share in his mission. Being called, being with and being sent constituted the basic features of discipleship with Jesus.

Martin Hengel has examined the New Testament traditions bearing on Jesus' calling of disciples and, apropos of Matthew 8:21-22, argues that it is authentically of the pre-Easter Jesus because there are no parallels to it in Judaism or the Hellenistic world.[41] In calling his disciples, Jesus was effectively saying a shocking thing: Come, follow me, and participate in the reign of God that is already breaking in, an event which takes precedence over both sacred taboos and the fourth commandment of the Decalogue given to Moses and Israel by God. Jesus said to a man, "Let those dead to the arriving kingdom and its primacy bury those who have

40. E. P. Sanders, *Jesus and Judaism*, 326–27.

41. *The Charismatic Leader and His Followers*, trans. J. Greig (New York: Crossroad, 1981).

physically died.'' The only parallel to this unconditional kind of call that Hengel could find was Yahweh's calling of prophets in the Old Testament. Coming from an untutored, wandering teacher, Jesus's call would necessarily be offensive to pious Jews. His call was explicitly and focally soteriological, that is, it concerned the saving reign of God, but it also implied a special, indeed extraordinary, authority on Jesus' part, which of itself was ambiguous and productive of very diverse responses and interpretations: Some followed him and others rejected him as belonging to the Evil One. But it is not surprising that even the most genuinely religious Jews at the time would have found such a command, with its implied authority, a stumbling block to commitment to Jesus.

Those who did commit themselves to one degree or another and began to follow Jesus joined this preacher's company, became schooled in his intentions and values, and learned the cost of discipleship. They left everything to follow Jesus, undergoing a conversion which resembled that of Gentiles becoming Jews (who, similarly, had to leave all social and personal goods to ''follow after'' Yahweh), the most significant difference being that their focus was not the Torah but Jesus as the way. There is no scholarly agreement that Jesus proclaimed to his followers, ''If any would come after me, let them deny themselves and take up their cross and follow me'' (Mark 8:34 par.). But it did not take them very long to realize that in following the Master they would be involved in conflicts that had the potential of becoming life-threatening.

Thus in Jesus' call to discipleship we find another expression of his sense of special delegation by God, the authority of the eschatological prophet who addresses people with the urgency of God's final emissary to Israel.

The Our Father. Jesus taught his disciples a prayer as a mark of their discipleship relationship to him. The Our Father is a thoroughly Jewish prayer, differing from almost all other instances of known Jewish prayer of that time in its marked brevity, its sequence of invocations followed by petitions, and its rather inclusive tenor. Luke's version (11:2-4) stands closer to Q and to the way Jesus taught the prayer, while Matthew's version (6:9-13), the more familiar one, preserves some of the more original wording in the parts common to both gospels.[42] The original Aramaic prayer *may* have looked something like this:

> Father!
> May your name be sanctified!
> May your kingdom come!
> Give us this day our bread for subsistence.
> Forgive us our debts

---

42. Lambrecht, *Sermon on the Mount*, 130.

> as we have forgiven our debtors.
> And bring us not into temptation.[43]

The prayer is addressed to Abba, God as Jesus was accustomed to address the divine Thou in his life. There follow two invocations and then three petitions. Both invocations bear on deeds which God can and will do, namely, sanctifying the divine name before all the nations at the end of the age, and bringing about the eschatological fullness of the divine reign. Next the basic needs of Jesus' followers are brought to God as requests: bread each day for the body; forgiveness of sins, and protection from *peirasmos*, that is, from the final test or tribulation in which our faith-relationship to God and God's Christ would be in danger of being betrayed.[44]

Jesus and the Rich and the Poor

Jesus himself was raised in the household of a craftsman, a carpenter, in what we might call a lower-middle-class environment, which at the beginning of the Common Era in Galilee, would not have been the most economically secure position; but his family was hardly destitute. In his ministry he traveled much, although Capernaum seems to have been the center of his Galilean ministry. He was dependent on some women of means for support during his travels and apparently did not work at a trade himself.

In his dealings with people of differing economic backgrounds, his most striking concern was their relationship to God's reign. Thus the relatively prosperous Zacchaeus was told that salvation had come to his house with the advent of Jesus, and in response he vowed to pay back those whom he had defrauded.[45] Jesus dined with wealthy publicans and challenged them to recognize the one dining with them. In the story of the rich man and Lazarus, Jesus contrasted the fate of the wealthy man and the wretch who lay at his doorstep.[46] On the other hand, Jesus was very much at home with the poor. The crowds which followed him no doubt numbered among them many of the economically poor in Palestine. In the story of the widow's mite, Jesus observed that the poor widow gave of her substance to support the Temple (Mark 12:41-44; Luke 21:1-4). This has often been taken to be a statement in praise of the widow for her wholehearted devotion, but Joseph Fitzmyer believes that Jesus more likely intended his

---

43. Thus Fitzmyer, *Luke X–XXIV*, 901.

44. Ibid., 141–42.

45. On the historicity of this incident see, among others, J. Fitzmyer, *Luke (X–XXIV)* 1218–19.

46. On the probability that the core of this parable goes back to Jesus, see ibid., 1127.

remark as a critique of an oppressive aspect of the religious system of the time.[47] Indeed, Jesus' whole ministry was pervaded by compassion toward the multitude, for they were like sheep without a shepherd (Mark 6:34; Matt 9:36).

The gift offered by Jesus to both rich and poor was the blessing of the reign of God. That blessing consisted in their radical acceptance by God, leading to forgiveness of their sins and conversion to the values of the kingdom.

Can one say that Jesus acted in solidarity with the poor, that he made an option for the poor? Luke's Gospel has certainly impressed that reading of Jesus' ministry deeply on the consciousness of many Christians, even in our own day. Liberation theology has rightfully developed this Lukan perspective in many challenging ways. Jesus' own earthly ministry, as far as historical-critical research discloses, seems rather to have cut across the divisions between rich and poor by the urgency of his message regarding the inbreaking reign. It is in Luke's Gospel that a clearly defined portrait of Jesus as acting in favor of the poor over against the rich emerges. In his own ministry, Jesus was not inaugurating a program of gradual amelioration. To us who live two thousand years later, such a program would make a lot of sense. But in light of the eschatologically impending reign of God, gradualism made no sense at all. The power of sin in its many forms was the obstacle to participation in the blessings of the kingdom. Jesus sided with the good creatureliness of both rich and poor and the possibility of their sharing in the kingdom, while opposing their sin, whatever forms it might take. It would seem that Jesus extended a welcoming hand to all those who were excluded and marginalized in his society, inviting them inside the compassionate embrace of his Father.

Jesus and Women

Each age brings its own perspectives to the study of Jesus, and those perspectives are colored by the issues and concerns of the period in question. In our own time the struggle of women to achieve equal status and true partnership with men has permitted us to appreciate Jesus' own attitudes toward women, which did not reflect contemporary Jewish or pagan thinking about them. Indeed, his approach was not going to acquire institutional form in the Church as the centuries unfolded.

Jesus showed a respect for women which recognized in them adult children of God who were not to be treated as chattel or possessions of men but as persons in their own right. There were women of means who supported his ministry; there were others who were disciples in a more inti-

47. Ibid., 1321.

mate sense.[48] Jesus took the woman caught in adultery seriously as an individual and refused to be drawn into a collective condemnation of her, but instead cared enough to recognize her contrition (John 7:53–8:11). Responding to the woman who anointed his feet with her tears, he comfortably received what ordinarily would have been a very sensual sign and recognized in it not sexual seduction but great love born of forgiveness (Luke 7:37-50). He was affected by the Canaanite woman's quickness of wit and led beyond his previous viewpoint on the place of Gentiles in his ministry (Matt 15:21-28).

Jesus himself was willing to compare God to the housewife who searched and searched until she found the lost coin. Looking down on his beloved Jerusalem, he felt like a hen who yearns to gather her chicks under her wing. Indeed, Jesus saw himself as a sophia (wisdom) figure sent by Sophia God.[49]

Research into Jesus' way of relating to women and the role of women in the New Testament and early Church has been extensive in recent years. This is an excellent example of the way texts (in this case the Gospels) show forth more of their meaning when approached with new questions and issues.

Jesus Names Himself

The New Testament portraits of Jesus involve the use of many titles and names which express the faith of the various New Testament communities in him: Christ or Messiah, Son of God, the Word or Wisdom of God, Son of Man, Son of David, Bread of Life, Shepherd, the Prophet who is to come, Servant of Yahweh, and Savior. These titles or names are the distillation of responses to the presence and action of Jesus as experienced in faith by the earliest communities. Thus they did not simply denote preconceived notions that were applied to Jesus. In fact, as we shall see, most of them were quite fluid in their meaning and received much of their significance from Jesus, the one to whom the communities were responding. Thus one must consider the history of each term and, even more, the person to whom the term was addressed.

48. B. Witherington III, *Women in the Ministry of Jesus: A Study of Jesus' Attitudes to Women and Their Roles as Reflected in His Earthly Life* (Cambridge and New York: Cambridge University Press, 1984); E. Schüssler Fiorenza, *In Memory of Her: A Feminist Theological Reconstruction of Christian Origins* (New York: Crossroad, 1983); E. Tetlow, *Women and Ministry in the New Testament* (New York and Mahwah: Paulist, 1980).

49. E. Schüssler Fiorenza, *In Memory of Her*, 130–37; see also S. Schneiders, *Women and the Word: The Gender of God in the New Testament and the Spirituality of Women* (New York and Mahwah: Paulist, 1986).

At this point we shall ask whether there are any titles or names that the pre-Easter Jesus used to speak of himself and what these might indicate, however indirectly, about his own sense of himself. The most significant titles or names that may have been employed by Jesus of himself are Messiah or Christ, Son of God, and Son of Man. Let us see whether Jesus did use these expressions as self-designations, and if so, how.

Messiah or Christ

In the Old Testament the title Messiah (*Christos* in Greek, both terms meaning the "anointed one") refers first of all to the anointed king of Israel such as Saul (1 Sam 10:1) and secondarily to the anointed priest (Lev 4:3). The "promised Messiah" of Israel originally meant the anointed king of the house, or line, of David, who would set his people free and usher in a lasting peace. Thus the messiah traditionally expected was a this-worldly king who would bring about a public, visible liberation and social well-being. In Jesus' time the notion of a king emancipating his people was still alive and flourishing, but there was also hope for the coming of an anointed figure (a "Messiah" or "Christ") who would be prophetic and not royal, who would realize the promise made by Moses in Deuteronomy 18:15: "The Lord your God will raise up for you a prophet like me from among you, from your brethren—him you shall heed." Further, Second and Third Isaiah contain mysterious words about a figure anointed by the Spirit who would bring good news to the poor and bind up the brokenhearted, proclaim liberty to the captives, and open up the prisons for those who were bound (Isa 61:1). Finally, hope existed as well for a Solomonic Son of David, a wise teacher and charismatic healer who would be God's anointed because he was anointed by the Spirit. As we saw above, in some recent studies this complex notion is summarized by the name or title "the eschatological prophet," although no such title was extant at the time of Jesus. The nearest we come to it in the Gospels is the phrase "the prophet who is to come" (John 6:14).

The Gospels present us with several moments when Jesus is associated with the title Messiah. The most dramatic one occurs at the midpoint of Mark's Gospel (8:29), where Jesus asks the disciples who they think he is, and Peter declares: "You are the Christ." As it stands in Mark, Jesus promptly teaches them about the Son of Man's having to suffer, be killed, and then rise again, a perspective on the Messiah which Peter finds unpalatable. When he dares to rebuke Jesus, Peter is rebuked in turn by Jesus in the strongest terms: "Get behind me, Satan! For you are not on the side of God, but of humans." Some scholars argue that the earlier form of the tradition had Jesus rebuking Peter immediately after the latter's confession of Jesus' messiahship. In any case, if Peter's confession goes back to Jesus' own earthly life, it occasioned a clear dissociation on Jesus' part from what Peter and the other disciples took the term "messiah" to mean. Another situation in which the title is referred to Jesus arises at his trial when, according to Mark 14:61, the high priest asks Jesus whether he is the Christ, the Son of the Blessed. Jesus answers, "I am," and then goes on to employ a different title, the Son of Man. Caution needs to be shown here, as with all the accounts of the trial, because it is notoriously difficult to determine the historical elements of the various versions of Jesus' last days in the Gospels. Given Mark's theology of the suffering and crucified Christ and Son of Man, it is not surprising that he shows Jesus accepting the title of Christ only when he has been bound over and is powerless in the hands of others, who think they can do with him as they will. Now Mark can say to his readers, this is the authentic Messiah, while at the same time he has Jesus speak about an exalted Son of Man coming on the clouds of heaven. In the Gospel of Matthew (26:64), to the question whether he is the Christ, the Son of God, Jesus responds, "You have said so," which can mean either that he accepts the title or that he rejects it. In Luke's Gospel (23:3) Pilate asks Jesus, "Are you the King of the Jews?" using the title that appears on the cross (23:38). The same ambiguous answer is offered here. Thus the trial scenes offer us no firm ground on which to stand regarding Jesus' acceptance of the Messiah title.

The two other pertinent texts, Matthew 23:10 ("you have one master, the Christ") and John 4:4-26 (Jesus with the Samaritan woman) do not go back to the pre-Easter Jesus. We may conclude, therefore, that we do not find any evidence of Jesus' calling himself the Messiah or Christ in either the kingly-nationalistic or the prophetic-eschatological sense. The fact that the title became a primary one, and among Gentile Christians a proper name, for Jesus after the resurrection suggests, on the one hand, how his own ministry, passion and death, and glorification gave content to the title when applied to him and, on the other hand, how the complex of signification which developed before his appearance in history gave the term a richness and flexibility that lent itself to Christological use.

Son of God

In the Old Testament the title Son of God referred either to the whole elected people of Israel or to the king, or later to a prophet or righteous person. The title evoked God's favor in electing and accepting a group or individual to execute the divine saving purposes. The idea of begetting or generating this Son of God never entered the picture for the Israelites, although their neighbors offered them options along this line which they abhorred. Jesus never referred to himself as *the* Son of God or even as *a* son of God in the New Testament. As we have seen, when he was asked by the high priest in the Gospel of Matthew whether he were the Son of God, he gives an ambiguous answer, just as he did in Luke's Gospel to the question about his being the Son of the Blessed One.

A notable passage in Matthew's Gospel seems at first sight to indicate that Jesus understood himself to be *the* Son of God: "All things have been delivered to me by my Father; and no one knows the Son except the Father, and no one knows the Father except the Son and anyone to whom the Son chooses to reveal him" (11:27). Even if the core of this passage goes back to the pre-Easter Jesus, there is good evidence that the saying about father and son derives from a Palestinian proverb about the apprenticeship of sons with fathers in the father's trade.[50] To be sure, in the church after Easter the proverb acquired a richer, Christological meaning. Indeed, John's Gospel developed this theme eloquently. But its use by Jesus does not indicate that he explicitly spoke of himself as *the* Son of God.

Much more important is Jesus' custom of naming God "Abba." His use of this name surely points to a sense on Jesus' part of being a son of God, and indeed in a very special but not fully defined way. Here we encounter the firmest ground in Jesus' own pattern of speaking for the early Church's confident titling of him as Son of God. The early Church's understanding of God's empowerment of Jesus at Easter gave full Christological content to this title as prayerful response to Jesus' presence in the community. Before that its implied use by the earthly Jesus expressed his sense of election and favor from God involving both call and mission to Israel.

Son of Man

We now turn to the most difficult title, difficult because of the vast amount of inconclusive scholarship expended on deciphering what meaning(s) it might have in the New Testament, whether Jesus might have used it as a self-designation, and if so with what significance.

With few exceptions Jesus is the one who uses this title in the New Testament. It shows up about seventy times in the Synoptic Gospels and a dozen in the Fourth Gospel, although some of these occurrences are clearly additions of the evangelist or of prior textual traditions. In two places the title is used by others (Acts 7:56; John 12:34). It is clearly Aramaic. Jesus is never portrayed as saying outright, "I am the Son of Man," but there are times when the Gospels seem to portray him as referring to himself when using the title, e.g., Matthew 8:20; Mark 8:31.

---

50. Jeremias, *New Testament Theology*, 59–60.

Biblical scholars generally agree that the Aramaic expression *bar 'enas(a')* was not a title before the formation of the New Testament, and some would insist that even in the New Testament it does not function as other titles do. For example, during his ministry Jesus is never addressed as Son of Man, and the title is never a matter of controversy or discussion. It is generally agreed that the title can mean "a human being," or can have the indefinite sense of "someone." Its possible use as a circumlocution for "I" when an individual is speaking has been much discussed recently without resolution.[51] The evangelists felt free to use the title as a substitute for "I," as we find by a comparison of Mark 8:27c with its parallel, Matthew 16:13. In Ezekiel, God addresses the prophet with this phrase, and here it simply means "man." In the apocalyptic Book of Daniel (7:13), the one "like a son of Man" is actually a representative of the faithful saints of Israel. The phrase occurs also in the apocalyptic Book of Enoch, but there is no agreement among scholars regarding its use as a title there.

It has frequently been noted that there are three different and unrelated classes of Son of Man sayings in the New Testament found on Jesus' lips: (1) Jesus as the earthly, lowly Son of Man (e.g., Luke 9:58); (2) Jesus as the suffering Son of Man (e.g., Mark 8:31); and (3) Jesus as the Son of Man coming in glory or judgment (e.g., Matt 24:27).

Some exegetes would maintain that the Aramaic phrase "the son of man" was indeed used by Jesus as a generic self-designation that needed to receive content, as it were, from Jesus himself.[52] To them it seems very probable that Jesus used the phrase Son of Man, given the well-nigh complete consistency with which it is put on his lips, whereas it seems improbable that he used it as a kind of title to refer to another, exalted figure who would come at the final judgment. Some scholars do hold this latter view.[53] But it is extremely difficult to square an expectation on Jesus' part of an eschatological figure distinct from himself with his own sense of authority in relation to the arrival of God's reign.

To the view that Jesus used the term of himself in a generic, allusive way is added the further point that the early community took over Jesus' usage and filled it out with eschatological content in the light of Easter and the faith-conviction that Jesus would soon return to judge the living and the dead. The fact that the Gospels never show Jesus as explicitly naming himself the coming Son of Man would indicate the early Church's de-

51. J. R. Donahue, "Recent Studies on the Origin of 'Son of Man' in the Gospels," *Catholic Biblical Quarterly* 48 (1986) 486–90.

52. L. Hurtado, "New Testament Christology: A Critique of Bousset's Influence," *Theological Studies* 40 (1979) 311–12.

53. For example, R. H. Fuller, *Foundations of New Testament Christology* (New York: Scribner, 1965) 123.

sire to respect the fact that Jesus never so named himself during his earthly ministry. The identification of Jesus with the exalted Son of Man by the early Church did not lead to confusion between the earthly stage and the exalted, post-resurrection stage, as is proved by the sense of otherness preserved in the portrait of the Jesus of the ministry speaking about the coming Son of Man.

Another view would hold that, in the absence of new documentation, we shall never achieve any clarity about the links between the title and the pre-Easter Jesus, and that we would do better to see it in relation to the development of the gospel as such. Advocates of this view continue that the title serves as a strand representing the earthly Jesus, human like us, who was vindicated at the resurrection and given power and glory after being rejected and suffering "many things."[54]

What does appear very clearly is that we cannot learn anything about Jesus' self-understanding from the use of the phrase "Son of Man" in the Gospels.

The Christological title Son of Man did not last long as a living title in the early Church beyond the circle of Aramaic-speaking Jewish Christians, because it derives from a current of tradition that was foreign to Greek-speaking Jews of the Diaspora. Nonetheless, because it was firmly rooted in its tradition it continued to be used until the end of the first century (even if its Greek translation makes for a barbarism). In the second century, beginning with Ignatius of Antioch (d. ca. 107) and Irenaeus of Lyons (d. ca. 200), the expression lost all apocalyptic and eschatological significance and came to designate Jesus Christ's humanity as distinguished from his divinity.

Upon examination, the issue of Jesus' naming of himself reveals itself to be a complicated one. He seemed to name himself relationally in his responsive naming of God as Abba and in his behavior as the final representative of God's reign. God and God's reign as spelling ultimate blessing and transformation for humankind were Jesus' ultimate concerns, and these concerns disclose his meaning much more accurately than any inherited title or newly forged name. The early Church soon realized all too well that Jesus transcends every partial identification and title even as he responds to all the human concerns embedded in those identifications and titles.

The Provocative Act in the Temple

Jesus' saying about the destruction of the Temple functions in the Synoptic Gospels as one of the accusations laid against him at his trial

---

54. Donahue, "Recent Studies," 498.

(Mark 14:58 par.). Allied to this saying was his act of overthrowing the moneychangers' tables in the Temple (Mark 11:15-19 par.) which occurred just before the trial. In John's Gospel this event occurs at the beginning of Jesus' ministry (2:13-16) but has a similar effect of setting the Jewish authorities (particularly the Sadducees, the guardians of the Temple) against him. The event is anchored securely in Jesus' public life, although neither the time of the act nor the intention underlying it are completely certain. Only John alludes explicitly to Zechariah 14:21, but scholars like Jeremias, who view the conduct of the merchants as a profanation of the Temple which Jesus then "cleansed," see Jesus acting as the end-time prophet fulfilling the word of prophecy: "And there shall no longer be a trader in the house of the Lord of hosts on that day [i.e., on the Day of Yahweh]."[55] Jesus' dramatic gesture no doubt took place in the court of the Gentiles, where traders were permitted to sell sacrificial animals and exchange the pilgrims' money so that they could purchase those animals. More recently it has been maintained that there was no question of an unclean situation in the Temple being cleansed, since what was going on there was completely legitimate, i.e., in accord with God's Law and essential to the functioning of the Temple.[56]

The deed finds a possible interpretation in the Temple saying attributed to Jesus by John: "Destroy this temple and in three days I will raise it up" (2:19). In Mark 13:1-2 Jesus predicts the destruction of the Temple and, as we saw, in Mark 14:58 he is accused of threatening its destruction himself. E. P. Sanders connects the deed with the Temple saying and considers it historical fact: Jesus' act in the Temple was intended by him as its symbolic destruction.[57] Whether the gesture of overturning tables qualifies as a symbol of destruction is questionable, but it may well have signified the symbolic *interruption* of the Temple's (legitimate) functioning.

In the new age, according to Jewish belief, there would be a new Temple, and the old Temple would be no more. Jesus' act could thus have signified that he was ushering in the new age, which would spell the end of the old Temple. Such a claim of authority with regard to the Temple and agency regarding the arrival of the new age, God's reign, would have been profoundly provocative and infuriating to the priests who—rightfully— served God in their service of the Temple.

The Jesus of the Ministry in the Q-Source and the Four Gospels

We have examined some of the principal traits of the pre-Easter Jesus insofar as literary and historical-critical study can arrive at some degree

---

55. Jeremias, *New Testament Theology*, 145.

56. Sanders, *Jesus and Judaism*, 63.

57. Ibid., 75.

of certainty about them. But Jesus' ministry is retrievable not only in a fragmentary way in stage one of the gospel tradition, namely, his pre-Easter life, but in the two other stages as well: stage two being Jesus' ministry in the pre-gospel traditions (oral and written) of the post-Easter Christian community and (most confidently of all) stage three, the ministry of Jesus in the final redaction (edition) of the Gospels as we now have them.

At this point it would be good to take a brief look at the major interpretations of Jesus' ministry which the New Testament offers, namely those in the Q-source and in the four Gospels. Here I will restrict my comments to the parts of these documents which portray Jesus as engaged in ministry; thus I will allude only secondarily to Christological motifs in the infancy narratives (Matthew and Luke), to the passion narratives (all four Gospels), and to the resurrection appearances (Matthew, Luke and John).

This brief summary can serve to remind us that the revelation of who Jesus Christ is comes to us primarily in the New Testament as a whole, which is the Word of God in human words, and only secondarily in the reconstructions of historians.[58]

The Jesus of the Ministry in the Q-Source

The Q-source is a document postulated by New Testament scholars to help explain the textual agreement of Matthew and Luke in material which is not from Mark (taking Mark as the first Gospel written). Matthew and Luke have about 235 verses in common, which do not derive from Mark. Earl Richard offers a helpful summary of the material from Q:

> The Q-passages constitute a sayings source consisting of prophetic, eschatological, sapiential (wisdom) and oracular sayings with little narrative. We use the following convenient form-critical classification: parables (well over a dozen, among others: the marriage feast/great supper, the stray/lost sheep, and talents/pounds), oracles (against the Galilean cities) or woes (against the Pharisees and scribes/lawyers), beatitudes, prophetic pronouncements (promises, present/future correlatives, and sentences of holy law), wisdom words (on love of enemies, on judgment), exhortations (Lord's prayer, advice on forgiveness and final judgment), and lastly narratives. The last is poorly represented. . . .[59]

It appears that the community from which the Q-document originated was apocalyptic in its thinking. This community believed that the present

58. This is a main concern of the recent statement by the Pontifical Biblical Commission on Scripture and Christology. See J. A. Fitzmyer, *Scripture and Christology: A Statement of the Biblical Commission with a Commentary* (New York and Mahwah: Paulist, 1986).

59. E. Richard, *Jesus One and Many: The Christological Concept of New Testament Authors* (Wilmington, Del.: Michael Glazier, 1988) 86. I am indebted to Richard for what follows.

world is full of evil but soon, after a time of great tribulation, it will give way to God's judgment, which will mean salvation for the elect and condemnation for those who have rejected God's emissary. Of particular concern to the community was God's reign, radical obedience to the Law in line with Jesus' view of the Law, Jesus' claim on disciples to leave all to follow him, and the expectation of the imminent arrival of the end-time. Much has been made of the fact that the cross and resurrection do not figure in its theology but pride of place goes to Jesus as the coming Son of Man who will exercise judgment on Israel.

Jesus himself in Q is primarily the Son of Man who will come as eschatological judge. In his ministry he is an emissary of Wisdom sent to Israel to reveal the long-hidden secrets of his Father (Matt 11:25 and Luke 10:21-22). His ministry is to Israel, it is a saving mission which involves an urgent call to repentance and full discipleship or unqualified commitment (Matt 11:21-23; Luke 10:13-15). The reign of God belongs to those who suffer for the sake of the Son of Man (Matt 5:3-12; Luke 6:20-23). Jesus' actions will be a cause of division (Matt 10:34-36; Luke 12:51-53). Those who acknowledge Jesus in his ministry will be acknowledged by the eschatological Son of Man at the time of judgment (Matt 10:32-33; Luke 12:8-9). Rejection is an important theme of Q: Israel rejects God's emissaries, including Jesus, and that rejection will spell condemnation for God's elect and the opening of salvation to the Gentiles (Matt 8:11; Luke 13:29).

The Jesus of the Ministry in Mark

The first of the written Gospels presents the story of the good news of Jesus Christ (1:1, variant reading). The literary character of Mark, and of the Gospels which follow, owes much to the Hellenistic form of heroic "biography." Most of Mark's Gospel is devoted to Jesus' ministry; the dramatic unfolding of his identity occurs mainly through the evangelist's adroit structuring of the narrative of that ministry. Indeed, the entire Gospel is a narrative of the progressive revelation of Jesus' true identity, articulated in two main divisions. The first division begins with Jesus' baptism and concludes with Peter's confession of him as the Christ (8:29-30). During this part of the narrative the reader is witness to the so-called messianic secret, by which Jesus seeks to keep his identity concealed so that his activity and person will be understood only in relation to the Church's kerygma of Cross and resurrection. The second part runs from the first prediction of the passion and resurrection (8:31) to the end of the Gospel, when the disciples are sent on mission to the Galilee of the Gentiles. In this part Jesus' identity is revealed: He is the Christ manifested and commissioned as God's Son, who will suffer and rise as the Son of Man and be professed as the Son of God when the eschatological signs of God's vindication have occurred (the great darkness and the rending of the curtain of the Temple).

At three crucial points in the narrative, God signals his revelation of who Jesus is: the beginning of part one (the heavenly voice speaking only to Jesus at the baptism), the beginning of part two (the heavenly voice speaking to those with Jesus at the transfiguration) and the end of the Gospel (the words of the young man [= angel] to the women at the tomb after the resurrection). In part one the people greatly appreciate Jesus for his teaching and deeds of power; but Jesus' true identity is not revealed by the Gospel writer, and only the demons recognize who he is. In part two the reader is led into the revelation of Jesus as the suffering and rising Son of Man. Jesus teaches his disciples about his own suffering and rising, and it is this teaching that the heavenly voice at the transfiguration commends to those who are in Jesus' company. In the second part there are no human confessions of Jesus' identity until the centurion's confession at the foot of the cross.

The title Son of Man is used by Mark to link the coming eschatological Jesus with the suffering and rising Jesus. Christ as a title occurs at crucial points in Mark as well: at the beginning of the Gospel, as the content of Peter's confession, and in a question put by the high priest. Finally, "teacher" is a significant Markan title for Jesus, with the emphasis shifting from his teaching of general audiences in part one to his focus on the disciples in part two.

The Jesus of the Ministry in Matthew

It has been suggested that "Jesus" is the most significant name or title for the hero of Matthew's Gospel. This Jesus is the Christ, promised in multiple ways by the Scriptures, who is Son of God in a special way (see below). While Son of Man is a fairly frequent term in Matthew, it does not carry the same importance for him that Christ, Son of God, or indeed the name of Jesus does.

In the Matthean infancy narrative Jesus is shown to be Son of God, because God is his Father, and son of David through Joseph of the house of David. The structure of the Gospel reveals Jesus to be one greater than Moses; he is the divinely sent, final, and unsurpassable teacher of the eternally valid law of God. Indeed, the entire central portion of the Gospel is divided into five sections ("books"), each containing a narrative and a discourse by Jesus and concluding with the phrase "and when Jesus had finished . . ." (7:28; 11:1; 13:53; 19:1; 26:1). This arrangement has convinced some scholars that Jesus' teaching was regarded by Matthew as the new Torah addressed not to Israel but to the Christian Church.

In addition to the five-book division, another way of dividing Matthew's Gospel is according to the main elements of classical biography: the presentation of the hero (1:1–4:16), his accomplishments (4:17–16:20) and his fate (16:21–28:20). Earl Richard sees the first arrangement as stemming from the evangelist's purpose (to present the teachings of the Risen Christ) and the second as occasioned by the genre within which he was writing (classical biography).

Matthew's Christology is higher (more exalted) than Mark's for several reasons. First of all, unlike Mark (and Q), the teacher in the Matthean ministry is not simply an emissary of Wisdom but Wisdom itself, who has dispatched the other envoys (10:40). This involves the important Old Testament notion of *shaliach* (authorized messenger or apostle), according to which the welcome extended to the emissary is effectively a welcome to the one who sent the envoy.[60] Second, Matthew goes beyond Mark in declaring that Jesus is God's Son in the explicit sense that God alone is Jesus' Father. This idea comes to expression in the infancy narrative and at numerous times when Jesus of the ministry refers to God as his Father. Matthew's higher Christology is strikingly indicated by his location of Jesus' teaching and Easter revelation on the "mountain," the place where God has taught the chosen people. Further, Jesus' permanent presence to the community is proclaimed at the beginning of the Gospel by the title Emmanuel and at its close by the words of the Risen One himself.

Jesus' audience in the great discourses of the Gospel is the Church, and the concerns addressed are theirs. Matthew wrote his Gospel after the Jewish-Roman war when Pharisaism had assumed the leadership of Judaism after the destruction of the Temple. Jesus affirms the Matthean Church, which was probably composed of Jewish and Gentile Christians, as the true Israel over against Matthew's opponents who will soon become organized in the form later known as Jamnian Pharisaism; thus he reveals himself as the fulfiller, not abolisher, of the whole law and the prophets. Portrayed as thoroughly Jewish himself, Jesus is nonetheless profoundly polemical toward all Jewish leaders and groups on the grounds of their hypocrisy and failure to be faithful to the most important matters of the Law (23:23). At the same time, Gentiles are often shown in a positive light and are included in the Church's universal mission (28:19).

The Jesus of the Ministry in Luke

A full appreciation of Lukan theology and Christology requires a reading of the third Gospel and the Acts of the Apostles as a two-volume work

---

60. G. Kittel and G. Friedrich, eds., *Theological Dictionary of the New Testament*, abridged in one volume by G. W. Bromiley (Grand Rapids: Eerdmans, 1985), s. v. "apostolos."

by a single author. For our purposes it is sufficient to consider Luke's understanding of the Jesus of the ministry in the Gospel, provided we remember that, in Luke's overall scheme, the ministry of the early Church as portrayed in Acts participates in the power of the same Spirit which led Jesus in his pre-Easter prophetic service of others, and shares in the same unitary saving plan of God for all people.

Luke's Jesus is the agent of God par excellence in a narrative that is ultimately theological, for it gives great prominence to the divine visitation to God's people and the divine activity aimed at realizing a plan of emphatically universal salvation. Many things "must" (*dei*) happen for the fulfillment of the divine plan. Everything Jesus is and does is an expression of it. Earl Richard calls this an "agency Christology."[61] Jesus is the Son of God, Son of Man and the prophet. The most important title is Christ, but Luke's favorite title is Lord. In his inaugural appearance in the synagogue, Jesus presents himself as the Isaian servant-prophet, filled with God's Spirit. Furthermore, Jesus is Lord before his birth, during his earthly ministry, and at his resurrection. In fact, Luke identifies the earthly and exalted Jesus by his employment of titles.

The Lukan Jesus of the ministry is given the most human and appealing portrait in the Gospels. In Luke we find parables that occur nowhere else, such as the good Samaritan (10:29-37), the prodigal son (15:11-32), the rich man and Lazarus (16:19-31), and the Pharisee and the publican (18:9-14). Jesus is the compassionate, Spirit-led prophet who opts for the poor, the marginalized, and the broken in mind and body. It is Luke's Jesus who castigates the rich and holds out hope and help to the poor. "It is principally Luke who attributes to Jesus such humanistic traits as forgiveness, mercy, love of enemy, stress upon doing rather than saying, upon giving, joy, and frequent prayer."[62] While the Lukan Jesus is unmistakably Jewish, he often alludes in his ministry to the mission to the Gentiles. Peculiar to Luke is the organization of a major portion of Jesus' ministry into a journey to Jerusalem (9:51-19:27).

The Jesus of the Ministry in John

In John's Gospel the Johannine community reveals its struggle with Judaism and its own internal conflicts about its relationship to and understanding of Jesus. The entire Gospel is divided into a "Book of Signs" and a "Book of Glory." In the first book Jesus performs a series of signs which gradually reveal his identity and his origin as *the* Son of the heavenly

61. E. Richard, *Jesus One and Many*, 178.
62. Ibid., 179.

Father, amid clashes with those who are opposed to him. The second book portrays Jesus' self-presentation to his disciples.

The Jesus of John's Gospel does not show the same common humanity that is found in the Synoptics. His prayer is for the sake of his audience (11:42). His knowledge seems unbounded (6:6) and his word all-powerful (18:6). The Jesus of the Johannine ministry is fully aware that he is the descending and ascending Son of Man, sent by the Father to do his will by revealing the Father's glory. He is Wisdom itself, possessing all the qualities ascribed to her, for example, preexistence and the ability to expose humankind and its evil deeds as well as to offer blessing to those who are willing to receive it; also, like Wisdom, he comes from God and returns to God. Jesus does not simply give saving knowledge symbolized by food and drink, but is himself true bread and wine, and the water which will take away all thirst. Jesus is Wisdom and greater than Wisdom. As the Son he enjoys a unique union with the Father, a union which he opens to those who believe in him.

Conclusion

We have seen that there is no obvious, linear continuity between the Christological titles employed by the early Church and Jesus' self-designations. But there is important continuity between those Christological titles and Jesus' exercise of authority and sense of his own intimate involvement in the arrival of God's reign. His preaching of God's reign as imminent and connected with his own activity, his prophetic act in the Temple, and his sense of authority led some to see him as conspiring with the Evil One, while others recognized in him the agency of the God of Israel.

Some authors speak of an implicit Christology at work in Jesus' ministry and person, one which Easter makes explicit. Others prefer to say that the pre-Easter Jesus, his person and message and activity, manifested a soteriology which "acquired personality," that is, became explicit Christology, in the light of his resurrection. However expressed, the necessary point is that, within the framework of his circumstances and the linguistic and conceptual possibilities at his disposal, Jesus was aware of God's working in and through him in a very special way to effect the divine saving purposes. His ministry was rooted profoundly in Judaism, but there is a scandalous "more" involved in his claim and way of proceeding which could alienate many. As one biblical scholar recently wrote:

> What brought Jesus to the cross may have been no one aspect of his ministry, but rather the fact that his ministry offended *so* many groups—including pious Jews—in *so* many different ways that he had few influen-

tial supporters when the final clash came between himself and the rulers in Jerusalem over the attacks on the temple.[63]

And so we are brought now to the fact and the mystery of the Cross, that "stumbling block" and "folly" (1 Cor 1:23).

---

63. J. P. Meier, "The Bible as a Source of Theology," *Proceedings of the Forty-Third Annual Convention of the Catholic Theological Society of America* (Louisville: Bellarmine College, 1988) 4.

3

The Death of Jesus of Nazareth

Jesus died at the hands of the Romans the death that was considered the most execrable at that time: death by crucifixion. A study of the earliest traditions in the New Testament shows that his death was a profoundly disturbing experience for the first Christians. Not, to be sure, because executions of prophets were unheard of, or because people who ran afoul of the Roman *imperium* were never executed, but because of their memory of Jesus as someone who stood in a special relationship with God and their realization of what the resurrection and exaltation revealed about Jesus' identity and his role as God's agent in human history. Both they and we need to ask what point there was to such a death, and what bearing it had on Jesus' message and ministry for the sake of God's inbreaking reign. And we need to ask a contemporary, critical question as well: Was his crucifixion an eventuality which Jesus foresaw and, if so, what meaning did it have for him? Such are the questions that will occupy us in this chapter.

We have already seen that Jesus' message and activity were capable of producing two pronounced responses, either acceptance or rejection. People interpreted his activity as either the work of God or the work of the Evil One. The early and main part of his ministry occurred in Galilee, where he initially met with success, but opposition was not slow in developing. At some point in the Galilean ministry he sent out the Twelve, two by two, to towns and villages to preach the message of God's reign and cast out demons. The disciples experienced what they regarded as success. Jesus, however, was apparently concerned about both the mounting opposition and the crowd's enthusiasm, and began to move the disciples away from mission to a closer relationship with himself, in order to strengthen them in the face of the growing enmity.

Historical Reflections on the Death of Jesus

Jesus' Opponents

We would do well to focus on the context of Jesus' ministry by surveying various religious movements active in Jesus' day, and by considering his effect on them and their response to him in order to determine who would have been sufficiently motivated to have him captured, tried, and executed.

Until recently, numerous Christian scholars were convinced that the Pharisees saw in Jesus a dangerous foe because he called them up short on the discrepancy between their teaching and their personal conduct. Even when these scholars recognized that Jesus' polemic against the Pharisees, as we know it in the Synoptic Gospels, shows signs of the early Church's efforts to separate itself from Judaism (whose only effective leadership after 70 C.E. came from the Pharisees), they still maintained that Jesus himself clearly challenged the Pharisees for giving false priority to human achievement in relationship with God. Today we need to be much more cautious about this assumption. It is striking that the Synoptic passion narratives do not explicitly mention the Pharisees when Jesus is being tried, although there were Pharisees on the Sanhedrin, or Jewish supreme council. John alone refers briefly to some officers of the chief priests and Pharisees who came out to capture Jesus (John 18:3). It is strange that, after all the reports of their opposition in Galilee, they are almost completely absent from the accounts of the trial in all four Gospels.

As we saw in the preceding chapter, Jesus could well have criticized some Pharisees for hypocrisy and for a marked discrepancy between what they said and what they did, but historical Pharisaism as such had in common with Jesus the desire to reform Judaism. The fact that Jesus did not follow the prescriptions of the Pharisees, who applied to their ordinary life the purity laws of the Temple, did not make him their enemy, as was mentioned earlier. They did not oppose others simply for not being Pharisees.[1]

There is no historically secure evidence that anything Jesus said or did would have *specifically* motivated the Pharisees to instigate Jesus' execution.

The Essenes were a community of reform-minded Jews who lived in the desert away from Jerusalem and the Temple. They were an elite sect seeking to be faithful to Yahweh, apart from all those who had compromised themselves with the Romans or with half-hearted fidelity to God. We do not have any traditions indicating a relationship between them and

---

1. On the difficulties involved in determining the social role of the Pharisees at the time of Jesus, see A. Saldarini, *Pharisees, Scribes and Sadducees: A Sociological Approach.*

Jesus. What is clear is that Jesus' whole approach was opposed to that of the Essenes, since he actually favored the "people of the land," who were faithful to the Temple and the basic prescriptions of the Law. The Essenes would have been angered even more by the blurring of the distinction between the righteous and sinners which Jesus' praxis encouraged. But such behavior did not make the Essenes his primary opponents; all Jewish groups would have found this attitude offensive. Jesus' way of proceeding was anything but monastic; his parables and teaching reveal someone who found God in the ordinary, everyday course of events, even as he preached that God was turning that course of events upside down with the approaching kingdom. However, this difference between Jesus and the Essenes would not have motivated them to seek his death. His action in the Temple would not have offended them particularly, because they were already committed to a new, eschatological Temple and refused to have anything to do with the Temple in Jerusalem.

The Zealots may or may not have been an organized group in Jesus' day.[2] Certainly they were such in the next generation. They regarded the Roman occupation of their country as an abomination, and sought to bring about God's triumph over Israel's enemy by anticipating God's exercise of power through their own use of violent force. Filled with righteousness for God and God's elected nation, they wished to spur God to action on behalf of their country.

Several things need to be considered when examining Jesus' relations with the Zealots. First, there is no record of Jesus' condemning the Zealots in the fashion that he attacked the Pharisees. Second, Jesus had in his company at least one disciple described as a Zealot (Simon the Zealot, Luke 6:15; or Simon the Cananaean, Mark 3:18 and Matt 10:4) and one or more who bore arms (Mark 14:47). Third, there is a passage in Luke (22:35-38) where Jesus seems to suggest that the disciples should become armed if they are not already. Considerations such as these have led S. G. F. Brandon, among others, to argue that Jesus was in many respects like the Zealots, and that the early Church tried to eliminate these features from the gospel portraits of Jesus. Other scholars have vigorously taken issue with this contention of Brandon.[3]

There are several major points which render Brandon's view very improbable. For one thing, Jesus did not preach the violent overthrow of

2. On the Zealots see R. Horsley and J. Hanson, *Bandits, Prophets and Messiahs: Popular Movements in the Time of Jesus* (Minneapolis: Winston, 1985) and M. Hengel, *The Zealots: Investigations into the Jewish Freedom Movement in the Period from Herod I until 70 A.D.*, trans. D. Smith (Edinburgh: T and T Clark, 1989).

3. S. G. F. Brandon, *Jesus and the Zealots* (New York: Scribner, 1967); for a critique see E. Bammel and C. F. D. Moule, eds., *Jesus and the Politics of His Day* (Cambridge: Cambridge University Press, 1984); and R. Horsley, *Jesus and the Spiral of Violence: Popular Jewish Resistance in Roman Palestine* (San Francisco: Harper and Row, 1987).

the Roman occupiers, and nothing in his message suggested that humans could or should force God's hand to hasten the arrival of the kingdom. Furthermore, he had by all accounts little direct contact with the Romans before his arrest and trial. Finally, his doctrine of love of enemies would have been judged outrageous by any Zealots. In any case, any opposition to Jesus on the part of the Zealots would not have been settled by cooperation with the hated Romans. The latter, for their part, may well have associated Jesus with the Zealots insofar as his miracles drew enthusiastic crowds and his action in the Temple was of a provocative sort.

Recently critical voices have been heard which remind us that it is unfruitful and, indeed inaccurate, to separate the religious and the political in Israel at the time of Jesus. What Jesus said and did had political-religious consequences, and both the Romans and the leaders of Judaism recognized that.[4]

The Sadducees, or priestly class, were a hereditary group associated with the Temple cult. They showed themselves willing to collaborate with the Romans to protect this essential feature of Jewish life and to preserve their own status. They were theologically conservative; for example, they did not subscribe to the relatively recent doctrine of the resurrection of the dead (as did the Pharisees). The Sadducees were threatened in several ways by Jesus. First, Jesus' action in the Temple must have provoked them, because by this gesture Jesus seemed to be proclaiming his authorization from God to interrupt or even terminate the functioning of the Temple as a religious institution. Second, Jesus' prophecy about the destruction of the Temple and his rebuilding it in three days had to be profoundly offensive to the Sadducees, again because of the sense of authority it shockingly conveyed. Third, any preaching Jesus did against those who were "lovers of money" (Luke 16:14) may historically have been aimed at the Sadducees rather than the Pharisees.

A growing number of scholars regard the Sadducees as the primary opponents of Jesus in connection with his arrest, trial, and execution, although this conclusion does not imply that only the Sadducees were offended by Jesus' action and sayings about the Temple.[5] All devout Jews who viewed the Temple as the privileged place where the service of God took place could have been scandalized by Jesus' action. As we saw, the passion accounts hardly mention the Pharisees during Jesus' last days, but they do give a prominent role to the high priests and to the Sanhedrin, on which the Sadducees probably formed the majority.

4. R. A. Horsley and J. S. Hanson, *Bandits, Prophets, and Messiahs: Popular Movements at the Time of Jesus.*

5. See, for example, G. S. Sloyan, *Jesus on Trial: The Development of the Passion Narratives and Their Historical and Ecumenical Implications* (Philadelphia: Fortress, 1973).

Did Jesus Reckon with His Own Death?

In recent years a heated controversy among exegetes, particularly in Europe, has revolved around this question, with some scholars maintaining that the New Testament presents no authentic Jesus-tradition suggesting that Jesus even foresaw his own death, much less expressed his understanding of its saving significance.[6] According to their argument, Jesus hoped that his message would be accepted and that Israel would be converted to the coming Reign of God; his arrest and death spelled the frustration and failure of what he intended. These scholars seem to be reacting in part to a widespread view among Christians (which has no basis in the Gospels) that Jesus' life and ministry were simply a prelude to the real and only truly significant event of his life, namely, his death, which in turn led to his resurrection.

Other scholars have disputed this argument and maintained to the contrary that it is highly improbable that Jesus did not reckon with the possibility of his own violent death.[7] The beheading of John the Baptist, someone with whom Jesus had at one time been closely allied, must have made a profound impression on him and suggested a similar destiny for himself. A second factor is the fate of prophets in the Old Testament. It could not have been lost on Jesus that those who rose up in Israel to challenge the religious-political status quo on behalf of God had often met with rejection and sometimes experienced violent death.

Authentic *logia* about the possibility of Jesus being killed are few in number in the gospel accounts. When Jesus was warned that Herod Antipas, the executioner of John the Baptist, wanted to kill him, he is described as saying: ". . . I must go on my way today and tomorrow and the day following; for it cannot be that a prophet should perish away from Jerusalem" (Luke 13:33). Earlier in Luke's Gospel, he linked himself with previous prophets:

> Woe to you! for you build the tombs of the prophets whom your fathers killed. So you are witnesses and consent to the deeds of your fathers: for they killed them, and you build their tombs. Therefore also the Wisdom of God said, "I will send them prophets and apostles, some of whom they will kill and persecute," that the blood of all the prophets, shed from the foundation of the world, may be required of this generation (Luke 11:47-50).

An additional question concerns Jesus' understanding in the last days of his life of the violent end which, with increasing threat, loomed before

6. For a summary of some recent views, see J. Galvin, "Jesus' Approach to Death," *Theological Studies* 41 (1980) 713-44.

7. For example, Schillebeeckx, *Jesus: An Experiment in Christology*, 298-303.

him. Did he believe that God's reign, the very core of his message and activity, would arrive despite the rejection of his person and message? Did he simply trust unconditionally that God's will would be accomplished despite his failure? Or are there signs that Jesus sensed that God's reign would occur in and through this very rejection of himself as representative of that reign?

Here we must be very careful not to place in Jesus' mind the theological reflections of the early Church, which went in several directions as we shall see. At the moment we are concerned with the issue of whether the pre-Easter Jesus expressed an understanding of the violent death that seemed increasingly to threaten him.

We find several important places in the Gospels which may point to Jesus' attributing significance to his prospective violent death. In Mark's Gospel Jesus says: "For the Son of Man also came not to be served but to serve, and to give his life as a ransom for many" (10:45). This saying goes back to a pre-Markan source, and the first half of it is basically authentic. It can be argued that the context which gave it meaning was the memory of Jesus serving others during a meal. The "serving" did not refer simply to waiting on others at table, but also to drawing his guests into relationship with the arriving rule and reign of God. The text further shows the early Church's connection of Jesus' table service with his death, viewed as redemptive of others ("ransom for many"). It has been suggested that the early Church's bringing together of the motifs of service and redemptive death was made possible by memories of the Last Supper. A verse from Luke's Gospel calls for attention as well, when Jesus says: "For which is the greater, one who sits at table or one who serves? Is it not the one who sits at table? But I am among you as one who serves" (22:27). The Aramaic "I am among you" seems to refer to a concrete situation of being at table, in which Jesus offers his disciples fellowship with himself.[8]

If we add Luke 12:37b (the master who will wait on his servants) and John 13:2-16 (the footwashing), we see a picture emerging of the early Christian interpretation of Jesus' ministry as essentially service to others, pointedly associated with the Last Supper, when Jesus offered table fellowship (a relationship of mutual trust and sharing of life) to the disciples for the last time before his death. Thus his death was seen by certain early Christians as service of an expiatory kind, that is, as something done for others that they could not do for themselves, namely, the removal of their own sin and guilt.

But is there a basis in the historical Jesus for this early interpretation of his death? Can we go beyond the general sense that Jesus viewed his

8. Ibid., 304.

life and ministry as service of others for God's sake, and affirm that he saw his death too as service of others?

Here we need to look more carefully at the gospel traditions concerning the Last Supper.

Those traditions, as we find them in the Gospels and First Corinthians, show strong signs of being shaped by the liturgical practice of the early Church. But embedded within them, we encounter a precious fragment of authentic material going back to Jesus (as determined by the criteria discussed in chapter 2). For Jesus is portrayed as saying something that makes sense only in the context of the Last Supper and does not, as far as we know, become part of later liturgical tradition: "Truly, I say to you, I shall not drink again of the fruit of the vine until that day when I drink it new in the kingdom of God" (Mark 14:25).

Several important points come together in this text and its context. First, Jesus was having a final meal with his friends just before he was to die. This meal stood in significant continuity with all the table fellowship he had offered to disciples and many others during the course of his ministry. But this meal was different, because he was offering fellowship with himself and the reign of God in the face of his impending death. The prospect of death was part of the climate and horizon of the deed of extending table fellowship at this particular moment. Second, Jesus said that he would not drink from the cup again until he drank it new in God's kingdom. This was tantamount to saying that, even though he was going to die, the reign of God would still occur. Here it is important to remember that God's kingdom or reign was not, for Jesus, already a fully constituted reality, a celestial place, as it were, that death would allow him to "enter." Rather, it was an event, indeed, *the* event of salvation that was already arriving but had not yet fully arrived. Jesus expressed in this statement his confidence that God's salvation would indeed fully occur, and would not be contradicted by his own death.

But even if this much is true, was Jesus saying that God's salvation in the form of a divine reign would occur *in and through* his death or simply *despite* that death? That was our original question.

Drawing on the work of exegetes, E. Schillebeeckx seems to find as much as one possibly could in this *logion* of Jesus:

> But there is no getting round the historical fact that in the very face of death Jesus offers the cup of fellowship to his disciples; this is a token that he is not just passively allowing death to overcome him but has actively integrated it into his total mission, in other words, that he understands and is undergoing his death as a final and extreme service to the cause of God as the cause of men, and that he has communicated this

self-understanding to his intimate disciples under the veiled sign of extending to them the fellowship-at-table shared with his friends.[9]

Schillebeeckx may actually be getting just a bit more from the *logion* than is derivable by a straight reading. Earlier he is more circumspect: "One is bound to say that in fact no certain logion of Jesus is to be found in which Jesus himself might be thought to ascribe a salvific import to his death."[10]

The most assured results of a historical-critical examination of this Last Supper saying can be summarized by remarking that, at that climactic meal, Jesus related in a significant but unelaborated way three realities of the first importance: his ministry as epitomized, even "unto death," in table fellowship; his death itself; and the coming of salvation in the form of God's rule. It will be up to various communities in the post-Easter period to develop more explicit Christological and soteriological (i.e., salvation-oriented) interpretations of the meaning of his death on the cross and his resurrection.

But this memory of the Last Supper will provide a precious starting point for their reflections.

Jesus' Trial in Historical Perspective

The question of the legal grounds for Jesus' execution, together with the issue of responsibility for his death, is obviously an enormously important and ecumenically most sensitive one in Jewish-Christian relations. Over the centuries Christians have unjustly accused Jews of the crime of deicide because of Jesus' crucifixion and have persecuted members of Jesus' race, using that charge as the justification for their hatred. The Second Vatican Council made an attempt at reconciliation from the Catholic side, when it declared:

> True, authorities of the Jews and those who followed their lead pressed for the death of Christ (cf. Jn. 19:6); still, what happened in His passion cannot be blamed upon all the Jews then living, without distinction, nor upon the Jews of today. Although the Church is the new People of God, the Jews should not be presented as repudiated or cursed by God, as if such views followed from the Holy Scriptures.[11]

9. Ibid., 311.

10. Ibid., 310.

11. *Nostra Aetate,* "Declaration on the Relation of the Church to Non-Christian Religions," in W. M. Abbott and J. Gallagher, *The Documents of Vatican II*, 665–66.

The contemporary scholarly discussion of the trial(s) and condemnation of Jesus reveals just how complex and divided opinion on the subject is. There is neither ecumenical agreement on the topic nor agreement among scholars of the same faith. It would be helpful to review some of the more important recent contributions to the discussion in order to appreciate how carefully one must tread in this area.

Three Jewish Views.[12] Haim Cohn, a justice on Israel's Supreme Court, has made a study of the New Testament accounts of Jesus' trial in light of what is known about legal procedures at that time.[13] After extensive discussion he concludes that Jesus was not the victim of a perversion of judgment ("judicial murder"), but was condemned to death legally and according to due process by the Romans because he pleaded guilty to the charge brought against him, namely, that in claiming to be a king he was not authorized by the Roman emperor (John 18:37); perhaps Jesus pleaded guilty so that the prophecies he regarded as concerning him might be fulfilled.[14] Cohn is convinced that Jesus was brought before the high priest's court so that it could have the chance of saving him from the Roman cross. Not being a Scripture scholar, Cohn is not able to deal with the texts as literary constructions, and this severely hampers his approach.

His final statement is worth noting:

> Hundreds of generations of Jews, throughout the Christian world, have been indiscriminately mulcted for a crime which neither they nor their ancestors committed. Worse still, they have for centuries, for millennia, been made to suffer all manner of torment, persecution, and degradation for the alleged part of their forefathers in the trial and crucifixion of Jesus, when, in solemn truth, their forefathers took no part in them but did all that they possibly and humanly could to save Jesus, whom they dearly loved and cherished as one of their own, from his tragic end at the hands of the Roman oppressor.[15]

Paul Winter, a Jewish lawyer originally from Czechoslovakia, enumerates several "assured results" regarding Jesus' trial and condemnation.[16] According to him, Jesus was arrested by the Romans for political reasons and brought by them to a local Jewish administrative official during the

---

12. For a history of modern Jewish interpretation of Jesus' trial(s), see D. R. Catchpole, *The Trial of Jesus: A Study of the Gospels and Jewish Historiography from 1770 to the Present Day* (Leiden: Brill, 1971).

13. H. Cohn, *The Trial and Death of Jesus* (New York: Harper and Row, 1971).

14. Ibid., 328.

15. Ibid., 331.

16. P. Winter, *On the Trial of Jesus*, ed. T. A. Burkill and G. Vermes, 2nd rev. ed. (Berlin and New York: De Gruyter, 1974).

same night. The following morning, after a brief deliberation by Jewish authorities, he was handed back to the Romans for trial. After being sentenced to death by crucifixion, he was killed. Not assured but probable, Winter concludes, are the following: On the night of Jesus' arrest, during the interval between his being brought to a local Jewish official and the morning deliberation in the council hall, Jesus was interrogated by a member of the high priest's staff, who questioned witnesses as well. He drew up charges which were approved by Jewish magistrates on the morning following the arrest. Jesus was subjected to derision by the soldiers who were to execute him. The questions which most interest us cannot be answered with any certainty at all: What the immediate cause of Jesus' arrest was, who took the initiative in arresting him, and what Jesus did to provoke political action against himself.

A third Jewish scholar, Ellis Rivkin, looks to the ancient Jewish historian Josephus for an understanding of the political and religious landscape of Israel in Jesus' day.[17] He distinguishes between the Sanhedrin and the *bêt din* (Greek *boulê*). The former was a kind of privy council of the Roman-appointed high priest in Jerusalem, which could be made up of Sadducees and Scribes-Pharisees (synonyms for Rivkin). It had no religious jurisdiction at all but was a temporary group to advise the high priest on strictly political issues, that is, on issues pertaining to relations between the Jews and the Romans.[18] The otherwise sharply divided Jewish groups could meet in the Sanhedrin because they all subscribed to a two-realm theory, giving to Caesar what belonged to Caesar and to God what belonged to God. A *bêt din* or *boulê* was a permanent body religious in nature; it could comprise only members of one group of Jews, e.g., the Pharisees.[19] It had authority to deal only with the issues of that group and could not judge matters pertaining to another group. This restriction was due to a second major principle operative at the time among the Jewish groups, according to Josephus: Live and let live.

Rivkin, following Josephus, paints a portrait of Jesus' time, particularly the decades preceding his appearance, to show how nervous the high priest and the Romans were about any revolutionary (or non-revolutionary) charismatic who excited the crowds. The uneasy and fragile alliance between the Romans and the high priest could be permanently destroyed if a disruptive person were allowed the freedom to preach and gather crowds.

Briefly put, Rivkin argues that Jesus was "tried" by Caiaphas and his privy council on the exclusively political question of the potential politi-

17. E. Rivkin, *What Crucified Jesus? The Political Execution of a Charismatic* (Nashville: Abingdon, 1984).

18. Ibid., 17.

19. Ibid., 18.

cal consequences of Jesus' claims regarding the arrival of God's kingdom in relation to his preaching and ministry.[20] He was then handed over to Pilate, who wasted no time in having him crucified, because he presented a threat to the emperor: The charge was simply and straightforwardly lese majesty. Religious issues such as blasphemy never entered the picture because the religious groups at the time, for all their hostility toward one another, never went beyond argument and vituperation in their battles; they exercised legislation only among their own. Rivkin sees the Synoptic Gospels as basically credible because they implicate with historical accuracy an ad hoc Sanhedrin, but exonerate the religious and more permanent *bêt din*, or *boulê*, of any involvement in Jesus' trial and death.[21] A charismatic like Jesus, who did not fit into what Rivkin calls the threefold mosaic of Judaism (Sadducees, Scribes-Pharisees, and Essenes), was a threat to the high priest because of his responsibility to keep the peace with the Romans. It did not really matter what Jesus' actual intentions were. The enthusiasm of the crowd(s) and Jesus' talk of the impending arrival of God's kingdom (without any authorization from the emperor!) were damning enough.

For Rivkin it was not a "who" but a "what" that killed Jesus: the Roman imperial system. This system was incarnated in a high priest who was a tool of the occupiers of Israel, a Sanhedrin which was not grounded in the onefold (written) law of the Sadducees or the twofold (written and oral) law of the Pharisees, a Roman procurator, and a Roman mode of execution.[22] Rivkin counts three victims of the system in addition to Jesus: the Jewish people, the Roman people, and the Spirit of God.

He concludes by reflecting that the fact that Caiaphas and the Romans may both have misunderstood what Jesus was about does not mean that the implications of Jesus' activity and preaching were not profoundly political in their own way. The maxim of Jesus' opponents (according to Rivkin), which is even ascribed to Jesus, "Give to Caesar the things that are Caesar's and to God the things that are God's" (Mark 12:17), is not a maxim with a simple meaning. Thus, in agreement with Cohn and Winter, Rivkin finds that Jesus was not purely a religious phenomenon bracketed off from the political realm, and that a political interpretation of his ministry and death was therefore not amiss.

Four Christian Views. Josef Blinzler devoted a volume to the trial of Jesus in 1955, which he revised several times up until 1969.[23] He concludes

---

20. Ibid., 51.

21. Ibid., 64.

22. Ibid., 95.

23. J. Blinzler, *Der Prozess Jesu*, 4th rev. ed. (Regensburg: Pustet, 1969); ET *The Trial of Jesus*, trans. I. and F. McHugh, 2nd ed. reprinted (Westminster, Md.: Newman, 1959).

that, from a formal-juridical point of view, the Jewish authorities and the Romans were equally responsible for Jesus' death but that, from a moral point of view (guilt), the Jews were more responsible because they changed the charge against Jesus when they handed him over to the Romans. In their own proceedings they accused him of blasphemy; but to Pilate they charged him with pretensions of being an earthly king and enemy of Caesar, a charge that they must have known was untrue and not warranted by the nature of Jesus' self-presentation in his ministry.[24] Blinzler takes as historical the gospel descriptions of the great pressure put on Pilate by the leaders of the Jews and the crowd(s), pressure to which he finally yielded.

Earlier I referred to S. G. F. Brandon. The most historically assured fact for him is the Roman execution of Jesus for sedition:[25] Pilate was convinced of Jesus' guilt and had him crucified. Brandon argues that Jesus continued the Baptist's apocalyptic preaching of God's kingdom, the establishment of which would involve the overthrow of the existing political and social order. Unlike John, Jesus saw himself as the primary agent of the kingdom's arrival, and indeed considered himself the kingly Messiah. He included some Zealots among his closest followers and, supported by his followers and the enthusiastic crowd, attempted at the end of his public life to overthrow the priestly leadership in Jerusalem, and therefore to strike as well at the Romans who were using the priests for their own oppressive purposes. His efforts failed and, thanks to Judas' betrayal, he was captured by his Jewish enemies. The Sanhedrin or the high priest determined that Jesus did have messianic (and thus seditious) pretensions, and so they gave him to Pilate, who had him executed as an insurgent. He died between two Zealots, which was fitting enough.

A Catholic scholar, Gerald S. Sloyan, gives careful attention to the trial narratives in his study published in 1973.[26] He concludes that (1) the Gospels were chiefly interested in showing that the death of Jesus was a juridically inexplicable event in light of his obvious innocence; (2) the Gospels as we have them state that the Jewish priestly leadership plotted Jesus' death on political charges; (3) at the trial with Pilate Jesus' political posture and perhaps even the question of his messiahship came up, assuming that the *titulus* (title) on the cross is historical; (4) historically there was antipathy between Jesus and certain leaders among the Temple priests; (5) there may have been a Barabbas involved but not as described in the narrative; (6) chief priests, scribes, and elders may have made up the group

24. Ibid., 292–93.

25. Brandon, *Jesus and the Zealots*, 141. On what follows see his chapter 6: "The Historical Reality: What Did Happen?" 140–50.

26. Sloyan, *Jesus on Trial: The Development of the Passion Narratives and Their Historical and Ecumenical Implications* (Philadelphia: Fortress, 1973).

which confronted Jesus; and (7) Pilate may not have seen in Jesus any great threat to the Roman Empire, which may have constituted the historical basis for the portrayal of his diffidence.

Edward Schillebeeckx argues that the members of the Sanhedrin were able to reach an agreement about Jesus on the basis of Deuteronomy 17:12, although they may have differed in their reasoning.[27] That verse refers to false teachers: "The one who acts presumptuously, by not obeying the priest who stands to minister there before the Lord your God, or the judge, that one shall die; so you shall purge the evil from Israel." Schillebeeckx maintains that this was not a uniformly interpreted rule of law until after 70 C.E., and that it was impossible to get the whole Sanhedrin to agree on its application to Jesus. Jesus' position was exacerbated when he remained silent before the Sanhedrin, for by that gesture he was refusing to submit his mission and ministry to the authority of Judaism. Positively, Jesus' silence was intended to assert that God was the sole warrant for what he had been about and that there was no room for human authentication of his mission. Such silence—which Schillebeeckx takes to be the historically most reliable aspect of the scene before the high priest as we find it depicted in the Synoptics—would have angered even those previously less antagonistic to him.

In any case the Sanhedrin did make one unanimous decision, in a second session, namely, to hand Jesus over to the Romans as someone who was perceived as a threat to the public order. That order the Romans were determined to preserve at whatever cost.

Some Basic Points. In reviewing these various opinions about the trial and condemnation of Jesus, we find several basic points emerging. First, Jesus died a political death on a political charge ("King of the Jews"). Second, both Sadducees and Romans were agents of his death. This can be said while taking into account that the Gospels, especially Luke and John, seem intent on heightening the responsibility of the Jewish leaders and people and lightening the responsibility of the Romans. Third, it may be impossible to reach clarity about the kind of trial(s) to which Jesus was subjected because of the degree of theological interpretation involved in the evangelists' presentations of the trial and passion. For one thing, they wanted to make it clear that the God of the Old Testament was at work in and through all the machinations of human beings as they did Jesus in.

The Nature of Crucifixion. Martin Hengel has published a fine study of the meaning of crucifixion at the time of Jesus.[28] In the Roman Em-

---

27. Schillebeeckx, *Jesus*, 312–18: "The Historical Grounds in Law for Jesus' Execution."

28. M. Hengel, *Crucifixion in the Ancient World and the Folly of the Message of the Cross*, trans. J. Bowden (Philadelphia: Fortress, 1977).

pire crucifixion was considered an execrable form of execution. It was reserved for slaves and any who rebelled against the *pax Romana* (the "peace" enforced by Rome). In effect, this mode of execution proclaimed to all spectators that the person being crucified was subhuman (precisely the status of a slave). Crucifixion was the final mockery of anyone who aspired to be free, to be a "somebody" in the face of Roman domination. Thus the violence involved in crucifying someone did not stop with physical torture, but struck at the very soul of the victim, attempting to desecrate him. Ultimate success would occur, of course, when and if the victim consented internally to the subhuman status being imposed on him. Victimization is not totally successful—for all the horrible things it can do unilaterally—until the victim says yes to the verdict of the executioner. Withholding that yes, the victim retains a certain power, the "power of the weak."[29]

Crucifixion, a desecration of the human, is a dark and terrible act. If Jesus had offered an illuminating interpretation of his death as a saving event, one would expect the early Church to have made use of it from the beginning. Instead, we find it grappling with Jesus' death in a variety of ways in an effort to make sense of it. Wolfhart Pannenberg has noted that, when it occurred, the Easter event carried a great deal of significance. Within an apocalyptic horizon of understanding, the resurrection of one who had preached the imminent coming of God's reign would carry enormous intrinsic meaning.[30] Jesus' execution was a different matter. His closeness with God and his authority to announce the kingdom of God, even to associate that reign's arrival with his own prophetic activity, made his death a dark and unintelligible event for those who had cast their lot with him. If God's cause and Jesus' cause were so intimately bound up with one another—more so than in the case of any previous prophet— how could God let Jesus die that way, an apparent failure?

New Testament Theologies of Jesus' Death

The Passion Narratives and the Old Testament

Mark's Gospel has been described as a passion narrative with an extended introduction. Certainly in Mark's narrative the revelation of Jesus' true identity occurs most fully in relation to his passion and death. But in all of the Gospels the passion assumes a very prominent place. In telling the story of Jesus' passion, the early Church made abundant use of the Old Testament. Psalm 22 is an excellent example. Earl Richard has

29. E. Janeway, *The Powers of the Weak* (New York: Knopf, 1980).

30. W. Pannenberg, *Jesus—God and Man*, trans. D. Priebe (Philadelphia: Westminster, 1968) 66–73.

correlated elements of the psalm with aspects of the passion narratives in a helpful way, to show how influential the Old Testament was on the early Christian understanding of Jesus' passion and death:[31]

Psalm 22	*Mark (et al)*
1 "forsake"	15:34 citation
2 cry by day—no answer cry by night—no rest	15:34 cry on cross 14:34 prayed at Gethsemane
4 and 8 trust in God— deliver	[Matt 27:43]
6 scorned by men	passion generally
7 mocking, making mouths at, wagging heads	15:29-31 deriding, wagging heads, mocking
11 there is none to help	15:31
14 bones out of joint	[John 19:32-33]
15 tongue cleaves to jaws	15:23 and 36 gave to drink
16 encircled by company of evildoers	death scene generally
piercing	crucifixion
18 dividing garments	15:24 dividing garments [John 19:24 cites text]
casting lots	15:23 casting lots
20 the sword	[John 19:34 piercing spear]

A comprehensive listing such as this offers striking evidence of how theological the passion narratives are, and how essential the traditions of the Old Testament were for their telling. As terrible as it was, the passion of Jesus constituted a story of fulfillment in relation to ancient texts, which were appreciated—in the "light" of Jesus' passion—as prophecies of that series of dark events.

Three New Testament Interpretations of Jesus' Death

After Easter, Jesus' followers used the classical Deuteronomic notion of Israel's stiff-necked rejection of the prophets vindicated by God as a

31. Richard, *Jesus, One and Many: The Christological Concept of New Testament Authors*, 81–82.

way of making sense of his death.[32] The pattern of human rejection in conjunction with divine vindication comes strongly to the fore in the Acts of the Apostles, particularly in the missionary sermons. These sermons, as we find them in Acts, are literary creations of Luke; but they make use of traditional material, and it is not difficult to find fragments in them of this early Jewish-Christian theology of the death of Jesus: "Let all the house of Israel therefore know assuredly that God has made him both Lord and Christ, this Jesus whom you crucified" (2:36; also 2:22-24; 4:10; 5:30-31; 10:39-40). This interpretation of Jesus' death restricts itself simply to speaking of what the persecutors of Jesus did and then, by contrast, of what God did to Jesus. Absent is any mention of Jesus' death as saving for others. God offered Jesus personal vindication, for he was the just and faithful servant of God (Acts 3:26).

This rejection-vindication scheme connects up with a theme from the pre-Easter Jesus' ministry, the controversy about the source of Jesus' authority and power, which persisted in the early Church's arguments with Jews about Jesus. Was Jesus the divinely authorized teacher of God's Law and prophet of the end-time, or was he an instrument of the Evil One, of the Antichrist? The scheme implies that certain Jewish leaders were implicated in his execution because they took him to be an enemy of God's Law. God, the only one who could decide the issue in a definitive way, revealed in the resurrection that Jesus was the authentic teacher of the Law of God, and that his authority was from God and no one else. His persecutors were revealed by the resurrection to be true children of stiff-necked Israel who, not for the first time, had killed the prophet sent to it by God (Neh 9:26).

A second interpretation of Jesus' death, which appears very early, situated it in salvation history (Luke 24:13-32): His death occurred by divine preordination and divine necessity, indicated by the Greek word *dei*, meaning "it is necessary." The risen Jesus asked the disciples at Emmaus, "Was it not necessary that the Christ should suffer these things and enter into his glory?" (Luke 24:26). Jesus' passion and death were those of the suffering righteous person, who suffers because of fidelity to God's Law. This widespread view in the Old Testament and intertestamental literature regarded suffering as a sign of God's election of the just person, and was convinced that suffering had to be the destiny of those who stayed faithful to God's commandments when the surrounding culture (for example, the late Hellenistic world) hated them for it. Numerous psalms speak of such a *zadik* (righteous person), whose woes are many and whose confidence is in God alone (e.g., Pss 54, 64, and 86). At some points God is seen as the vindicator of the just person; at other points God is the agent

---

32. I am indebted to Schillebeeckx, *Jesus*, 273–94, for what follows.

who sets in motion the whole pattern of events leading to the *zadik's* death (e.g., Acts 2:23). The just ones may be brought very low, but they will be exalted by God.

The passion narrative in Mark is shaped by this conviction that God was at work in all that happened to Jesus. As we have seen, prayerful reflection on Old Testament texts stands behind the narrative and gives it its theological thrust. This concern to make sense of Jesus' execution in terms of the suffering righteous one was an intra-ecclesial, catechetical interest and not an apologetic one, i.e, one that aimed itself at outsiders (unlike the "rejected prophet" scheme discussed above).

Among the principal Old Testament texts underlying this second non-soteriological interpretation of Jesus' death are Psalm 34; Wisdom 2:12-20; 5:1-7; and 4 Maccabees 18:6b-19. These texts and others like them are implicit in the Synoptic passion accounts and explicit in the Johannine narrative. The accent falls in any case on God as the one at work in the narrative course of events. Jesus' suffering and death do not yet possess a saving efficacy. Theology, not soteriology, is dominant so far.

It is time now to turn to the third interpretation of Jesus' suffering and death, the directly soteriological one, which perceived Jesus' death as redemptive and atoning for sins. The key words for this interpretation are the Greek prepositions *hyper* and *anti*: He died *for* us, *on account of* our sins. We find them in Galatians 1:4; Romans 4:25; 5:8; 8:32; Ephesians 5:2; 1 Corinthians 15:3b-5; Mark 10:45; and 1 Peter 2:21-24. This interpretation of the passion and death most probably relied on the early Church's application of Isaiah 53 to the story of Jesus: "But he [i.e., Yahweh's servant] was wounded for our transgressions, he was bruised for our iniquities, upon him was the chastisement that made us whole, and with his stripes we are healed" (Isa 53:5). E. Schillebeeckx asks whether the origin of the understanding of Jesus' death as an atoning one has a basis in the historical life of Jesus, which would explain the early Church's turning to the fourth Servant Song of Second Isaiah as a principal clue to the meaning of Jesus' death.

As we might expect, he finds this basis in Jesus' understanding of himself as a servant of others, particularly through table fellowship culminating in the Last Supper just before his arrest. The "for the sake of others" was thus inscribed in Jesus' mode of life. It was inscribed as well in his death as the culmination of his life of service, given final expression in the extension of the cup to his disciples in the face of death.

> Jesus' whole life is the hermeneusis of his death. The very substance of salvation is sufficiently present in it, which could be and was in fact articulated later on in various ways through faith in him. Although the historico-critical method cannot produce knock-down arguments on this score, still less can it assert categorically that so far as history goes we do not

know how Jesus understood his own death. Jesus' understanding of that death as part and parcel of his mission of tendering salvation seems to me, therefore, a fact preceding Easter—and demonstrably so, at least for Jesus' self-understanding in the final days of his life.[33]

Thus Jesus' way of living and dying grounds New Testament talk of his death as sacrifice. The accounts of the institution of the Eucharist allude to Exodus 24:5-8 and the blood of the covenant. Ephesians 5:2 expresses this motif as well: "And walk in love, as Christ loved us and gave himself up for us, a fragrant offering and sacrifice to God." It is the Letter to the Hebrews which first explicates, extensively, the joint themes of Jesus as the great high priest and of his death as sacrificial (Hebrews 9-10).

We have, therefore, three complexes of interpretation regarding Jesus' death which are all quite early, even if they cannot be chronologically ordered. Two are theological and one is soteriological. In later developments they will be combined in various ways, a possibility already suggested by a key source, the Isaian Servant Songs, which bring together the motifs of prophet, righteous sufferer, atoning death and God's vindication. But more importantly, Jesus' own life exemplified the traits of prophet, righteous sufferer, and servant of others. And by Easter God was shown to be the ultimate agent at work in all that Jesus said and did and suffered.[34]

A Suffering Messiah

One of the important issues early Christians had to struggle with was that their Jewish heritage had not prepared them to connect the notion of suffering with the notion of Messiah in its primarily royal and dynastic sense. There were plenty of examples of prophets sent from God who suffered for their message; some were even killed. But the linking of rejection, suffering and violent death with the expectation of a dynastic, Davidic king had not occurred. When and if this Messiah arrived, he would usher in the new age of enduring peace and justice. He would triumph over evil because he would be filled with the power of the one who sent him. There would be combat, the eschatological woes, as the Antichrist or evil powers defended themselves. But the Messiah would triumph by virtue of superior strength.

The early Jewish-Christians had to work hard to bring these notions together. The experience of Easter had assured them that, after his death, Jesus was enthroned at God's right hand and invested with universal

33. Ibid., 311.

34. For an extended treatment of the soteriologies and doctrines of grace and sin in all the books of the New Testament, with the exception of the Synoptic Gospels, see E. Schillebeeckx, *Christ: The Christian Experience in the Modern World*, trans. J. Bowden (New York: Crossroad, 1980).

authority. At first they expected the reign of God to occur immediately and to spell the consummation of all things. Although this expectation had to give way to the so-called delay of the parousia (the return of Christ in glory), the conviction remained that upon raising Jesus from the dead God had installed him as anointed ruler of all. Over time the Church began to view Jesus' life as messianic in this dynastic, royal sense. Eventually, instead of being anointed Messiah at the resurrection, Jesus became the Messiah at his conception (in Matthew's and Luke's infancy narratives). Thus, as it "messianized" Jesus' life, the Church had to discover how God could have let the kingly Messiah suffer and die a violent death.

The task was eased considerably by the fact that, at the time of the beginnings of the Church, the notion of Messiah had become a complex one. The term had ceased to refer only to a dynastic, royal figure. Indeed, Wisdom literature saw in Solomon, the Son of David, a truly prophetic figure whose teaching was the very model of God's wisdom. Anointed with the royal oil and filled with the wisdom of God, Solomon combined in his person the dynastic and prophetic forms of messiahship. As wise man, Solomon was son, servant, and child of God (Wis 2:13, 16d, 18 and 9:4b, 5a). The wise man would reveal his true identity through suffering and exposure to a shameful death (Wis 2:19). This tradition made it possible for Christian writers to draw on texts which spoke of an anointed servant of God who would suffer and be rejected in the service of God, and whose suffering and death would redound to the good of others. The fourth Servant Song of Isaiah (52:13–53:12) became a precious source for them also, and they applied many of its verses to Jesus. This is all the more striking because we do not have any evidence from before Jesus' time that writers employed these texts for either their view of vicarious suffering or their relating of the two ideas of (prophetic) anointed one and vicarious sufferer.

Paul on Christ's Saving Work

Paul saw Christ's death, in inseparable conjunction with his resurrection, as effecting liberation for those who believe (Rom 8:21). This liberation was like the emancipation of a slave, an act of redemption. Yet Paul does not belabor the image of redemption. While the price was Christ's blood, no real purchase occurred, for there was no payee, whether Satan or sin or another agent. The emancipation was not for the sake of lonely independence, but rather for full membership in God and Christ. In Paul's striking language, the Christian has moved from being a slave of sin to being a "slave" of God and Christ. Freedom and belonging cannot be contrasted in Paul; what matters is to whom or to what we belong and the quality of the belonging. For Paul, the liberation wrought by Christ was fourfold and bears on the deepest dimensions of human existence. Jesus' death and resurrection have freed us from the bondage of sin, of the Law, of death, and of the false self (Rom 5-8).

When writing about the bondage of sin, Paul did not have in mind simply the individual faults we commit. Instead he perceived sin as an archetypal figure walking on the world stage and seeking to hold people in its thrall (Rom 5:12). This personification of sin allowed him to emphasize the power it can have in human life. Jesus' death and resurrection have broken the back of that power, so that it cannot have the last word in human history, no matter how dark that history becomes. Universally, Christ's presence and power reign supreme as the ultimate context and condition of all history (Rom 5:20-21). Sin can have power in individual lives and in the lives of societies, and Paul addresses this problem regularly (e.g., Rom 6:12), but it can have *final* power only if individuals and groups give it that role in their lives.

Jesus' death and resurrection have freed us from bondage to the Law as well (Gal 3:13). There are several dimensions to this liberation. For Paul, the Law of Moses was holy and of God (Rom 7:12). He himself never apologized for his fidelity to the Law (Gal 1:14). It would be a complete misreading of him to suggest that he saw his conversion as a movement away from the evil and self-righteousness signified by observance of the Law to the goodness revealed in Jesus Christ by grace. Jews believed, and still believe, that only God can save and that salvation is by grace. The Law is a gift of God to Israel, intended by God to express the covenant relationship between Israel and Yahweh. Paul saw his conversion as a movement away from the Law in the role of the definitive, God-given mediator of God's blessings to Christ as that definitive mediator: his passage was from grace to yet greater grace. But the Law, meant to be grace, could be turned into an instrument of harm if it were used to justify rejection of the yet greater grace who was Christ. When Paul ran into harsh opposition from those who insisted that Gentile converts needed to become Jews in order to become Christians, he was confronted with a use of the Law which he considered profoundly wrong. The Law was being reified, i.e., made into a thing, a source of security per se, and thus an idol. Turning the Law into an obstacle to grace was the very opposite of God's intention. Instead of being a way, it became an ultimate reality; and if related to as such, it would endanger the salvation of those who professed fidelity to it.[35] Grace was intended to open us up to a gracious God and the initiatives of God, not to provide a safe haven from further growth.

35. See E. P. Sanders, *Paul, The Law and the Jewish People* (Philadelphia: Fortress, 1983), and J. A. Fitzmyer, "Paul and the Law," *To Advance the Gospel* (New York: Crossroad, 1981) 186-201.

Thus the legalistic misuse of the Law (exemplified for Paul by his opponents, and not by Judaism as such) was a form of bondage from which Jesus' death and resurrection has freed us. Turning a means into an end, or what is not God into our heart's absolute, comes down to a fatal misunderstanding of final security as our own achievement rather than as something that is securely ours only as gift. Such a misunderstanding marks the undoing of the human being as image of God, as a creature who is in truth the person she or he is only by *ultimately* relating to the true God in trustful surrender.

The third form of bondage from which Jesus freed us, according to Paul, is the power of death (Rom 6:5-9; 1 Cor 15:20-22). Death is not only the cessation of biological life for Paul but, more profoundly, full and final separation from God and from community. It is the "wages of sin," the full revelation of sin's horrendous might when left unchecked. And fear of death, when we let it dominate us, leads us to seek security in what is manipulable (the sin of idolatry), cherishing things and means as we are meant to cherish only the personal, and committing ourselves ultimately to the non-divine though we are meant to belong finally only to God.

The fourth form of bondage is the false self. The false self is dominated by the principle of sin, so that the self is incapable of living righteously. The false self is a stranger to the person and yet, paradoxically, the agent of the self's intentions. Unless the guiding principle in the person changes, everything chosen and done will lead to greater and greater captivity.

It is evident that for Paul these four forms of bondage were deeply intertwined: the power of sin, the misuse of the Law which plays into the hands of sin, the destructive separation of death as sin's full and final issue, and the false self who is the captive of sin.

For Paul the notions of bondage, or enslavement, and redemption were correlative. Christ's death and resurrection brought new life to those who had all died in Adam. Adam and Christ were corporate and representative figures for Paul. In their choices the destiny of the human race was decided, while Christ's choice unto death undid the consequences of Adam's sin insofar as the latter had created a universal situation, or condition, into which all were born. Now the universal situation of humankind in its ultimate depths had been altered. Where sin had abounded grace was abounding all the more (Rom 5:20).

The principal notions employed by Paul to express the saving significance of the Cross, in addition to redemption, were expiation or propitiation, reconciliation, and justification. All these terms will reappear regularly in the development of soteriology throughout the Christian centuries (as we shall see in chapter 6).

Expiation, or propitiation, refers to the removal of an offense which blocks relationship with another. Paul does not use the normal noun or verb for this but rather the term *hilasterion*, which can mean either a means or instrument of expiation in a general way or, more specifically, "the mercy seat," with an allusion to the part of the inner Temple which was ritually sprinkled with blood on the Day of Atonement (Rom 3:25). Expiation is associated with blood, because in the Old Testament the blood of an animal was used for ritual purification of objects belonging to God's service which had been defiled, or for their introduction into the sacred sphere from the profane. Moreover, the person performing such a ritual action was dedicated to God. For Paul, Jesus' death was expiatory because by his blood those who believe in him have been dedicated to God and belong to God, after having been estranged. The English language has added a theological term to soteriology: atonement, at-one-ment. It is usually taken to be a synonym for expiation and, like that term, refers to Jesus' role, although in its more general meaning it could connote reconciliation (see below) as well, and in that sense be viewed as an activity of God the Father.

In Paul's writings propitiation does not denote the appeasement of God's anger. The idea of God's anger can certainly be found in Paul (e.g., 1 Thess 2:16; Rom 1:18; 2:5; 4:15; 9:22) and in the New Testament generally. But ordinarily in Paul's usage anger or wrath is an eschatological concept referring to God's relationship to those who, on the Day of the Lord, definitively reject God's salvation. Jesus saves believers from that eschatological wrath (Rom 5:9).

Reconciliation (*katallagê*: Rom 5:10-11; 2 Cor 5:18-20) refers to the rejoining of warring parties and the peace which ensues as a result of that rejoining, here applied to the relationship between sinners and God. It is implied that the rejoining of the estranged parties can be a costly endeavor for the mediator or agent of reconciliation. In the view of Paul and the other New Testament writers, it is sinners who need to be reconciled to God, never God who needs to be reconciled to sinners. Moreover, for Paul it is God who initiates the reconciliation process and God who provides the mediator, Jesus, God's Son.

Jesus' Passion in the Four Gospels

Several form-critical scholars of the first half of this century were convinced that there existed a fairly well-developed passion narrative prior to Mark, and that such an early, continuous narrative stood in striking contrast to the rest of the Gospels, which are made up of discrete units of tradition brought together by the evangelists or the traditions they inherited. On the other hand, most contemporary research emphasizes the close kinship between each passion narrative and the theology of the respective evangelist.[36] While there are a number of common elements in all the Synoptic passion stories, we find significant differences as well.[37]

Basic motifs in Mark's Gospel give structure to the passion narrative: Jesus' royal sonship, which is declared by God in the main part of the Gospel, is recognized in truth only when he becomes the crucified one; the blindness and misunderstanding of the disciples during Jesus' ministry lead to their flight during the passion; Jesus' cleansing of the Temple becomes a principal charge and taunt against him; and, finally, Jesus suffers full of confidence that at a future moment he will return as the vindicated and glorious Son of Man to judge all (14:62).

Matthew's passion account is heavily dependent on Mark while at the same time reflecting major themes from the earlier part of his own Gospel, themes that are both Christological and ecclesiological (i.e., having to do with one's understanding of the Church). Jesus is the royal Son of David and Son of God who suffers as the model of righteousness, trusting in God and not resisting arrest nor taking an oath, in fidelity to his own Sermon on the Mount. The new age begins with Jesus' death, when Israel's blessings and legacy are opened to the Gentiles, as the Jews reject Jesus and shout that his blood is upon their heads.

We find in Luke a passion narrative that is quite different from the two preceding ones but similar in its echo of major Gospel themes. Some of Luke's themes are: Jesus' passion as his divine destiny; Jesus' passion as a model of what discipleship means; Jesus' suffering as the process whereby he is rejected as the (last of) the prophets; and, finally, Jesus' passion as the death of the royal Son of God.

Finally, in the distinctive Johannine passion narrative the same pattern of correspondence with the earlier part of the Gospel occurs, although John seems to rework a different tradition from that of the Synoptics.[38] Jesus is fully conscious that he is the one sent by his Father and, rather than being a victim, is fully in command of the situation. He witnesses to the truth in his passion as he did in his ministry. He is opposed by "the Jews" (meaning the leaders of the Jews) during the passion as he was earlier for making himself God's Son, i.e., equal to God and God's intimate. His death is the consummation of everything for which the Father has sent him. In his death he is the model shepherd. He pours out the promised Spirit, symbolized by the water and blood (cf. 1 John 5:6-8). Since it is

36. See, for example, F. J. Matera, *Passion Narratives and Gospel Theologies: Interpreting the Synoptics through Their Passion Stories* (New York and Mahwah: Paulist, 1986).

37. Ibid., 222-23. Matera lists eight common elements. I am grateful to him for what follows.

38. See R. E. Brown, *The Gospel According to John XIII-XXI* (Garden City, New York: Doubleday, 1966) 910-16.

his "hour," he shows his care for his own in entrusting his disciples (in the person of the Beloved Disciple) and the New Israel (in the person of Mary) to each other. In his appearance before Pilate he explains his kingdom, and in his torment he is mocked as a king. Indeed, his crucifixion is his enthronement, i.e, his glorification, as well. Finally, in the symbolism of the seamless garment, he shows himself the priest of God.

Theological Reflections on the New Testament Understanding of Jesus' Death

Jesus' Freedom in Dying

Some years ago Rudolf Bultmann wrote of Jesus' passion and death that we cannot determine how Jesus understood his death, and that we must be open to the possibility that he collapsed on the cross.[39] His devaluation of the historical features of Jesus' death stems from his theological position, which we have already considered, namely, that faith cannot be legitimated by the "work" of historical research.

Bultmann's opinion may appear to have a basis in what some think is the oldest piece of tradition about Jesus as he died: the terse and terrible Markan statement "And Jesus uttered a loud cry, and breathed his last" (15:37). One might be tempted to hear in these words a cry of despair on Jesus' part, but such a reading would be speculation rather than exegesis. This is not to gainsay the fact that the verse, which Matthew retains substantially (27:50) and Luke (23:46) and John (19:30) qualify in their respective ways, poses serious questions to theologians about the nature of Jesus' death. Nevertheless, it will not convey an inside view of Jesus' self-awareness, although a cry of agony while a human being is dying on a cross is both understandable and capable of representing a number of possible interior dispositions.

Along with the Last Supper scene, which we examined to some extent above, the agony in the garden is an important narrative in connection with the question of Jesus' disposition as he faced death. There was a tendency in the past for authors and preachers to attribute Jesus' great pain in the garden principally to the fact that he was mentally present to all the sins and sinners of history past and history to come, the sinners for whose redemption he was about to die. In the light of contemporary biblical exegesis, we are much more cautious about what the text can deliver in the way of historical information.[40] There can be no doubt that the

---

39. R. Bultmann, "The Primitive Christian Kerygma and the Historical Jesus," in *The Historical Jesus and the Kerygmatic Christ*, ed. C. E. Braaten and R. A. Harrisville (New York and Nashville: Abingdon, 1964) 24.

40. G. O'Collins refers to Ferdinand Prat's *Jesus Christ: His Life, His Teaching, and His Work*, which was a popular work thirty years ago, as an example of this maximalist view of Jesus' un-

narrative in the three Synoptic Gospels contains a number of features that express the early Church's theological understanding of Jesus' progress toward the cross, for example, the triple failure of the three disciples to watch with Jesus in his agony, as well as the sayings of Jesus, which were ostensibly not heard by the sleeping three. In the present form of the account, there seems to be an exhortation (*parainesis*), directed at the early Christian community, to be faithful in difficult times. But a historical basis for the memory behind the narrative seems indisputable, since it hardly squares comfortably with the early community's desire to show Jesus as the exalted, plenipotentiary Messiah.

One possibility allowed by the account of the agony in the garden is that Jesus did not desire the death before him: ". . . remove this cup from me" (Mark 14:36 par.). The cup he was referring to was arguably the cup of eschatological woe, the terrible period of trial which, according to much apocalyptic literature, must precede the coming of God's salvation. What he did want above all else, however, was to be obedient to God his Father: "But not my will but yours be done" (Mark 14:36). This unity of will and desire with God-Abba was the paramount value of Jesus' life, and even a completely understandable resistance to drinking the eschatological cup of suffering and woe—that ultimate test in which everything might collapse—yielded to his commitment to the Father's will.

The theological point that the early community wanted to make here about the pre-Easter Jesus was that he went to his death freely, not in the sense that, once captured, he could have miraculously escaped from the hands of his captors, but rather that he *chose* to go to the cross. In other words, his disposition toward what was happening to him was one of free acceptance of what God wanted in the situation. The episode of the agony in the garden expresses in narrative form this crucial theological point. Paul's letters speak succinctly of Jesus' obedience, but the Synoptic Gospels narrate it dramatically, not by way of explanation but as a *story*.

John's Gospel is even more emphatic about Jesus' freedom in choosing his death, but thereby risks the danger of making Jesus a superhuman creature who in sovereign freedom does what he wants (10:17-18), the others in his life being so many instruments of his own plans and choosing. For example, when the soldiers and officers confront Jesus in the garden to arrest him, they fall to the ground at his acknowledgement of who he is. The "I am he" (John 18:6) turns out to be a very powerful

derstanding of his own death. See his *Interpreting Jesus* (New York and Ramsey: Paulist, 1983) 80–81; F. Prat, *Jesus Christ: His Life, His Teaching, His Work*, 16th ed., trans. J. J. Heenan (Milwaukee: Bruce, 1950), vol. 2, 319. For a contemporary exegetical treatment, see D. M. Stanley, *Jesus in Gethsemane: The Early Church Reflects on the Suffering of Jesus* (New York and Ramsey: Paulist, 1980).

word indeed! In the Synoptic accounts of the agony, there is a more convincing mixture of human weakness and resolution.

The freedom with which Jesus went to his death was not the freedom to remain a captive or to escape, but the kind of freedom that exists within the human limits of a human situation, the freedom to choose how to relate to those limits. Jesus' freedom lay in choosing a radical dependence on God, and in choosing how to relate to those around him, his disciples, his captors, his judges, and his executioners. Just as with us, his relationship with God-Abba and himself became visible and incarnate in his way of relating to his "neighbor" in those very straitened circumstances. The passion narratives are the story of Jesus' freedom in the narrowest of circumstances. In that plight he had, at least, the powers of the weak.

God's Will and Jesus' Death

Among the fundamental questions which need to be addressed are these: Did God want Jesus to suffer and die a violent death? What was God's will for Jesus here, according to the New Testament?

Now it is true that there are places in the New Testament where we are told that God handed Jesus over to those who then killed him. "The son of man will be delivered into the hands of men" (Mark 9:31). Here the passive voice could be the so-called theological passive, referring to God without explicitly naming the divine. With complete explicitness Paul wrote about God as "he who did not spare his own Son but gave him up for us all" (Rom 8:32). At an early stage in the development of the gospel traditions of Jesus' passion and death, the view developed that God was "behind" everything that went on. Evil men did not have their way with Jesus in such wise that God was "left out in the cold," as it were. Even what *they* did was caught up in a larger, beneficent plan that was God's alone.

But it is one thing to say that God's saving plan encompassed the suffering and death of Jesus, another to argue that God wanted or wants suffering. There is no basis in the New Testament for contending that God, the one who was Abba in Jesus' life, desired in some simple way that Jesus suffer and die a violent death. After all, God is God of the living, not the dead, and God wants everyone to have life and have it abundantly. The God of the New Testament (and here I am not implying a contrast with the Old Testament) is revealed in Jesus' ministry where Jesus engages in combat with the evil powers and despoils them (Mark 3:27 par.). The God of Jesus fights sin and the violence, oppression, and death that are sin's manifestations. God did not want Jesus to be a victim of sinners' violence but, it would seem, God did want Jesus, and through Jesus God's own self, to draw as close as possible to sinners (and thus, necessarily, to their violence) in the hope of opening them up to transformation. If Jesus freely chose to be in solidarity with sinners (as well as the sick, possessed, and oppressed), then he would be exposed to all that they might choose to do to him.

This is an example of how an understanding of Jesus' ministry can shed light on the interpretation of his passion and death. A dynamic occurs in the passion and death that is an intensification, and indeed climax, of what was going on all along in the public ministry.

Thus when it is said that it was God's will for Jesus to suffer and die, it is essential to make some distinctions. What is it that God wanted, and what it is that God not only did not want but fought and fights against? Another way of framing the question: What costs was Jesus willing to take on, and what costs was God, in and through Jesus, willing to take on for the sake of coming infinitely close to sinners so as to invite them in the most profound way to reconciliation, forgiveness, and transformation? Enduring a means, or set of means, for the sake of a goal is no strange thing. If you want the goal, you have to want the means; but that second "wanting" may perhaps, at times, be better termed an "enduring."

Jesus' Life and Death as Representative Acts

The understanding of Jesus' death as expiatory, as happening on account of and for the sake of sinners so that their sin and guilt would be taken away, was not, as noted above, the only very early interpretation. But it became the dominant one in the later development of tradition.

The Old Testament provides a background for this interpretation. The Servant Songs of Second Isaiah, as we have seen, speak of the sufferings of one being the source of healing for others. Two Books of Maccabees (2 Macc 7:37-38; 4 Macc 6:27-29; 17:12; 18:4) contain a theology of martyrdom which views the death of the Jewish martyr as able to expiate the sins of others. In the period between the two testaments, the notion of an expiatory death gained currency and lay at hand for use by Christian writers seeking to express the meaning of Jesus' death. The application of this theology to Jesus was not merely extrinsic, but derived from an appreciation of Jesus' life and ministry as essentially for the sake of others. It is the concept of representation, with reference to Jesus' ministry in life and death, that we shall need to examine in more detail in chapter 6.

The Trinity and the Cross

Recent theology has reminded the Church that the passion and death of Jesus cannot be adequately understood apart from the doctrine of the Trinity. Jürgen Moltmann, a German Reformed theologian, has argued dramatically for the profound joining of these two themes in his work

The Crucified God.[41] Some critics disagree with Moltmann's interpretation of Jesus' cry in Mark's Gospel as a cry in the face of God's abandonment of him. They have accused him of turning a historical, momentary experience, itself not easily interpreted, into an eternal, intradivine moment in God's life, somewhat as G. W. F. Hegel idealistically sublimated history into the divine life. But one major contribution of Moltmann has been his contention that God the Father must be thought of as fully and intimately involved in the suffering and death of his Son, indeed, that we must realize that in his own way the Father participated in the suffering and death of his Son.[42] The classic doctrine of the impassive and impassible God must give way to a view informed by the revelation of the Cross.

Catholic theologians have given new attention to Cross and Trinity as well. Hans Urs von Balthasar and, more recently, John O'Donnell have argued that the Trinity expresses and communicates its full identity in the event of the Cross (united with the resurrection). As O'Donnell writes:

> . . . the mission of Jesus which is fulfilled in the Cross has its origins in the eternal Trinity. If we conceive of the event of the Cross as a divine drama involving the Father and the Son, then as Balthasar argues, this drama must be grounded in the eternal background of the divine life. The cross is the working out in history of the drama, which surpasses every drama, namely the eternal action within God himself. In other words, the only way to avoid seeing the cross as the imposition of an alien obedience is to situate the dramatic action within the eternal trinitarian drama. This is the merit of Balthasar's trinitarian theology. Balthasar wants to stress that the cross is a separation of Father and Son, but the dramatic caesura that rends the heart of God on Calvary has already been embraced from all eternity by the divine Trinity. For from all eternity the Father has given himself away to the Son, has risked his being on the Son, and from eternity the Son has been a yes to the Father, a surrender to obedience. Thus the Father's risk of himself creates a space for the Son. The Father separates himself from himself, so that the Son can be. But this separation is also bridged over in eternity by the Holy Spirit, the communion of love of the Father and the Son.[43]

41. J. Moltmann, *The Crucified God: The Cross of Christ as the Foundation and Criticism of Christian Theology*, trans. R. A. Wilson and J. Bowden (New York: Harper and Row, 1974); see also his *The Trinity and the Kingdom of God: The Doctrine of God*, trans. M. Kohl (New York: Harper and Row, 1981) ch. 2.

42. Moltmann, *The Crucified God*, 244–47.

43. J. O'Donnell, *The Mystery of the Triune God* (New York: Paulist, 1989) 65. He refers to H. Urs von Balthasar, *Theodramatik* III (Einsiedeln: Benziger, 1980) 297–305 and *Herrlichkeit* III, 2, Teil 2 (Einsiedeln: Benziger, 1969) 208. See von Balthasar's essay *Life Out of Death: Meditations on the Easter Mystery* (Philadelphia: Fortress, 1985).

Conclusion

In this chapter we have considered the passion and death of Jesus from historical and New Testament theological perspectives. The New Testament documents do not make it easy to determine in any detail either the legal or quasi-legal procedures by which Jesus was tried. Nor do they make it clear who was responsible for his death, beyond the likelihood that both Jewish leaders and Romans were responsible. It is quite possible that he was not tried on religious charges at all. But the complexities of the historical question have not prevented Christians from seeing in Jesus' death the plan and purpose of God as well as a profound consistency between Jesus' ministry and his death, for in both he gave himself fully on behalf of God his Father and on behalf of his brothers and sisters. He died freely and with a sense of trust in God that somehow the salvation symbolized in the kingdom he had preached would arrive. He died in total solidarity with sinners, with the broken of mind and body, with all victims of violence, and with all those who, down the full length of human history, have been pushed to the margins of society. His death for the sake of sinners was paradoxically the triumph of the Father's love and his own, united in the Spirit. The Cross has been the primary Christian symbol because in its mystery it embraces the meeting of divine-human love and sin, the enemy of human nature, while expressing the hidden but ultimately effective victory of that love.

4

The Resurrection of Jesus

Christian faith depends essentially on the resurrection of Jesus. Certainly for Paul, "If Christ has not been raised, then our preaching is in vain and your faith is in vain" (1 Cor 15:14). In other words, without the resurrection of Jesus, the apostolic preaching would not be full of God's saving power. But he also means that Jesus' not being raised would give the lie to that preaching, for its truth derived from Jesus' victory over death. Looking back, it is not hard to see why most Christians have been convinced that if Jesus had died rejected by some of the Jewish leaders, executed by the Roman occupiers of Israel, and deserted by his disciples, without anything more occurring beyond that, then his story would have remained that of a striking spokesman for God and for the welfare of God's people who was done in by events. The movement that is Christianity would never have gotten off the ground.

But very soon after the crucifixion of Jesus, the disciples began to spread the word: "Jesus is not dead but alive and will return soon in glory to judge the living and the dead." From this moment on the disciples were convinced that the reign of God, preached by Jesus and signed forth in his healings and exorcisms, was now occurring in its fullness and that, in the terms of Jewish apocalyptic thought, the universal resurrection of the dead was commencing, with Jesus the first of those who were raised, the representative "first fruits" of those who had fallen asleep (1 Cor 15:20). Eschatological redemption was happening. In quick succession Jesus and then others would enter the new age wrought by God.

As time went on and it became apparent that the universal resurrection and the consummation of all things in God's reign were not going to occur immediately, Christians gave further thought to Jesus' role in salvation and the relationship of others to that salvation (see, e.g., 1 Thess 4:13-18). In various ways they found expression for their conviction that Easter meant the reversal of all that was negative in his death, the vindication of his message and claim, and his installation as God's anointed.

In order to come to some appreciation of the significance of Jesus' resurrection for both the New Testament writers and present day Christology, and for Christian faith itself, we shall consider several topics in this chapter. First, we shall examine the question of the *genesis* of Easter faith by surveying the earliest New Testament data regarding Jesus' resurrection and looking at the Easter event from a historical point of view, which means exploring the nature of the "Easter experience." Next, we shall reflect on the *meaning* of Easter in the New Testament as an eschatological, soteriological, and theological event, and as an event that revealed Jesus' identity. This will lead us into some of the hermeneutical paths provided by contemporary theology as we seek to approach the Church's talk about resurrection meaningfully. Then we shall consider the question of the *truth* of Easter faith. Finally, it will be useful to review several of the principal understandings of Jesus which developed in the New Testament canon in the light of Easter and which paved the way for post-New Testament Christology.

The Genesis of Easter Faith: The Earliest New Testament Data

Pheme Perkins counts three sources of primitive Easter tradition behind the gospel narratives of the resurrection appearances, the narratives that have primarily shaped the Christian imagination and understanding of Easter. The first source is the kerygmatic tradition, which has left some of its earliest traces in 1 Cor 15:5-8. The second is the tradition that associates some women with the empty tomb, of which Mark 16 contains the oldest version we possess. The third is the witness of early Christian prophets who, in Jesus' name, proclaimed his exaltation.[1]

We shall now examine each of these sources for information about the origins of Easter faith.

Easter and Kerygma: Paul

Kerygmatic or preaching formulas do not come down to us in their original contexts, for they were essentially oral events which then entered into the literary traditions of the New Testament. These formulas are of two different types. The first type speaks of the antithesis of death and

---

1. P. Perkins, *Resurrection: New Testament Witness and Contemporary Reflection* (Garden City, New York: Doubleday, 1984) 137.

resurrection, for example, in Romans 14:9: "Christ died and lived again," and 1 Thessalonians 4:14a: "since we believe that Jesus died and rose again." The second type speaks of Christ as raised but does not mention his death. One of the earliest kerygmatic formulas of this type is found in 1 Thessalonians: "to wait for his Son from heaven, whom God raised from the dead, Jesus who delivers us from the wrath to come" (1:10). There are other pre-Pauline kerygmatic statements in Paul's writings, such as Rom 1:3-4; 4:24-25; 8:34; 10:9.[2]

But it is 1 Corinthians 15:3-8 which calls for more extensive attention. In the fifteenth chapter of this letter, Paul is telling his readers that he and all other apostolic leaders in the Church teach one and the same doctrine of the resurrection, which is opposed to the one-sided view of some in the Corinthian community who maintain that Christians are already completely resurrected and redeemed and thus free of all constraints of law and obligation. Paul refers to this shared teaching by quoting elements of already venerable tradition, linking up these elements with the Greek word for "that" (*hoti*), which functions like quotation marks.

He introduces the traditional material with technical terms about receiving and passing on tradition, to assure his readers that he is faithfully communicating to them what was first entrusted to him. There is a structure to what he recounts as sacred tradition:

Christ died
for our sins
in accordance with the Scriptures

and was buried;

he was raised
on the third day
in accordance with the Scriptures

and he appeared to Cephas
then to the twelve
then to more than five hundred brethren at one time
then to James,
then to all the apostles.

The first thing we notice here is that "Christ," originally a title, has already been elided into a proper name for Jesus. Then we notice that we have two parallel sentences, each containing a statement of fact (Christ died; Christ was raised) followed by what may be taken to be an interpretation, or amplification, of that fact (his death was for our sins; it was on the third day that he was raised). The origin of the phrase "on the third

2. Ibid., 217–28.

day" may be due to the post-Easter appearances beginning on the third day after Jesus' resurrection, but may also connote that Jesus' resurrection by God was a decisive, eschatological act, for, according to the Old Testament, God acts in a decisive, saving way on the third day (Hos 6:2). This death and being raised are the fulfillment of the Old Testament. The parallelisms continue with Jesus' burial, mentioned as confirmation of the fact of his death, and a list of appearances to named witnesses confirming his being raised from the dead.

A plausible interpretation of the list of recipients of appearances runs this way: Since Cephas and the Twelve were the leaders of the Jerusalem community, and the "more than five hundred brethren" (some of whom, Paul adds, are still alive as he writes) could be a reference to the Pentecost event recounted by Luke, what we have so far are appearances of the risen Jesus as Church-founding events. James and all the apostles, mentioned next, are the missionaries who spread the gospel beyond Jerusalem and Israel.[3] This dual perspective shows up in the Easter narratives of Matthew, Luke, and John as well: Church-founding and Church-sending as two effects, or dimensions, of the experience of the Risen One.

Finally, Paul adds something about himself: Last of all, as to an *ektrôma*, Christ appeared also to him. Now *ektrôma* can mean a monster or monstrous birth, or it can mean a fetus that has been surgically removed from its dying mother's womb and so has never laid eyes on the one who gave it birth.[4] Both senses might be intended by Paul, because he had persecuted the Church of Christ out of zeal for the Law and had never seen the earthly Jesus.

Thus we find in these few verses of Paul a most succinct account of the pivotal events of Easter, and the core of the apostolic kerygma. The passage contains no descriptions of appearances, only the simple mention of them. From it we learn about the crucial relationship between leaders in the earliest communities and being recipients of appearances. And we note that the function of the appearances is Church-founding and Church-sending.

Easter, Kerygma, and Empty Tomb: Mark

Let us now turn our attention to the original ending of Mark's Gospel (16:1-8). Even at an early stage it seemed strange to those familiar with the Gospels of Matthew and Luke and with the traditions that led to their accounts of the resurrection appearances, that Mark's ending did not con-

---

3. R. H. Fuller, *The Formation of the Resurrection Narratives* (New York: Macmillan, 1971) 34–38.

4. E. Schillebeeckx, *Jesus: An Experiment in Christology*, 708, n. 87.

tain accounts of Easter appearances. As compensation for this apparent omission someone imported traditional material similar to that found elsewhere in the New Testament, to "round off" what seemed to be a very abrupt ending to the second Gospel. (The original version of Mark even ends with a particle, a not unknown literary occurrence in antiquity but a very infrequent one.) There is general scholarly agreement, however, that verse 8 concludes the original version of Mark's Gospel.

Many scholars also agree in isolating a core of traditional material from Mark 16:1-8 that is very old and among the oldest texts bearing on the events after Jesus' death. The earliest material seems to read more or less as follows:

> And very early on the first day of the week, they [some women] went to the tomb when the sun had risen. And looking up, they saw that the stone was rolled back; for it was very large. And entering the tomb, they saw a young man sitting on the right side, dressed in a white robe; and they were amazed. And he said to them, "Do not be amazed; you seek Jesus of Nazareth, who was crucified. He has risen, he is not here; see the place where they laid him." And they went out and fled from the tomb; for trembling and astonishment had come upon them.

The story here is one of an angelophany, composed in what (to the original readers or hearers) would have been a standard Jewish manner. The young man dressed in white is an angel. He strikes holy terror into the hearts of the women, the expected reaction in this type of literature. The women come looking for Jesus' body and instead encounter someone from God, a heavenly messenger (*angelos*) who illuminates the situation. He proclaims the Church's kerygma; that Jesus of Nazareth, the crucified one, has risen and is not here in the tomb; Jesus is alive and not among the dead. This truth God reveals to the frightened women.

The point of the story is not the discovery of the empty tomb, for there is no mention of the women ascertaining for themselves that the tomb was indeed empty. The point lies rather in the proclamation from God of Jesus' resurrection. Mark's Gospel ends, then, not with appearances of the Easter Jesus, but with the Church's proclamation of Jesus' resurrection as divine revelation. Peculiar to this story is the fact that only here in the New Testament is the kerygma connected with a particular geographical location: the site where Jesus was buried.

This fact has led some scholars to theorize that the ancient tradition embedded in Mark 16:1-8 originated from, or at least was associated with, an annual celebration of Easter in Jerusalem at the tomb.[5] Several presuppositions come into play here: first, that the Jerusalem community knew

---

5. For a summary of this view with references, see ibid., 329–31, 334–37.

the location of the tomb,[6] second, that it was regularly venerated, as were tombs of other holy people before and after Jesus; and third, that there was a liturgical celebration at the tomb during which, at a climactic moment, the liturgical leader would point to the site of the tomb and utter the words of the angelic messenger.

The conclusions that are reasonably sure are these: First, an ancient tradition connects some women with the discovery of the empty tomb. The names of the women vary, excepting Mary of Magdala (about whom we know only that Jesus cast seven demons out of her). Second, the correct interpretation of the meaning of the empty tomb is given by the resurrection of Jesus and its proclamation in faith and, ultimately, by God's own revelation; the tomb does not communicate its own significance. Third, the early Church was quite comfortable with the conviction that women were told the good news of the resurrection apart from appearances of Jesus to the "official" witnesses, Peter and the Twelve. (But notice that Mark, in his addition to the ancient story, states that the women disobeyed the angelic command in his inherited material and said nothing to anyone because of their fear. In this way, some argue, Mark preserved the primacy of both the apostles' experience of the Risen One and their preaching of the Easter kerygma.)

The two more extended ancient traditions that we have been examining contain some common elements. In both 1 Corinthians 15 and Mark 16, we are dealing with the basic proclamation of the early Church: Jesus who died, rose or, better, was raised from the dead. Each tradition also names witnesses to the truth of the kerygma and in each case God is the ultimate agent. The two passages speak of Jesus' *being raised* which is the "theological passive" affirming that God is the agent of the resurrection. Regarding the revelation of the resurrection, in the early material employed by Paul, divine activity is probably suggested by the verb *ôphthê*, which in the Septuagint often means "was revealed," with the implication that God did the revealing (see, for example, Gen 12:7 and 26:2).[7] In his traditional material, Mark used the presence and words of the young man to indicate God's action in making known Jesus' resurrection.

There are also several important differences between the two passages. First, the traditions used by Paul in 1 Corinthians 15:3-8 were just that, pieces of tradition, which may have been combined even before Paul included them in his letter. On the other hand, the tradition taken over by Mark was a coherent story. Second, Paul's traditions do not refer to a tomb (nor does Paul do so anywhere in his writings), whereas the tomb is a key factor in the Markan story, and Jesus' absence from it is explained

6. See R. E. Brown, "The Burial of Jesus (Mark 15:42-47)," *Catholic Biblical Quarterly* 50 (1988) 233-45.

7. Fuller, *Formation*, 32-33.

by his resurrection. Third, the witnesses named in the Pauline passage are all men (although the "more than five hundred" probably did include women), while Mark's account affirms that women were the earliest recipients of the good news of the resurrection.

Easter and the Sayings of the Risen Lord

The third early source for the development of the traditions regarding the resurrection consisted of proclamations of Jesus' messianic exaltation by early Christian prophets speaking in his name. Several examples are presented as sayings of the risen Jesus at the end of Matthew's Gospel (28:18-20): "All authority in heaven and on earth has been given to me. Go therefore and make disciples of all nations, baptizing them in the name of the Father and of the Son and of the Holy Spirit, teaching them to observe all that I have commanded you: and lo, I am with you always, to the close of the age." These *logia* were first uttered by Christian prophets under the influence of Jesus' Spirit, who spoke for him as the exalted Son of Man (with an allusion to Dan 7:14). Matthew combined them as we find here.[8]

The Genesis of Easter Faith: The Appearance Narratives and History

Tradition-critical and redaction-critical study of the appearance narratives as we find them in Matthew, Luke, and John makes it abundantly clear that their composition involved inherited material and the theological reflection of the evangelists, just as was the case with the passion narratives and indeed the individual Gospels in their entirety. Christological and ecclesiological concerns of each of these three Gospels are echoed in the stories of the risen Jesus with his disciples. We find this to be the case in Matthew, for example, where Jesus the teacher and revealer on the mount of the Sermon becomes the teacher and revealer on the mount of the resurrection-presence. We see it again in Luke, where the Jesus who ate and drank with his friends in the days of his ministry does the same in the days between his resurrection and ascension. In John, the Jesus who had promised in his last discourse that, when he was glorified, he would send the Paraclete now breathes it forth on his own.

When we remember that Matthew's and Luke's Gospels were composed after 70 C.E., and that the Fourth Gospel received its final redaction at the end of the first century, we realize that a lot of Church life and ministry, as well as prayer to Christ and witness in his name, occurred while these

8. M. E. Boring, *Sayings of the Risen Jesus: Christian Prophecy in the Synoptic Tradition* (Cambridge: Cambridge University Press, 1982) 195-225.

narratives were acquiring their final form. Thus any attempt to use the appearance narratives as texts offering direct access to the Easter experiences of the disciples soon after Jesus' death would be completely misplaced.

Edward Schillebeeckx has well expressed the basic structure of the appearance narratives:

> The element of "manifestation" points in a "vertical" way to the apostolic *kerygma* and the praxis or actual conduct of the Church as being characterized by grace and revelation. In the verticality of the manifestation, as the ancient expression for an "epiphany" or "disclosure of God," is concentrated the grace, impacted with the saving events of history, of what has for years been occurring (horizontally) in the Matthean, Lucan and Johannine churches: the preaching of the gospel to Jew and pagan, Christian baptism and the ministry of reconciliation, in faith-inspired assurance that in all of this Jesus is at work. The activity of the heavenly Jesus in the Church is expressed in terms of epiphany. The matter or "substance" of the manifestation is supplied out of the concrete life of the Church as the "community of Christ."[9]

One of the most frequently emphasized features in any discussion of the gospel appearance narratives is the tremendous discrepancy among the stories. By comparison the passion narratives, for all their differences, describe a fairly uniform sequence of events. The original ending of Mark differs from those of the other Gospels in that it contains no appearance stories but only a reference to Jesus' going before the disciples to Galilee where they will see him. R. H. Fuller offers this summary of the two major discrepancies in the appearance narratives:

> First, Mark implies, while Matthew and John 21 state, that the appearances are located in Galilee but, in Luke and John 20, the appearances take place in Jerusalem. Second, in Matthew and John 21 (and perhaps also by implication in Mark), the appearances seem to be manifestations of an already risen and ascended One and of a more "spiritual" kind, whereas the appearance to the women on the way from the tomb in Matthew, the Lucan Emmaus story, and the Christophany to the eleven in Luke and in John 20 are of a risen but not yet ascended Lord whose corporal manifestation is emphasized (he is touched and he eats). John throws the picture into further confusion by implying that the ascension took place between the appearance to Mary Magdalene and the encounter with Thomas. Yet Thomas is invited to touch him. One would expect touching to be characteristic of the preascension Christophanies, as in

---

9. Schillebeeckx, *Jesus*, 358.

Luke, but John has a different view. For him Christ apparently ascends between the appearance to Mary Magdalene and the appearance to the disciples a week later.[10]

Thus when we move from the oldest literary sources to the gospel appearance narratives as we meet them in the New Testament we move from relative simplicity to considerable variation. It is quite possible that there was only one appearance to the eleven, which was retold differently in the various early communities and located in Galilee in some traditions and in Jerusalem in others. The stories of appearances of Jesus to women were a conflation of previous distinct traditions about women discovering the empty tomb and appearances to male disciples.

Even if we do not have "reports" which spell out exactly what the events were, in regard to the beginnings of Easter faith, we can safely say the following: that (1) soon after Jesus' death some of those who had followed Jesus during his ministry (and at least one who did not: Paul) had experiences which convinced them that this crucified Jesus of Nazareth was now alive and in God's *doxa*, glory; (2) they believed that these experiences were initiated by Jesus and God; (3) these experiences allowed the disciples to identify the reality experienced as being that of Jesus, the one they all (except Paul) had known before his death, not resuscitated, i.e., having returned to ongoing earthly life (like Lazarus in John's Gospel), but living a completely new, eschatological mode of existence; (4) they experienced a renewal and profound transformation of their relationship with Jesus as his disciples; and, (5) they experienced the revelation of his being alive with eschatological life as entailing a charge or mission for themselves.

The Easter Experience

The word experience is used throughout this summary. Oceans of ink have been spilled over the centuries in attempting to determine the nature of the "Easter experience."

It would be instructive to contrast two recent Roman Catholic theologians' approaches to the notion of the "Easter experience," for they represent two major positions in the present-day discussion. The theologians are Edward Schillebeeckx (Belgian) and Gerald O'Collins (Australian).

Schillebeeckx argues from the absence of any mention of the resurrection or appearances in the Q-source that the reality denoted by "Easter experience" was independent of the tomb tradition and the appearance tradition.[11] Moreover, resurrection is just one possible model by which

---

10. Fuller, *Formation*, 5.

11. Schillebeeckx, *Jesus*, 396–97.

to interpret what happened to Jesus after his death. Rapture or "being taken up to God" is another model, and may have been the one used by the community behind the Q-source. There is no doubt that later on resurrection and traditions about appearances dominated the New Testament and subsequent witness.

For Schillebeeckx, God really brought Jesus from death to a whole new mode of life. That truth is not in dispute at all: it is as central to his view as it is to Christianity.[12] He insists, however, that the Easter experiences of the disciples were not empirical experiences of a historical reality, but rather faith-motivated experiences of grace and forgiveness. The conviction that Jesus was with God in a whole new way after being killed developed out of a combination of factors. Immediately after Jesus' death the disciples still possessed some (small) degree of faith in their master, despite his apparent defeat on the cross (remembering perhaps that he spoke of the coming of God's reign in the face of his impending death). Regathered by Peter, they recalled his ministry and presence among them and his sense of closeness with God-Abba.[13] Conjoined with those memories and reflections was a new element occurring after his death: a new experience of the grace of forgiveness. Sensing that their desertion of their master was now being forgiven *by him* after his death, they concluded that Jesus was alive and with God, because a dead person cannot forgive.[14] The movement to Easter faith was expressed in terms of a model from Judaism of the conversion of Gentiles to the light of Yahweh and the covenant faith of Judaism.[15] The disciples' Easter experience was essentially a conversion experience, which led them to conclude that Jesus was alive and with God. They found a number of ways of interpreting this experience of conversion with reference to Jesus: that he was raised by God, or taken up to God, or exalted at God's right hand. But the reality to be interpreted was the remembered earthly Jesus of Nazareth and the grace and forgiveness experienced after his death. As Schillebeeckx puts it:

> Thus we end up in a remarkable hermeneutical circle: Jesus' living and dying on earth suggested to Christians, in virtue of their experiences after Jesus' death, the idea of the resurrection or the coming Parousia of Jesus, while on the basis of their faith in the risen or coming crucified One they relate the story of Jesus in the gospels; in other words, these gospel stories of Jesus are themselves a hermeneusis of Jesus' Parousia and resurrection, while belief in the Parousia or in the resurrection was engendered by things remembered of the historical Jesus. The "matter to be

12. Ibid., 644–50.
13. Ibid., 385.
14. Ibid., 391.
15. Ibid., 383.

interpreted''—Jesus of Nazareth—came eventually to be interpreted in and through the faith-inspired affirmation of his resurrection (Parousia), while that resurrection or Parousia is in its turn the "object of interpretation" which is then interpreted through the gospel narratives as remembrances of Jesus' earthly life, as also in the light of his resurrection or coming Parousia.[16]

For Schillebeeckx, the Easter experiences of the disciples were like other experiences of grace. They were, of course, conditioned by historical factors like all human experiences. Sensory elements, including visual ones, may even have been involved, but these would have been in the nature of redundancy experiences. To imagine that the core Easter experience was empirical would be to denature an essentially faith-motivated experience of grace joined with reflection on the pre-Easter Jesus' life and death. No visual element could have served as the ground of the disciples' Easter faith.[17]

Gerald O'Collins has disputed Schillebeeckx's position in a number of publications.[18] He recognizes, however, that Schillebeeckx is not seeking to reduce all talk of resurrection, exaltation, and so on to a transformation of the disciples after Jesus' death. At issue is the nature of the disciples' experience. O'Collins argues that the Easter experience of the disciples is inadequately described as a faith-motivated experience of grace and forgiveness conjoined with memories of the earthly Jesus and with the inference that a forgiving Jesus must be alive. Crucial for O'Collins is the disciples' conviction of Jesus being alive in God's glory. They experienced not only forgiveness but also *Jesus* personally alive. The affirmation that Jesus was alive in God's *doxa* was not an interpretive inference for the disciples, but an essential dimension of their experience. While experience and interpretation are deeply intertwined in all human encounters, in this instance the affirmation that Jesus was alive in a whole new way after his death was not simply an interpretation of the earthly Jesus in light of a forgiveness experience; rather, the affirmation expressed the fact that it was *he* who was the very reality experienced. On Schillebeeckx's terms the disciples could have concluded from their experience of grace that *God* forgave them. But why was Jesus, personally, the agent of for-

16. Ibid., 402.

17. E. Schillebeeckx, *An Interim Report on the Books "Jesus" and "Christ"* (New York: Crossroad, 1982) 75.

18. G. O'Collins, *What Are They Saying About the Resurrection?* (New York and Ramsey: Paulist, 1978); *Interpreting Jesus*, 120–24 and *Jesus Risen* (New York and Ramsey: Paulist, 1987). The last-named volume gives a helpful historical survey of views of the resurrection. Most recently O'Collins has published *Interpreting the Resurrection: Examining the Major Problems in the Stories of Jesus' Resurrection* (New York and Ramsey: Paulist, 1988). See also J. Galvin, "The Resurrection of Jesus in Catholic Systematics," *Heythrop Journal* 20 (1979) 123–45.

giveness? (O'Collins insists that the forgiveness motif is not a major one in the Easter accounts and should not be overstressed.)

O'Collins sees in Schillebeeckx's argument theological presuppositions which make the latter leery of any reference to experiences of Jesus after his death. Those presuppositions need to be addressed. Could Jesus, newly alive in God's glory, make himself known as a transhistorical (eschatological) reality to human beings still living in history? O'Collins responds yes.[19] The experience would be human and within history as far as the disciples were concerned, but the one experienced would be known in God's eschatological glory. Jesus' appearances would not presuppose the disciples' faith but would be a reason for it, as the New Testament, including Paul, seems to state.[20] The initiative would be Jesus'. O'Collins is arguing for the uniqueness of this experience, as befits the uniqueness of Jesus' eschatological character and of the Church's primary witness to Jesus' presence and action in the world. God gave the chosen disciples the capacity to see the Risen Christ. The Easter experience had a visual element but not in the sense of ordinary sight; it was a "graced power of perception: in which the recipients of the appearances were to some extent rendered connatural to the eschatologial reality they were perceiving."[21] In O'Collins' view, the ancient *ôphthê*-formula is not simply second-level interpretation but intimately allied with the original experience. This important point in his argument has yet to be further developed by him. Because he defines biblical seeing as normally involving some kind of ocular sight, he contends that the disciples probably saw not an internal, subjective vision but rather an external, objective vision of a kind that did not compel their faith but invited it.[22] Presumably such a vision would have differed from later Christian mystical experiences, which are not considered normative revelation in a Church-founding sense.

In his critique of Schillbeeckx, O'Collins argues strongly for a traditional approach. I think he has discovered a serious flaw in Schillebeeckx's argument.[23] The latter has not offered an adequate explanation for the identification of Jesus of Nazareth as alive in God's glory. Even Schillebeeckx has to admit that "early Christian local churches did nevertheless all have an experience of Easter, that is, knew the reality which other churches explicitly referred to as 'resurrection.' "[24] The Q-community's *maranatha*-Christology meant that its members had had an experience

19. O'Collins, *Interpreting Jesus*, 123.

20. Ibid., 123.

21. O'Collins, *Jesus Risen*, 119–20.

22. Ibid., 118–19.

23. For another critique of Schillebeeckx, see P. Carnley, *The Structure of Resurrection Belief* (Oxford: Clarendon Press, 1987) 199–222.

24. Schillebeeckx, *Jesus*, 396.

which convinced them that Jesus was personally with God and would return soon as judge and Savior. An adequate *explanation* of their faith calls for there being given (by God and Jesus) a means of identifying this man Jesus as the one who is "with God" and will "come soon as judge and Savior." Even if we cannot describe in detail the original experiences which generated Easter faith, we may argue from a less satisfactory explanation to a more satisfactory one. In this case the more satisfactory explanation has on its side what Schillebeeckx himself acknowledges is a "centuries-old hermeneutical tradition" rooted in the New Testament.[25] We can readily agree that the appearance narratives as we have them are Christological and ecclesiological elaborations of the early Church, which cannot be used to determine the original experiences in any detail. But the notion of appearance can still be affirmed as part of the originating experience, because it is a necessary component of an adequate explanation for the emergence of Easter faith.[26]

An important question in regard to the early disciples' Easter experiences is how they differed from later Christians' experiences of Jesus. The faith of those disciples was similar to and different from ours: similar because both faiths were and are responses to the presence of the Risen Christ, grounded ultimately in the fidelity and initiative of God in Christ; and different because our faith comes to us in and through the Church and its witness to the Risen Christ in the power of the Spirit. We are embedded in the Easter tradition, since that has become the tradition of the Church. The disciples, on the other hand, stood at the beginnings of the Church, at the very origins of the Easter tradition. To be sure, they (with the exception of Paul) had been called and gathered by the pre-Easter Jesus and had ministered in association with him. They had had a kind of faith-relationship to him before his death. They knew that at the Last Supper he had taken his death into account and still believed in the arrival of God's reign despite the deadly opposition which his ministry had aroused. Nevertheless Jesus' crucifixion set a huge question mark against his preaching that the reign of God would arrive. The fact that Jesus the crucified became, by God's mighty act, the kingdom of God in person called for an experience which could make that foundational identifying act and a profoundly new faith possible.

The New Testament clearly distinguishes the apostolic experiences of the Risen One from those of later disciples, and later Church teaching recognizes the apostolic experiences as normative for the relationship of later Christians to Christ. We have seen how in 1 Corinthians 15:8 Paul

---

25. Ibid., 710, n. 119. Here Schillebeeckx contends that the object of Christian faith is not the Easter appearances. He is right. The object of Easter faith is the person of Jesus the Christ.

26. See G. J. Hughes on interpretation and explanation: "Dead Theories, Live Metaphors and the Resurrection," *Heythrop Journal* 29 (1988) 313–28.

refers to himself as the last to receive the founding revelation. He distinguishes between the apostolic revelation he has received and his other "visions" of Christ (2 Cor 12:1-5; cf. Gal 1:12; 1 Cor 9:1). John's Gospel distinguishes between those who have seen and believed and those who have not seen and yet believed, affirming that the latter, although in a different situation, are blessed (John 20:29). As far as we know, with the exception of Paul, all the disciples who experienced "Easter" had known Jesus in his ministry and could identify him as the Risen One. This act of identification lies at the heart of the Gospels, founding and inaugurating the Christian tradition, which will nurture the faith of later Christians.

The Meaning of Easter: The New Testament

Whether the climactic event in Jesus' life and death is called resurrection, exaltation, or glorification, all these ways of referring to it have the following elements in common: (1) the three terms express the inauguration of the "new age" (*eschaton*) by God in and through what happened to Jesus; (2) they indicate that what happened to Jesus was the climax of God's saving action in Israel's history for the sake of Israel and "the nations"; (3) they refer to God as the ultimate agent of revelation and salvation in and through what happened to Jesus; (4) they refer to the event which reveals Jesus in his full identity in relation to God and his brothers and sisters.

Let us briefly consider each of these four elements in order to gain an initial appreciation of the meaning of Easter in the New Testament.

Easter as Eschatological Event

We have seen that at the center of Jesus' preaching was the coming reign of God. The fullness of that reign pertained to the *eschaton*, to the final condition intended by God for the chosen people and through them for all the nations. Thus Jesus, as charismatic preacher of that reign and healer who signed forth its proleptic presence, was an eschatological figure, and his followers associated him with the coming reign which he had preached and for which he had suffered. When the conviction developed that he had been raised from the dead and exalted as the Son of Man, they realized that the reign of God was already decisively and irrevocably occurring. The resurrection of Jesus was the first installment (Acts 26:23; 1 Cor 15:20-21; Col 1:18) in a story whose denouement they expected to follow very shortly. When it became clear that the end of history and the consummation of all things would not happen so soon after Jesus' death and resurrection, they needed to reinterpret the situation. But the understanding that Jesus' resurrection was in some sense the precursor of the end of history did not lose its hold on their minds and hearts.

In the ministry of Jesus, there are some sayings which seem to indicate that the reign of God is already present (Luke 11:20 and Matt 12:28) and others which refer to a future action of God (for example, the petition in the Our Father "Your kingdom come!" [Matt 6:10 and Luke 11:2]). Likewise, Christians in the early decades of the Church's life who meditated on the significance of the resurrection recognized that there was a duality to God's reign in their experience. Paul, concerned that some of the Corinthian Christians were professing an exclusively present understanding of the resurrection, argued that Christians do not yet share fully in Christ's glory, that there is an order among those who participate:

> For as in Adam all die, so also in Christ shall all be made alive. But each in his own order: Christ the first fruits, then at his coming those who belong to Christ. Then comes the end, when he delivers the kingdom to God the Father after destroying every rule and every authority and power (1 Cor 15:22-24).

There is a consensus in present-day exegesis and theology that a completely realized eschatology does not do justice to what we know about the New Testament witness, and surely does not fit our own experience. Nor does a totally futuristic eschatology do justice to the New Testament or ongoing Christian praxis.[27] Christian hope for the salvation and well-being of the human race is directed to a future when God will be "all in all and everything to everyone": this is the "not-yet" dimension of Christian eschatology. But Christian hope is also based on Jesus' having been raised by God the Father in the power of the Spirit, and on the signs of resurrection which are given to those who strive by grace to live as Jesus lived, in compassion for the outcast, the poor, the violated and the oppressed: This is the "already" dimension of that same Christian eschatology. Paul praises his communities for the gifts of the Spirit that they have received as they wait for the final revealing of Christ (e.g., 1 Cor 1:4-8). Christian faith is meant to be both prophetically sacramental and sacramentally prophetic. In other words, it needs to learn again and again in changing circumstances how to witness to Christ's resurrection as both presence to be celebrated and challenge to be met in justice and love.

Easter as Soteriological Event

For a long time theologians tended to view Easter as mainly offering apologetic proof of the divinity of Jesus and the truth of the Christian faith. More recent, biblically oriented theology has stressed, however, that the death of Jesus was not the only saving event but that the totality of

---

27. A proponent of realized eschatology in the New Testament was the British Scripture scholar C. H. Dodd. A thoroughgoing futuristic interpretation of New Testament eschatology is exemplified by J. Weiss and A. Schweitzer.

Easter, in profound unity with Jesus' life and death, constitutes saving news for Jesus, the disciples, Israel, and God's larger world as well.

Let us consider Jesus, first of all, in terms of his message and his person and activity. We have seen how the primary symbol of salvation in Jesus' message was the reign of God. It occurs in the Gospels with a frequency that is unparalleled in the Old Testament or intertestamental literature. Moreover, we saw that Jesus intimated that the reign of God about which he preached, and thus its saving power, was beginning to happen in and through his speaking and acting. He even regarded his suffering and death as in some unspecified way in keeping with the coming of that reign, judging from the authentic *logion* at the Last Supper.

Easter is the occurrence of the reign of God in the exaltation of Jesus, and for the New Testament writers this exaltation was the long-awaited soteriological event (Phil 2:9-11; Eph 4:8-10; Heb 12:2). The universal resurrection of the dead, in the apocalyptic context in which it possessed meaning, was bound up with God's judgment of the righteous and the sinful. As the Son of Man, Jesus was constituted by the resurrection/exaltation as God's viceroy, God's agent in this ultimate act of salvation and judgment. Paul expressed Jesus' role succinctly in speaking of him as the one who was "crucified for our trespasses and raised for our justification" (Rom 4:25).

We can approach the soteriological character of the resurrection by a different, though allied, route. His exaltation and resurrection by God the Father in the Spirit meant, among other things, the divine vindication of *Jesus' person and his way of living and acting* (Phil 2:6-11). Jesus' activity in his ministry sought the welfare of people in relation to God and to each other: the twofold commandment of love of God and love of neighbor. He put himself on the line for the outcast, the despised, the guilt-ridden, the oppressed of body and mind, the poor, and those trapped as victimizers and victims in social systems (e.g., tax collectors). His life and ministry were about total dedication to God-Abba who saves, and total cooperation with the Father's saving work. On this fundamental point the Synoptics and John's Gospel are in total agreement.

In contemporary language we could say that Jesus was engaged in a liberative praxis in his ministry—not a programmatic, systematic praxis, but one which gave anticipatory expression to what, in human terms, the fullness of God's reign "looks like." In his resurrection/exaltation this Jesus with his way of living was vindicated by God and delivered from the restrictions of time and space. The resurrection was saving event first of all because it was God's event for Jesus and us. The power of sin and death tried to do in Jesus and all that he represented; God transformed the Jesus killed by sinners into God's personal way of liberating and saving people from the power of sin as it seeks to victimize people through guilt, oppression, and degrading poverty.

The disciples shared in the saving deed which was the resurrection of the crucified one. Peter had betrayed Jesus and most of the other disciples had fled in fear (some women stood at a distance). It seems correct to maintain that the Easter experiences involved forgiveness and peace for the disciples even though their conversion is not a significant motif in the appearance narratives as we have them. (It is almost as if the ensuing years of Church life have made the Easter conversion of the first disciples not a matter of concern.)

Paul is the only one who writes in the first person about his own Easter experience (in 1 Cor 9:1; 15:8; Gal 1:12, 16), and he does so in the barest of words, speaking of having seen the Lord (1 Cor 9:1), of Christ appearing to him as the last of the official witnesses (1 Cor 15:8), of the gospel which came to him through a revelation of Jesus Christ (Gal 1:12), and of how God was pleased to reveal his Son to him (Gal 1:16). Paul was certainly changed by his Damascus experience, but that experience did not save him from a personally sinful life as much as it converted him in the sense of changing his allegiance. By his own account this change was from being a well-intentioned persecutor of the Church to being a zealous apostle of Christ; from being zealous for the Law as the definitive revelation of God's saving plan (*mystêrion*) to being firmly committed to Christ as that definitive revelation; and from viewing membership in Israel as the way to salvation to acknowledging membership in Christ as that way and to recognizing that Gentiles had equal access with Jews to salvation (Gal 1:13-16). This is not to say that all of these changes occurred in Paul in a flash on the road to Damascus. Not at all. But the encounter on the road strikingly began the process of conversion which would lead him first to Ananias in Damascus (Acts 9:10-17) and then to the wide world of the Gentiles (Acts, *passim*).

The emphasis in Paul's letters (unlike the *Confessions* of St. Augustine) is not on Paul's own personal redemption by Christ from a life of sin, but rather on the universal plan or project which God has revealed in Christ. Jesus' resurrection, in unity with his death, has introduced the new age (2 Cor 5:17) that had been hoped for by Paul's Jewish brothers and sisters. While evil still abounds in the world (1 Cor 10:11; Gal 1:4), the back of sin has been broken; it has no definitive power anymore and is doomed to pass away (1 Cor 2:6). God has been faithful not only to Israel's hopes for a new age but to creation itself, not simply by restoring it to some former, imagined glory but by initiating its definitive movement toward a hitherto undreamt-of consummation. In God's and Jesus' free gift of self, there is an excess that goes beyond what happened at the beginning (Rom 5:15-16). Even in the present Paul could proclaim that anyone who is in Christ is "a new creation" (2 Cor 5:17; cf. Gal 6:15). This new creation has been inaugurated by God in raising Jesus from the dead: "But if Christ is in you, although your bodies are dead because of sin, your spirits are alive because of righteousness. If the Spirit of him who raised Jesus from the dead dwells in you, he who raised Christ Jesus from the dead will give life to your mortal bodies also through his Spirit which dwells in you" (Rom 8:10-11). For Paul, it is baptism which initiates the Christian's participation in the saving power of Jesus' death and resurrection (Rom 6:3-11).

It is clear from the preceding that in Jesus' destiny eschatology and soteriology were profoundly united. Without the crucifixion, the resurrection would have been a strange and glorious victory, omitting any engagement with the enemy that would have made it be a truly saving event. Without the resurrection, the crucifixion would have meant the death of a profoundly devout and strikingly authoritative prophet who had appeared to act in God's name but whose life and death, it turned out, were quite separable from the reign of God whose coming he preached. The resurrection constituted the life and death of Jesus as a saving event of world-historical significance, because it has the event which embraced world history as the precursor of its final future consummation. *The person of Jesus and his and God's cause, the salvation of the world, are now forever inseparable.*

Jesus' death by crucifixion and his resurrection cannot be collapsed into one undifferentiated event. They are distinguishable though inseparable. The reign of God, preached and enacted in anticipatory ways by Jesus in his earthly ministry unto death, occurred decisively and definitively in Jesus' exaltation as the beginning of the saving *eschaton* of God. Jesus the crucified eschatological prophet of the reign of God became that reign in person. Thus that reign and person still bear the marks of the Cross, as does the risen Jesus of Luke's and John's Gospels; and the way to further the values of God's reign must always involve a critical, practical, and loving *imitatio Christi*.

Easter as Theological Event

The resurrection has everything to do with Jesus and God. Some writers in ancient times and in the modern, post-Enlightenment period have wanted to reduce the Easter event to a change in the disciples after Jesus' death; they eliminate any talk of something having been done to and for Jesus by God in that event. According to these writers, the disciples reassembled after Calvary and, reflecting on the Jesus they had known, found that their trust in God and Jesus was rekindled despite Jesus' ignominious death. Or else the disciples had some sort of hallucinatory or ecstatic experience, which they interpreted as signifying the resurrection of Jesus but which really had to do only with their own psychological and spiritual state. But the New Testament shows great consistency in maintaining that the Easter event was something effected by God and something that happened to the dead Jesus, making him alive in a new, eschatological mode of existence beyond sin and death. The frequent use of two verbs for "raise" in the so-called theological passive witnesses to this (e.g., Mark 16:6; Luke 24:34; John 21:14; Rom 4:25; 2 Tim 2:8). Thus Easter, for the New Testament writers, was the event of God's faithful, creative love, making the dead newly alive and inaugurating the new creation (cf. the Old Testament, e.g., Isa 26:19; Dan 12:2). God was revealed as God of the living, as the redeemer of those victimized by the final victimizer, death.

The resurrection was therefore thoroughly theo-logical; that is, it was rooted in and effected by God, and it revealed God in the ultimate depths of divinity as victorious agent of the new creation, first for Jesus and then, in and through Jesus' resurrection, for all creation which until now has groaned for God's redemption (Rom 8:18-23).

Easter and the Revelation of Christ

The Easter event also has everything to do with Jesus. The dead Jesus was transformed into a newly alive, eschatological reality; the same Jesus, the same personal someone, now in a radically new mode of existence. Both continuity and discontinuity come into play here. What was "sown a physical body . . ., is raised a spiritual body," Paul wrote of the resurrection of the dead, and this applies to Jesus as well (1 Cor 15:44). Jesus' resurrected body is spiritual in the sense that it is now suffused with the Spirit of God; it belongs completely to the Spirit's "sphere of influence" and no longer to the sphere of corruption and decay (Acts 13:34).

The canonical New Testament nowhere describes the actual transformation of Jesus, nor is any mention made of witnesses to Jesus' entrance into eschatological existence. This is as it should be, since this transformation was transempirical. The *terminus a quo*, the deceased Jesus, was historical, and the resurrection is predicated of this Jesus; but the event of transformation exceeds any ordinary human perception, just as the new age, inaugurated in Jesus' glorification, exceeds ordinary, unfinished human history as its God-created consummation. (Only apocryphal works such as the Gospel of Peter attempt to describe the resurrection as a physical exiting from the tomb.) Thus we can say that the resurrection of Jesus is not only a theo-logical event but also a Christo-logical one, for through it Jesus is definitively revealed as the Lord, Christ, Son of God in power, the exalted and coming Son of Man.

Some scholars distinguish between the disciples' *de facto* psychological need for appearances after Jesus' death and a *de jure* need for such appearances to accomplish the grounding of Christianity and the full revelation of the significance of Jesus as the Christ.[28] At issue here is the question of the revelatory nature of the resurrection in relation to the earthly Jesus including his death.

One thing must be said at the beginning. Jesus' resurrection does not add a chapter or chapters to Jesus' biography. The personal identity of Jesus of Nazareth is constituted by the single life Jesus lived from conception to death. The one he became through all of that living is the one he is: the Easter Jesus. Thus we must not play off the pre-Easter Jesus against the Easter Jesus. Easter, the exaltation/resurrection, did not give Jesus more freedom, graciousness, generosity, or servant character than he had developed during his earthly life unto death. There is but one Jesus of Nazareth, and the content of his identity is the one life he lived on this earth unto death. At death we become who we have been becoming until then. (And we become this at the price of having to let go of it all.)

Then what difference does resurrection make Christologically, that is, for Jesus' reality as revelation to us?

There are several differences which Jesus' resurrection makes Christologically, so to speak. First, Jesus is disclosed by God to be fully of God, in God's glory, filled with God's life and God's power. This happens to the entire Jesus, the one who lived his complete life unto death. All that Jesus is, is now united to God's life and God's rule over all creation. This can only happen beyond death, just as Jesus cannot be fully of God until he, Jesus, comes to be himself in his full earthly becoming unto death. Second, Jesus through his resurrection and exaltation becomes universally present, beyond the restrictions of time and space, restrictions that were bound up with his being a pilgrim on earth. Resurrection involves a coming-to-presence for Jesus. He shares fully now in God's presence to the world.[29] The presence he offered others during his life is now transformed by God's Spirit into a universal presence. Third, Jesus is now encounterable in faith at all times and places in human history. Indeed, he precedes the Church's missionary efforts to witness explicitly to the good news. He is thoroughly accessible to all who call on his name. Each of these ways of speaking about resurrection as affecting Jesus revelationally concerns his relationships. The one he became through his life and death is now present, available, encounterable in faith and the Spirit, filled with the fullness of God's life and power, and fully united with God in ways which the Church during its first centuries will explore and clarify. But the human Jesus, the one who is so related and encounterable, is the one whose human identity was fashioned on the anvil of his daily life in Pales-

---

28. See J. P. Galvin's previously cited discussion of the views of two German scholars, Rudolf Pesch and Hansjuergen Verweyen, "The Origins of Faith in the Resurrection of Jesus: Two Recent Perspectives," *Theological Studies* 49 (1988) 25–44.

29. P. Hodgson, *Jesus: Word and Presence* (Philadelphia: Fortress, 1971) 241–54.

tine until his death. Thus faith in Jesus' presence and power in and beyond the Church must be amplified again and again with the stories about Jesus the earthly eschatological prophet of God, for that role is the stuff of his identity.

In other words, there are not two sources of Christological revelation, the pre-Easter Jesus and the Easter Jesus; there is only one source of revelation: the Jesus of the earthly life, ministry, and death who in one sense is now totally achieved in his own individual identity and related to God and the world out of that achieved identity. In another sense, as the "whole Christ" whose body is membered by his countless brothers and sisters, his larger identity is still incomplete insofar as they and their history and world are incomplete (1 Cor 12:12-27).

Some would maintain that the earthly life of Jesus was ambiguous in itself, and that the resurrection removes that ambiguity.[30] Others argue that the resurrection cannot make up for a revelational lack in the pre-Easter Jesus.[31] Let us look at these two opinions for a moment. The ambiguity was not Jesus in relation to God or himself or others. The ambiguity existed among people reacting and responding to Jesus. The question was, Did Jesus speak and act in the power of God or of the Evil One? We have seen that people interpreted Jesus either one way or the other. Moreover, there was a deficiency when Jesus died, because his ministry was so tied up with the coming reign of God that the failure of that reign to occur overtly in connection with his life and death could have invited his disciples to separate Jesus from the future divine reign and to see him simply as another spokesman for it whose life and death had proceeded apart from it. The revelational lack in the earthly life and ministry of Jesus was the lack inherent in one who was still on the way toward achieving his own personal identity and relationships and whose special claims about God, God's reign, and his own functions regarding that reign were called into radical question by God's silence at the time of his death.

The Empty Tomb and the Bodily Character of the Resurrection

A further interpretive issue arises with regard to the empty tomb and the corporeal nature of Jesus' resurrection. In the minds of most Christians, Jesus' resurrection and the fact of the empty tomb are inextricably intertwined, with the former being the obvious cause of the latter and the latter in turn being a proof of the former. By contrast, one of the results of the tradition-historical approach to the New Testament resurrection narratives has been the conclusion that, originally, the tomb tradition and

30. Pannenberg, *Jesus—God and Man*, 67.

31. See note 28.

the appearance traditions were separate, and only later were they integrated.

History and Tradition

Historically we have no record of anyone maintaining that the whereabouts of the tomb were unknown or that the tomb was not empty. Matthew's Gospel seems to allude to an early Jewish polemical argument to the effect that the apostles had stolen the body (27:62-66). But this argument also presumes that the tomb was empty. Nevertheless, even if we agree that Jesus was buried in a tomb with a known location, it would still not be possible to prove in any final way that the tomb was empty or to eliminate definitively all inner-worldly causes for its being empty. There are limits to what historical research can deliver.

A number of exegetes and theologians have argued that it would have been impossible to preach Jesus' resurrection in Jerusalem if it had been possible to point to Jesus' corpse.[32] But other scholars have appealed to what they see as a pluralism of views at that time with regard to the connection before resurrection and the fate of the bodily remains. Jerome Murphy-O'Connor, for example, is convinced that in Palestine at that time resurrection and empty tomb would not have been allied so tightly in people's thinking.[33] Thus here, too, there is historical unclarity.

As we move on to a biblical-theological consideration of this question, we recall first of all that in a pre-Markan source the tradition of the empty tomb is joined with the tradition of the Church's kerygma so that Jesus' resurrection by God accounts for the tomb's emptiness. This is a good theological reminder to us that the empty tomb does not prove Jesus' resurrection, but is a powerful sign of it *after* faith in the resurrection has illuminated the significance of the tomb's emptiness. Christians do not believe in the empty tomb but in the resurrected Christ, and faith in Christ offers the light which interprets the tomb. Until modern times Christians have joined faith in the resurrection with a conviction that the tomb was empty because of the bodily character of the resurrection. The Catholic Church has certainly taught and preached down through the centuries that the resurrection entailed an empty tomb.

---

32. For example, R. E. Brown, "The Resurrection of Jesus" in *The New Jerome Biblical Commentary* (Englewood Cliffs, New Jersey: Prentice-Hall, 1990) 1374; Pannenberg, *Jesus—God and Man*, 100.

33. In a review of Perkins' books in *Heythrop Journal* 19 (1988) 350. But he goes on to say that, without the empty tomb, appearances of a dead person would not have suggested resurrection rather than immortality, the latter being a concept widespread in Palestine at the time of Jesus' death.

Such a joining of the two traditions of resurrection and empty tomb makes powerful symbolic sense on a number of counts. First, Jesus died an ignominious death and his body bore the marks of sin's efforts to do him in. Through the Spirit God transformed that body with its marks of the "old eon" into the body of the "new eon," God's new creation, without any residue or remainder. The empty tomb, in the light of Easter, suggests that God wastes nothing; the only waste comes from the obduracy of sinners. Thus all of Jesus' reality, including his corpse, was gathered into the new eschatological age and totally transformed. Second, this understanding of the mutual implication of resurrection and empty tomb vividly expresses the personal continuity of the pre-Easter Jesus with the Easter Lord; for his earthly body was transformed into a spiritual body, i.e, a body belonging completely to the sphere of God's Spirit. Third, within this framework a strong message of hope is addressed to all of material creation. Even *the body* of our good works done in grace and of our suffering endured in love will have a future with God and, through God, with our brothers and sisters. Fourth, the empty tomb joined with the resurrection says something about the difference between Jesus and ourselves. Jesus was not simply the first to be resurrected, the one in and through whom others will be raised. He was and is the Son of God and Savior of all, and so it is supremely fitting that his destiny be both related to ours and different from ours. God's act of keeping Jesus' body from decomposing through its total transformation into the new age conveys Jesus' unique role in our salvation. Finally, the conjunction of resurrection and empty tomb gives powerful expression to God's involvement in the course of history as God brings it to the fulfillment for which it has been destined. This involvement could be conceived classically as an intervention from outside and above history. Or it could be thought of, more critically, as an involvement from within history by virtue of the Spirit's immanence-through-transcendence in history. God's Spirit has been working throughout history to prepare it for the acceptance of God's humanizing and consummating self-communication.

Contemporary Issues

This review of the symbolic and theological significance of resurrection belief in conjunction with the sign of the empty tomb helps to explain why it has claimed the imaginations and assent of Christians over the centuries. But contemporary theology must also address the self-understanding of present-day people, both to learn how to communicate the good news of the resurrection to them and to deepen its own critical understanding of what Christians now actually believe about Christ's resurrection and its significance for the destiny of all others.

For people of the twentieth century, the question of personal identity and its connection with the body is a complex one. The human body is both that which a living person *is* and that which a living person *has*. My relationship to my body is ambiguous. As phenomenologists have reminded us, I reveal myself to others in and through my body with its gestures and signs, and I hide from others through it as well. I am at times betrayed by my body, for example, by the spontaneous sign of blushing, and at other times I can manipulate my body, thus treating it as a quasi-object. My body is constantly changing as a system of living cells, so that at any moment I am not simply identical with my biological self. I can lose certain parts of my body and remain essentially the same person.

There exists, of course, an entire synthesis of information in my body—in its neurons and nervous system—which constitutes my bodily history, the effect on my body of stimuli, sensory experiences, memories, and choices made, all stored up in a way that is beyond my control but which provides a somatic context for further experiencing and further choices. This bodily history is not simply identical with my body as a system of ever-changing cells.

From another angle we need to consider the fact that each of our bodies meshes intricately with the whole material world in ever-widening circles of interaction and interconnection. In individual human beings and in the societal web of human beings, matter comes to a certain focus of concentrated energy, sensitivity, and perception. From this perspective we cannot speak only of the redemption of individuals or of society, but must include the question of the redemption of the material universe, the matrix and perduring home of the human. Any and all material, given the appropriate chemical changes, can be humanized and become part of human beings; and all the material of the human body can, and at death does, become part of the nonhuman cosmos. There exists here an affinity bonding the human and the prehuman which argues strongly for their common destiny in the providence of God under any authentically Christian hope for resurrection. "Resurrection of the body" speaks strikingly to this modern perception. "Body" in biblical, certainly Pauline, terms means the person in all his or her worldly (corporate!) relationships,[34] a notion which is often forgotten in theological discussion. A certain totality is intended by the term. All that is human about persons, individually and collectively, will be resurrected. The consummation of the human person cannot prescind from the bodily history of that person, which moves out in ever-widening circles. But bodily history need not refer to the body of the person during his or her earthly life. Since personal identity and em-

---

34. J. A. T. Robinson, *The Body: A Study in Pauline Theology* (London: SCM, 1952).

bodiment are neither separable nor flatly one and the same, it is possible to conceive of a mode of human, personal existence that would stand in continuity with our present, earthly mode of existence (he or she would be the same person) yet would be material in a different, thoroughly personalized and integrated way. When in writing about the destiny of those who will share in Christ's resurrection, Paul speaks of a "spiritual body" which comes after the "physical body" (1 Cor 15:44) he is speaking about continuity and difference. We can imagine the possibility of a fully personal and integrated materiality without being able directly to represent what such a mode of existence would be like in detail. We may hope for such a destiny based on our conviction that Jesus is indeed raised from the dead as the first fruits of those who have fallen asleep.

At this juncture it would be good for us to remember rather humbly that we do not really understand the nature of matter. Natural science explores and makes predictions regarding functional relationships among physical phenomena but such investigation, vastly fruitful as it is, does not disclose what matter itself is. Furthermore, we are able to recognize that the relationship of human beings in their personal identities to matter is a highly complex affair. All of which confirms the point that Christian talk of the "resurrection of the body" need not be contrary to human reason and our scientific understanding of the human being or the material world, but may point beyond both our present knowledge and our present mode of existence as creatures in this world. It is possible to affirm a nondualistic destiny for human beings which in some way involves a transformed materiality, without any need to refer to the dispersed material residue that was once a corpse and earlier the living body of the person.

Christological Significance

But for the theologian general anthropological reflections about the Christian hope regarding those who have died and will die do not of themselves answer the specifically Christological question of Jesus' destiny. It is historically probable that Jesus was buried at a known location, that the tomb was discovered empty, and that the body had not been stolen.[35] No one will ever be able to prove historically that the reason why the tomb was empty was because God raised Jesus from the dead. And in fact the point of the resurrection proclamation of the earliest believers was not to clarify the meaning of the empty tomb (the tomb tradition seems to have possessed significance for the Jerusalem community but not beyond it). The resurrection acquires its significance from a considerably wider

---

35. See Brown, "Resurrection of Jesus," 791–92.

context, namely, God's creative fidelity to the covenant with Israel, and through Israel to all human history and all creation, as that creative fidelity came to a climax in the divine saving action in Jesus.

But even here the empty tomb offers eloquent testimony (when considered in the context of the preaching of eschatological salvation) that God is doing something fully new, inaugurating a new creation that is transformative of *all* that has gone before, without remainder, except whatever the obduracy of sinners might entail. The fact that Jesus' body did not decompose but was totally changed into a new creation signified both the power of God as consummator of history and the unique role of Jesus in salvation history. But the truly significant difference between Jesus' resurrection and our own is not that Jesus' material remains are nowhere in Palestine while our corpses will decompose in the grave. The difference has to do with who Jesus was, his relationship to God and the reign of God, and the unity of God and Jesus in the power of the Holy Spirit. It also consists in the fact that through and in Jesus' resurrection the promise of our future resurrection is made totally firm, beyond the power of sin and death to undo it.

For some these reflections are all much too subtle. How can the good news involve such subtlety? Perhaps the question is better expressed, How can the Christian hope in resurrection involve such mystery—the mystery of human persons and their corporate destiny, and the absolute, infinite Mystery of God who redeems historical beings within, through, and beyond their own histories?

Hermeneutical Reflections: The Meaning of Easter for Today

We have been considering the biblical data regarding Jesus' resurrection and some historical and theological perspectives on the event prompted by the New Testament witness. Now it is time to move from the early Christian era to our own time. We need to involve ourselves briefly in the task of hermeneutics. The hermeneutical question is basically this: What can talk about the resurrection of an individual in the context of the apocalyptic and eschatological expectations of two thousand years ago mean for us today? Or, to express it differently: How it is possible for modern people to approach all this talk about the resurrection of Jesus?

Many Christian theologians, both Catholic and Protestant, have given attention to this important question. One of the most promising routes of access to New Testament faith in Jesus' resurrection, for some, is the route of our own humanity and our quest for meaning. Thus for these Christians the hermeneutical question becomes an anthropological one.

Resurrection and the Humanity of Our Hope

Karl Rahner, a German Catholic theologian who died in 1984, devoted much thought to the relationship between our humanity and Christian talk about Jesus' resurrection.[36] For Rahner, it is very important that we examine our human lives to discover in the welter of thoughts, decisions, and activities that make up our daily life the deepest aspirations of our hearts, the deepest orientation of our personality. By deepest aspirations and deepest orientation, he is not referring to one particular aspiration or orientation that we may or may not entertain at a given moment in our minds. Rather, he means the most basic dynamism of our personality, which makes all our thinking and choosing possible, even if that most basic dynamism does not "show up" as one particular decision or thought among others. He called this dynamism the "a priori condition of possibility of all our knowing and choosing." According to Rahner, the most basic dynamism of our personality as thinking, deciding people is a dynamism of hope. We are essentially people of hope, not in the sense that our mood is always hopeful (of course not), but rather in the sense that in all our knowing and deciding we are seeking more and more truth and value. We may lie and we may injure ourselves and others by choosing disvalues, yet even our missteps in their own strange way bear witness to a ceaseless quest for more knowledge and more value. Then the question is posed, can that quest be satisfied?[37]

Rahner takes a second tack as well. He considers the history of the choices which make up our life. When we choose a way of life, or form a friendship, or decide to move to another country, we are choosing good A over good B. But for Rahner, there is something more profound going on. He would insist that we are mainly choosing ourselves, that our choices are primarily about the kind of person I want to be. In addition, Rahner sees in all our choosing of who we will be as persons not an endless chain of choices which just happen accidentally to be ended by death. He would say that an endless chain of choices in human life would render any particular choice empty of all meaning, because it could simply be replaced at a later date by a different choice. Rahner maintains that our history of choices has an end, a goal, that the basic dynamism of all our choosing is toward the definitive, toward who I shall be definitively. Each choice,

36. See, for example, K. Rahner, *Foundations of Christian Faith*, trans. W. Dych (New York: Seabury, 1978) 266-85; on Rahner, see L. J. O'Donovan ed., *A World of Grace: Themes and Foundations of Karl Rahner's Theology* (New York: Seabury, 1980), especially chap. 11; G. Vass, *Understanding Karl Rahner, vol. 1: A Theologian in Search of a Philosophy* (London: Sheed and Ward, 1985).

37. For a similar, Protestant hermeneutical approach see Pannenberg, *Jesus—God and Man*, 82-88.

each conversion of myself as chooser, contributes to the definitive one I shall be. "Freedom is for finality" is Rahner's lapidary way of expressing this point.[38]

If our thinking and choosing is oriented toward more truth and more goodness, if this restless pursuit of the more is not just the personality trait of certain industrious people but the dynamism which underlies all people's thinking and deciding, and if all our choosing is about becoming someone definitive, then we have to face foursquare the mystery of death. Because death is the end of our choosing and the end of our pursuit of the more. Does our life, geared to the more and to the definitive, end in nullity, in zero? Or are we the beings who in all our thinking and willing hope for eternal life, for a final transformation and consummation of all that is most human and personal and good about us?

Rahner suggests that in our experience of the death of others there is something that is human and something that is antihuman, something that should not be.[39] What is human about death we experience when someone who has lived a full life lovingly surrenders it, having again and again graciously died little and not so little deaths *within* life before dying the ultimate death. Such a person dies full of years, with a graciously accepted finitude marking his or her spirit. Here death is a completion.

But death shows a different face very often, when someone who dies not full of years but cut off from life in its prime or even before there was any chance to live life at all. Then there is death by violence, that of another's savagery or the violence, say, of cancer, which day by day changes a person from the one we knew, loved, and intimately communicated with to a stranger who gradually—or suddenly—becomes alienated from himself or herself and the friends who surround the hospital bed. There is something about this kind of death that should not be, and we protest against it. It calls the human project in its goodness into radical question, and tempts us to give up on that project.

Thus, Rahner reflects, death has a dimension which reflects and reminds us of our good finitude and a dimension which speaks of the power of evil, the enemy of our human nature. Does this duality not suggest that death as the narrow door of transformation and death as the threatened waste of the whole human project have two different sources?

If we attend to reflections like these, Rahner believes, we cannot prove the truth of Christian statements about Jesus' resurrection. But what such reflections on our human existence in the world can do is to provide a thought-context within which the early Church's proclamation about Jesus'

38. See K. Rahner, "Theology of Freedom," in *Theological Investigations*, trans. K.-H. and B. Kruger (Baltimore: Helicon, 1969), vol. 6, 178–96.

39. K. Rahner, *On the Theology of Death*, 2nd ed., trans. W. J. O'Hara (New York: Herder, 1967) 32–55.

resurrection as the beginning of a universal resurrection demonstrates its credibility.

The early Christian Church proclaimed that one human being died into resurrection (to use a terse expression of Rahner's) and that all other human beings may have a share in that resurrection. Rahner himself would say that they will share in that resurrection if they lead lives that are open to the mystery of their lives, including the Holy Mystery whom Christians call God, whether that openness is a matter of explicit confession or implicit in their love of neighbor, which contains the "full measure of the law." Christian faith in Jesus' resurrection involves the conviction that one of our human race has been raised from the dead, given definitive existence in the life of God, and made by God the sign and instrument of the redemption of his brothers and sisters from death.

The hope which impels us to search for more and more truth and goodness, and the dynamism which leads us to choose our way through life toward finality as we seek to become ourselves in relation to all else, have their term in resurrection by the God of Jesus Christ. That is the good news spoken by the Church and by Christians to all human beings.

While not proving the truth of the Christian claim, these hermeneutical reflections serve to show that the early Church's proclamation is not about some strange, disconnected, esoteric event but that it touches on the mainspring of human initiative and enterprise, the dynamism of human understanding, choosing, and pursuit of meaning.

This way of approaching the Easter event moves in a full circle. Not only can hermeneutical reflections lead some people to recognize in the Easter message of the Church what they were unknowingly looking for all along; the Easter message can also alert others to recognize within themselves and the larger society of their fellow human beings this hunger for the more and this drive to choose unto finality. The search for the more and the constant choosing through which we come to finality are not simply philosophical ideas which came to Rahner independently of his own concrete experience. He would say that the light of Christian revelation, precisely as Easter revelation, has helped him to recognize dimensions of the human phenomenon which are indeed there to be recognized, but which Christian faith highlights through its solid confidence in redeemable (because redeemed) humankind, thanks to Christ's saving work in the Holy Spirit.

Resurrection and the Liberative Praxis of Love

Another approach to the present-day meaningfulness of the Church's message of salvation is taken by contemporary political and liberation theologians. The German theologian Johann Baptist Metz offers one version of this approach in his *Faith in History and Society*.[40] He points out that among the enormous shortcomings of modern theories of emancipation and liberation such as Karl Marx's is their inability to include the fallen victims of oppression in their message of revolutionary hope. Although the longed-for classless society will benefit those at the end of the history of struggle, it will have no room for those who preceded them. The emancipation and liberation for which revolutionaries fight falls dismally short of universality.

Metz argues that the dangerous memory of the crucified and resurrected one and the liberative praxis entailed by following Christ extend the hope of a universal emancipation and liberation that speaks good news not only to those at the purported conclusion of a long historical struggle, but also to those defeated and rendered mute by oppressors during the bloody course of history.[41] In addition to its partial basis in an honest reading of Church history (the Church's record on this score is a mixed one), such a view is verified by the activity of Christians in history on behalf of the oppressed and in opposition to the structures which oppress them. Christianity is vindicated in this respect by its faith in the God who is God of history and God of the living *and* the dead, and who in Jesus Christ and the Spirit has committed God's self to the emancipation and liberation of all peoples from the powers of sin and death. The home of resurrection talk is apocalyptic, where God's judgment on this evil age entails a reversal of values, with a new age of justice and peace being inaugurated in full intimacy with the God who frees.

In Metz's confrontation with Marxism, a symbol of New Testament faith and an element of the ancient creeds have taken on new significance. In the Apostles' Creed, Christians confess that Christ descended into hell. This reflects 1 Peter 3:18-20a: "For Christ also died for sins once for all, the righteous for the unrighteous, that he might bring us to God, being put to death in the flesh but made alive in the spirit; in which he went and preached to the spirits in prison, who formerly did not obey, when God's patience waited in the days of Noah. . . ."[42] This text, which was very popular in the Middle Ages, can be taken to mean that, by virtue of his death and resurrection, Christ is the Savior of those who died before the time of his appearance in history. Time and space, and particularly death, do not limit the saving efficacy of the Cross and resurrection. Another interpretation of the passage is that, in the death he died, Christ

---

40. Metz, *Faith in History and Society: Toward A Practical Fundamental Theology*, trans. D. Smith (New York: Seabury, 1980).

41. Ibid., ch. 11.

42. On the notion of the "harrowing of hell" see F. W. Dillistone, *The Christian Understanding of Atonement*, 2nd ed. (Minneapolis: Fortress/Augsburg, 1988) 98–102.

was in solidarity with the dead who felt abandoned because they were awaiting salvation from God in an uncertain state.[43]

Once again, such considerations do not prove the truth of the Christian confession of Christ's resurrection. Rather, they demonstrate the potential power of the central Christian metaphor of resurrection for those who struggle to humanize and liberate this world. Resurrection does not mean "pie in the sky when you die"; it justifies our confidence that the struggle to improve human life, both societal and personal, on this earth need not be thought of as doomed by some "constraints of history."

Juan Luis Segundo has pursued an allied approach in his liberation Christology. He wrote his five-volume exploration of Christ for non-believers, aiming to show the resources of Christian faith to those who struggle against oppression and victimization. The resurrection of Jesus serves as a symbolically powerful hypothesis for Segundo. It suggests that our deeds of justice and love for our neighbor have a future, indeed that they last forever. Instead of death and our world's constant tendency toward entropy having the final word, something is building in human history that death, sin, and oppression cannot undo. That "something" is a kingdom of justice and love, which is fully human and thoroughly of God's doing. It is growing like a mustard seed, often seemingly invisible and yet composed of all those things that have been done in love for the neighbor. Resurrection does not confer value on human efforts to liberate people; those efforts have intrinsic value. But resurrection does offer hope that what people are striving for when they struggle to emancipate themselves and others is not going to be the victim of a negative power more resourceful than itself. There is an infinite Being whose nature is love and who is on the side of justice, truth, and solidarity in love. The body of our good works has a future. That is what authentic Christian hope in resurrection means.

Resurrection and Creative Evolution

A third, kindred line of thought has been developed by the priest-paleontologist, Pierre Teilhard de Chardin.[44] Teilhard recognizes that there are two principal vectors of force operating in our universe, the vector of entropy and the vector of evolution. The first vector is the tendency of matter to move to the least level of organization: the second law of thermodynamics. The second vector is the contrary development of in-

---

43. H. Urs von Balthasar, among others, offers this interpretation. See his "Triduum Mortis," *Mysterium Salutis: Grundriss Heilsgeschichtlicher Dogmatik*, ed. J. Feiner and M. Loehrer (Einsiedeln: Benziger, 1969) vol. 3/2, 227–55.

44. P. Teilhard de Chardin, *The Phenomenon of Man*, trans. B. Wall (New York: Harper and Row, 1959).

creasingly sophisticated systems of matter, culminating in human beings and the "noosphere," which is made up of the "thinking envelop" that spans our globe. The second vector is haunted by the first. What will be the issue of the world process? Is it worthwhile to contribute to the advancement of humanity and its "noogenesis"?

Teilhard believed that the cosmic Christ of Paul spoke to this question. The Christ of Colossians and Ephesians is a Christ in whom God intends, in the fullness of time, to unite all beings on heaven and earth (Eph 1:10); this Christ fills all in all (Eph 1:23), and in him and for him all things have been created (Col 1:16-17).[45] For Teilhard, the destiny of humankind and the destiny of the material cosmos that is our home are one: We are not souls meant for heaven and bodies meant for entropy, for corruption. We are unitary beings who are spiritual-corporeal. We are capable of reflection and love, *and* we belong thoroughly to (and have emerged from) mother earth. The Christian doctrine of the bodily resurrection of Jesus and the bodily resurrection of those who will be saved is capable of making sense to those who wrestle with the question whether there is a meaningful "issue" and outcome to evolution.

The Truth of Easter Faith

We have examined the genesis of Easter faith by looking at some of the earliest data from the New Testament and discussing the role of appearances of the Risen Christ and the empty tomb. Then we looked at the meaning of Christ's resurrection in the contexts of the New Testament and the twentieth century. Now we need to consider the truth of Easter faith.

Modern Catholic theology has tended to treat this question in fundamental theology as part of an apologetic argument for the credibility of Christ as divinely sent and of the Church he founded.[46] In the present study only certain lines of inquiry can be suggested.

There is no question of attempting to prove the truth of Easter faith, faith that Jesus was raised from the dead and is living in God's life as Son, Savior, and Christ. One can offer, with St. Thomas Aquinas, evidence that "shows forth" the truthfulness of Christian faith, but this is not a matter of ironclad proof.[47] Knowledge of anything really important is by participation, not by distance and externality. The most comprehen-

---

45. C. Mooney, *Teilhard de Chardin and the Mystery of Christ* (New York and San Francisco: Harper and Row, 1966).

46. See the critical evaluation of this tradition in E. Schüssler Fiorenza, *Foundational Theology: Jesus and the Church* (New York: Crossroad, 1986).

47. *Summa Theologiae*, 3a, q. 55, a. 5 and 6 (vol. 55, Blackfriars ed., trans. C. T. Moore [New York: McGraw-Hill, 1976] 53–65).

sively and fundamentally objective truths are the most profoundly subjective as well, requiring that they be known by the whole person and the whole person's self-investment. Still, it is possible to offer considerations which, in the best Catholic tradition, show that (1) the act of faith in the Risen Christ is not an imprudent or rash act contradicting what is rationally known or morally imperative; and (2) faith in the Risen Christ can help individuals and communities to engage more deeply with the reality of the historical journey and the mystery of their own humanity in its quest for truth, justice, and peace.

The truth of an important affirmation such as "God raised Jesus," implies an event which transcended ordinary empirical experience. Nonetheless, it must be gauged by the basic criteria for any statement: first by its ability to explain certain data which require explanation; second, by its internal consistency; and third, by its heuristic fruitfulness, that is, its power to generate understanding of ever-widening ranges of data. With regard to the first criterion, there are data after Jesus' death that require satisfactory explanation. Among them are (1) the transformation of the disciples into witnesses to Christ and his values, which went qualitatively beyond their relationship to him before his death; (2) their conviction that he had appeared to them after his death and that his appearances, coupled with their memory of him, caused the transformation; (3) the emergence, in a very brief time, of Christianity as a world religion; and (4) the correspondence of Easter faith to the deep hunger in humankind for ultimate meaning and for a secure future for all the good that human freedom achieves in history. Are these data best explained by the Christian affirmation that God raised Jesus from the dead? If so, then his resurrection, even though a transhistorical event would count as fact, indeed, a supremely important fact.[48]

The truth of Easter faith also depends on the consistency of the affirmation that God raised Jesus from the dead. I will cite just two examples of the kinds of issues involved here. First, does the manner of Jesus' living and dying give evidence of his being the kind of person whom the God of the covenant would raise from the dead? While of itself this is evidence that does not suffice, it is necessary evidence. The "who was raised" is all-important. Was he trustworthy? Did he live a life which helps to make sense of his resurrection?[49] The New Testament addresses these questions when it tells the story of Jesus' ministry and death as a hermeneusis of his resurrection. On this level, there is the theoretical possibility of Christian faith being disproved if, for example, it could be conclusively shown

---

48. "Facts are what statements (when true) state, not what statements are about." Thus N. Lash quotes P. F. Strawson in "Easter Meaning," *Heythrop Journal* 25 (1984) 12. In other words, facts belong to the realm of meaning and are not the external referents of assertions.

49. See N. Lash, "Easter Meaning," 3–18.

that Jesus was a charlatan in his dealings with people. Second, is the assertion that God raised Jesus coherent with our understanding of the relations between matter and spirit and matter and personal reality? Recent theologies such as Karl Rahner's help us understand better the coherence between them.[50]

The third criterion of truth—heuristic fruitfulness—focuses on the generative power of Easter faith for further insight. A theologian such as Wolfhart Pannenberg has developed some of the intellectual implications of Easter for a philosophy of history that seeks to determine the meaning of all history while it is still unfinished.[51] Liberation theologians, on the other hand, would stress the transformative power of Easter faith beyond the cognitive domain, that is, its power to motivate people to persevere in the struggle for a just society. As Jon Sobrino writes:

> . . . the hermeneutics designed to comprehend the resurrection must be political. This means that it is possible to verify the truth of what happened in the resurrection only through a transforming praxis based on the ideals of the resurrection. The elements of misery and protest in the biblical texts can be understood only in an active process of change which transforms the present, in a concrete effort to implement the promises of history here and now. . . . Given the fact of a world that is presently unredeemed, the resurrection can be understood only through a praxis that seeks to transform the world. This means that our *approach to the resurrection is continually in process of formation.*[52]

The exclusive claim involved here I find objectionable, but Sobrino and others have touched on a crucial line of inquiry: What kinds of lives do those who believe in the resurrection of Jesus live? What is the quality of their lives as community members and mission bearers to the world? In conjunction with other lines of inquiry, this praxis-oriented one can be very important—and immensely challenging to the Christian Churches. Those individuals and communities share in the gift of the resurrection who live and die as Jesus lived and died not in slavish imitation of his unique unrepeatable life, but in dedication to the values of the kingdom he preached and for which he suffered, and in reliance on the same Holy Spirit of God.[53]

50. K. Rahner, "The Unity of Spirit and Matter in the Christian Understanding of Faith," *Theological Investigations*, vol. 6, 153–77.

51. W. Pannenberg, "Eschatology and the Experience of Meaning," in *Basic Questions in Theology* vol. 3, trans. R. A. Wilson (London: SCM Press, 1973) 192–210.

52. J. Sobrino, *Christology at the Crossroads: A Latin American Approach*, trans. J. Drury (Maryknoll, New York: Orbis, 1978) 255. The italics are Sobrino's.

53. Cf. G. O'Collins' five tests of the truth of Christian faith in Jesus' resurrection presented in *Jesus Risen*, 137–47. See also his notion of "experiential correlate" in *The Resurrection of*

Resurrection and New Testament Christological Developments

As the early communities of faith assimilated the good news of Jesus' resurrection and sought to articulate their faith in Jesus and its significance for their lives, they found many resources on which to draw: There were traditions enshrining memories of the pre-Easter Jesus, i. e., early kerygmatic, creedal, and narrative traditions that could be simply taken over or modified; and finally the Old Testament and intertestamental material giving voice to various traditions of expectation such as the dynastic and prophetic, as well as Wisdom and apocalytic literature.

As we saw in chapter 2, the traditions concerning the Son of Man did not prove to be a lasting resource for Christological development, because they did not have significance for Gentile Christians. Son of Man Christology remains a permanent part of Christian tradition because of the Synoptists' use of it, but it does not continue to any large extent beyond them. Those traditions did not "travel" well. When the early Fathers, beginning with Ignatius of Antioch and Irenaeus of Lyons, started to refer to Jesus in his humanity as opposed to his divinity as the "son of man," it was clear that the expression had completely lost its Danielic, apocalyptic significance.

The New Testament Christological titles that exercised the greatest influence in the history of Christian thought are Son of God, Christ, the Last Adam, and the Wisdom and Word of God. These titles did travel well, for they could be understood (or misunderstood) in semantic contexts beyond both Aramaic-speaking Judaism and Judaism altogether. After all, "son of God" was a term used of the Emperor, and "sons of God" of charismatically gifted men in the Hellenistic-Roman world.[54] "Anointed one" ("christos") had significance beyond Judaism because royal anointing was practiced in Roman-Hellenistic culture, and Christ soon became part of Jesus' proper name. The Last Adam could connect with philosophical speculation on the origins and destiny of humankind, and Wisdom and Logos struck up strong resonances with Greek thinkers interested in cosmology and salvation. While all these titles and the ideas associated with them were firmly anchored in Judaism, they could also speak meaningfully to non-Jewish Christians.

Jesus Christ (Valley Forge, Penn.: Judson, 1973) 69–73. Schüssler Fiorenza, *Foundational Theology*, argues for a pattern of foundational theologizing that includes reconstructive interpretation of the New Testament traditions regarding the resurrection (determining the literary genres involved), retroductive warrants in support of that tradition (assessing the illuminative power of belief in the resurrection) and background theories relevant to the resurrection (determining the validity of historical testimony and deciding whether our present-day understanding of the relation between matter and spirit makes talk of resurrection coherent).

54. M. Hengel, *The Son of God: The Oirigin of Christology and the History of Jewish-Christian Religion*, trans. J. Bowden (Philadelphia: Fortress, 1976).

A principal development in the New Testament period, which was equally important to Jewish and Gentile Christians, concerned Jesus' unity with God. From the conviction that in Jesus' life, death, and resurrection God's saving plan had reached a decisive, eschatological climax and God had revealed a unity with Jesus that was not comparable to the unity between God and any human person previously, there developed the belief that Jesus' unity with God did not begin at the resurrection/exaltation (as we find, for example, in Rom 1:4) but had already existed during his lifetime. One of the points made by the Markan account of Jesus' baptism by John was that the Father declared, and thus constituted, Jesus the beloved Son during that event (e.g., Mark 1:11). The unity of Jesus with God as God's Son was pushed back even further in the Lukan and Matthean infancy narratives. In Luke Jesus becomes Son of the Most High and Son of God at his conception by Mary when she is overshadowed by the Spirit (1:35). According to Matthew Jesus is conceived of the Holy Spirit and will save the people from their sins as God's Son and Emmanuel (1:20-23). Thus the entire life of Jesus is "Christologized," that is, recognized as the life of the anointed one of God from conception to exaltation. But it is the resurrection/exaltation which both makes this movement backward in time possible and marks its starting point. The backward movement does not stop there, however. Jesus' unity with God will be pushed back even to the time before his conception and earthly life.

Wisdom and Word Christology

John's prologue offers elements of a Christology that will be fateful for all later developments. The pre-Johannine hymn that it employs focuses on a reality called "the Word." Here is a plausible reconstruction of the original hymn, following James D. G. Dunn:[55]

In the beginning was the Word,
and the Word was with God,
and the Word was God.
(He was in the beginning with God.)
All things were made through him,
and without him was not anything made that was made.

In him was life;
and the life was the light of men.
The light shines in the darkness,

55. J. D. G. Dunn, *Christology in the Making: An Inquiry into the Origins of the Doctrine of the Incarnation* (Philadelphia: Westminster, 1980) 240. I am indebted to Dunn for what follows on the Word, Son of God, and Last Adam.

and the darkness has not overcome it.
(The true light that enlightens every man was coming into the world.)

He was in the world
(and the world was made through him),
yet the world knew him not.
He came to his own home,
and his own people received him not.
But to all who received him,
he gave power to become children of God.

And the Word became flesh
and dwelt among us,
full of grace and truth;
we have beheld his glory,
glory as of the only Son from the Father
and from his fullness
have we all received,
grace upon grace.

It is fairly universally agreed now among scholars that the Johannine prologue draws on Wisdom literature and shows resemblances to Philo of Alexandria's philosophy of the divine Logos, which itself is an adaptation of Wisdom motifs together with themes from Stoic philosophy.

A brief mention of basic Wisdom themes will suggest the degree of influence by Wisdom literature on the New Testament. In the Book of Wisdom we are told that "with you [God] is wisdom, who knows your works and was present when you made the world" (9:9; cf. John 1:1 and Col 1:15-20). In Sirach we find these words: "The one who created me assigned a place for my tent. And he said, 'Make your dwelling in Jacob'(24:8; cf. John 1:14). Again in Wisdom: "For she [Wisdom] is an initiate in the knowledge of God, and an associate in his works. If riches are a desirable possession in life, what is richer than wisdom, who effects all things? And if understanding is effective, who more than she is fashioner of what exists?" (8:4-6; cf. John 1:3 and 1 Cor 8:6).

But what was it that led Christians to identify Jesus of Nazareth with preexistent Wisdom, the agent of creation who came and tented among God's people, thereby giving Jesus a cosmic role as well as introducing the notion of incarnation? In the Wisdom literature we are dealing with a poetic figure, not with a substantial reality next to God or a personally preexistent being. Wisdom, God's Spirit, Torah, Shekinah, and other such terms are so many ways of speaking about God's own creative and salvific involvement in the world. They are poetic prolongations of God's personality, extensions of God's activity among us.

But the New Testament writers boldly identified a particular historical human being with Wisdom. What was the basis for this identification?

First, as we have seen, it is probable that Jesus used Wisdom motifs in his own preaching. Jesus introduced his disciples into a sense of God and God's kingdom that was the fruit of Jesus' own intimacy with "Abba." As already noted, it did not prove at all difficult to interpret Jesus as an envoy of Wisdom, a view of him that we find in Q and one to which Luke stays faithful (see, e.g., Luke 7:31-35; 11:25-27; 11:49). Matthew, on the other hand, edits the Q-data so that Jesus presents himself as Wisdom herself (see, e.g., Matt 11:19; 23:34; and possibly Matt 23:37-39). Matthew is the only Synoptic evangelist who does this.

Second, the Jewish tradition of Hasidism (a tradition of strict observance which sought to consecrate daily life to God) rejected all assimilation to Hellenism. They joined together prophecy, Wisdom, and apocalyptic motifs in their efforts to observe the Law with pious strictness. The Hasidim regarded those faithful to the Law (the "righteous") as the only truly wise persons, and looked upon them as initiates into the mysteries of God with some understanding of the eschatological reversal that God planned for all things. These Hasidim did not indulge in Hellenistic speculation about Wisdom as a "hypostasis," that is, a figure "next to" God. Thus from a Hasidic perspective, Jesus' preaching of God's reign as the final act of God's salvation could have resulted in a close association of him with Wisdom after Easter.

Third, Jesus' exaltation at Easter, his vindication as *the* just one of God, and the pouring out of the eschatological Spirit as part of that exaltation, led some Christians to make bold use of Hellenistic-Jewish models of Wisdom as "someone" preexistent and to identify Jesus with that Wisdom. Jesus, who was not God-Abba, was Wisdom. The one in and through whom God was inaugurating the new creation was also principal agent (under God-Abba) of the first creation. It appears that eschatology and protology (the doctrine of the end and the doctrine of the beginning, respectively) were easily amalgamated by those Christians, who could move from the faith-conviction of Jesus' resurrection/exaltation to attributing a role at the beginning of the created universe to Jesus the exalted one.

Thus *both* elements of Jesus' public ministry (his Wisdom sayings, and his eschatological message of the inbreaking reign of God with its apocalyptic associations) plus the conviction of his exaltation by God after his death enabled some communities of Greek-speaking Jewish-Christians to envisage Jesus first as associated with Wisdom, and then as identified with her and with the roles ascribed to her.

In terms of the future unfolding of Christology, we have here one of the most important developments within the canonical New Testament: the ascription to Jesus, thanks to his intimacy with God as evinced in his ministry and vindicated in his exaltation, of a preexistent relationship with God and a cosmic role in creation and redemption. It is within this framework that one must look for the background to the verse in John's prologue which, from the second century, will dominate Christian reflection on Jesus Christ, namely, John 1:14: "And the Word became flesh and dwelt among us." It is Wisdom theologies that make possible a Wisdom-Word Christology of incarnation. Although it is only one strand of New Testament thought about Jesus, incarnation Christology will become the preeminent theme in the later history of Christological traditions.

Whereas earlier in this century scholars sought to explain the origins of incarnation theology in Gentile myths of descending and ascending savior gods, there is now a consensus that it is sufficient to look to the various trajectories in Wisdom literature to find the basis for the New Testament view of Jesus as Wisdom and Word of God. Philo of Alexandria made use of Wisdom literature to develop a philosophy of the cosmic *Logos* (Word) that he hoped would appeal to sophisticated Gentile readers. Similarly, some early Christians mined the Wisdom theologies in their efforts to describe or define the role of Christ in the cosmos and salvation history and to make him attractive to the Hellenistic world.

Adam Christology

The notion of the Last Adam is a peculiarly Pauline one. Paul employs Wisdom speculation in writing about the first Adam as he existed before the Fall, and draws a contrast between the first and last Adam. While the first Adam was made in the image of God and by rights was not liable to death, he disobeyed God's will and so became subject to death and corruption. The Last Adam, on the other hand, was likewise made in the image of God and by rights not liable to death and corruption; but because he obeyed God's will by choosing to suffer and die an ignominious death, he was exalted to God's right hand where he receives the homage of all creation.

The principal texts for Paul's Last Adam Christology are Philippians 2:6-11 and Romans 5:12-21. The former was originally a hymn, which Paul adapted for his own purposes. The original hymn has been reconstructed to read thus:

[Christ Jesus]
who though he was in the form of God
did not count equality with God a thing to be grasped,
but emptied himself,
taking the form of a servant,
being born in the likeness of men.

And being found in human form,
he humbled himself
and became obedient to death . . .

Wherefore God has highly exalted him
and bestowed on him the name which is above every name,
that at the name of Jesus every knee should bow . . .
and every tongue confess
that Jesus Christ is Lord. . . .[56]

Many exegetes take the movement in this hymn to be the classic one of *katabasis-anabasis*, that is, the descent and ascent of a heavenly being. They argue or assume that the hymn presupposes the preexistence of the one who is in the form (image) of God.[57] According to their interpretation, the hymn would be saying the following: Although Jesus Christ was preexistent as God's image (and thus did not have to die, being a sharer in divine immortality), he did not consider his likeness to God something to hold on to or to grasp at (as if to master it and thus make it his own and not let it remain gift). He emptied himself by becoming a human being, looking like all other human beings (i.e., as one liable to death although he was not). He lowered himself yet more during the course of his life by dying in obedience to God. God reversed all that by exalting Jesus to be Lord of all.

But one must ask whether the self-emptying and assuming the likeness of humans and the being found in the likeness of humans and humbling himself and becoming obedient unto death are all the same event or successive events. In the latter case, we are to imagine incarnation (and thus preexistence), followed by choice during his earthly career, followed in turn by his death.

In any case we meet here a pre-Pauline Christology that sees Jesus as the one who by virtue of his likeness to God, that is, by virtue of his being in the image of God (human as God intended humans to be), should be a slave to no one and/or no thing, yet freely chooses to become subject to death out of obedience to God.

Paul makes several additions to the hymn: He adds in verse 8 the phrase "even death on a cross" and in verse 10 the phrase "in heaven and on earth and under the earth," but the original hymn quite definitely comes from those Christians of the 40s and 50s who expressed their faith in terms of an Adam Christology.

James D. G. Dunn addresses well the question of a possible reference to preexistence in the hymn:

56. Ibid., 115, 117.

57. Representative is the influential article of E. Käsemann, "A Critical Analysis of Philippians 2:5-11," *Journal for Theology and Church* 5 (1968) 45–88.

. . . the language throughout, and not least at these points [viz., where the hymn speaks of "being in the form of God" and "being born in the likeness of men"] is wholly determined by the creation narratives and by the contrast between what Adam grasped at and what he in consequence became. It was Adam who was "in the form of God," Adam who "became what men now are" (in contrast to what God had intended for them). The language was used *not* because it is first and foremost appropriate to *Christ*, but because it is appropriate to *Adam*, drawn from the account of Adam's creation and fall. *It was used of Christ therefore to bring out the Adamic character of Christ's life, death and resurrection.* So archetypal was Jesus' work in its effect that it can be described in language appropriate to archetypal man and as a reversal of the archetypal sin.[58]

In other words, there is no more allusion to preexistence here than there is in the story of Adam in Genesis. Adam's and Christ's choices both refer not to a moment in their lives but to the whole character of their existence.

Son of God Christology

We have already seen in chapter 2 that Jesus indicated in various ways that he had a special relationship with the God of Israel. While we have no authentic *logion* in which he refers to himself as the Son of God, we have impressive evidence that he called God "Abba" and that he acted with a sense of special authorization from Abba for what he said and did. We also know that his addressing God as Abba was characteristic of him, that this practice was an unusual one, and that he introduced others into his way of praying so as to make their experience of being "sons of God" dependent on his. The teaching of the Our Father had this precise effect.

Jesus' own sense of sonship was eschatological; in other words, it was bound up with his sense of being the chosen emissary of God to inaugurate the end-time of salvation. There is no evidence that Jesus thought of himself as the preexistent Son of God. John's Gospel develops a portrait of Jesus in which he does repeatedly show such a self-awareness, but this portrait has to be attributed to the evangelist and not to any authentic Jesus-tradition. In Matthew 11:27 we receive a striking indication of Jesus' sense of intimacy with the Father: "All things have been delivered to me by my Father; and no one knows the Son except the Father, and no one knows the Father except the Son and any one to whom the Son chooses to reveal him." This saying is probably based on a piece of native wisdom about the relationship between father and son engendered by the son's learning a family trade from the father. As spoken by Jesus

58. Dunn, *Christology in the Making*, 120.

it suggests, though not in any specific way, the intimacy between Jesus and Abba. This type of saying in the Synoptic tradition became a principal emphasis of John's Gospel.

According to Romans 1:3-4, which in the main is pre-Pauline, Jesus was constituted, installed, and designated the Son of God by God on the basis of the resurrection of the dead. The Greek makes two important points: (1) God made Jesus the Son of God (in power)—it is not just a matter of God's revealing something that was already the case; and (2) this installation was on the basis of the (general) resurrection of the dead, which presumably was already beginning in Jesus' resurrection as the first fruits. Here the title Son of God is thoroughly eschatological, without reference to Jesus' earthly history, and closely connected with resurrection. Resurrection as a general saving event and the exaltation of Jesus are intertwined.

A second pre-Pauline reference to Jesus' sonship is preserved in Acts 13:32-33: "And we bring you the good news that what God promised to the fathers, this he has fulfilled to us their children by raising Jesus; as also it is written in the second psalm, 'Thou art my Son, today I have begotten thee.'" This psalm quotation functions in the New Testament as a very significant "proof-text" at various other places as well (Mark 1:11; Luke 3:22; Heb 1:5; 5:5). In its earliest occurrence it expresses an idea similar to that of Romans 1:3, namely, that Jesus was made Son of God at his resurrection. Psalm 2, which concerns the Lord's anointed and a king whom God has set on Zion, lent itself to dynastic messianic interpretation and was used by Christians at an early stage with reference to Jesus.

Following the bits of tradition that we possess from the period of the earliest preaching of Jesus' sonship is Paul's contribution. Lord is a term much more frequently employed by him than Son, but the latter term appears at some important moments: 1 Thessalonians 1:9-10 and 1 Corinthians 15:24-28 both have to do with Jesus' sonship in an eschatological context. Other texts deal with the exalted Jesus' sonship in relation to believers: Galatians 1:16 (in relation to Paul's own conversion); Romans 8:15-17 (in relation to the believers' freedom to pray to Abba through the Spirit of sonship that they share in dependence on Jesus); Galatians 2:20 (in relation to Jesus' death: Jesus as the Son "who loved me and gave himself for me"); and, finally, Jesus as the Son sent by the Father (Gal 4:4; Rom 8:3).

These last two texts deserve special attention, because they have often been cited as evidence for a notion of preexistence in Paul's Christology. However, Dunn and others have argued persuasively that neither text need be read that way and that, in fact, the more likely interpretation situates them in another context. With regard to Galatians 4:4, [the verse] can be understood quite adequately and comprehensively as a version of the familiar Pauline association between Jesus' sonship and his redemptive death. . . . Jesus as the Son of God sent by God as one born of woman, born under the law to redeem (by his death) those likewise under the law and bring those likewise born of woman to share in the relation of sonship which he had himself enjoyed during his ministry and now could "dispense" to others as the first born of the eschatological family of God.[59]

In Romans 8:3 a similar pattern of thought is recognizable. The phrase "in the likeness of sinful flesh" depicts Jesus' sonship as it was before his "sacrifice for sin": which signifies that his "sacrifice for sin" involved a condemnation of sin in the flesh. This seems to be another instance of Pauline Adam Christology rather than a Christology of incarnation.[60]

In Mark's Gospel the Son of God title does not occur very frequently, but it plays an important role at several key places. We are told in the very first verse (according to some manuscripts) that this is the Gospel of Jesus Christ, the Son of God. Near the close of the Gospel we find the climactic recognition of Jesus in his true identity, when the centurion, seeing how he died, declares: "Truly this man was (the) Son of God" (15:39). Earlier in the Gospel the unclean spirits over whom Jesus shows mastery confess him as Son of God, but he silences them (3:11). At the baptism in the Jordan he is declared "my beloved Son" by the voice from heaven (1:11); here Mark uses Psalm 2:7, which had hitherto been used only in relation to Jesus' resurrection. Thus it appears to be the case that Mark regarded Jesus' sonship as beginning at his baptism, not at his resurrection. At the transfiguration Jesus is again declared "my beloved Son" by the voice from the cloud (9:7). After the first declaration, Jesus goes into the desert and is tempted; after the second declaration, he predicts his passion. The only time he admits explicitly to being Son of God in Mark is at the trial before the Sanhedrin, when he says "I am" in reply to the question of the high priest: "Are you the Christ, the Son of the Blessed?" (14:61).

Mark wanted his readers to realize that Son of God as a name for Jesus and a way of understanding him can only be properly employed with reference to the crucified Jesus, who was tempted, suffered, and died. Mark found no room for an independent "theology of glory," that is, for a view of the exalted and powerful Jesus divorced from his humiliation, suffering, and death. Rather, the author of this Gospel presents Jesus as Paul presents him, one whose true identity manifested itself through weakness and the mystery of the Cross. It is not in encounters with God per

59. Ibid., 44.
60. Ibid., 45.

se (baptism and transfiguration), or in resurrection and exaltation, that Jesus is revealed as the Son of God, but in his crucifying death. That is Mark's contribution to a Son of God Christology of Jesus.

In Matthew's Gospel we are given a portrait of Jesus as the authentic Son of God who is the definitive teacher of Israel and interpreter of the Law, urging his followers to a greater righteousness than that of the Jews. As we have seen, Matthew regards Jesus' sonship as beginning not at his baptism, but at his conception, and characterizing the entirety of his life. This notion, however, does not express incarnation as we later come to understand it. There is no question here of preexistence, which is a component of the complex notion of incarnation. Matthew remains within the confines of Jesus' historical existence when he presents his understanding of the origins of Jesus' life and sonship. While the terminology of sonship does not appear here, Matthew is suggesting that Jesus' conception is his begetting as God's Son, and that it is a virginal conception, so that Jesus is Son of David, but, more importantly, the one whose coming-to-be was due to the overshadowing of Mary by the Most High. This is a divine begetting, which did not in any way involve intercourse between the deity and the human mother, but resulted from God's initiative.

Luke-Acts does not tell us much about Jesus as Son of God, for the title does not play a significant role in Luke's eyes.

The Letter to the Hebrews, James D. G. Dunn argues, is the first New Testament writing to make use of the theme of a pre-existent divine sonship.[61] However, it does so against the background of Platonic idealism. In other words, the pre-existence of the Son is an ideal preexistence; the Son exists in God's eternal intention. There is really no thought of an individual preexistent reality that then becomes incarnate. Indeed this letter reveals two views of the Son, that are not reconciled by the author: the Son of God who becomes the eschatological high priest through suffering; and the ideal, heavenly Son who exists in God's mind, and as such "pre-exists" the drama of Jesus' life of obedience and suffering.

It is in the Johannine writings that Son of God has pride of place and has shaped later Christological thinking in the most decisive way.

John's Gospel seeks to lead its readers to the confession that Jesus is the Christ and Son of God, so that believing they may have life in his name (20:31). The relationship between Jesus and his Father, which in the Synoptic Gospels is one of special intimacy and eschatological in nature, in John's Gospel becomes a unique matter of unity or oneness between Jesus and his Father that is eternal (not beginning at some moment of Jesus' earthly life), protological (at the beginning of all things, not only

61. Ibid., 51–56.

at their consummation), and preexistent (existent prior to Jesus' earthly life). Jesus' earthly life, death, and glorification neither diminish nor enhance that relationship. It is revealed in the flesh by becoming flesh, but it also existed before Jesus' conception and continues after his glorification. There is no room for Matthew and Luke's idea that Jesus is the begotten Son of God at his conception; nor is there room for the conviction that Jesus is constituted or installed Son of God at his resurrection. And there is most assuredly no possibility of Jesus' becoming Son of God at his baptism by John, or being reliably revealed as Son of God in his humiliation on the cross, where he is portrayed in the exclusively stark terms of Mark's account.

John's Gospel offers the only unambiguous expression of incarnational Christology in the New Testament, that is, a Christology that speaks of a personally preexistent Son (and Word) being made flesh or coming into the world from a preexistent condition with God. Here it is not a question of ideal preexistence, as in the Letter to the Hebrews, but of personal preexistence. Jesus is portrayed as fully conscious of his personal preexistence and as quite explicit in speaking about it with other people, a state of affairs that must be attributed to the author of this Gospel, because its absence from earlier strata of the tradition is inconceivable if it in fact derives from the pre-Easter Jesus.

The Johannine presentation of Jesus as the eternal Son of God made flesh has become the dominant one since the second century, with the other Gospel accounts being subordinated to it. But the various portraits of Jesus in the New Testament documents are different enough so that they cannot be exegetically harmonized. Faithfulness to Scripture demands that the pluralism in the New Testament be respected as such. We cannot regard the other views of Jesus as complementary and incomplete next to John's allegedly comprehensive scriptural view. John's view is one among a number of Christologies of the Son of God in the New Testament.

Nevertheless, John's understanding of Jesus is unparalleled in the New Testament. The unity of Jesus and the Father is a unity of origin, love, and obedience. All that Jesus is comes from the Father, all the truth he teaches comes from that source; the Father and Jesus love each other in the most profound way; and Jesus does all that he sees the Father doing and is sent by the Father and obeys the Father fully. There is a tension between the unity of Father and Son and the subordination of Son to Father, which in the fourth century supplied ammunition to both the Arians and the orthodox interpreters of the Council of Nicea.

The Christological reflection of the second century and beyond was decisively shaped by this theological departure on the part of John. He brought together in his Gospel both Word Christology and Son of God Christology. By identifying Jesus Christ as the Word become flesh and the only-begotten

Son, he went beyond all previous Christological reflection in the New Testament. From then on the preexistence of Christ will be thought of as personal, not impersonal or simply ideal. From then on some*one* was preexistent, not just some*thing* (for example, God's plan or *mystêrion* of salvation, or a personification of God's revealing and saving power in the world). Here the cosmic (the Word of God as God's creative and provident power) and the intimate-personal (the Son of God and the Father as intimates, totally united in love and truth) are joined in a union full of tension and richness. Later centuries will wrestle with a variety of possible interpretations of this conjunction.

Regarding the Word, a certain development is traceable in the New Testament. First, attention was given to the Word of God, the good news that Jesus preached and then entrusted to the Church. This Word had been predetermined by God from the beginning of the world as the Word of salvation. Then the conviction developed that at his resurrection/exaltation Jesus became that gospel, that Word of God; he became the content of his own preaching, the good news of salvation that God had predetermined from the very beginning. At this stage of development there existed a way of speaking about the Christ-event, "whose ambiguity seems to hover hesitatingly between the idea of the divine predetermination of that which is proclaimed and a conception of the actual pre-existence of that which was predetermined."[62]

Preexistence does not of itself connote divinity, certainly not divinity in the full sense that later Christian tradition will affirm of Jesus Christ. But the roles that are ascribed to Christ in both creation and redemption, while remaining within the bounds of Jewish monotheism in the New Testament, bring Jesus functionally closer and closer to the Godhead, without ever confusing him with God-Abba, generally termed *hô theos* or *hô patêr* in the New Testament. The post-New Testament Church will carry this process much further, as the next chapter will explore.

Conclusion

In this chapter we have considered Christ's resurrection in both its historical setting and its biblical and theological significance. In union with his life, ministry, and death, Jesus' resurrection stands at the center of Christian faith and expresses both his role in salvation and the hope that Christians entertain for our world and ourselves. In focusing on two key aspects of the resurrection, namely, the appearances and the empty tomb, we found that presuppositions about the way God acts in and for history come into play as we approach the historical and biblical-literary data. The resur-

---

62. Ibid., 248–49.

rection can offer firm hope to those who commit their energies to fostering the human in an oppressive, dangerous world and can speak to the radical human desire that what we begin to become in this life may at last join the living God and all our predecessors in the human family. Finally, we have traced some of the principal identifications of Jesus that resurrection faith made possible and that started the Church on the road toward deepening Christological reflection.

5

Jesus Christ, God's Total Self-Gift

One of the most significant contributions of modern biblical exegesis has been the profound awareness it has given us of the development of Christology as reflected in the canonical New Testament. Rather than serving as a static mirror or photograph, the New Testament bears the imprint of a dynamic process that unfolded during several generations of early Church life. As a result, we can no longer regard the New Testament as an immobile starting point, a set of premises, for example, to be used to generate the Church's later doctrinal formulations. Moreover, the New Testament witness to Christ is not only dynamic; it is pluriform as well, indeed to the point at places where the texts are not logically coherent because of conflicting assertions about Christ. The New Testament offers us not a compendium of answers but a journey of revelation and discovery, as we observe the earliest Christian communities struggling to make sense of their faith in relation to the problems and opportunities of their particular religious, cultural, and political situations.

What the New Testament does provide is a paradigm for the development of doctrine itself, in which we appreciate the profound historicity of revelation and the fact that history, in the sense of the concrete life-experience of the different communities with their specific circumstances and concerns, was the place where the Risen Christ's revelation occurred in the power and light of the Holy Spirit.

Toward the end of the period of New Testament Christological development, some Christians came to the realization that God was so intimately involved in Jesus' life, death, and resurrection that Jesus' relationship with God transcended beyond all measure that of any other human or angelic being; those Christians began to worship Jesus under the inspiration of the Pentecostal Spirit. In this chapter we shall consider instances of the New Testament's affirmation of Jesus' divinity and then trace that affirmation as it developed in the first four centuries of the Church's life, marking off what is specific to Christianity from the competing claims of contemporary religions and ideologies. This in turn will lead us to some theological reflections on the mystery of God as revealed in Jesus Christ.

The Divinity of Jesus Christ in the New Testament

The Relevant Texts

The divinity of Jesus does not constitute one of the dominant motifs of the New Testament writings. In fact, we do not find many texts which unambiguously attribute divine status to him. More often the New Testament authors tend to associate Jesus closely with activities that are proper to God, without ascribing full divinity to him.

An example of such an association would be one by Paul in his First Letter to the Corinthians:

> Hence, as to the eating of food offered to idols, we know that "an idol has no real existence," and that "there is no God but one." For although there may be so-called gods in heaven or on earth—as indeed there are many "gods" and many "lords"—yet for us there is one God, the Father, from whom are all things and for whom we exist, and one Lord, Jesus Christ, through whom are all things and through whom we exist (8:4-6).

In his analysis of this passage, James D. G. Dunn argues that Paul is here employing Wisdom thought-patterns to express the insight that, thanks to his resurrection/exaltation, Jesus now shares in the divine rule over all created things and all believers, "and therefore his Lordship is the continuation and fullest expression of God's own creative power," that is, of God's wisdom.[1] The type of passage represented by this text brings Jesus very close to God in a functional way, but it falls short of affirming him as sharing equal status with God the Father.

A deutero-Pauline text deserves attention here as well, for it also brings God and Jesus closely together. The author employs a hymn, which he has adapted for his own purposes by adding the phrases in parentheses:

---

1. J. D. G. Dunn, *Christology in the Making*, 182.

He [the beloved Son] is the image of the invisible God, the
   firstborn of all creation;
for in him all things were created, in heaven and on earth,
   (visible and invisible, whether thrones or dominions
   or principalities or authorities—)
all things were created through him and for him.
He is before all things,
   and in him all things hold together.
He is the head of the body, (the church).

He is the beginning, the first-born from the dead,
   that in everything he might be pre-eminent.
For in him the fulness of God was pleased to dwell,
and through him to reconcile to himself all things,
   making peace (by the blood of his cross)
whether on earth or in heaven (Col 1:15-20).[2]

Several of the clauses and phrases in this hymn deserve attention. The
notion of "image" (*eikôn*) comes from Wisdom literature. Christ, like
Wisdom, is the image of God. The "firstborn of all creation" is a difficult phrase to interpret. It can mean one of two things: either that the
referent is the first (in time?) of all creatures or the one who in some way
precedes (in rank?) all creatures (and thus is perhaps not himself a creature). The ambiguity here is proper to Wisdom conceptuality, where Wisdom is both creature (Sir 1:4) and the agent by which creation comes to
be (Prov 3:19). The ambivalence of Wisdom literature on this point will
arm all parties to the fourth-century controversies about the Word/Son
of God. The next significant clause is "in him all things were created."
Dunn and others point out that it probably refers to God's primordial
intention for creation. The meaning then would be that all were created
"in him in intention, as the one predetermined by God to be the fullest
expression of his wise ordering of the world and its history."[3] Another
significant clause is "in him all the fulness of God was pleased to dwell."
Seeking its meaning within the thought world of Hellenistic Judaism, Dunn
interprets this statement as saying that Christ is the cosmic presence of
God, in other words, "The action and manifestation of God which in one
sense is inescapable throughout the cosmos has been focused in the man
Jesus, or better, in the whole 'Christ-event.' "[4] Finally, the clause "he
is before all things" seems to possess the same ambiguity as "the first-

---

2. Following Dunn's reconstruction, ibid., 188.

3. Ibid., 190.

4. Ibid., 193.

born.'' All in all, the hymn speaks eloquently of Christ as the fullest expression of God's wisdom and creative power.

In his discussion of the question whether the New Testament actually calls Jesus God, Raymond Brown has pointed to texts that appear to affirm Jesus' divinity but that, upon critical analysis, do not: Galatians 2:20; Acts 20:28; Colossians 2:2; and 2 Thessalonians 1:12. Five other texts he regards as probably asserting Jesus' divinity: Titus 2:13; John 1:18; 1 John 5:20; Romans 9:5; and 2 Peter 1:1.[5] The texts that affirm Jesus' divinity most clearly are Hebrews 1:8-9; John 1:1; and John 20:28. In the first case, the author of Hebrews cites a psalm in such a way that God is saying to the Son, "Your throne, O God, is forever and ever." While the point of the passage in Hebrews is not Jesus' divinity but his superiority to the angels, the fact that the psalm is cited so that Jesus is called God had to be an object of the author's awareness and a deliberate choice on his part. In the second instance, the first verse of John's Gospel calls the Word *theos*. Although the article that is used when referring to God the Father is missing here, it is likely that more than simply "divine" is intended, since there is a Greek adjective meaning "divine," which the author chose not to use. The end of the prologue speaks of God the only Son (*monogenês theos*), and the original ending of the whole Gospel has Thomas calling the risen Jesus my God (*ho theos mou*). Brown takes the first verse of the Gospel to be functioning as the first element in a literary inclusion for both the ending of the hymn and the ending of the Gospel.[6] The third instance is the scene just referred to in which Thomas responds to the invitation to touch Jesus' wounds by exclaiming, "My Lord and my God." Here the article is used with *theos*. Brown considers this the clearest instance of Jesus' being called God in the New Testament.

Functional and Metaphysical Conceptions of Jesus' Divinity

As the Christian Church expanded throughout all of the known world and began to develop the canon of the New Testament writings and to employ those writings as the basis of its preaching, catechesis, and missionary proclamation, it eventually became apparent that the language and thought of the New Testament needed to be interpreted and explained with language and thought patterns that were not themselves biblical. The Bible could not remain a self-interpreting set of documents.

We have seen that the early Christians mined the Old Testament and intertestamental writings in order to reach some understanding of Jesus' relationship to God and to themselves. They used traditional materials,

---

5. R. Brown, "Does the New Testament Call Jesus God?" in *Jesus—God and Man: Modern Biblical Reflections* (New York: Macmillan, 1967) 10–23.

6. Ibid., 27.

which first circulated orally and were then committed to writing—the so-called Jesus-traditions—and they reflected as well on their own experiences of God in and through the Spirit of Jesus Christ active in the community. These expressions of faith—prayers, inspired utterances, hymns and stories of the Risen Lord's healing power and governing rule in the community and the larger world, and missionary proclamations calling nonbelievers to faith—were essential parts of the ongoing development of the community's life of discipleship.

In all of this we are dealing not simply with a purely linear development of faith-understanding but a much more complex kind of growth. One of the most important and central issues facing early Christians was the need to reconcile the unquestioned monotheism of all Christians—Jewish and Gentile Christians alike—with those statements in the New Testament that seemed to ascribe full divinity to the exalted Lord Jesus without identifying him with God-Abba. Moreover, the spontaneous prayer experiences that may well have stood at the origin of the more adventurous New Testament statements about Jesus' divinity were giving way to the more regular practice in the Christian communities of worshiping the risen Jesus with the kind of worship hitherto reserved only for God the Creator of all.[7]

There was no developed "orthodoxy" (right thinking) or rule of faith available to these Christians that would provide clear norms for thinking and acting. They confronted an immense conflict in their faith-life, where belief in the uniqueness of God and the uniqueness of the worship of the true God seemed to collide head on with what appeared to be a Spirit-inspired practice of worshiping the exalted Jesus. Sacred Scripture—both the Old and the New Testament—was explicit and eloquent in defense of monotheism (or *monarchia*, "the sole rule [of God]," to use the ancient, more dynamic term). The New Testament contained texts that manifestly subordinated Jesus the Son to God the Father, and yet included other texts indicating that Christ could be worshiped as "Lord and God." It would not do simply to quote Scripture in order to clarify Scripture.

Thus the search for nonscriptural ways of thinking and speaking not only answered a missionary need of the Church to explain itself to Gentile intellectuals and others of "civilized" cultures. Christian faith needed such formulations for its own authentic self-understanding. And there would be no clear guidelines by which, in the midst of the fray, one could easily know which formulation was "orthodox" and which "heretical."

The transition from a New Testament way of speaking about Jesus Christ to a postbiblical, philosophical one has often been summarized as

---

7. See L. Hurtado, *One God, One Lord: Early Christian Devotion and Ancient Jewish Monotheism* (Philadelphia: Fortress, 1988); and the classic study by J. Jungmann, *The Place of Christ in Liturgical Prayer*, trans. A. Peeler, 2nd, rev. ed. (Staten Island: Alba, 1965).

the shift from a functional to a metaphysical mode of interpretation. A few reflections on this transition will serve to introduce the first major doctrinal achievement in Christology, which the Church produced in the fourth century.

The person of Jesus Christ is undoubtedly of paramount importance in the New Testament—not his biography or physical characteristics, to be sure, but his personal role as the center of the saving events wrought by God in and through his life, death, and resurrection. The New Testament, from beginning to end, is about the salvation God has wrought for Israel and the whole cosmos, and the promise that God intends to bring that salvation, already decisively inaugurated, to completion. The "what" of salvation is anchored in a "who," Christ the Lord. Scripture has myriad ways of describing the role of Christ: He is God's image, the good shepherd, the prophet, the Lord, and Son. Indeed, there are about forty titles and images for Jesus in the New Testament. Even the scriptural title Son, which bespeaks his most intimate relationship with God-Abba, is a term denoting function. The Son is the one who has been favored by God and sent for a divinely commissioned purpose. And, as we noted above, the Old Testament attributes to the representative or emissary the authority of the one who sends him.[8] Paul and John generally associate Jesus' sonship with a sending (e.g., Gal 4:4; John 3:16). Such an emphasis means that the relationship between Jesus and his Father remains descriptive, metaphorical, and functional.

Contemporary theology and philosophy of religion appreciate the power and irreplaceable richness of metaphorical language in religious discourse in a way that some previous ages did not.[9] Yet symbol and metaphor can lead one's thoughts on contradictory paths, and so critical reflection must stand in healthy tension with metaphor if the authentic understanding of Christian faith is to be well served. The evocative breadth of metaphor and the conceptual control of definition each plays its role in faith's self-expression and self-understanding.

The New Testament's articulation of Christian faith made it abundantly clear to the Christians of the first centuries that Jesus Christ now formed part of the definition of God. God had revealed the divine self definitively in Jesus, so that as a Christian one could not think of God without reference to Jesus. God was revealed as the "God and Father of our Lord Jesus Christ." But if Jesus now shared in the divine *monarchia*, how was that sharing to be understood?

8. See ch. 2, n. 60.

9. See, for example, S. McFague, *Metaphorical Theology: Models of God in Religious Language* (Philadelphia: Fortress, 1982); and J. M. Soskice, *Metaphor and Religious Language* (New York: Oxford University Press, 1985).

Jesus' Becoming Word, Son, and Lord

The relationship of Jesus to God-Abba was not the only major theological issue posed by the New Testament writings. A second problem was that of the earthly Jesus in relation to the titles Word, Son, and Lord. We noted earlier the divergent ways in which the New Testament authors speak about Jesus in connection with these titles. In Mark's Gospel, Jesus first accepts the titles Christ and Son when he is Pilate's prisoner, and is confessed for the first time as Son of God without restriction when he is dying on the cross. In the Gospel of Matthew, Jesus is from the beginning of his life, the one "conceived of the Holy Spirit," Son, Emmanuel, and the one who "will save his people from their sins." In Luke, Jesus is from conception the "Son of the Most High," destined to be king in the Davidic line, the child who will be called holy, the Son of God. In John, the Word of God preexists Jesus' earthly life and becomes flesh in time.

In the Synoptics, as we have seen, the baptismal scene at the Jordan contains a tradition which sees that event as the beginning of Jesus' sonship. Yet the earliest texts in Paul's letters and Acts take the resurrection/exaltation to be the event that constitutes Jesus as Lord and Messiah and Son.

Now these traditions cannot be harmonized among themselves on purely scriptural principles. They each represent a different Christological idea. But the early Church will attempt to harmonize them by making one of them dominant, namely, the idea of incarnation contained in John's prologue (1:14).

Several related questions posed by these diverse traditions but not answerable by them were, Did Jesus *become* Word and Son and Messiah and Lord, and if so when? Was there a time in his earthly life when he was not Word and Son and Messiah and Lord? The Word became flesh, John's Gospel tells us. Did the flesh (i.e., human life) of Jesus become divine Word as well?

Of course, these questions were not systematically addressed by the New Testament authors. We have seen how it is possible to construe the hymn in Philippians 2 as expressing the character of Jesus' whole life and death, and not necessarily concerning a chronological sequence of events: incarnation, ministry, and death culminating in exaltation. So too, the other texts that seem to date Jesus' becoming Lord and Christ and Son are not pressing a systematic-theological point, but rather noting pivotal moments in the relationship between Jesus and his Father without articulating the connection between those moments and others.

Doubtless, later tradition will give such pride of place to protology, that is, to the eternal existence of the Word and the incarnation, that the precedence accorded by the New Testament to the eschatological event of resurrection/exaltation will to a large extent be lost from view. The Greeks, as represented by Aristotle, considered true knowledge of something to be the knowledge of its principle or beginning, and thus its past.[10] The eschatological perspective of the Bible suggests that priority belongs to the consummation of reality which, in the biblical perspective, involves (1) the revelation of a reality's true nature and (2) its full constitution as that reality.

The first point is the easier to substantiate from the New Testament. Few will question the finding of modern biblical exegesis that, in the epistemological order, Jesus' resurrection provided the basis for the infancy narratives and eventually for the Johannine statement of the incarnation, as well as for the Church's application to Jesus of exalted titles such as Son of God, Messiah, coming Son of Man, Word, and Wisdom. The resurrection unveiled the basis for recognizing dimensions of Jesus' earthly life that otherwise would have remained concealed.

But the second point goes further, for it is not only epistemological but also ontological. Beyond acknowledging that our faith-knowledge of Jesus Christ depends on the resurrection, does Jesus Christ's being and identity depend on his being raised? I am asking not only about his transformed humanity, but also his very identity as the personal unity of the divine and human. Can an eschatological event exert influence on a reality that, from a temporal point of view, preceded it? There are contemporary theologians who are convinced that the biblical conception of reality has not been given sufficient scope in our ontological conception of reality, and that the Greek view that the nature of something is "what it has been" leads unduly to our according priority to the past over the future.[11]

Certainly we must avoid an error that emerged in early Christianity. A group of Jewish-Christians known as Ebionites (from the Hebrew word for "poor") believed that Jesus became the Christ at his baptism by John, and that he was human and only human. Later Theodotus the Tanner (second century) and Theodotus the Banker (early third century), and then Bishop Paul of Samosata (third century), taught that Jesus was filled with an impersonal divine force at his baptism and before that was merely human ("psiloanthropism"). This "adoptionist" position labors under the theological difficulty of implying that only certain portions of Jesus' life were and are revelatory of God and saving of us. The advantage of the incarnation doctrine (and a good deal of its attraction and power) comes from the fact that it excludes nothing; it recognizes in the entire career and destiny of Jesus' revelatory and redemptive significance (even though many later generations would narrow the redemptive significance

10. F. J. van Beeck, *Christ Proclaimed: Christology as Rhetoric*, 278-79.

11. See, for example, W. Pannenberg, *Jesus: God and Man*, 135-38, on the retroactive power of the resurrection as eschatological event.

of Jesus' life and ministry to the dimensions of his becoming incarnate and being crucified).

An exaggeratedly incarnational Christology would render the resurrection otiose, unnecessary, no more than the lifting of wraps under which Jesus' true identity had lain hidden. In this conception the resurrection loses its genuine futurity vis-à-vis the earthly life of Jesus in addition to its content, communicated by the New Testament, as God's decisive act on Jesus' behalf and for the sake of all humankind. A resurrection-based Christology admits of an incarnational perspective, provided that the incarnation is not identified with the moment of Jesus human conception but designates the character of Jesus' whole earthly life (unto consummation) as the eternal Word become human.

Resurrection and incarnation are alike in that both pertain to and qualify the one and entire Jesus of Nazareth, who was and is the human being he is because of and in and through the one life he lived unto death. Resurrection and incarnation differ in that the former is eschatologically, and the latter protologically, conceived. Incarnation can be predicated of Jesus' whole life from its beginning in time. Resurrection can refer to Jesus' whole life, but only from the viewpoint of its consummation at his death. This difference is an important one, and here lies the tension between them. However, it is not a contradiction, and Christianity has not seen it as a contradiction. But the predominance, until recently, of the incarntion (Christmas) over the resurrection (Easter) in the consciousness not only of ordinary believers but of theologians, too, is not a healthy state of affairs.

Basic issues are at stake here about how reality is constituted and how profoundly historical it is as well as issues such as the immutability of God and God's involvement in human history. Does God do new things for us that are "old stuff" for God, or does this prevalent way of thinking fail to let God be the always new one who acts with fresh as well as faithful freedom at all times?

Worship and the Rhetoric of Christology

Of those places in the New Testament where the divinity of Jesus is most clearly affirmed, it is striking that one is a hymn (John 1:14), one occurs on the "first day of the week," that is, Sunday (John 20:28), and the third is a psalm text (Heb 1:8-9). Most of the passages which Raymond Brown identifies as probable assertions of Jesus' divinity have a liturgical provenance as well. It would appear that early Christians' praise of the God who had done the decisive, saving deed in Christ gathered up Jesus, as it were, into the object of their praise. At this stage of development it is not the Jesus of the ministry who is the one called God, but the protological Word or the eschatological Lord. The logic of praise is more spontaneous than doctrinal thinking, and it is plausible that the widening of the name God to include Jesus would happen first in Spirit-inspired responsive acts of praise and thanksgiving.

Joseph Fitzmyer has shown that the absolute use of the Greek *kyrios* (Lord) with reference to Jesus derived from the Palestinian-Semitic religious sphere and not from the Greek pagan world. He writes: "From the various evidence available today it seems quite likely that there was an incipient custom among both Semitic- and Greek-speaking Jews of Palestine to call Yahweh *'âdn, mare,* or *kyrios.*"[12] Palestinian Jewish-Christians borrowed the title and applied it to Jesus in order to express his regal and transcendent status, thereby asserting Jesus' equality with Yahweh without identifying Jesus and Abba.

The same scholar has argued that *maranatha* as found in 1 Corinthians 16:22 and in *Didache* 10:6 is best translated as an imperative ("Lord Jesus, come") alluding to Jesus' parousiac coming, and connoting his eschatological and regal significance. The probably original context of this usage would have been a primitive liturgical setting.[13]

This last point raises another, larger question. What is the proper context in which the meaning of final Christian utterances is disclosed? Frans Jozef van Beeck reminds us that Christian language conveys its full meaning only in the context of "worship and witness." Calling Jesus God or, better, Son of God is not grounded ultimately in the historical analysis of his ministry or death, or in the scholarly retrieval of the events of Easter, but in the full-bodied response to Christ evoked from the worshiping and witnessing community by his resurrection-presence in the Holy Spirit.[14]

This means, among other things, that Christian statements need to be returned again and again to the context in which they reveal their full significance, after the very important work of exegesis and hermeneutics has been done. A second naivete is called for when we turn from analysis to the Christ met in proclamation, sacrament, and witness to the world.

Struggling Toward Orthodoxy: The First Four Centuries

The Divinity of Jesus in the Early Church Fathers

The earliest post-New Testament writers, known as the Apostolic Fathers, continued the development that had emerged in the later New

---

12. "*Kyrios* and *Maranatha* and Their Aramaic Background," *To Advance the Gospel: New Testament Studies* (New York: Crossroad, 1981) 222.

13. Ibid., 228.

14. van Beeck, *Christ Proclaimed*, 66–104.

Testament period of calling Jesus God. Ignatius of Antioch, writing in the second century to the Ephesians, declares, "Jesus Christ our God was conceived of Mary" (Eph 18:2) and, "God was now appearing in human form" (Eph 19:3). In *Smyrnaeans* 1:1 Ignatius salutes "Jesus Christ, the Divine One who has gifted you with such wisdom." The homily erroneously called the Second Letter of Clement frankly states, "It is fitting that you should think of Jesus Christ as of God."[15]

The confrontation between Christianity and the pagan cultures of Rome and Hellenism began, of course, in the New Testament period and continued to hold center stage in the defense (*apologia*) of the faith and its propagation throughout the civilized world. Among the first post-New Testament writers to expound the values of Christianity in direct relation to pagan philosophy were Justin Martyr and Clement of Alexandria. For both of them, Christ was the fulfillment not only of the Jewish covenant but of the deepest aspirations of pagans as well. In the first "ecumenical" theology, they maintained that the Word, which pervades all creation and receives fragmentary expression in the best of what the ancient philosophers wrote, in the last days came among us completely and definitively in Jesus Christ.[16]

As was briefly mentioned above, the most profound problem facing Christianity's development was that of the divine monarchy, the Jewish religious belief and Greek philosophical view that the ultimate reality—God—stands alone (*monos*) as source (*archē*) and governor of the world. If Jesus were God, how could this truth be reconciled with the exclusive character of the divine monarchy?

In the second and third centuries two views emerged that attempted to square the divine monarchy with Jesus' divinity. The so-called dynamic monarchianists, the two Theodotuses and Paul of Samosata to whom I referred above, maintained that Jesus was possessed of an impersonal divine power (*dynamis*) that made him superior to other creatures but no threat to the Father's monarchy. Other thinkers, known collectively as modalistic monarchianists, sought reconciliation of the conflict by insisting that the Word or Son and the Holy Spirit were different ways (modes) in which the one undivided and undifferentiated God appeared in salvation history, but that these modes were not present in God's own being. Three men who defended this view were Praxeas, Noetus, and Sabellius. In later Church history, modalistic monarchianism would be termed Sabel-

---

15. Cited in Brown, "Does the New Testament?," 31–32. For an English translation of these early letters, see *Early Christian Writings: The Apostolic Fathers*, trans. M. Staniforth (Baltimore: Penguin, 1968). For 2 Clement, *The Ante-Nicene Christian Library*, vol. 1: The Apostolic Fathers, ed. A. Roberts and J. Donaldson (Edinburgh: T. and T. Clark, 1867). See also R. M. Grant, *Greek Apologists of the Second Century* (Philadelphia: Westminster, 1988).

16. See, for example, Justin, *Apologia*, II, 8, 3; 13, 3.

lianism. Another name for it was patripassianism, an uncomplimentary term coined by Tertullian (d. 225), because he had heard these thinkers saying that the Father had suffered on the cross in his mode of appearance called the Son. To be sure, the question of how the Father is related to or involved in Jesus' crucifixion reasserted itself later, but the Sabellian answer negated the distinct reality of the Word or Son.[17]

The giant of the third century, Origen of Alexandria (d. 254), developed a major synthesis of Christian doctrine employing Middle Platonism and Stoic notions. He assigned a prominent role to preexistence in his theology. Not only was the Word or Son preexistent, but Jesus' human soul and indeed all human souls were also. Jesus' soul distinguished itself by not falling, as did all the others. Thus Jesus' special role in salvation history would be a result of his moral development. (This would become a favorite theme of the Arians.) The Word manifested himself in various aspects (*epinoiai*) or "structures of knowledge," some pertaining to the Word in himself and in relation to the Father, and others pertaining to the Word in relation to human beings.[18] Fatefully, however, Origen asserted that there were three hypostases, the Father, the Son, and the Holy Spirit, sequentially subordinate in rank and being. He distinguished between God as *ho theos* and God as simply *theos* (following John 1:1). The Son and the Father were morally united, but not one in nature.

Arius of Alexandria

The name associated with the First Ecumenical Council at Nicaea, Arius of Alexandria (d. 336), has become famous in subsequent ages, although his extant writings are few and he was not a true founder of a "school" in his lifetime. Most of the references to his theology that we do possess are found in the words of authors who were ill-disposed toward him and who eventually triumphed over him; thus they must be read with great care. Arius was a presbyter in good standing when the controversy over his views began. The bishop of his diocese of Alexandria at the time was Alexander, a strong critic of Arius. Arius's philosophical background was eclectic. Scholars can find elements of Platonism and Aristotelianism in him, and possibly Stoicism as well. He taught that the Son was created, begotten, and made by God's will and counsel.[19] He was created not out

17. On the dynamic and modalistic monarchianists, see J. N. D. Kelly, *Early Christian Doctrines*, 5th ed. (San Francisco: Harper and Row, 1978) 115–26.

18. Ibid., 132–37, 158–62.

19. It would be a long while before Christian authors carefully distinguished between two important Greek terms employed in the controversy: *genetos* and *gennetos* and their alpha-privative forms. Eventually the first term would come to mean "coming into existence," "transitory," "created," or "made"; the second would mean "begotten," excluding all the definitions of *genetos*.

of some existing principle, certainly not out of God's being, but out of nonexistence. The Son existed before the time of all other creatures, but was not eternal: "There was a time when the Son was not."

A major concern of Arius was the relation between Jesus' passion and God. It was essential that divinity and suffering be united, otherwise we would not have been saved. However, God the ultimate, unbegotten one could not have been the divine one who suffered and died, because this "highest God" could neither suffer, nor perish, nor undergo any sort of change. Thus Arius maintained that the Son who became flesh, suffered, and died was neither God the unbegotten one nor a "part" of the unbegotten one (for God is indivisible and unchangeable), but rather an entity that was divine in a secondary sense, superior to all other creatures, in a class by itself, yet ultimately a creature. Such an entity was fully capable of entering into the incarnation, passion, and death and could experience the resurrection as the reversal of reality that it was.

Arius was clearly struggling with several interconnected issues: the transcendence of God the Father, the wholly unbegotten one; the immanence, and indeed full involvement, of divinity in the life and death of Jesus of Nazareth; and the preservation of perfect *monarchia* without denying the first two points, which Scripture seemed to insist on as fundamental truths of Christian faith.

Now Arius did not develop his views in opposition to a clear orthodoxy available to Christians at the time. His efforts were condemned and vilified later, but he was seeking to preserve genuine values, even though his solution failed to take full account of the revolution that the Christ-event implied for our understanding of the nature of God and of the relationship of divinity to human history and suffering.

As R. P. C. Hanson recently wrote in a major study of Arius and Arianism:

> We can, . . . I believe, give him the credit for attempting to solve questions which were not simply those raised by Greek philosophy. It is not just to dismiss him as one wholly preoccupied with philosophy. The very fact of his eclecticism suggests that he has some ultimate purpose for which he is using the tools of philosophy, but which itself is not philosophical but theological. He was in his way attempting to discover or construct a rational Christian doctrine of God, and for this his chief source was necessarily not the ideas of Plato or Aristotle or Zeno, but the Bible. Even after this long examination of the background of his ideas, we are left with a sense of incompleteness.[20]

20. R. P. C. Hanson, *The Search for the Christian Doctrine of God: The Arian Controversy 318-381* (Edinburgh: T. and T. Clark, 1988) 98. In this section, and the one following, I am indebted to Hanson's study.

The First General Council, Nicaea I (325)

In the town of Nicaea, modern Iznik in Turkey, the First General or Ecumenical Council of the Church met to deal with several topics, including the ideas of Arius and those who were sympathetic to them. The council, which consisted mainly of Eastern bishops, was called by the Emperor Constantine, who at the time was not a Christian, and probably not even a catechumen. He hoped that it would restore some measure of order to his empire, in which political unity and religious harmony were deeply intertwined.

The Council of Nicaea is remembered principally for the Creed that it issued, along with attendant anathemas, or condemnations. The text reads thus:

> We believe in one God, the Father almighty, maker of all things, visible and invisible.
>
> And in one Lord Jesus Christ, the Son of God, the only-begotten generated from the Father, that is from the being (*ousias*) of the Father, God from God, Light from Light, true God from true God, begotten, not made, one in being (*homoousion*) with the Father, through whom all things were made, those in heaven and those on earth. For us and for our salvation He came down, and became flesh, was made man, suffered, and rose again on the third day. He ascended to the heavens and shall come again to judge the living and the dead.
>
> And in the Holy Spirit.

As for those who say: "There was a time when He was not" and "Before being begotten He was not," and who declare that He was made from nothing (*ek ouk ontôn*), or that the Son of God is from a different substance (*hypostaseôs*) or being (*ousias*), that is, created (*ktistos*) or subject to change and alteration,—(such persons) the Catholic Church condemns.[21]

Eusebius of Caesarea, a participant at the council, states that the basis of the Nicene Creed was the baptismal creed of his diocese, but modern scholarship finds it impossible to identify with certainty the document that formed the starting point for this declaration of faith.[22] The most significant elements are two: the technical phrases that were added to the Creed, and the condemnations.

Some of the phrases that were added were "from the being (*ousias*) of the Father" and "one in being (*homoousion*) with the Father." The mean-

---

21. J. Neuner and J. Dupuis, eds., *The Christian Faith in the Doctrinal Documents of the Catholic Church*, rev. ed. (Westminster, Md.: Christian Classics, 1975) 5–6; the translation given here is slightly amended.

22. On the difficulty of determining the creedal background to the Nicene Creed, see J. N. D. Kelly, *Early Christian Creeds*, 3rd ed. (London: Longmans, 1972) 227–30.

ing these expressions would have had for the signers of the Creed is not at all clear to scholars of our time.

The first phrase uses a Greek term which ordinarily meant "distinct entity" or "nature." The intent of the expression was to deny that the Son was a creature made from nothing, or generated from some principle of being other than God. For Arius, the conception of the Son's generation from the being of the Father possessed a necessarily materialistic meaning, involving either the splitting-off of a portion of the Father's being or an addition made to that being.

The most famous word in the Creed was, of course, *homoousios*, translated in English as "one in being" or "consubstantial." What can be said with certainty about the term as it appears at Nicaea is that it was unacceptable to Arius and thus attractive to those opposed to him. The term did not recommend itself for two reasons: On the face of it, it carried a material connotation; it meant "of the same or similar stuff." It had also been used by the Gnostic thinker Valentinus to refer to emanations from the ultimate principle, and thus connoted likeness, dependence, and subordination vis-à-vis a higher principle of being. Thus in this context the consubstantiality works in one direction. The lower is in some respects like the higher, but the higher is not like the lower. (According to Hanson, the term never seems to lose this one-directionality, even in the mature thought of Athanasius.)

Since the term was not defined in the Creed, or by the council fathers, it carried the meanings that the various bishop-theologians wanted it to have. It was not a rallying point at the council, because of its ambiguity. Its principal service then seems to have been its ability to stake out a clearly anti-Arian position, since Arius thought that use of the term implied the reprehensible idea that the Father's being, or *ousia*, needed something additional in order to be complete.

The Council of Nicaea is an example of a council in which the clarification of doctrine occurred after the assembly, indeed a number of years later (see below). A given term employed by the council, but at the time indeterminate in meaning, will finally achieve definition and recognition for its representation of the truth of the faith as the result of hard conceptual work after the council. Until that work of clarification occurs, though, it will be the source of much confusion.[23]

The anathemas aim directly at the doctrine of the Arians. They taught that the Son existed before all other creatures, but was not eternally existent (only the Father, the "highest God," was such). They also taught that he was "created out of nothing." The phrase "from a different substance (*hypostaseôs*) or being (*ousias*)" refers to their view that the Son was other

23. On the circumstances of the council and the formulation of the Creed and anathemas, see R. P. C. Hanson, *The Search for the Christian Doctrine of God*, 152–78.

than the Father in nature, being a creature, even if the supreme creature. The statement that the Son was of the substance of the Father was new teaching at Nicaea. But the use of the two terms *hypostasis* (subsistent being) and *ousia* (concrete nature) as synonyms indicates the theological limitations of the statement; for the time being the way was closed to finding an accurate manner of speaking about the One and the Three. The council was far from the later thought that God is one and identical as *ousia*, and distinct as *hypostaseis*. Indeed, this latter phrase will sound Sabellian to some for a good part of the fourth century.

The council marked a critical turning point in the history of Christian doctrine, not because it had consciously offered a terminological solution, but because it was instinctively correct in believing that Arius' solution to the problem of *monarchia* and a suffering God was wrong and dangerous, and because it did employ a term which (once it had received an accurate, and scripturally faithful, interpretation) would preserve the very core of the good news of God's *self*-communication in Jesus Christ through the Holy Spirit.

Defenders of Nicaea: Athanasius of Alexandria and Hilary of Poitiers

It is time now to turn to Athanasius (d. 373) and Hilary (d. 367), the crucial figures in the East and West, respectively, with regard to the future of the Nicene Council and its doctrine of *homoousios*.

At the time of the council itself, Athanasius was a deacon and certainly a minor figure. He first mentions *homoousios* in his *Orationes contra Arianos* (written between 339 and 345), but the reference is a brief one: The Son is "true God, by origin consubstantial with the true Father."[24] After that he says nothing about the term until some twenty years later. Then he writes that "the Son is all that the Father is, except for the name 'Father.' "[25] He uses the expression "identity of nature" (*tautotêta tês phuseôs*);[26] and he adds that the Father and Son are one "in the peculiarity and particularity of their nature" (*te idiôteti kai oikeiôteti tes physeôs*).[27] Thus Athanasius was able to find other ways of expressing what he took to be the intention of Nicaea without resorting to the term *homoousios*.

However, he did defend the Nicene term vigorously in his later years. He was convinced that it did not have to have either a materialistic or a Gnostic-emanational connotation. The term could be technically defined as meaning that the two realities, Father and Son, although distinct in some respects, are of one and the same substance, with one reality (the

24. *Or. con. Ar.* I.9, cited in Hanson, *The Search*, 436.
25. Ibid., III.4.
26. Ibid., III.22.
27. Ibid., III.4.

Son) being derived from (generated by) the other. Athanasius acknowledges that there is no analogy in the created order for this state of affairs. The human analogies of father-son and begetter-begotten are inadequate because they constitute two separate substances.

For Athanasius, the basis for the truthful use of this technical term was the long-standing tradition of worshiping Jesus Christ as God's equal, yet no second god, and of experiencing that worship as divinizing (*theiopoiêsis*) and as the first installment of the promised total victory over corruption and the root of all sin and death, corruptibility. If Jesus Christ could communicate divine life as redemption from corruptibility, then he was the one true God (yet not the Father), because only the one true God could communicate the gift of eternal life and its first fruits tasted in faith, love, and hope.

In the context of Arian efforts to solve the genuine problem of God's *monarchia* and God's involvement in suffering, sin, and death, *homoousios* and allied terms provided the technical instruments by which the good news could be interpreted and protected. For the champion of that term, Athanasius, the basic problem was not a suffering God (that question did not interest him although it was to recur in later Church history); rather, it was a God who is totally self-revealing and self-communicating to human history.

The word *homoousios* is Greek, of course, but its meaning is not "Hellenic-philosophical"; it is philosophically and theologically Christian.[28] Arius represented an attempt to solve the problem of the "monarchical" God's involvement in human history in terms that fell short of the full good news expressed in the Christian idea of incarnation, remaining instead within the confines of the given "orthodoxies" of the day. As Walter Kasper puts it, Arius' triumph would have meant the triumph of Hellenization.[29] Among the victors in his wake would have been two groups: the "Homoian" Arians such as Eudoxius (d. 370), who always avoided the words *ousia* and *homoousios*, preferring to speak of the Father and Son as simply alike (although *homoousios* ordinarily meant this) and the "Homoiousians" (also known polemically as "semi-Arians") such as Basil of Ancyra (d. ca. 360), who believed that only corporeal substances could be *homoousios* yet were opposed to the Sabellianists and the extreme Arians, the so-called Neo-Arians. It is among the latter group that one finds this Hellenization in its most undiluted form. The chief representatives of this group, Aetius (d. ca. 367) and Eunomius (d. 395), were thoroughgoing rationalists in their arguments for the creaturely charac-

---

28. "[Athanasius] was capable, perhaps alone among his contemporaries, of freeing himself from the enticing but damaging tendency to speculation about the relation of the pre-existent Son to the *Logos* of the philosophers" (Hanson, *The Search*, 422).

29. W. Kasper, *Jesus the Christ*, trans. V. Green (New York: Paulist, 1976) 178.

ter of the Son. Their view that the Son is unlike (*anhomoios*) the Father with respect to *ousia* would be strongly opposed by the three famous Cappadocian fathers, Basil of Caesarea (d. 379), Gregory of Nazianzus (d. 390), and Gregory of Nyssa (d. 394).

Athanasius made it clear that the Godhead did not need a mediator in relation to the divine being (as Origen and Arius thought), nor did God the Father need a cosmological mediator who would substitute for the "highest God" by getting involved in the world.[30] The eternally begotten Son mediates the Father soteriologically, in the incarnation, by being the full coming of the Father into the world. To the question "If the Father loved us so much, why didn't he come in person, instead of sending an emissary, the Son?" Athanasius long ago gave the answer: The Son's coming in the Spirit *is* the full and complete arrival of the Father; the incarnate Son is the full *self*-communication of the Father and the only, and completely adequate, way in which the Father comes into the world.

A second major defender of Nicaea, this time in the Western Church, was Hilary of Poitiers. Some have called him the Latin Athanasius, not because his theology was similar or because he was greatly influenced by Athanasius (he was not), but because of his originality and intelligence. His greatest work was *De Trinitate*, in twelve books, written from around 356 to 360.[31] The theological influences on his work were mainly from the Latin Fathers, particularly Tertullian.

In *De Trinitate* Hilary wrote that Jesus Christ "is to be confessed as nothing else than God in the fullness of Godhead" (I.13). And further that "They (Father and Son) in our belief are each one reality, not [together] one Person, and we do not profess that the Two are the same nor some compromise between a true and a false (God); because his birth does not permit him who is born as God from God to be either identical or separate" (II.1). The union between Father and Son was not just a moral and voluntary one but an actual, metaphysical unity. Hilary preferred to speak of an essential rather than substantial unity, and that led some scholars to wonder whether he thought this unity was generic rather than substantial. Hanson finds Hilary's thought fluid with regard to numerical or generic identity.[32]

About the unity of Father and Son Hilary maintained, "God the Father and God the Son are One unconditionally (*absolute*), not by identity (*unione*) of Person, but by unity (*unitate*) of substance" (IV.42).

---

30. Hanson calls Athanasius' idea that the mediating activity of the Son is to be located not within the Godhead (thus making up for the "highest God's" inability to have immediate contact with creatures) but in its becoming incarnate: "a new, indeed revolutionary, theological idea and one entirely consonant with Scripture" (*The Search*, 424; cf. 447).

31. References are given in the text.

32. Hanson, *The Search*, 480.

And in a passage that Hanson thinks recalls Origen and anticipates the twentieth-century Reformed theologian Karl Barth (d. 1968), Hilary speaks of God being God through God:[33]

> The Father therefore is in the Son and the Son in the Father, God in God; not by a meeting of two types joining together, not by the implanting of the nature of a more capacious substance . . . but through the generation of a nature which is living from the Living One; seeing that the situation does not alter, that generation does not damage the nature of God, that nothing is produced other than the birth of God into God from God, that there is here no novelty, nothing extrinsic, nothing detachable . . . . (VII.39).

God as one as distinguished from three is expressed by Hilary as *natura*. Sometimes *genus* serves as a synonym, but never *substantia* or *essentia*. One deficiency in Hilary's thought is his use of *substantia* at times to mean what God is as three and at other times what God is as one.

In *De Trinitate* Hilary uses phrases approximating *homoousios* such as "uniformity of an inseparable nature" and "nature preserving through generation the authenticity of substance."[34] He gives extended treatment to *homoousion* only once in this work:

> These arguments have been stated in case any suspicion should linger about the mention of *homoousion* as adopted by the Fathers and in that creed which was to last for ever, so that it should be recognized that the Son exists (*subsistere*) in the substance in which he was generated from the Father, and that nothing of the substance in which he was existing was removed from the Father by the generation of the Son, and that it was not registered that the Son is *homoousios* with the Father by men who were holy and zealous for the doctrine of God for the wrong reasons (*vitiis causisque*) listed above; in case anybody should think that the generation of the only-begotten was abolished by means of *ousia* because he was said to be *homoousios* with the Father (IV.6).

In *De Synodis* Hilary explores the word *homoousion*. He translates Tertullian's phrase *unius substantiae* with it, and says that if we are speaking of likeness of nature, we rightly mention only one *substantia*: "One substance, as long as it does not abolish the Person who exists distinctly (*personam subsistentem*) nor divide one substance separated into two, will be maintained in an orthodox sense."[35] At one place he offers a precise definition of what he means by *homoousion*: "By [this term] . . . I under-

---

33. Ibid., 480.

34. Ibid., 488.

35. *De syn.* 67, in Hanson, *The Search*, 489.

stand God from God, not of a different substance (*essentiae*), not divided off but born, and from the substance of the ingenerate God a co-generated only-begotten birth for the Son, according to likeness."[36] Here he is interpreting *homoousion* to accord as far as possible with *homoiousion*. For he was also willing to accept this latter term as it was employed by the followers of Basil of Ancyra, and he tried to reconcile the two.

Toward a Solution: The Cappadocian Fathers

The fourth-century controversies regarding the nature of the Son who became incarnate in Jesus of Nazareth moved toward resolution thanks not only to Athanasius and Hilary, but in a special way to three theologians from Cappadocia in Asia Minor: Basil of Caesarea, his brother Gregory of Nyssa, and their friend Gregory of Nazianzus. While each of their three theologies stands on its own as a distinctive achievement, together they also made a common contribution to the struggle for orthodoxy, which can be summarized in four points.

First, the Cappadocian Fathers made it clear to future ages that the Son cannot be considered a reality subordinate to the Father, or a necessary means by which the Father is related to creation either as Creator or Redeemer. They laid to rest for good that earlier "orthodoxy" which Athanasius had also assailed, namely, the notion that the ultimate origin of all reality could not have direct dealings with creation because that ultimate principle was the "highest God." As we saw earlier in Athanasius, God the *pantokratôr* (almighty one) "needed" the Son not in order to be present to creation as God but, through the Son's becoming incarnate, to be fully in creation as a member of the human race. They made a second affirmation that decisively clarified an issue central for the Arians. They maintained that ingenerateness (not being begotten), while an attribute of God's nature, was not constitutive of that nature. Thus the Father as God is ingenerate, but the Son as fully and equally God is generate, begotten. Third, they stoutly maintained the Father's eternal begetting of the Son and taught that this begetting was an operation of God's will and nature in concert, not will only (as in creation) or nature only (i.e., a compulsive, quasi-physical action such as the Arians feared). Finally, while making abundant use of philosophy, they showed a profound sensitivity to the limits of analogical thinking about God's nature and, as Hanson expresses it, "no inclination at all to impose particular formulae as the immutable test of orthodoxy."[37]

One of Basil's finest contributions to the whole discussion was his elaboration of terms for the One and the Three in the Godhead. He defined

---

36. *De syn.* 58, in Hanson, *The Search*, 490.

37. Ibid., 731.

God as the one substance (*ousia*), nature (*physis*), or substratum (*hypokeimenon*). One of the definitions employed by Basil to elaborate the notion of *hypostasis* as distinct from *ousia* was "that which presents and circumscribes that which is general and uncircumscribed within any object by means of the peculiarities which are manifested."[38] It is interesting to note that one of his terms for person, *tropos hyparxeôs* ("mode of subsistence"), which was later employed by Bonaventure and Thomas Aquinas, would be revived by Karl Rahner in the twentieth century as a "distinct mode of subsistence."[39]

Another major achievement of this period was the development of the doctrine of the Holy Spirit. Many of those who disputed the full divinity of the Holy Spirit in the fourth century were called "Macedonians" (i.e., followers of Macedonius of Constantinople) or "Pneumatomachians" ("assailants of the Spirit"), although the first term is historically inaccurate and the second suggests that there was an established orthodoxy that "heretics" were combatting (another example of the victors, with hindsight, labeling the losers). The three Cappadocians all affirmed the divinity of the Spirit, Gregory of Nazianzus arguing that the one who attaches us to the Father and the Son cannot be a creature.[40]

However, only Gregory of Nazianzus was willing, on several occasions, to call the Spirit "God" and *homoousios* with the Father and the Son. Basil never made either affirmation, and Gregory of Nyssa rarely used either term of the Third in the Godhead. All three Cappadocians had to contend with the fact that the Scriptures of themselves do not provide full support for the notion that the Holy Spirit is a distinct hypostasis. They appealed to the baptismal practice of the Church (baptizing in the three names), as well as to four centuries of religious experience by the Church as supplementary support for that teaching.

Toward a Solution: The Second General Council, Constantinople I (381)

The first Council of Constantinople, which by virtue of its reception at the Council of Chalcedon (451) became the Church's Second General or Ecumenical Council, met in the spring and summer of 381. We have no reports of the day-to-day proceedings of the assembly. Gregory of Nyssa described the popular atmosphere surrounding the council:

---

38. Ep. 38.3, cited in Hanson, *The Search*, 690.

39. Basil of Caesarea, *Adv. Eun.* 2.17; Bonaventure, *De Trinitate* 3.2 and ad 13; Thomas Aquinas, *In I Sent.* d. 23, q. 1, a. 3; Rahner, *The Trinity*, trans. J. Donceel (New York: Herder and Herder) 109.

40. *Epp. 226.3*; cf. Hanson, *The Search*, 375.

> If you ask for change, the man launches into a theological discussion about begotten and unbegotten; if you enquire about the price of bread, the answer is given that the Father is greater and the Son subordinate; if you remark that the bath is nice, the man pronounces that the Son is from non-existence.[41]

What has come down to us from this council are four canons, one of them of doctrinal significance, and a creed.

The first canon offers a reaffirmation of the Nicene Creed, and denounces "Eunomians or 'Anomaeans,' Arians or Eudoxians, the Semi-Arians or Pneumatomachs, Sabellians, Marcellians, Photinians and Apollinarists."[42]

The creed reads:

> We believe in one God, the Father almighty, maker of heaven and earth, of all things visible and invisible.
>
> And in one Lord Jesus Christ, the only-begotten Son of God, generated from the Father before all ages, Light from Light, true God from true God, begotten not made, one in being (*homoousion*) with the Father, through whom all things were made. For us and for our salvation He came down from the heavens, and became flesh from the Holy Spirit and the Virgin Mary and was made man. For our sake too He was crucified under Pontius Pilate, suffered and was buried. On the third day He rose again according to the Scriptures, He ascended to the heavens and is seated at the right hand of the Father. He shall come again in glory to judge the living and the dead; to His Kingdom there will be no end. And in the Holy Spirit, the Lord (*to Kyrion*) and Giver of life, who proceeds (*ekporeuomenon*) from the Father, who together with the Father and the Son is worshipped and glorified, who has spoken through the prophets. (And) in one Holy Catholic and apostolic Church. We acknowledge one baptism for the forgiveness of sins. We expect the resurrection of the dead and the life of the world to come. Amen.[43]

Among the twelve differences between this creed and the one from Nicaea, several are considered noteworthy. The creed of 381 omits the phrase "that is, of the substance (*ousia*) of the Father." Hanson believes the phrase was omitted for no particular reason.[44] The clause "To his kingdom there will be no end" was directed against Marcellus of Ancyra (d. ca. 374), who taught that, unlike the Father's reign, Jesus' would not be eternal. The addition to the article on the Holy Spirit offers a succinct

41. *PG* 46 557, quoted in Hanson, *The Search*, 806.

42. Neuner and Dupuis, *Christian Faith*, 10.

43. Ibid., 9.

44. Hanson, *The Search*, 818.

summary of Basil of Caesarea's teaching. It does not call the Holy Spirit "God" in any direct way, and it does not use *homoousios* of the Spirit; but the Spirit is the object of equal worship with the other two Persons.

The creed of 381 was based, not on the Nicene formula, but on an unknown creed that apparently already contained the references to the Church, baptism, and resurrection.[45]

One of the most significant contributions of this council was that it explicitly affirmed the principle of tradition. By resoundingly reaffirming the First Ecumenical Council, and yet not simply repeating it but moving forward to deal with new issues, the council of 381 exemplified the "creative fidelity" which is the mark of a living tradition that is both guided by the Holy Spirit and deeply intertwined with the contingencies of history.

A combination of the two conciliar creeds, the Nicene-Constantinopolitan Creed, is the one recited in the Eucharistic Liturgy on Sundays and major feast days.

Theological Reflections on the God Revealed in the History of Jesus Christ

From the Economic to the Immanent Trinity

If we look back from the concerns of this chapter to those of the three preceding chapters, we see that a dramatic shift has occurred. In the earlier chapters we traced the principal features of Jesus' ministry and death, followed by the rise of resurrection faith. We devoted a good deal of attention to what historical research can tell us about the historical Jesus. Even the discussion about the earliest traditions concerning his resurrection bore a certain historical "modesty." In this chapter we seem to have left history and are watching very intelligent people discuss the inner nature of the infinite, invisible God. What justifies this transition?

The early Fathers used to make a distinction between *oikonomia* and *theologia*, the economy of salvation and the eternal life of God. The way of discovery moves from the faith-experience of Jesus Christ in the Holy Spirit in our history to the God who is revealed and communicated to us through Christ in the Spirit. The fourth-century Christological controversies culminated in a conviction that, in Jesus Christ and in the Spirit-inspired experience of Christ, we have to do with the very God and no lesser being. The Church's experience of Christ in the Spirit can be trusted to bring us into the very life of God.

The most basic concern of the fourth-century theologians (and their predecessors) was soteriological. Arius and the Arians, as we saw, were convinced that only a God who could undergo suffering and death could

---

45. Kelly, *Early Christian Creeds*, 304.

save sinners. The difficulty for them was that the God who is the ultimate source of all being could not thus compromise the divine transcendence, and so a lesser "god" had to become incarnate. But at the root of all the arguing and battling over such ideas (and the struggles for power) lay the question of the meaning of human life and the age-old question of who or what can give ultimate significance to human life by transforming it beyond its present, broken condition.

The answer of the Church in the fourth century consisted in the firm affirmation that only God, and no other, could be the ultimate source of human salvation, of definitive human well-being. No other reality, be it an angel, a "lower god," or a deified human wonder-worker, could effect the salvation of the human. This implied a whole anthropology, a comprehensive view of what it means to be human. Nothing less than God's own infinite life, God's holiness and integrity, God's truth and love, could be the definitive "home" of the authentically human. Any reality less than God, grasped and treated as ultimate, would end up denaturing the human person or the community of persons that "idolized" it. This did not mean that God wants only the divine life to be our final companion and total salvation, in a kind of *solus cum soli* ("alone with the alone"), but that the ultimate salvation of the human consists in total relationship to God and relationship to all else only as found in God. For the moment it is sufficient to emphasize this principal contribution of the fourth-century Church.

One finds a deep continuity between Judaism and Christianity in this conviction. Both of these religions are religions of grace, faiths which proclaim that God alone offers salvation to the human and that men and women are meant to respond to the divine initiative by "walking in the ways of God." The profound difference between the two faiths is measured by their divergent beliefs about the "way of God": for Jews, obedience to the Torah is the path of salvation, and for Christians it is the obedience of faith in Jesus Christ by the grace of the Holy Spirit. The definitive grace bears the name "Torah" for Jews and "Christ" for Christians, and this difference cannot be gainsaid in ecumenical encounter between the two faiths. (The promising aspect of this encounter is that Christians are getting over their penchant for contrasting Judaism as a religion of law, in the sense of legalism and "works righteousness," to Christianity as a religion of grace.)

The discovery of the fourth century that permanently stamped Christology can be expressed in terms of mediation. Jesus Christ is other than God as Abba, God as the divine Thou of Jesus' prayer, obedience, and service. And yet the resurrection revealed to faith that Jesus Christ is fully God, communicating as his own to give the divine gift of divine life as well as the forgiveness of sins that liberates human beings so that they can share in that divine life. Thus Jesus Christ receives all that the Father is, all the being and life of the Father, and in turn communicates it to those who are open to the gift of the Holy Spirit, the self-gift of God the Father in and through the person of Jesus Christ. The foremost insight of this crucial epoch in the development of the Church's understanding of its faith comes down to this: God mediates God to humankind. This is not the full story, to be sure. The next chapter will complete the picture. But this much must be clearly affirmed: God gives God to us. No reality less than God can of itself and by itself give God to us.

There is more, though. We discover in the Christ-event that God can give God's self away to us, and through us to all creation. The actuality of God's historical self-communication in Jesus Christ reveals a capacity in God that is rooted in an actuality in God. God can communicate God's self to history because God is essentially self-communicative in the eternal divine life. God exists in a total unity with Self that is full of divine life and divine movement: the Father, the unoriginated origin of all reality and source of all divinity, communicates, "gives away" the Father's being to the Word/Son, revealing to us thereby that one of the deepest characteristics of reality is to share itself by expressing itself, and in that way to be fully actual. As Karl Rahner puts it, the Father's self-utterance in the eternal Word/Son in the abundance of the divine life is the condition of possibility of the utterance of the Father's life in the Word/Son into the nondivine creation in the person of Jesus Christ.[46]

The fourth century not only affirmed the full divinity of the eternal Son; it came, through much struggle and hesitation, to the conviction that the Holy Spirit was fully divine as well, equal in being and status to the Father and Son, not ingenerate (the characteristic of the Father), nor generated (the characteristic of the Son), but spirated, "breathed forth." The Holy Spirit is the divine gift that renders finite, forgiven sinners able to receive the Father's self-communication of the Son. While respecting our finite frame, the Spirit prepares us for uncreated grace, for the gift of the Father in and through the Son. The Holy Spirit operates "on our side," as it were, communicating to us the divine welcome to the Father's self-utterance. In the Godhead the Spirit is the bond of love between the Father and the Son, the uniting unity of their love. Another way of putting it is to say that the Holy Spirit is the totally adequate reception of the Father's self-communication in the Son. Its full reception is an essential "dimension" of the abundant actuality of this communication (which here is not, of course, a message but the Father's *self*-communication in the Son).[47]

46. "On the Theology of the Incarnation," *Theological Investigations*, trans. K. Smyth (Baltimore: Helicon, 1966) vol. 4, 115.

47. Rahner, *The Trinity*, 337, n. 40. Instead of the classical Augustinian psychological model of the Trinity, which employs the tripartite structure of the human soul (memory, intellect and

The great Reformed theologian in the Calvinist tradition, Karl Barth, elaborated the good news of the consubstantiality of the Son incarnate in the Holy Spirit as follows. In having to do with the God of Jesus Christ, we have to do not with only one side of God, a side that happens to be turned toward us in mercy and saving grace. No, all that God is, without remainder, has drawn close to us in Jesus and the Spirit. God is not like the moon, with an undisclosed face hidden from the earth. God is present in the Christ-event so totally and thoroughly that we can completely trust this self-revelation of the invisible, infinite, all-holy One, who is infinitely other than we creatures, yet completely with us, Emmanuel, God with us.[48]

The economic and the immanent Trinity are one and the same, Rahner would say. The truth that is met in history in Jesus Christ (truth in the sense of the Word that is faithful self-presentation, self-utterance) and the Love that is experienced in history in the Holy Spirit (love as the bond uniting the opposites in a way that allows healthy differences to flourish) are the very same truth (Word) and love (Spirit) as the self-utterance and bond of love within the divine life. God relates in free, self-giving love to creation in the same manner that God is related to God's self through all eternity.

Thus twentieth-century theology tries to find words to express this contribution of the fourth century.

The inner Word of God, the eternal Son, is incomprehensible, and all analogical language about that Word is inadequate. The Cappadocian theologians, and all major Christian theologians since them, have taught this truth with great force. Yet we can use analogical ways of speaking of God as the source of the creaturely, historical world that we directly experience, and as infinitely transcendent of that creaturely world. Furthermore, we can employ the analogy of faith, which is a process of comparing and relating the different truths of faith in order to arrive at a deeper faith-understanding of Jesus Christ. And finally, we can relate what we know in faith about God in Christ to our last end.[49]

The humanity of Jesus is the human revelation of God's life in the disclosing light of the Holy Spirit. In Jesus' life, his manner of living and of being with others, we find the human version of the divine Son and Word, the Son and Word spelt out in human, immediately intelligible terms (without that humanity losing its own mystery; for even the human in its

will or mind, thought and love) as the analogy for God's triunity, Rahner uses a communications model: the communicator, the communicated, and the actual reception of the communicated (ibid., 34–38, 87–99).

48. K. Barth, *Church Dogmatics* II/2: *The Doctrine of God*, trans. G. W. Bromiley et al. (Edinburgh: T. and T. Clark, 1957) 3–34.

49. Thus the First Vatican Council, *Dei Filius*, "The Dogmatic Constitution on the Catholic Faith," in Neuner and Dupuis, *Christian Faith*, 45, n. 132.

own finite way is mystery, nonobjectifiable depth of meaning and possibility).

Thus the dimensions of Jesus that we described in chapters 2 and 3 are once again significant: Jesus' relationship to Abba in the openness of the Spirit; his relationship to other human beings, and his relationship to the natural world. In his relationship to Abba (as the Synoptics, but most especially John's Gospel, tell us) Jesus received all that he was from the Father in gratitude and existed in dedication and obedience to the Father, returning all to Abba. Jesus invited others to share his unity with the Father, even though it was unique (the distinction between "my Father and your Father"), and for that purpose he considered himself sent by the Father. In his relations with others, Jesus was open and accessible to all, extending unconditional acceptance and hospitality, especially to sinners and outcasts, the poor and needy, in solidarity with them even to the curse of crucifixion. He presented himself as consistent in word and deed, without deceit or dissimulation, with the frankness and courtesy of love. In relation to the material world, Jesus showed his respect and attentiveness toward nature in his stories and parables, where he let ordinary natural rhythms become involved in the happening of God's reign. Can we not see in the historical Jesus something of the character of the eternal Word and Son? All that the Word and Son is comes from the Father, and that Word returns all to the Father in a unity whose liberality and openness are infinite. The divine other in the Godhead is the divine "space" and ground of possibility within which the material world can come to be from nonexistence: "Through him all things were made, both visible and invisible." Finally, the Jesus who patiently works and suffers so that, in the fullness of time, God may be all in all reveals the Word as the one in the Godhead who lives in complete dedication to the Father and wants to bring all history to its consummation for the Father's glory. The identity of the economic and immanent Trinity allows us to find in Jesus' threefold dimensionality clues to the character of the Word who became enfleshed in his life and death.

Preexistence

We have seen how faith in Jesus' resurrection/exaltation led to believers' drawing on Old Testament images and concepts to express his unity with God's creative and salvific purposes in history. A principal source lay at hand in Wisdom literature. If Jesus was the Wisdom of God come among us (see John's prologue), was he not in some way preexistent, i.e., did he not exist in some real way before living an earthly life in human history bounded by time and space?

Preexistence is not a concept restricted to Wisdom literature. Ancient thinkers often believed that really important historical events also occur in "heaven," a realm prior and superior to temporal existence. Apocalyptic thinking reckoned with heavenly figures held in reserve in the heavenly realm before their appearance on earth.[50] Protology, that is, the knowledge of origins "in the beginning" or before the beginning, takes precedence in this type of thinking. And for sophisticated Greeks the eternal, immutable ideas were "really real" in comparison with the transitory and corruptible imitations found in the world.

Yet even if one does not share the mythic thinking of the ancients regarding the preexistence of the significant in heaven before its emergence in history, the notion of preexistence is unavoidable in Christology. Christian faith's identification of Jesus with the eternal Word/Son of God who is one in being (*homoousios*) with the eternal Father means that the divine reality who became incarnate in Jesus of Nazareth exists vis-à-vis all created reality (including Jesus' humanity) just as God exists vis-à-vis creation. That existence is often termed preexistence; God preexists all creaturely reality, but in a very specific sense.

We shall return to this idea shortly, but first it is necessary to say a word about Jesus' human reality. The only sense in which that reality was preexistent (existent before Jesus' conception in Mary's womb) was that it possessed intentional preexistence, that is, it existed in God's mind and God's intention. Before the historical conception of Jesus at a concrete time and place, however, his humanity possessed no actuality at all. Our concern here is, therefore, exclusively with the actual existence of the eternal Word/Son before the conception of Jesus.

We can hardly avoid a kind of mythological thinking in this context, by thinking of God in terms of time and space. We seem forced to represent preexistence as one kind of existence which is temporally prior to another kind of existence. But that perception is wrong when we are contemplating the existence of God in relation to all creatures. God's being is prior to that of all creatures not because God's temporality extends "further back" than any creature, but because God's being transcends infinitely all creaturely reality as its ultimate source and final goal. The priority is ontological, not temporal.[51]

Having said that, though, there still remains the immense problem of seeking the least inadequate way of representing the relationship of history to God and God to history. During the long course of the Church's existence, a stubborn desire contrary to the good news has revealed itself: the

50. See J. J. Collins, *The Apocalyptic Imagination: An Introduction to the Jewish Matrix of Christianity* (New York: Crossroad, 1984).

51. A recent debate has brought the myth-dimension of Christianity, and particularly the central belief in the incarnation, onto center stage. See J. Hick, ed. *The Myth of God Incarnate* (Philadelphia: Westminster, 1977); M. Green, *The Truth of God Incarnate* (Grand Rapids, Mich.: Eerdmans, 1977); M. Goulder, ed., *Incarnation and Myth: The Debate Continued* (Grand Rapids, Mich.: Eerdmans, 1979).

desire to denigrate the creaturely in comparison with the divine, rather than recognizing that God's loving creation and self-communication are the ground of creaturely *substantiality*. This desire, as we shall see in the next chapter, appears as a docetic or monophysitic tendency in Christology when Christians reflectively (or unreflectively!) try to hold together the unity of the divine and human in Jesus Christ, at the expense of the latter. However, must God and the human always be thought of as in competition, even when sin is not in the picture? Must the divine supplant or remove the creaturely, so as to make room, as it were, for the divine to be completely present among us?[52]

It would seem to be in full keeping with the good news to maintain that where God is most present and at work, there one finds creatures (and particularly, the free creature: humankind) most fully alive, responsible, and "substantially" present. At many junctures in his theological career, Karl Rahner reminded Christians that the healthy autonomy and subsistence of creaturely beings is directly, not inversely, proportionate to their dependence on God.[53]

But how are we to represent the divine Word/Son who becomes incarnate in Jesus of Nazareth? We can fall into the trap of letting our imagination rule our thinking, and represent the Word in the Godhead as a kind of invisible human person waiting to be conceived in time. If we move to a more sophisticated level, going beyond imagination to a concept of the immanent Word/Son as a person in the modern sense of the term, i.e, as a distinctly subsisting reality with an individual center of consciousness, then we have succeeded in thinking not of the one God subsisting in three persons (as the tradition has taught) but rather of three gods: tritheism. For in the Godhead there is one divine life, one divine consciousness, and one divine freedom subsisting in and shared by three distinct personal modes of being. The Father, the Word/Son, and the Holy Spirit are one and the same *qua* nature but distinct precisely as persons, or more exactly, different in their relations of opposition to each other. But none of the Three possesses a separate consciousness over against the other two, which is the case with finite, created human persons. Each of the divine persons is self-conscious and conscious of the other two by means of the one divine consciousness that each of them shares in its own unique way. Unlike human persons, the Three are subsistent relations. We recognize that relationships with our fellow humans are utterly essential for our fulfillment, but we remain ontologically human persons, possessing human dignity even when we radically fail to develop loving relationships. We must *have* relationships because, unlike the Three in the Godhead, we are

---

52. P. Schoonenberg, "God or Man: A False Dilemma," in *The Christ*, trans. D. Couling (New York: Herder and Herder, 1972) 13–49.

53. Rahner, "Theology of the Incarnation," 117.

not subsistent relations ourselves.

Piet Schoonenberg represents a recent Catholic attempt to rethink preexistence in a way which will allow us to say that Jesus Christ is a human person. With regard to the immanent Trinity, he suggests that (1) the immanent Word (he prefers this term to "Son" for the immanent utterance of the Father) exists in the Godhead eternally but perhaps not necessarily; (2) the Word is not a person (in the modern sense of one who possesses an individual center of consciousness) or involved in personal relationships (in the modern sense) until the incarnation; and (3) we cannot say whether or not there would have been an actual Word in the Godhead if the incarnation had not occurred.[54] Schoonenberg's reason for maintaining this agnostic stance is that we could affirm such preexistence of the Word "if the relationship between God's immutability and his free self-determination were accessible to us. Because this is not the case, the question remains unanswered and unanswerable. It is thereby eliminated from theology as a meaningless question."[55] Elsewhere he writes that the relationship among the Three is immanently modal (prescinding from the incarnation?) but economically personal. That is, the Word has a personal relationship (in the modern sense) to the Father only as the incarnate Word, and the Spirit is personal (in the modern sense) only as poured forth in the Church and in the lives of believers.[56]

We may remember that Basil of Caesarea was willing to call the Three in the Godhead "modes of subsistence" as an alternative to *hypostaseis*. Karl Rahner, as we saw, recommends a return to such usage, given the modern meaning of person. What Schoonenberg is saying, then, is that in the incarnation of the Word and the outpouring of the Spirit these two divine modes of subsistence become personal in the contemporary meaning of the term. In the incarnation, the Word becomes present in an unsurpassable way in the human person Jesus Christ; and in its outpouring, the Spirit analogously (i. e., in a way similar to and different from the incarnation) becomes the source of new life in the community of baptized human persons.

The difficulty in Schoonenberg's position appears with the notion that God generates the Word freely and that the Word's generation depends on God's free decision to communicate the divine life to human history. Schoonenberg is seeking a way out of the impasse that he sees in the tradition's refusal to call Jesus a human person, and the theological and pas-

---

54. For a similar challenging of the traditional view of Christ's preexistence as personal preexistence, see M. K. Hellwig, *Jesus, The Compassion of God* (Wilmington, Del.: Michael Glazier, 1983).

55. P. Schoonenberg, "Trinity—the Consummated Covenant: Theses on the Doctrine of the Trinitarian God," *Studies in Religion* 5 (1975–76) 112.

56. Schoonenberg, *The Christ*, 83–87.

toral problems caused by the exclusively divine personhood of Jesus. But Schoonenberg has not satisfied his critics that his solution is not a modern form of modalism. He certainly is not advocating modalism in the Sabellian sense of three names for an internally undifferentiated Godhead. But he is open to the possibility that God *could have been* eternally, internally undifferentiated, a possibility that is not the actual case, to be sure. This point seems contrary to the long-standing tradition that God's triunity for the world reveals the triunity that is God's eternal and necessary self-identity. In other words, the classic teaching is that God is not triune only in order to become God-for-us; God is "already" triune as God for God. God freely relates to the world through the relationships by which God is necessarily related to God's own self. It would seem that formulating a more adequate treatment of Jesus' full humanity, without suggesting a free, "economically" dependent generation of the Word (and spiration of the Spirit), would be a more satisfactory way to proceed. But he has unforgettably alerted us to the problems associated with the use of the term "person" of the preexistent reality and activity that became incarnate in Jesus. We shall return to this topic when discussing the hypostatic union.[57]

God in Relation to Change and Suffering

We saw earlier that one of the chief concerns of the Arians was the ability of God to be involved in suffering, and thus able to save sinners. The "highest God," the source of all being, had to remain untouched by all change and suffering, because any such involvement would compromise the ultimate deity. So the Arians postulated that a "second god," superior to all other creatures, yet in the final analysis itself a creature, became incarnate, suffered, and died. Their doctrine was ill-fated and inadequate, but the question they pondered still remains for theology, and specifically, Christology: Is the triune God involved in the human Jesus' suffering and death, and if so, how?

One of the classical characteristics of the divine in antiquity was *apatheia*, freedom from all change and suffering.[58] Transitoriness, corruptibility, and contingency were the marks of the nondivine. The Fathers

---

57. For recent official statements on Christology, with particular reference to the question of preexistence, see the Congregation for the Doctrine of the Faith's Declaration "Regarding the Safeguarding of Faith in the Mysteries of the Incarnation and of the Most Blessed Trinity from Some Recent Errors," *Origins* 1 (1972) 666–68; see as well The International Theological Commission, *Select Questions on Christology: September 1980* (Washington, D.C.: United States Catholic Conference, 1980).

58. See G. L. Prestige, *God in Patristic Thought* 2nd rev. ed. (London: S.P.C.K., 1952); for classical texts, see C. Hartshorne and W. L. Reese, eds., *Philosophers Speak of God* (Chicago: University of Chicago Press, 1953) Part I.

of the Church agreed that *apatheia* was the essential condition of God, which Christians, through a lifetime of faithfulness to grace and discipline, could come to experience by participation. The notion owed much to Stoic philosophy and its image of the philosopher who, by dint of struggle and slow assimilation to the good, achieved a centeredness and self-possession that allowed him to rise above, and thus gain freedom from, the pull of passions and the inner tyranny that pain and loss can work in "lesser mortals." The world of corruption and corruptibility, where events and people come and go in all their transitoriness, was contrasted to the world of the spirit, which shares in the unchanging, utterly reliable divine life. Perfection consisted in the good that is or has become free from change.

And yet, at the heart of the Christian good news we hear John's message: "And the Word became flesh and dwelt among us" (1:14). One of the single most influential verses in the whole New Testament, it still challenges theologians and Christian philosophers. Scripture says of the Word that it *became*. This affirmation acquired greater depth when the Church of the fourth century recognized after a major struggle that this Word was not simply the Old Testament Wisdom of God but the eternal, consubstantial Word and only-begotten Son. Then it appeared as though revelation was predicating change of God in the incarnation of the Person of the Word/Son.

Karl Rahner, in a classic article that has been referred to above, asks whether Christians have given this incarnational insight its due.[59]

In the space of four centuries, the Church came to the profoundly novel and revolutionary view that the absolute simplicity of God's being was in no way compromised or negated by the actuality of three persons subsisting in the one divine nature. Here the conservative, fundamentalistic readers of the New Testament (the Arians) and their rationalistic successors (the Neo-Arians) were the ones who missed the truth of Scripture that had to be framed in terms other than those of Scripture. In the Godhead there exists an infinite "otherness," an infinite distinction, which does not diminish the infinite divine unity but expresses its lively abundance. This "Christian metaphysics" was the fruit of attention to revelation, and ran counter to the canons of Greek philosophy of every stripe.

Rahner asks whether we are not being invited to recognize that God's being can enter into change, that—to use a phrase of the German Protestant theologian, Eberhard Jüngel—in the Christ-event it is revealed to us that God's being is in becoming (*"Gottes Sein ist im Werden"*).[60] The point at issue here is not the same as with the "unity in distinction" of the Trinity. In the latter case, we are reflecting in faith on the immanent

59. K. Rahner, "Theology of the Incarnation," 112–16.

60. E. Jüngel, *The Doctrine of the Trinity: God's Being Is in Becoming*, trans. H. Harris (Grand Rapids, Mich.: Eerdmans, 1976).

unity in distinction of the three hypostases of the immanent Godhead. In the case Rahner is proposing—the incarnation—we are considering the immanent Word/Son remaining itself while becoming the economic Word, the Word incarnate, the Word rendered a historical, developing, mortal human being, Jesus of Nazareth. But the two situations are similar in that we predicate both unity and threeness as really of God, and we predicate both sameness and becoming as really of God the Word.

The traditional doctrine of God as represented, for example, by Thomas Aquinas, maintained that God's inability to change or become in any sense was due to the absolute perfection of the divine being, which excluded all composition.[61] All change involved the actuation of potency, and only finite being had potency; God was the totally actual one, the subsistent act of existence (*ipsum esse subsistens*).[62]

Various attempts have been made in modern times to reconsider God as a relational being and as a being who can change, receive, and suffer. A commanding thinker in this regard is the German idealist philosopher G. F. W. Hegel. He conceived of world history and the history of nature as a vast movement. In outline, he sought to rethink the reality of God not as substance but as absolute Spirit, which comes to itself in full actuality through a process of externalization or "othering forth" (Being-in-itself becoming Being-for-itself) and of reconciliation or reunion with that "other" (Spirit moving from the stage of Being-for-itself to the stage of Being-in-and-for-itself). This endless process by which absolute Spirit comes to full actuality occurs in and through the worldly processes of sensation, thought, moral activity, politics, art, religion and finally philosophy. It is a threefold process of sublation (*Aufhebung*) during which each unfolding moment is negated, transcended, and preserved in its truth. The historical emergence of Jesus Christ and the emergence of the community of the Church in the power of the Spirit mark the beginning of the culmination of this process; then absolute Spirit becomes both a particular historical individual within the process as well as the community that continues his presence thanks to the "negation of the negation," the resurrection as the event of the Spirit that cancels the destructive aspects of the Cross. Hegel labored to think of God as genuinely infinite, not therefore *a* being to be compared to or contrasted with others, for that would finitize God. The infinite God differs from finite reality in a way that does not render God finite. God's being is both other than and inclusive of, all other reality. For Hegel, the unity of the selfsame and the different

---

61. *Summa Theologiae* I, q. 3 (Blackfriars ed. vol. 6, ed. C. Velecky [New York: McGraw-Hill, 1976]). For a noteworthy effort to show Aquinas' openness to contemporary "relational" concerns see W. N. Clarke, "A New Look at the Immutability of God," in R. J. Roth, ed., *God Knowable and Unknowable* (New York: Fordham University Press, 1973) 43–72.

62. *S. T.*, I, q. 3, a. 4.

occurs through a historical process of unification. God, as absolute Spirit, is no stranger to change and development; on the contrary, the concrete life of Spirit consists in a "lawful" process of self-development.

After a very extensive study of Hegel's Christology, Hans Küng, who finds it in many respects enormously challenging to traditional theology, reflected:

> . . . we may now fittingly register yet again all those reservations which the preceding two chapters have developed in detail concerning Hegel's major printed works. In the last analysis, the same factors have pressed themselves on our attention regarding the paths of the World Spirit in world history and of the Absolute Spirit in art, religion and philosophy that we were already able to observe and indeed obliged to call into question in the *Phenomenology, Logic, Encyclopaedia* and *Philosophy of Right*: the element of "being sublated" in a graceless necessity and dialectic of being, in an insight of reason and science of history which upstage any proper role of faith.[63]

In the sixteenth and seventeenth centuries, and then later in the nineteenth century, certain Protestant theologians developed a trajectory of thought that has been called "kenotic theology" because they tried to interpret, more radically than in previous centuries, the famous statement in the Philippians hymn, "[Christ Jesus] emptied himself, taking the form of a servant" (2:7). As we saw above, an increasing number of exegetes are interpreting this hymn to be about the entire career of Jesus as the one who, though fully in God's image and thus not liable to death, freely identified with sinners in obedience to God even unto death. The more traditional view sees Jesus' self-emptying or *kenôsis* as occurring at the incarnation, which is understood to be the transition from heavenly preexistence to earthly existence. Martin Chemnitz (d. 1586) and the Giessen theologians taught that during his earthly career Christ, the Son of God incarnate, chose to give up the use of the attributes of the divine majesty. Others, like Johann Brenz (d. 1570) of Tübingen, asserted that he continued to use them but not publicly. In the nineteenth century, Gottfried Thomasius (d. 1875) and others held that the eternal Son engaged in a self-limitation of his own divinity by renouncing the world-related attributes of divinity (omniscience, omnipresence, omnipotence), while retaining the immanent, essential attributes (holiness, truth, power, love). Wolfgang Friedrich Gess (d. 1891) went even further and affirmed that the eternal Son surrendered both the world-related and the essential attributes, as well as his eternal self-consciousness, in the incarnation. English theologians such as Charles Gore (d. 1932) and William Temple (d. 1944)

---

63. H. Küng, *The Incarnation of God: A Study of Hegel's Theological Thought as Prolegomena to a Future Christology*, trans. J. R. Stephenson (New York: Crossroad, 1987) 385.

attempted more moderate types of kenoticism, while Russian writers including Vladimir Sergeyevich Solovyev (d. 1900), Pavel Alexandrovich Florensky (d. 1943?), and Sergey Nikolayevich Bulgakov (d. 1944) represent Russian efforts to develop kenotic theories.[64]

Among twentieth-century Roman Catholic theologians, Hans Urs von Balthasar stands out for his attempt to think of God in Christ in relation to change, especially suffering and the "curse" of crucifixion. For Barth, God's self-emptying in the incarnation is rooted in the eternal self-emptying that occurs in the Godhead in the threefold personal self-gift. The three divine persons are described not as standing in themselves but as centered outside themselves.[65]

The process philosophy of Alfred North Whitehead and Charles Hartshorne has influenced American theologians like John Cobb and Shubert Ogden in their efforts to rethink the relationality and immutability of God.[66] Since this line of reflection involves postulating two ultimate dimensions of God—an indeterminate, infinite, unchanging aspect full of possibility, and a concrete, finite, changeable aspect, full of actuality—the reality of God becomes philosophically and conceptually more intelligible at the expense of the actually infinite God of traditional Christianity. The historical, finite, changing which, according to traditional Christianity, is freely entered into in the incarnation of the Son and the outpouring of the Holy Spirit, is here wrongly incorporated into the nature of God as an ultimate dimension of God *qua* divine, rather than God *qua* incarnate.[67]

We began with Karl Rahner's question about the becoming of God in the incarnation. No response to this question that compromises the infinite actuality of God or God's character as the all-determining reality will be faithful to the core of the Christian tradition. For Christian faith recognizes that these "properties" of God are intertwined with the biblical conviction that God is utterly and immutably faithful and reliable, truth itself, in all divine dealing with human history. God's relationship to the world is thoroughly grounded in *who* God is in God's own self.

64. On German writers of kenotic theology see C. Welch, *Protestant Thought in the Nineteenth Century* (New Haven: Yale University Press, 1965); for Russian developments see F. C. Copleston, *Russian Religious Philosophy: Selected Aspects* (Notre Dame, Ind: Notre Dame University Press, 1988).

65. H. Urs von Balthasar, "Mysterium Paschale" in J. Feiner and M. Loehrer, eds., *Mysterium Salutis: Grundriss Heilsgeschichtlicher Dogmatik* (Einsiedeln: Benziger, 1969), vol. III/2, 143–54.

66. A. N. Whitehead, *Process and Reality: An Essay in Cosmology*, corrected ed. (New York: Free Press, 1978); C. Hartshorne, *The Divine Relativity: A Social Conception of God* (New Haven: Yale University Press, 1948); J. B. Cobb, *A Christian Natural Theology* (Philadelphia: Westminster, 1965); S. Ogden, *The Reality of God and Other Essays* (New York: Harper and Row, 1966).

67. See D. Burrell, "Does Process Theology Rest on a Mistake?," *Theological Studies* 43 (1982) 123–35.

Rahner himself proposes that God, who is unchangeable in God's self, is able to change and does actually change in the other, through the divine Word's becoming the other, the human Jesus, and its living the reality of the other as the very (historical) reality of God. In German he expresses it thus: "Gott ändert sich am andern": "God changes in the other." Thus the actuality of the incarnation reveals a real possibility in God, a possiblity known not to philosophy as such but to those who recognize the Christ-event for what it is. Rahner continues (referring in the classic way to incarnation as *kenôsis*):

> The Absolute, or more correctly, he who is the absolute, has, in the pure freedom of his infinite and abiding unrelatedness, the possibility of himself becoming that other thing, the finite; God, in and by the fact that he empties *himself* gives away *himself*, *poses* the other as his reality. The basic element to begin with is not the concept of an assumption [i.e., the idea that the Logos assumed Jesus' human nature as its own], which presupposes what is to be assumed as something obvious, and has nothing more to do than assign it to the taker—a term, however, which it never really reaches, since it is rejected by immutability and may never affect him, since he is unchangeable, when his immutability is considered undialectically and in isolation —in static concepts. On the contrary, the basic element, according to our faith, is the *self*-emptying, the coming to be, the *kenôsis* and *genesis* of God himself, who can come to be by *becoming* another thing, derivative, in the act of constituting it, without having to change in his own proper reality which is the unoriginated origin.[68]

The good news of the Christ-event is not only that God has come among us and is one of us in a real becoming, but that "God is love" (1 John 4:8). Yet because, in the Aristotelian scheme often employed by Christian philosophy and theology, relation was an accident inhering in a substance (indeed, the least real of all realities) and involved dependence on the reality to which the relation was oriented, Christian philosophers and theologians have maintained that God does not stand in real relation to creatures. This is because the divine being has no accidents (i.e., qualities that cannot exist on their own but depend on another) and is not dependent on any nondivine reality. The only relation to creatures that Thomas Aquinas, for example, predicates of God is a *relatio rationis* ("relation of reason"), which means that we need to think of the deity as related to us (by Aristotelian relation) but that relation exists only in our mind. Christologically, this comes down to saying that the statement "The Word

68. K. Rahner, "The Theology of the Incarnation," 112. For a Roman Catholic Christology whose central key is the kenotic process, see L. Richard, *A Kenotic Christology: In the Humanity of Jesus The Christ, The Compassion of Our God* (Washington, D.C.: University Press of America, 1982).

became flesh'' signifies the Word entering into a relation of reason with Jesus' humanity, while his humanity entered into a real relation with the Word.

But how does this square with the conviction, drawn from revelation, that God loves humankind by means of a total self-communication in the person of Jesus Christ and through the gift of the Holy Spirit poured out in the Church and in the individual Christian; and that through the Church's witness, that divine self-gift is offered to the whole world, for we know that God "desires all . . . to be saved and to come to the knowledge of the truth" (1 Tim 2:4)?[69] Talk of God's nonrelatedness to the world becomes even more difficult to accept when, as a theologian has recently expressed the matter, the Three in the Godhead are thought of in relation both to us and within the divine being as lover and beloved and the gift of love:

> The Father is purely a giver and sender. He is thus the unoriginated origin of divine love, a pure source, a pure outflowing. The Son receives life, glory and power from the Father; but he does not receive it in order to keep it for himself, to possess it, and to take full enjoyment of it for himself; rather, he receives it in order to empty himself of it (Phil. 2.6f.) and to pass it on. . . . Finally, in the Spirit the faithful receive the gift of the Father through the Son, so that they may share in this gift. The Spirit is nothing by himself; he is a pure receiving, pure donation and gift; as such he is pure fulfillment, eternal joy and blessedness, pure endless completion. Since he is the expression of the ecstasy of love in God, God is, in and through him, an eternal movement of pure exuberance reaching beyond himself. As gift within God, the Spirit is God's eschatological gift to the world; he is the world's definitive sanctification and completion.[70]

The reality of God is the reality of three subsistent relations: the Father, source of all life in the Trinity, communicating life to the Son; and the Father, through the Son, (who receives all from the Father) communicating life to the Holy Spirit. The God revealed through Jesus Christ

---

69. Norris Clarke affirms a real intentional relation of God to the created universe: "Let us say, then, in conclusion, that the immutability which must be affirmed of God is the unchanging, indefectible steadfastness of an infinite plenitude of goodness and loving benevolence, but a benevolence which also expresses itself in a process, a progressive unfolding, of mutual interpersonal relationships, spread out in real temporal succession at our receiving end and matched by a distinct differentiation of intentional consciousness in God for each real external expression in us, in terms of which He is truly related to us by an intentional relation of personal consciousness" ("A New Look at the Immutability of God," 66–67).

70. W. Kasper, *The God of Jesus Christ*, trans. M. J. O'Connell (New York: Crossroad, 1983) 308. For a similar Roman Catholic interpretation of the Trinity as lover, beloved, and love see J. Bracken, "The Holy Trinity as a Community of Divine Persons," *Heythrop Journal* 2, 3 (1974) 166–82, 257–70.

in the Holy Spirit is the God who does not have relations but *is* relationship. Is theology being consistent with itself when it affirms the full relationality of God's own life on the basis of Christ and the Spirit, relationality that transcends Aristotle's categories, while denying that the Three in the Godhead are in real relation to the world? God's self-communicating love in the *oikonomia* led Christians to affirm that self-communicating love as a communion of infinite relationality in the Godhead. Would it not be possible to affirm that God's free creation and self-communication allow God to enter into real relationship with creatures in the incarnation of the Word/Son and the donation of the Spirit, relationship that expresses neither an accident of God's being nor poverty on God's part? This relatedness of God would transcend all categories and be more actual, not less, than all creaturely forms of relatedness.[71]

Contemporary theology, thanks to Rahner, has recaptured the pre-Augustinian insight that the Word alone could become flesh and the Spirit alone could be poured out. From Augustine on a tradition flourished which maintained that any one of the three persons could have become incarnate and been sent as our sanctification. That severance of the immanent from the economic Trinity has been overcome, since we have come to appreciate that God's ultimate gift to us is uncreated grace, i.e., God's own being, so that in Christ and the Spirit we receive the Father's truth and love. This recovery of the fundamental importance for Christian life of the communication of God's own being to humankind calls for an exploration of the gracious and free relatedness of God's life and being to creation in the economy of salvation. God is love, or subsistent Being-in-Love in God's self, and therefore able to be love, total self-gift, for us.[72]

Jesus Christ in the Spirit as the Consummation of Time

One of the unfortunate losses that occurred when Christianity began to feel at home in the Gentile world was the eclipse, to a large extent, of a sense of the eschatological dimension of the Christ-event. Of course

71. See C. M. La Cugna, "The Relational God: Aquinas and Beyond," *Theological Studies* 46 (1985) 647–63. She concludes that "the question whether God has a real relation to creation is clarified when it is considered in the context of trinitarian theology. Recast in light of a relational metaphysics, the question reads, whether the *triune* God has a real relation to creation. In its nontrinitarian form, the question must be answered in the negative (as Aquinas does). In its revised form, however, the question must be answered in the affirmative *and* the first question must be rejected as reflecting a theologically inadequate doctrine of God" (662).

72. For an exploration of the Trinity that employs Bernard Lonergan's analysis of intentionality and conceives of the Three of the Trinity as love (the Father), the expression of love (the Son), and the communication of love (the Holy Spirit), see A. Kelly, *The Trinity of Love: A Theology of the Christian God* (Wilmington, Del.: Michael Glazier, 1989). For a recent constructive study of the suffering of God in modern theology, see P. S. Fiddes, *The Creative Suffering of God* (Oxford: Clarendon, 1988).

the Western Church saw then and has since seen the emergence of eschatological and apocalyptic groups urging Christians to awaken to the imminent end of history. But overall attention shifted to the ongoing life of the Church with its graces, needs, and struggles. In modern times the pendulum has swung back and, thanks to the renewal of scriptural studies, theology has been able to reappropriate the eschatological dimension. Any theology of the God of Jesus Christ must reckon with the truth that that God is one who is coming, who is Advent, or as the German language expresses it, *Zu-kunft*, the God who is arriving and who is history's final future.

In the ministry of Jesus, the reign of God is the eschatological event in relation to which all human effort and suffering can begin to make sense. That reign, however, is not disincarnate, and its effect on human affairs is not totally reserved for some future happening. In his parables and other words of authority, in his deeds of healing and disciple-making, in his acted-out parables such as eating with sinners and interrupting the life of the Temple, Jesus anticipated in concrete, particular ways the shape of the reign to come. He made particular choices and chose limited, provisional tactics in order to serve the values of God's reign within history. The already/not-yet nature of God's reign showed itself in the living tension between anticipation and fulfillment.

The resurrection of Jesus was an event that was truly future with respect to his life and ministry. It did not lie "concealed," as it were, until after his death. Moreover, Jesus' resurrection is not now a past event in the same way that his life and death are. Although in our four principal Eucharistic Prayers we recall his death and resurrection and await his return, that should not lead us into thinking that his resurrection is timebound event like his death. Jesus' resurrection means his full and unrestricted presence among us in our ongoing human history. We have seen that one meaning of a principal Greek term for resurrection, *anastanai*, is "to cause to stand in the midst of or to be present," which is a fundamental dimension of what God did for Jesus after his death. That presence still carries eschatological tension, however, because Christ is not yet complete:

> For creation waits with eager longing for the revealing of the sons of God; for the creation was subjected to futility, not of its own will but by the will of him who subjected it in hope; because the creation itself will be set free from its bondage to decay and obtain the glorious liberty of the children of God. We know that the whole creation has been groaning in travail together until now; and not only the creation, but we ourselves, who have the first fruits of the Spirit, groan inwardly as we wait for adoption as sons, the redemption of our bodies (Rom 8:19-23).

By virtue of the resurrection, Jesus Christ's body is not only the transformed "body under the complete sway of Spirit" (*sôma pneumatikon*; see 1 Cor 15:44). It also consists of the body whose life and unity comes from the Holy Spirit active in our ongoing history. This body of Christ is made up of many members, not in the sense of members of an organization but of a living organism (Eph 5:29-30). The members do not all have the same role, nor is their contribution the same; like the members of the human body, their roles are complementary and interrelated (1 Cor 12). The body of Christ is not simply a by-product of the resurrection but part of its effective reality. The entrance of Jesus into eschatological life with the Father, and the emergence of the Church in the power of the Spirit within history, are two sides of the single victory of God over sin and division and death. The body of Christ needs continually to be "built up" until Christ comes to full stature (Eph 4:12-13).

Thus a freely chosen futurity pertains to the Word/Son of God in his becoming flesh even unto Easter and to the growing pains of the body of Christ until, at the consummation of all things, we are Christ's and Christ is God's (1 Cor 3:23).

Protology and the incarnation of the preexistent Word/Son, does not render eschatology otiose, because God's total involvement in history and commitment to its ultimate well-being do not render the unfolding of history in all its contingency and concreteness a mechanistic deployment of what already is, or an unwrapping of what is present but hidden. God's saving plan (*mystêrion*), of which Ephesians speaks (1:3-14) and which has been revealed to us in the Christ-event, requires human freedom for its accomplishment. The free decisions of human beings, made in grace or contrary to grace, give shape to the emergent body of the Lord, and omission and commission leave their mark on it. The creation of the final outcome of human history is not only the work of the preexistent creator God, but of Jesus Christ in the Spirit laboring in history, drawing men and women into God's future for them, and empowering them to contribute to the creation of the new humanity. It is through Jesus Christ that God the Father is creating and recreating all things, and it is Christ's Holy Spirit who lures all things forward into the communion that will last forever. When eternity, in the sense of the fullness of time, comes to be, the "whole" Jesus Christ in the Spirit will be fully recognized as the new humanity, which is the end and goal of the "kingdom project," for which all Christians are called to work and pray.

It is time now for us to turn our attention to Jesus Christ as the pioneer and source, in the Spirit, of that new humanity.

Conclusion

The path to the affirmation that Jesus Christ was truly divine, the incarnate second person of the Trinity, was strewn with controversy and struggles toward orthodoxy. In its affirmation that, at a particular historical moment, God entered history in a human being as the focus and culmination of all the divine dealings through creation and covenant, Nicaea transcended both Greek philosophy and Hebrew Scripture. This affirmation was first of all soteriological in its import. God alone can free humankind *from* the power of sin and *for* full participation in both the divine life and the new humanity intended by God for all human beings. No worldly creature or power can communicate that liberation of those gifts to us or initiate the process by which we grow into it. The freedom to live responsibly in this world engaged in the task of its authentic humanization paradoxically entails not only our graced humanity but also God's full and personal involvement in the process. The implications of this total involvement of God on behalf of humankind will unfold in the next chapter.

6

Jesus Christ, the First of the New Humanity

In chapter 5 we considered the divinity of Jesus Christ and examined some of the key stages in the Christian tradition's formulation of the unity and equality of Christ with the Father in the Holy Spirit. In the order of knowing, of course, Jesus' divinity was not the first reality encountered. The reason for treating the divinity of Christ before approaching the question of his integral humanity is that the former issue arose historically before the latter: it then posed challenges to Christ's humanity, challenges that for many Christians are still pressing today. In the present chapter we shall consider Christ's integral humanity and then his role as the first of the new humanity, that is, as the Savior, the one in and through whom God is working the liberation and salvation of all humankind. This dimension of Christology is classically known as soteriology.

The Integral Humanity of Jesus Christ

The revelation of Jesus' divinity occurred and occurs in and through his humanity.[1] The unsurpassable relation to the Father in the Holy Spirit that is the divine Word or divine Son is revealed to us humans in and through the graced quality of Jesus' human relationship to the Father and to his fellow humans, without the divine relationship being reducible to the human one. But God is not *a* being existing alongside other beings, and God's reality as infinite actuality is not juxtaposed to creaturely re-

---

1. K. Rahner, "On the Eternal Significance of the Humanity of Christ," *Theological Investigations*, trans. K.-H. and B. Kruger (Baltimore: Helicon, 1967), vol. 3, 35–46.

ality, even if for our understanding we find ourselves representing God this way. Thus the divine Word, as Jesus Christ's divine relation to the Father (and to us) in the spaciousness opened up by the Spirit, exists revelationally not alongside Jesus' human relationships but as the ground and creative source of his relationships to God-Abba and his neighbors, which are the more immediately and directly accessible realities for us human beings. (We shall return to this aspect of the matter in the next chapter.)

But it would be a mistake to think that the divinity of Jesus Christ is the mysterious and unknown "part" of his reality about which we need revelation whereas his humanity is the obvious and already known "part." Christian faith finds in the whole Jesus Christ the revelation of the true God, the revelation of the authentically human, and the revelation of the union between them. Thus we are not leaving the area of the mysterious when we move to a discussion of Jesus' humanity, nor are we proceeding without the help of revelation. Theology, as orderly speech about God and all reality in relation to God, continues on its path by considering the integral humanity of Jesus as the sacrament of our salvation and the first fruits of the new humanity that God intends for all of us.

Jesus' Humanity in the The New Testament

It is customary to assert that Jesus' humanity is not a problem for the New Testament, that it developed as an issue only in the post-New Testament Church. Such a view calls for some nuancing. To a certain extent the answer depends on who is doing the reading of the New Testament. As anyone knows who has preached or taught a religious studies class on texts such as Jesus' rebuking the waves (Mark 4:35-41 par.) or walking on the water (Mark 6:45-52 par.), there are passages in the Synoptic Gospels which suggest that Jesus was not like us in all things except sin (Heb 4:15) but that he possessed, on the contrary, rather extraordinary powers which set him apart. His more special miracles such as the multiplication of the loaves, events such as the transfiguration, and his seeming ability to get out of tight situations when he wanted to (Luke 4:30) all lend an air of difference to Jesus. At the same time, the Synoptists also portray Jesus as doing very ordinary things, eating and drinking with friends, displaying human emotions such as joy, grief, fear, and anger, having favorite friends whose homes he frequented, seeking at times solitude for prayer, and even dying with a sense of abandonment.

John's Gospel offers even greater challenge when it represents Jesus as not needing to pray, such is his great intimacy with the Father (11:42), as full of a sense of preexistence (e.g. John 8:58), and as absolutely capable in every situation, for example, when he knocks his would-be arresters to the ground by words alone (18:6). In John the notion begins to develop that Jesus said and did things for our instruction, but not as part of his own developing human experience.

My point here is that certain New Testament texts, taken at first blush, give cause for thinking of Jesus as not really like us. To be sure, each of these texts needs to be examined with the best resources of responsible Scripture scholarship, and our conclusion might be that what we can know historically about the earthly Jesus warrants our thinking of him as thoroughly human. But early readers of the Gospels did not have a lens through which to read the texts interpretively, nor do most Christians today.

Even within the New Testament canon, we find texts indicating that there were currents abroad that cast doubt on the coming in the flesh of the Word or Christ. A number of exegetes see in the climactic incarnational verse of John's prologue (1:14) a response to the claim that the Word did not truly become flesh. The First Letter of John makes the real coming in the flesh an article of faith, a standard by which to assess the orthodoxy of a Christian: "Who is the liar but he who denies that Jesus is the Christ?" (2:22). And again, "By this you know the Spirit of God: every spirit which confesses that Jesus Christ has come in the flesh is of God, and every spirit which does not confess Jesus is not of God" (4:2-3).[2] Paul makes a strikingly similar statement about the invisible Spirit of God and the fleshliness of he who is now the exalted one: "No one can say 'Jesus is Lord' except by the Holy Spirit" (1 Cor 12:3). It is possible that here, too, we are dealing with a movement in the community that denied the fleshly reality of the eschatologically exalted one.

Post-New Testament Denials of Jesus' Humanity

A major threat in the early Church that went to the core of the Christian faith was a view called docetism (from the Greek word *dokein*, "to seem"). Not so much a school of thought as a perspective that showed up in various intellectual contexts, docetism taught that the Son of God, or divine Word, only appeared to be incarnate and to suffer in Jesus; his humanity was not real or substantial but merely a veil hiding, and signaling the presence of, the only and really important reality, the eternal and divine.

Gnosticism was a principal form of docetism in the second century, with Basilides, Apelles, and Valentinus as its most noted proponents.[3]

---

2. E. Käsemann, *The Testament of Jesus: A Study of the Gospel of John in the Light of Chapter 17*, trans. G. Krodel (London: S.C.M., 1968) 26, 66; R. Brown, *The Gospel According to John I-XII* (Garden City, New York: Doubleday, 1966) lii-lvi.

3. See P. Perkins, *The Gnostic Dialogues: The Early Church and the Crisis of Gnosticism* (New York and Ramsey: Paulist, 1980).

The Gnostics maintained that genuine salvation occurred by means of an elite kind of knowledge (*gnôsis*) not given to all that brought emancipation from all that is material and sensible. The latter acts as a veil hiding the true, eternal, and spiritual nature of ultimate reality contained in all of us. The Gnostics were capable of developing elaborate cosmologies, with hierarchies of emanations which in descending order "fell away" from the supreme or ultimate reality. Gnosticism was not simply a Christian heresy but a complex (perhaps pre-Christian) pattern of thought that affected Judaism and Christianity in a way that was mortally dangerous to both. The goodness of creation and of the God of creation was at stake, as well as the intrinsic significance of concrete, spatial-temporal history, with its detail and contingency. Judeo-Christianity lives on the basis of God's action in and through and on behalf of history. Any effort to negate the value of history in favor of eternal, ever-present structures of reality, in relation to which concrete historical events are so many epiphenomena, is totally antithetical to that twofold religious tradition, which regards history and eschatology as essential.

Moreover, the primacy attributed to knowledge of an elite and exclusive kind is also contrary to Christianity (and Judaism), for which living faith is the way of participation in eschatological salvation. Faith is not a natural faculty that has simply been overladen with material and sensible concerns and illusions from which it must be freed. It is a gift of God freely and generously given and involving a genuine not-knowing, not-seeing that is partly due to the incompleteness of our pilgrim state on earth. This not-knowing derives also from the infinite, transcendent abundance of the divine life. That life will always be present to us as mystery to be explored, and never as reality to be grasped, much less simplistically identified with.

The concerns of Gnosticism and the deepest values of orthodox Christianity are at loggerheads, and necessarily so. Their respective readings of the nature of reality are contradictory. In a way, Gnosticism makes more systemic sense. It possesses a certain tidiness, and the notion that some people are more special than others because they are privy to important knowledge has its appeal. But Christianity and the good news it proclaims will not permit the affirmation of one portion of reality (the spiritual) at the expense of another (the material). Such "writing off" of a portion of the real is inherently anti-Christian and anti-Christological. Of course, many Christians, both official representatives and ordinary church members, have been antimaterial and antisexual. But in this attitude they have gone against the core of Christian conviction, which is grounded in the Genesis accounts of creation and the message contained in the life, death, and resurrection of Jesus. But the Gnostic "higher viewpoint" is a perennial temptation.

Two of the principal figures in the early Church who fought Gnosticism and its Christological docetism were Ignatius of Antioch (d. ca. 107) and Irenaeus of Lyons (d. ca. 200). Ignatius was adamant in his affirmation of the full corporeal reality of Jesus Christ. After upholding the basic facts of Jesus' life, he writes to the Smyrneans: "All this He submitted to for our sakes, that salvation might be ours. And suffer He did, verily and indeed; just as He did verily and indeed raise Himself again. His passion was no unreal illusion, as some sceptics aver who are all unreality themselves."[4] Irenaeus of Lyons, who could be called the first systematic theologian, wrote extensively against the Gnostics, particularly against Marcion, who distinguished between the God of the Old Testament and the God of the New Testament, asserting that the former, creator God was a wrathful, law-bound, "earthy" deity transcended by the loving, freedom-granting, "spiritual" deity revealed in Jesus Christ. Irenaeus countered Marcion's assertion by defending the identity of the creating and redeeming God, and the unity of the Old and New Testaments. He argued staunchly as well on behalf of the physicality of Christ and the bodiliness of his resurrection. He stressed the goodness of creation and the developmental character of all history, terming the historical process one of *anakephalaiosis*, in which all things spiritual and material were brought to a head, or summation, in Christ: Jesus Christ recapitulates in himself the process of the world's maturation in a twofold manner, first by passing through the various stages of growth himself, and then by being the goal or end who gathers up and unites in himself all the growth that has occurred in world history.[5]

A particular form of Gnosticism founded by a man named Mani of Babylonia flourished around the time of Saint Augustine. Manichaeism proved a very powerful attraction for the young Augustine. But with the help of Neoplatonic philosophy, he began to emerge from its grasp. Its teaching that there was an ultimate source of evil as well as an ultimate cause of good satisfied Augustine's inquiring mind for a while, until he came to the insight that some questions such as Whence comes evil? (*Unde malum?*) are insidious because they falsely promise an answer that cannot be given. That question implies that there is someone or something which is the cause or principle of evil, and further that evil is itself something, like an individual being. With the help of Plotinus, Augustine realized that the ultimate reality is one and good, and that evil is not something existing in and of itself (a "substance") but is the absence of goodness which ought to be present ("privation of the good").[6]

4. "The Epistle to the Smyrneans," in *Early Christian Writings: The Apostolic Fathers*, trans. M. Staniforth, n. 2, 119.

5. *Adv. Haer.* 3.22.3,4; 5.21.1.

6. S. N. C. Lieu, *Manichaeism in the Late Roman Empire and Medieval China: A Historical Survey* (Manchester: Manchester University Press, 1985). On Augustine's struggle with the na-

For Mani and his followers, material was evil and illusory, and sex and human desire deceitful and perverting. Augustine struggled long and hard with these beliefs, and in the enormous output of his writing one can see that he never fully freed himself from an attitude to the flesh and sexuality that does not square with the best of the good news about God's creation.

In the Middle Ages another form of Gnosticism was virulent, the so-called Albigensian heresy. The Albigensians flourished in southern Europe for the most part and considered themselves, in good Gnostic fashion, a spiritual elite who had been freed from the body and the constraints that go with bodily existence. Thus they abhorred marriage, which was appropriate for the common Christians who were still "fleshly," yet gave themselves to all kinds of profligacy in the name of their "spiritual freedom." The egregious bad faith of these people, who reminded Church authorities of the "strong" and "wise" members of the Corinthian community whom Paul had chastized, were harshly dealt with, in the spirit of the times, by those same authorities.[7]

The Integral Humanity of Jesus Christ

When in the prologue to John's Gospel, we are told that the Word became flesh (1:14), this is a biblical way of saying that the Word of God became a human being, in all its mortality, frailty, and contingency. "Flesh" in this context refers to the whole human being and not just a part of that reality. When Christianity moved into Hellenistic-Gentile areas, the word "flesh" became restricted to a part of the whole person, which was contrasted with another part termed "spirit." This division would inevitably pose problems for Christianity and its proclamation of the integral good news.

It soon became apparent that it was not sufficient simply to affirm the earthly, material, human reality of Jesus Christ. One needed to be specific about just what constituted his human reality. Many writers before the fifth century shared the implicit conviction that the divine Word's presence in Christ directly and immediately substituted for human spiritual faculties. This conviction was not contested for a long time. Arius of Alexandria believed it, and Athanasius, his bitter opponent on other issues, did not disagree with him about this one for many years. For Athanasius, the divine Word assumed a human body as instrument, or *organon*. This theologian practically ignored Christ's mind or soul.[8] Because Arius placed

ture of evil, see P. Brown, *Augustine of Hippo: A Biography* (Berkeley: University of California Press, 1967), Parts I and II.

7. *The New Catholic Encyclopedia*, s. v. "Albigenses."

8. See R. P. C. Hanson, *The Search for the Christian Doctrine of God: The Arian Controversy, 318–81)* 446–58.

such a strong accent on Christ's changeability and weakness, both as Word and as human being, Athanasius strove to eliminate as much change and weakness as possible from Christ, despite the New Testament witness. Thus he maintained that, during his earthly life, Jesus did not make genuine choices but was completely fixed in his moral purposes. Christ experienced no moral development. His life was an example to us of someone who is not only sinless but incorruptible. As we have seen in some of the Fathers, it is incorruptibility that must be overcome by the redemption, for it is the root of all sin. Because of his negative evaluation of Jesus as a moral agent, Athanasius was not able to offer a satisfactory account of salvation.[9]

The other great supporter of Christ's divine consubstantiality, Hilary of Poitiers, also had difficulties with the genuineness of Christ's humanity. He presented a striking view of divine *kenosis* by maintaining that the Word had abandoned the form, or appearance and condition, of divinity, without abandoning any of the powers of God and without ceasing to be God. Nevertheless, he affirmed that Christ possessed a human mind and a human will. Yet he simultaneously denied that Christ was in any way ignorant or that he felt hunger at the end of his "forty days" fast in the wilderness. Furthermore, Christ felt no fear in the garden before his arrest, nor did he know either sorrow for Lazarus' death or weakness on the cross. Indeed, he did not even suffer pain on the cross. Hilary managed to say all this by distinguishing between the infliction of pain on the body as an externally caused event and the experience of pain as an internal quality or feeling; the latter he stoutly denied of Christ. The paradox is that he affirmed the presence in Christ of the constituent elements of humanity (as understood at that time) more clearly than Athanasius did, but went further than Athanasius in the direction of a kind of "practical docetism."[10]

It was when Apollinarius of Laodicea (d. 390) explicitly argued for the absence of a human soul in Christ that an orthodox position on the matter began to emerge.[11]

Apollinarius asserted Christ's oneness of nature (*physis*) in the Alexandrian sense of one concrete, independent existence. To ensure this unity or oneness (he was the first to use the phrase "one incarnate nature of the divine Word," which would become a favorite expression of Cyril of Alexandria), he maintained that Jesus did not possess a higher spiritual soul, or *nous*, the faculty of reason and choice, but that the divine Word supplied that lack. The flesh is a complete being only when united with

9. Ibid., 452; A. Grillmeier, *Christ in Christian Tradition, vol. 1: From the Apostolic Age to Chalcedon*, trans. J. Bowden (Atlanta: John Knox, 1975) 286–87.

10. See Hanson, *The Search for the Christian Doctrine of God*, 492–502.

11. J. N. D. Kelly, *Early Christian Doctrines*, 289–95.

the Word as the sole governing principle within Christ, to the point of being the vivifying principle for Christ's body. The divine Word was complete in itself before the incarnation; once incarnate, the Word is complete with the flesh. But the flesh is incomplete apart from the Word, and what it lacks is the spiritual part of human reality, which is the basis for independence: *nous*. Because the united realities are not each complete beings in themselves, they can become one complete being. Apollinarius argued further that if Jesus Christ had possessed his own independent human *nous*, then he would have been genuinely free and so would have been able to sin. But Jesus was not able to sin; he could not frustrate God the Father's saving plan. Therefore, he did not possess his own individual human *nous*. The whole Christological tradition bears witness to the fact that Apollinarius was grappling with two of the most important issues in Christology: the personal unity of Christ and his human freedom. But his answers were premature and wrong, with the result that "Apollinarianism" became a designation for any view that held Christ to be deficient in some spiritual portion of his human nature.

We shall consider Jesus' personal unity in the following chapter, but for now it is sufficient to say that Apollinarius's first argument rests on the presupposition that God's reality as the infinitely actual one and human reality as a finite actuality can be "added up," so that one of them must be displaced in whole or in part for the other to be present. This kind of presupposition is erroneous, no matter how tempted we are to represent God and creaturely reality as two separate "quantities" of being. When it is a question of the union of the divine and the creaturely, one of the realities need not be deficient or curtailed for the other to be fully present. The second argument raises questions about Jesus' ability or inability to sin, which we will discuss later, but Apollinarius was wrong to insist that Jesus' possession of the higher human spiritual soul with its powers of reason and will would endanger our redemption. On the contrary, if Jesus had not enjoyed his own human freedom, which required that he have his own human power of choice and self-determination, our salvation would be completely undermined.

The classical response to Apollinarianism came from the pen of Gregory of Nazianzus who wrote: "What is not assumed is not healed; what is united with God is also saved."[12] This principle rests on a prior one: While God alone is our ultimate salvation, it is through like that like is saved. As bodily and spiritual beings, we are saved by one who is body informed by spirit and totally united with God.

Reaching further back, we also find that central to the New Testament understanding of our salvation is the conviction that Jesus' life, ministry,

---

12. *Ep.* 101.7 (*Patrologiae cursus completus*, ed. J. P. Migne, Series graeca [Paris, 1857–66] 37, 181C; hereafter *PG*).

and death were matters of his free obedience to God his "Abba" and his free solidarity with us sinners. *Because of* that free obedience, Jesus was exalted above every name (Phil 2:9). Moreover, opponents of Apollinarius, and Paul in Romans 5 before them, argued that, just as sin came into the world through misused human freedom, so our redemption from sin's power must be mediated to us through human freedom as well, if God is to take creation seriously in its freedom and not treat it simply as the passive object of divine initiatives. Finally, in contemporary Catholic theology no one has been more insistent than Karl Rahner that Jesus' free acceptance of God's self-communication is the way that God's forgiving and divinizing grace has entered completely and irrevocably into human history as a universal offer to all human beings throughout history.[13] This view is based on the more general consideration that only what occurs in human history in and from human freedom is truly historical. God's gift of the divine life to history becomes thoroughly historical only through Jesus' human freedom. In his lifelong acceptance of God's offer unto death and resurrection, the divine life becomes irrevocably present and available in and through the Church, the continuation of God's self-communication through Christ in the Spirit.

Thus Apollinarius' explicit denial of the human spiritual powers of reason and will in Jesus was a disastrous mistake; his view was condemned at the Synod of Alexandria (362), the First Council of Constantinople (381), and the Roman Synod of 382. In 451 the Council of Chalcedon declared that Christ was *homoousios hemin*, "one in being with us humans." In addition, it taught that Christ was "perfect in divinity and perfect in humanity, the same truly God and truly man, composed of rational soul (*ek psychês logikês*) and body."[14]

The tendency demonstrated in Apollinarius to accentuate the divinity of Jesus Christ and its completeness at the expense of his humanity was a powerfully attractive one, even for those who did not drive it to heretical extremes. The Alexandrian school of theology, with its *logos-sarx* (Word-flesh) Christology, laid great stress on the hegemony of the Logos in Christ's life. This meant that the active, directing principle in his life was the Word, and his human reality was an instrument in the hands of the Logos, as it were. A more pronounced version of this slighting of the reality of the human in Christ in favor of the divine was attributed by his opponents to a fourth-century individual by the name of Eutyches of Constantinople. "Eutycheanism" is an extreme form of Alexandrian

13. K. Rahner, *Foundations of Christian Faith: Introduction to the Idea of Christianity*, trans. W. V. Dych (New York: Seabury, 1984) 193–95.

14. J. Neuner and J. Dupuis, *The Teaching of the Catholic Church in the Doctrinal Documents of the Catholic Church*, 154. "Perfect" in this declaration can also be translated as "complete" or "whole."

Monophysitism, the view that Jesus Christ had one nature (using the Alexandrian definition of the term "nature," which is concrete existence). This view takes Cyril's position and exaggerates it excessively. Eutyches was accused of maintaining that in Christ the divine reality swamps the human, so that the latter is not truly substantial but is more a surface effect than genuine reality. We do know that the historical Eutyches refused to subscribe to the notion that Christ was consubstantial with other human beings. The reason for his refusal was his understanding of such consubstantiality to mean that Jesus was a human individual with an independent existence such as all other humans have; this in turn would mean for him that Christ was two beings. He was willing to say that *before* the union of the divine and human in Christ there were two natures (= independent existences) but after that union there was only one nature (= independent existence). The historical Eutyches was not Apollinarian in his views: Christ possessed a human mind and soul.[15] The "Eutychean" position (whether Eutyches actually held the position ascribed to him is doubtful) has often been given the general name Monophysitism. It is a heresy involving a quasidocetism, which has never died out in the Church. Any view of the Christ-child at Christmas that invests the child with an adult understanding of all that is going on around him; any view of Christ that denies that he lived a human life within human limits (sin is not limit but the deadly denial of the human) is a form of monophysitism. Monophysitism in its "Eutychean" form is a very tempting "theology" for some: either divine or human, but not both. The conversion that is required to change this perception is not always, exclusively, an intellectual change of mind, the graduation to a better theology; it may rather be a healing of the heart concerning the value of one's own humanity in the face of God and before the tribunal of one's own self.

For Cyril of Alexandria (d. 444), a towering figure of the fifth-century controversies who stressed the unity of Christ's reality, the human experiences of Jesus were not intrinsic to his own growth and development as a human being, but were intended as a moral example for us. Jesus did not have to cry, because he did not feel real sorrow as the Word of God incarnate. He did not really feel agony in the garden, but was setting an example of authentic discipleship in times of great anguish. He was not really ignorant of the hour of the Son of Man's coming but pretended to be, thus calling us to trust.[16] This way of seeing Jesus means that his humanity was not an essential part of the gift of salvation, but only the signal communicated to us that the really and sole important reality (God) is among us. It misses the main point of the good news, which is that salvation as God intends it for us does not consist simply in God-for-us but

15. Kelly, *Early Christian Doctrines*, 330–34.

16. Ibid., 322–23.

in God-with-us, God among and for us as one who makes us, in God as the supreme gift, gifts for each other as well, in our own substantial reality as graced and forgiven human beings. Any understanding of salvation that writes off the substantiality of the human in the name of a concept of God has not heard all the good news. For all his brilliance and great faith, Cyril did not hear all the good news.

Another dimension of Jesus' integral humanity *as saving good news* comes into focus when we consider the fact that Jesus was an individual human being: a first-century Jewish male, from a small town in Galilee, who lived only about thirty years and did not travel very far from home in his ministry. Did Jesus' particularity mean that he did not relate to those who were human like himself but different in their distinguishing, individualizing characteristics? The early Fathers were clear that, as far as salvation was concerned, what was important and necessary was that the divine Word assume a complete human nature *as such*. Of course, that complete human nature, to be concrete, had to be male or female, living at a particular time and place, possessing certain individual life-experiences, and so forth. But the incarnation was a movement of saving *inclusion*, not exclusion, so that the Chalcedonian affirmation of Jesus' human consubstantiality refers to human nature as such. When Gregory of Nyssa asserted that the Word assumed a human nature without individualizing characteristics, he was speaking technically and terminologically, as F. J. van Beeck has well pointed out.[17] Some later theologians would draw erroneous inferences from technical language and state that Christ's human nature was nothing in particular. This is called the doctrine of "nihilianism."[18] In the current discussion about the ordination of women, there is a danger of arguing for the significance of Jesus' maleness in ways that would effectively exclude women from salvation, which is certainly not intended. That Christ was male is a fact of his humanity as an individual; the individual must possess a gender. But Christ includes all men and women in his saving relation, and does so as the divine Logos incarnate in a concrete human nature. The tradition did not make Jesus' maleness (or Jewishness, or his being a person of the first century C.E.) a principle of salvation, whereas it vigorously made his human nature, as rooted in the divine Word and anointed by the Spirit, the principle of salvation.

Jesus' Self-Consciousness and Freedom

Thomas Aquinas can be taken as a classical interpreter of the question of Christ's self-consciousness and knowledge. For him, Christ possessed

---

17. Gregory of Nyssa, *PG* 45, 1276. See F. J. van Beeck, *Christ Proclaimed: Christology as Rhetoric*, 157.

18. Ibid.

an immediate, beatific vision of God all through his life, as well as infused knowledge and acquired, experimental knowledge.[19] Christ's soul did not fully comprehend God, since the finite cannot comprehend or exhaustively know the infinite God. But Christ's soul knew through the Word all that exists in the entire course of time: past, present, and future, in addition to the thoughts of human beings.[20]

Contemporary theologians such as Bernard Lonergan and Karl Rahner have addressed the conflict that has arisen in modern times between the results of competent exegesis and the traditional interpretation of Aquinas.[21] We now know that the gospel writers affirm some special qualities about the knowledge of the Jesus of the ministry in the light of Easter faith (e.g., Mark 2:6-8; John 4:18; 6:5; 6:64). But at the same time, there are texts that refer to his developing awareness (e.g., Luke 2:52) and his ignorance of matters of salvation (e.g., Mark 13:32).

Karl Rahner distinguishes between knowledge of particular objects and nonobjective consciousness. Immediate self-presence and presence to God as the ultimate goal of all our knowing and loving are forms of nonobjective consciousness, not knowledge of objects. Consciousness of self and of God as the goal of our spiritual dynamism are concomitant with our knowledge of objects, and compared with the latter can seem dark and fragile. Self and God as goal of our self-transcendence are indirectly given in consciousness through our implicit awareness of self as origin and God as ultimate "whither" of all our knowing and loving.

In Jesus' human consciousness God is not present as an object among objects, nor even as some supreme object, but rather as infinite, ungraspable Mystery. Rahner holds that the awareness of God is immediate though not beatifying, because the teaching that it was beatifying was never defined by the Church.[22]

I would try to express Rahner's point in Trinitarian terms this way. In Christ's human consciousness, God the Father is "known" in a nonobjectifying way as the ultimate source of his life and love, "known" as the divine Thou in Christ's life, to whom he was completely dedicated. In his human consciousness, the divine Word is "known" in a nonobjectifying way as the divine relation to the Father grounding Christ's human life and human loves. And in his human consciousness, the Holy Spirit

19. *Summa Theologiae*, Part II, q. 9 (Blackfriars ed., vol. 49, trans L. G. Walsh [New York: McGraw-Hill, 1974] 82–99).

20. Ibid., a. 2, resp.; 104–105.

21. B. J. F. Lonergan, "Christ as Subject: A Reply," in *Collection*, ed. F. E. Crowe (New York: Herder and Herder, 1967), 164–97; K. Rahner, "Dogmatic Reflections on the Knowledge and Self-Consciousness of Christ," *Theological Investigations*, trans. K.-H. Kruger (Baltimore: Helicon, 1966), vol. 5, 193–215. For a scriptural statement of the problem, see R. E. Brown, "How Much Did Jesus Know?" *Jesus—God and Man* (New York: Macmillan, 1967) 39–102.

22. Rahner, "Dogmatic Reflections," 199.

is "known," again in a nonobjectifying way, as the divine gift who unites the Father and the Son in the radiance and love of the gift. In this unitary and threefold consciousness, the humanity of Christ relates to God as Mystery more than we allow God to be Mystery for us. Mystery here is not a term for deficiency but for richness and abundance, abundance that Christ's finite human consciousness cannot encompass but "knows" to the degree that he lets God encompass him through the course of his life into the darkness and seeming abandonment of death.

Thus, as Rahner puts it, there is a nescience in Christ's human consciousness, a not-knowing, which is part of the finitude of his humanity. We perfectionists think that all not-knowing is due to our sinfulness, but there is a kind of not-knowing that is part of our human nature and required for us to be humanly free. So too with Christ.

Christians sometimes imagine that Christ's human consciousness, unlike ours, could dip into his divine consciousness whenever he wanted to make up for the deficiency in his human consciousness. Such a view ignores the fact that, in the incarnation, Christ lived his divine life *in and through* the limits (and gifts) of his human life. The Council of Chalcedon taught us that the creaturely reality of Christ related to the divine reality as creature to God, when it asserted that the unity of Jesus Christ is the ground for the distinction between the human and divine realities, not for their merger into a third human-divine mixture.

Being human involves not only consciousness and knowledge but freedom as well. We have seen that Christ's human freedom is essential to our salvation. Freedom consists not primarily in the ability to choose between finite objects but rather in the ability, through the course of a lifetime, to choose who one will be unto finality. As I have observed earlier, theologians such as Rahner insist that freedom's meaningfulness derives from its goal. That goal is complete union with God and union with all others in God as chosen in a way that involves human creativity. Freedom does not mean choosing a fulfillment for which God could have programmed human beings with greater efficiency and fewer disasters. We are made in the image and likeness of God, and one of the meanings of that rich phrase is that we are called to be, under grace, creaturely sharers in God's work of bringing about the new heaven and new earth. Within the framework of our finitude, we are called to contribute something unique: not only the works of our hands but *we ourselves*, insofar as we, emcompassed by God's prevenient grace, are the fruit of our own choosing.

So too with Christ. His freedom consisted in his creative cooperation with the Father in the Spirit in the proclaiming and signing forth of the reign of God. There was no divine blueprint telling him each day of his ministry whether, for example, he should take a gentle tack with people or a denunciatory one, whether to stay with fellow Jews or travel to other lands, whether to avoid capture or let himself be captured. Yet in and through his particular choices about strategy and tactics, he was choosing in obedience to the Father and as enlightened by the Spirit to become, more and more, Jesus and no other, to constitute who he was as a human reality in response to the divine initiative in his life.

But, if that is true, what about sin? Could Christ have sinned, since he was free? The Council of Chalcedon (451) declared Christ sinless.[23] The Second Council of Constantinople (553), in reaction to Theodore of Mopsuestia, defined Jesus' sinlessness as "impeccability," the inability to sin. The former signifies a de facto absence of sin, the latter, a metaphysical, or de jure, impossibility of sinning. Moreover, the former can mean that Christ was free not to sin, while the latter says that Jesus was not "free" to sin. Several reflections are in order here.

First of all, we should remember that Christ's sinlessness is not something that can be empirically verified. We have seen that people had three main reactions to Jesus in his ministry: They believed that he was mad, that he was of Satan (not unconnected with the first view), or that he was truly of God. The first two views presupposed that the power of sin held sway in Jesus' life and work. Moreover, during his ministry, it was more often sinners than the "righteous" who were able to recognize that Jesus was sent by God and not an instrument of the Evil One. In the light of faith, Christians claim to find in the life of Jesus the signs of his truly being of God. The resurrection offers the fullest testimony that Jesus was thoroughly of grace, of God. But there is no way that one can survey the entire life of Jesus and assert on historical grounds, "Jesus of Nazareth never sinned." History cannot decide such things. The affirmation of Christ's sinlessness is an affirmation of faith and a negative way of expressing his unique relationship to the Father in the Spirit. Thus his "sinlessness" is Christological; it is not just any kind of sinlessness, and it shares thoroughly in the mystery of his relationship with God.

Second, whatever we conclude about the nature of Jesus' sinlessness, we should remember that Paul was willing to state that God made him sin who knew no sin (2 Cor 5:21). Christ's sinlessness did not make him a person who felt superior to sinners, who excluded them from his company or looked down on them as if from some self-righteous height; cultic language about Christ's being a spotless victim (e.g., 2 Cor 5:21; 1 Pet 1:19) should not lead one to think in those terms. Christ's life defined what God's sinlessness is like: something quite different from what we sinners tend to imagine. Christ's sinlessness led him to spend all his time and energy on sinners, with a willingness to be taken for a sinner without protesting that his conscience was clean and his morals unassailable. On

23. Neuner and Dupuis, *The Teaching*, 172 n. 635.

the cross he died the death of a sinner and did so, according to Luke, in the company of sinners (23:32). In some respects, he let sin have its way with him in order that he might confront sinners with the enormity of their self-destructive ways and offer them the grace of full forgiveness.

Third, Jesus was able to be tempted, and part of himself was spontaneously attracted to "goods" that were not God's will (Heb 4:15). The temptations in the desert are highly theologized accounts, but they no doubt refer to a dimension of Jesus' life and ministry. In the garden of Gethsemane he asked that the cup of eschatological woes pass him by, but then added: "Father, your will, not mine, be done."

Fourth, Jesus' sinlessness ought not to be conceived as placing him in his ministry above the tragic ambiguities of human life. He apparently chose not to intervene in the case of John the Baptist's imprisonment and execution. He preached the good news to the Jews, thus excluding Gentiles for the most part from his ministrations. He had to deal with limited time, limited resources, and limited energy, so that all his major choices involved him in ambiguity.[24]

Was Jesus able to sin? Did his genuine freedom include such a capability, even if it were never actualized? When we consider the totality of his life from the vantage point of his resurrection, we are led by faith to say in summary of his completed life: Jesus' earthly life was that of the Son of God incarnate, the definitive self-communication of God to the world. As such, he could not have sinned; he could not have chosen contrary to his deepest character as the authentically human and the incarnate self-expression of God. But, given the supreme importance of his freedom for our salvation, when we consider Jesus as a *viator* on the way before his resurrection, then we do better to say that as he continued to choose the Father's will through the various stages of his life, it became increasingly impossible *morally* for Jesus to sin; his human will became developmentally more and more confirmed in grace, more and more "practiced" in choosing the values that pertained to God's reign, so that his death was not only the darkest and most "testing" period of his life but also the time when his freedom acquired definitive shape as fully belonging to God his Father and fully in solidarity with those for whom he lived and died.[25]

---

24. This is a favorite theme of the liberation philosopher and theologian J. L. Segundo. See his *An Evolutionary Approach to Jesus of Nazareth*, trans. J. Drury (Maryknoll, New York: Orbis, 1988), which is volume 5 of his *Jesus of Nazareth Yesterday and Today*.

25. Cf. G. O'Collins who, in his *Interpreting Jesus* (Ramsey: Paulist, 1983), likewise seeks to avoid speaking of the ontological impossibility of Jesus' sinning, especially if it implies that sinlessness was due to Jesus' subjective dispositions rather than to the role of divine providence in his life (194). Jesus was unable to sin because he was the incarnate Son of God; the mechanism by which he was sinless is another question, and here *de facto* sinlessness is the most appropriate formulation, given the importance of Jesus' real freedom (194–95).

Jesus' Faith

The belief that Jesus possessed the beatific vision during his lifetime made it impossible to affirm that he was a person of faith, for faith is the condition of the *viator*, the pilgrim who has not yet arrived at the fullness of light and life in the beatific vision of God. However, several contemporary theologians have stressed that Jesus was a person of faith during his earthly life. Among the Protestant theologians are Ernst Fuchs and Gerhard Ebeling, and among the Roman Catholics are Jon Sobrino, James Mackey, and Gerald O'Collins.[26] For them, faith is the relationship of someone "on the way" to the fullness of life with God, a relationship characterized by trust in God's Word. Several texts are usually referred to in this discussion. The first is Mark 9:23, which is taken as an implicit reference to Christ himself: "If you can! All things are possible to him who believes." The second is in Hebrews 12:2, in which Jesus is called "the pioneer and perfecter of our faith."[27] The third is a particular way of translating Galatians 2:16: "A man is not justified by works of the law but through the faith of Jesus Christ."

Jesus was a person of absolute trust in God his Abba and of obedient commitment to God, even in the darkness of Gethsemane and his passion. Even in the face of his own impending death (Mark 14:24), he trusted that God would bring about salvation in the future. What about Jesus' relationship to himself? His radical self-presence was a matter not of faith but, as Rahner would put it, of immediate self-consciousness. This is the origin of the supreme sense of authority and authorization that stamped his ministry of word and deed. His self-presence was not a matter of belief but of immediacy. However, the articulation of that self-presence in terms of his own Jewish heritage required a process of patient learning, experimentation, and choice. His radical self-presence was richly mysterious, not a ready source of certitudes and clarities that dispensed him from prayer, reflection, and decision about how to express his identity and mission. Moreover, his human consciousness of God was a consciousness of *the* incomprehensible Mystery, which is known to the extent that it is relied on and surrendered to.

In all these respects, apart from his radical self-presence, Jesus may definitely be called *the* person of faith par excellence. But it is already

---

26. E. Fuchs, "Jesus and Faith," *Studies of the Historical Jesus*, trans. A. Scobie (Naperville, Ill.: A. R. Allenson, 1964) 48–64; G. Ebeling, "Jesus and Faith," *Word and Faith*, trans. J. W. Leitch (Philadelphia: Fortress, 1963) 204–46; J. Sobrino, *Christology at the Crossroads: A Latin American Approach*, trans. J. Drury (Maryknoll, New York: Orbis, 1978) 79–145; J. Mackey, *Jesus, the Man and the Myth: A Contemporary Christology* (New York and Ramsey: Paulist, 1979) 159–71; G. O'Collins, *Interpreting Jesus*, 190–93.

27. The Greek lacks the "our" and speaks of Jesus as the pioneer and perfecter of faith; this is the nearest the New Testament comes to referring to him as one who believes.

clear that serious theological difficulties would ensue if it were proposed that he was simply like us in this respect. As "pioneer and perfecter of faith," he differs from us in that our relationship to God is mediated through his; this marks a structural and essential difference between his trust and ours. There is a mysterious lack of mediation in Jesus' relationship to Abba as compared with our relationship to God the Father. No Moses or "Christ figure" is a necessary or adequate mediator between Jesus and God the Father. By contrast, our faith-relationship to God is thoroughly structured and shaped by the mediation of Jesus Christ in the power of the Holy Spirit. Talk of Jesus as a person of faith must always keep this difference regarding mediation in view.

The Virginal Conception of Jesus

From the second until the eighteenth century, Christianity was unanimous in its conviction that Jesus was conceived virginally, that is, without the involvement of a human father. The infancy narratives in Matthew and Luke were taken to teach this doctrine as divine revelation.

In modern times many objections to the doctrine of the virginal conception have been advanced. Some critics have asserted that such a teaching amounts to the application of familiar religious views from the surrounding cultures to Jesus' mode of birth. After all, in antiquity many extraordinary persons were considered to be virginally conceived; their provenance was thereby divine, not merely human.[28] A more contemporary objection is that being human involves not just "having all the ingredients," but being genetically connected to the prehistory of the human race. This is something that the New Testament writers could not have been aware of. Without this genetic connection, Jesus of Nazareth would not be "like us in all things but sin." Furthermore, we know that genetically the Y chromosome that made Jesus a man did not come from Mary. Thus an additional wonder is called for beyond what Matthew and Luke had in mind: God had to supply the male chromosome. Others have objected that the divine doctrine of virginal conception devalues sex and sexual intercourse, as if it would be demeaning for Jesus to have come into this world through the sexual love of a man and woman. Finally, there are those who object to the doctrine because it belongs to the realm of the miraculous and of divine interventions in history, which they reject as impossible or as a threat to the integrity of creation and human history.

Several points need to be made here. First, there is a difference between the narration of the conception and birth of Jesus and that of other figures

---

28. For examples, see R. E. Brown, "The Problem of the Virginal Conception of Jesus," *The Virginal Conception and the Bodily Resurrection of Jesus* (New York and Ramsey: Paulist, 1973) 62–65.

in antiquity. The transcendence of God is maintained in the gospel narratives; there is no question of a "divine marriage," i.e., of Jesus' being conceived through a physical relationship between Mary and God. Second, the identity of Jesus Christ does not depend on a virginal conception. In other words, belief in the divinity of Jesus does not necessarily entail belief in his virginal conception. Third, historians will never be able to show, according to their methods, that there was no human father involved in the conception of Jesus. Indeed, there does not seem to be sufficient historical evidence to determine whether the Jewish charge that Jesus was illegitimate preceded or followed the development of the Christian tradition of Jesus' virginal conception.[29] Fourth, one must decide whether Matthew and Luke are offering a *theologoumenon*, a theological interpretation of the meaning of Jesus' identity and mission, or a fact about Jesus' historical origins.[30] Within the Catholic Church the problem has been explored by both exegetes and theologians, each recognizing that there is involved as well a question of the Church's teaching office, since Jesus' virginal conception has been taught by the Church down through the centuries and would appear to be a doctrine of the universal ordinary magisterium. The issue then becomes the broader, more fundamental one of the reformability or irreformability of the teaching of the ordinary magisterium.

Recently a Catholic scholar, Jane Schaberg, has argued that careful study of the Matthean and Lukan texts leaves open the possibility that Jesus was illegitimate. If this were so (and the author admits that, strictly speaking, it cannot be demonstrated), then Jesus' identification with the marginal and outcast would be even more dramatically actualized than had previously been thought: Jesus would be one with all those whom society has despised for not being "legitimate." Reviewers have judged her position to be hypothetical and speculative.[31]

One thing such a suggestion achieves is to raise once again the question whether Jesus Christ can do justice to every human concern. In this instance, the concern is with the inclusion of the excluded, specifically all illegitimate children down through history. Is Christ willing to identify with them in the historical ambiguity of the circumstances of his birth, an ambiguity that faith sees through (just as it does the charge that Jesus was a drunkard and glutton and sinful friend of sinners)? In defending the Church's belief in the virginal conception of Jesus, we must do so in

29. R. E. Brown, *The Birth of the Messiah: A Commentary on the Infancy Narratives in Matthew and Luke* (Garden City, New York: Doubleday, 1977) 542.

30. J. A. Fitzmyer, "The Virginal Conception of Jesus in the New Testament," *To Advance the Gospel: New Testament Studies* (New York: Crossroad, 1981) 41–78.

31. J. Schaberg, *The Illegitimacy of Jesus: A Feminist Theological Interpretation of the Infancy Narratives* (San Francisco: Harper and Row, 1987).

a way that offers hospitality to all who were ambiguously and illegitimately conceived. Jesus is ready to receive all names and titles, not because all are literally true, but because he has room for them in his compassionate person and can define their saving meaning out of the abundance of his presence as the Risen One.

A major point being made by the doctrine of the virginal conception is that Jesus' origins are not only human but divine. His emergence in history involves human initiative and freedom, a truth vividly expressed in Luke's annunciation scene (1:34-35), and "behind" that God's initiative for the sake of the world's salvation (expressed in Luke 1:30-31). If human beings are to be freed from all that oppresses them and if that liberation is to be one which lasts, its ultimate agent must be God, no one less. The virginal conception of Jesus gives expression to the transcendent origin of the Liberator and Savior of human history in the God who is infinitely free for us.

The Saving Work of Jesus Christ

The humanity of Jesus in the sense not only of his integral constitution as a human being (what the tradition has called "complete human nature") but also of his human openness to the incomprehensible God and to all that is human, is the real symbol in and through which the divine Word's openness to God-Abba and to human history have become present and effective within history.[32] The life, ministry, and death of Jesus, consummated in his exaltation/resurrection, were the incarnation, in a unique and definitive way, of God's saving purposes for all creation. Through the particular and individual, God did something that brought to a climax what God had been doing from the beginning of history: communicating God's self to and in history in a process that itself was a history. The Christ-event, considered as the foundational event of the Church in history, was a beginning as well as a climax. Since the outpouring of the Spirit and the emergence of the Church, there has been a divinely originated witness to Christ's eschatological victory over the power of sin and a divinely originated continuation of Christ's saving presence in history.

We have seen how Jesus' ministry, as well as his death and resurrection, need to be appreciated for the saving moments that they were. Jesus' person was about salvation, and the salvation God was and is effecting through Jesus has translated into the work of Jesus Christ in the power and breadth of the Spirit. It is time now to consider somewhat more extensively the saving work of Christ or, in other words, Christology as soteriology. As this historical review will show, there have been tendencies in

---

32. Rahner, "The Eternal Significance," 35-46.

the past to separate the person from the saving work of Christ. In contemporary theology there is a healthy effort afoot to reunite them.

Patristic Theologies of Redemption

Irenaeus of Lyons. The most "systematic" of early theologies was produced by Irenaeus, Bishop of Lyons, who though born in Asia Minor served the Church in the West both as Church leader and theologian. As we saw earlier, he wrote his *Contra Haereses* in opposition to the Gnostics and the Marcionites, against whom he argued forcefully and articulately for the unity of the Old and New Testaments, and for the identity of the creating God and the redeeming God. Irenaeus held that all of creation is good and sin is the distortion of that goodness. According to the divine plan, the good creation was meant to come to full stature, that is, to mature to the full dimensions intended by God. That plan was frustrated by the disobedience of Adam and Eve. But God's commitment to creation did not depend on how humans responded to divine commands. In continuing fidelity to creation, God sent Jesus Christ, Son of God, to enact a process that, as I noted earlier, Irenaeus called *anakephalaiosis*. The term crystallizes Irenaeus's soteriological thought, which involved several ideas. First, in Christ all the stages of human development—infancy, childhood, adolescence, and adulthood—and all the phases of salvation history are lived through ("recapitulated") in gracious obedience to God and in a reversal of Adam's sin. Irenaeus favored various antitheses in speaking about this reversal: Just as on a tree disobedience occurred, so too on the tree of the cross obedience flourished; just as through Eve's succumbing to the wiles of the devil sin entered the world, so too through Mary's yes to the divine invitation salvation came to dwell among us. Through this process there has occurred a restoration of creation to what God intended it to be. A second aspect of *anakephalaiosis* concerns the direction of history: All things are oriented upward toward (*ana*) Christ, in an ascent from the less to the more mature and developed. A third dimension is that all things are meant to be summed up in Christ, brought to a head (*kephalē*) and given final meaning in him as their saving goal.

According to this soteriology, the human reality of Christ is intrinsically important as a contributor to our salvation; it is not, as in some other patristic views, simply an instrument of the Logos, who is then regarded as the only truly saving principle. That Jesus Christ is the salvation of the world through all that he was, is, and will be is a basic element of the good news, which does not receive its due whenever Christians take our destiny to be God alone, exclusive of the human, rather than God eternally wanting to be God among and with us, so that in finding God we also find each other.

Divinization, Paideia, *and the Redemptive Assumption of Human Nature.*
It was Irenaeus who first expressed the most basic understanding of the
purpose of the incarnation of the divine Word: "God became human that
we humans might become God."[33] This motif of "divinization" (*theopoi-
ôsis*) was repeated in the fourth and fifth centuries by theologians such
as Athanasius and the two Cappadocian Gregories, and became a hall-
mark of Eastern theology, Orthodox and Uniate, during all subsequent
epochs. God shared our nature in the incarnation of the Word, that
through the bestowal of the Holy Spirit we might become unique par-
ticipants in the divine nature. For the Fathers, particularly the Greek
Fathers, God's ultimate design on our behalf is that we become totally
united with God, sharing the divine life, light, and love. No goal less than
union with God can fulfill human beings, because they were created in
God's image and likeness to be fully possessed by God and in that possession to achieve the fullness of beatitude. An important New Testament
text in this regard is found at 2 Peter 1:4: "that through these [promises]
you may escape from the corruption that is in the world because of passion, and become partakers of the divine nature."

From this perspective sin, whether original or personal, does not stand
as the primary point of reference for the understanding of salvation; God's
mysterion, or saving plan for humankind, as positive divinization by divine (i.e., uncreated) grace has pride of place. To be sure, salvation involves our sinfulness and the power of sin at work in the world, but these
cannot "frame" the dimensions of the gift God wants to give us, which
is God's own life in divine self-communication.

The Fathers, following Scripture, use a number of images to express
what Christ has done for us in relation to sin. His action is compared to
medical healing, to priestly sacrifice (where he is both offerer and victim), to illumination of the blind, to being clothed by another (immortal
life put on the corruptible body), to conquest (over the demons who hold
humans in thrall), and to payment of a ransom (to redeem, meaning "to
buy back" those held hostage by sin and the devil). This last image has
been dominant, certainly in the West, for the whole theology of "salvation" (which itself is the notion of "being made safe"). But redemption,
healing, and so forth are all images and analogies drawn from human experience, which have their limits as well as their strengths.

A striking example of the limits of these images is provided by the notion of ransom, which we considered earlier. One of the favorite theories
of our salvation, for the Fathers, was the idea of Christ as the ransom
emancipating human beings from the hostage-hold that the devil had on
them. Origen said that God paid the ransom (Christ) into the Devil's hands
but the Devil found he could not control it and was overpowered by God's

---

33. *Adv. Haer.* V, Preface, *PG* 7, col. 1120.

deceit. Gregory of Nazianzus, on the other hand, argued that overdevelopment of the implications of the ransom image would lead to absurdity. If we say that the ransom was paid to the Devil, this means that the divine life was given over to him. If we decide instead that the ransom was paid to the Father, this too is ridiculous, because the Father is the one who initiated the entire process of liberation.[34] Thus the point conveyed by the image must not be erroneously expanded by developing the narrative implied by the image, otherwise we miss the point altogether.

We need to remember that the debate about the divine *homoousia* of Jesus Christ was a debate about our present and future welfare as human beings. The concern was thoroughly soteriological: we are made for God, each of us in an absolutely unique way and all of us together as sharers in our common humanity. But the second *homoousia*, that Christ is completely human and like us in all things but sin is equally soteriological. "What was not assumed by Christ was not healed because it was not united to God." Gregory of Nazianzus would have interpreted this maxim to which I referred earlier in terms of a Platonic theory of universals which we find strange. Contemporary theologians would anchor Christ's universal inclusion of all humanity in his presence through the Spirit as the Risen One, but the point made remains true for Christians: in assuming human nature Christ assumed the whole of it and in taking to himself all that is concretely human (as good creation and sinfulness) through his ministry, death and resurrection, he saved it. Christ assumed fallen human nature and thus healed it.

The patristic tradition taught that the communication of divine life to Christians, made possible by the incarnation of the Word and the outpouring of the Spirit at Pentecost, was effectively mediated through the Church to them by the sacraments of initiation (baptism, confirmation, and Eucharist). These sacraments set Christians on a path of transformation from darkness to light, from corruption to immortal life, from thralldom to the evil powers of this world to authentic freedom, and from hatred of virtue to love of the good. The transformation envisioned is a Christian version of the Greek ideal of *paideia*, a pattern of education and upbringing that fashioned people in the image of the good through participation (*methexis*) in it. According to the *paideia Christoû*, he who is the image of the invisible God reveals the divine nature to those adopted in the Holy Spirit as sons and daughters belonging to the household of God, and that Spirit renders them more and more persons in the image of Christ.[35]

34. Origen, *Comm. in Math*, 16, 8; Gregory of Nazianzus, *Or.*, 45, 22.

35. See H. Rondet, *The Grace of Christ: A Brief History of the Theology of Grace*, trans. T. W. Guzie (New York: Paulist, 1967) ch. 5.

Sin is conceived not principally in moral terms as the fruit of individual choices, but rather as a condition of enslavement to an evil force or power leading those imprisoned into bodily and spiritual death. The only life that is stronger than the power of sin and death is divine grace, the divine nature, which not only can transform the corruptible into the incorruptible but also can unite human beings to divine nature, in which consists human fulfillment.

As Athanasius expresses it:

> [Christ], although powerful and the creator of the universe, fashioned for himself in the virgin a body as a temple, and appropriated it for his own as an instrument in which to be known and dwell. And thus taking a body like ours, since all were liable to the corruption of death, and surrendering it to death on behalf of all, he offered it to the Father. And this he did in his loving kindness in order that, as all die in him, the law concerning corruption in men might be abolished—since its power was concluded in the Lord's body and it would never again have influence over men who are like him—and in order that, as men had turned to corruption, he might turn them back again to incorruption and might give them life for death, in that he had made the body his own, and by the grace of the resurrection had rid them of death as straw is destroyed by fire.[36]

The type of soteriology formulated by the Fathers of the Church, again particularly in the East, has been called "natural" or "physical," in the sense that the focus falls on the divine nature communicated in Christ and on the Spirit transforming our human nature. This type has been contrasted to the more "juridical," ethical model, which was favored in the West and came to classic expression in the theory of Anselm of Canterbury (see below). Among the primary positive features of the patristic understanding of salvation are the importance given to the communication of divine life: the complementary, distinct but inseparable roles of Christ and the Holy Spirit; the balance between the sacrifice on the cross and the resurrection as both essential dimensions of God's saving act in Christ; the liberation wrought by Christ recognized as victory over death and emancipation of humans from the power of the demonic; and the restoration of all creation in a way that exceeds the "first creation."[37]

Among the Fathers, salvation is not separated off as a distinct treatise in theology but is integrated into theology in the strict sense, i.e., Trinitarian theology.

36. *De Incarn. Verbi* 8, in Athanasius, *Contra Gentes and De Incarnatione*, ed. and trans. R. W. Thomson (Oxford: Clarendon, 1971) 153.

37. See V. Lossky, *In the Image and Likeness of God*, trans. A. M. Allchin (Crestwood, New York: St. Vladimir, 1974) 102.

Medieval Theologies of Redemption

Anselm of Canterbury. The most famous single medieval theory of redemption was developed by Anselm of Canterbury (d. 1109). His book *Cur Deus Homo?* offered the first separate treatise dedicated to exploring the meaning of redemption with all the limits of an approach which is divorced from the rest of Christology. His views, which greatly influenced many succeeding soteriologies, have been the object of much criticism in modern times for being unbiblical and excessively juridical in their conception. Over the past ten or fifteen years, though, a number of theologians have reappraised Anselm's theory and found that his primary notions do have biblical roots. While recognizing the limitations of his theory, they have even compared it favorably to the structural concerns of liberation theology.[38]

Anselm seeks the "necessary reasons" for what Scripture has revealed to us about the will of God regarding our salvation. These "necessary reasons" are not a priori ideas, but the inner intelligibility of what God has done in Christ insofar as theology (faith seeking understanding) can discover it. As a product of the monastic theological tradition, Anselm was convinced that prayerful contemplation of, and absorption in, God's revealed truth could lead to true knowledge of its meaning with the aid of all the resources of human reason. He realized that theology must use analogies, recognizing that they are imperfect, and must fall short of directly describing the ineffable God. In the rhetorical tradition in which he stood, "necessary reasons" meant reasons that are founded on truth and capable of providing certitude. He believed that necessary reasons could be found, not for the object of faith but for how the object of faith exists.[39] For example, it is a fact for believers that the Son of God died on the cross for sinners. Theology needs to ask why it was necessary for redemption to occur this way, given two other facts for believers: that God freely chose to redeem us, and that God's infinite wisdom was involved in the choice of the means by which we were redeemed.

Anselm reminds the reader that the offense of sin should be measured by the stature, or honor, of the one offended. In this case, the infinite God is the one offended. Thus the offense is infinite. How can an infinite offense against God's infinite honor be made right? It is axiomatic for Anselm that, as in the case of any other offense, to right the wrong relationship between sinner and God, either punishment must be undergone or satisfaction made. In this case satisfaction and not punishment is what

---

38. G. Greshake, "Erlösung und Freiheit: Eine Neuinterpretation der Erlösungslehre Anselms von Canterbury" in *Gottes Heil—Glück des Menschen: Theologische Perspektiven* (Freiburg: Herder, 1983) 80–104; W. Kasper, *Jesus the Christ*, 219–21.

39. See Anselm, *Why God Became Man*, trans. J. M. Colleran (Albany: Magi Books, 1969) introduction, 37–42.

God decided on (a point ignored by many later theologians in their own theories of atonement).

Before proceeding further, we should note that Anselm makes a distinction in his theology between God's honor as it exists in itself (*honor Dei quantum in ipso*) and the honor of God insofar as it exists outside God, the latter referring to God's honor reflected in the integrity of creation as God intended it to be. Anselm explicitly says that God's honor as it exists in itself cannot be harmed or offended; rather, all the harm done by sin terminates in creation, injuring its rightful order and wholeness.[40] Thus Anselm never paints the portrait of a wrathful God whose personal honor has been injured and who therefore demands retributive justice to appease the divine anger.

These two ideas, the infinity of the object of offense and the fact that the offense harms only the fabric of creation, are not completely united in the development of his theory. Nevertheless, a moral agent is needed to repair the damage done by sin, and that moral agent must be both infinite, as God is infinite, and human, because it is human beings who have sinned. Thus Jesus Christ, one person who is completely divine and completely human, is the appropriate moral agent to repair the harm done by sin.

But why did Christ *have to* (in the sense of a "necessary reason" and with an allusion to the New Testament *dei*, "it is necessary") die on the cross in order to save us? Could not any act of the divine-human one have saved us? Anselm responds by saying that Christ had to do something that went beyond what he owed God, for only such a supererogatory act could serve as true satisfaction, and only in this way would there be an abundance of merit in which others could share. Now insofar as he was human, Christ owed God obedience, trust, love, service, and so forth. The one thing that Christ did not owe God, the one thing that he could do as a completely free, supererogatory act was to die. While all other human beings had to die because they shared in Adam and Eve's sin, Christ was the sinless one and thus did not have to die. Dying out of love for God and for human beings would be a free and gracious act that was not called for by the nature of who Christ was (not unlike the message of the hymn in 2 Philippians). But not only was it a free and gracious act as the death of the sinless human being, it was also an infinite act because it was the death of the Son of God incarnate. Thus Christ's death was capable of repairing the damage done by sin, which was an act that brought death into the world and harmed incalculably the fabric of God's "external honor," i.e., God's good creation.

For Anselm, at the heart of the mystery of Christ's death on the cross, two divine values are at work. The first is divine mercy. God chose out

40. Anselm, *Why God Became Man*, I, 15 (Colleran edition, 90-91).

of love to redeem the human race; God chose to reconcile the world to God's self. Anselm is perfectly faithful to the New Testament in affirming that creation has been estranged from God by sin, and in not suggesting that God has been estranged from creation. God does not need to be reconciled to us; we need to be reconciled to God. The second divine value revealed in redemption is justice, or righteousness. God's truth demands that God take the divine reality, the nature of creation, and the essence of sin into full account and do justice to all three, not overlooking any of them. This means that God does not want creation, specifically the human race, to be simply the *object* of divine compassion and forgiveness but rather an active *participant* in the redemption process. Thus God respects the very freedom by which humankind turned against the divine life. God does justice to who God is, and to who God primordially wants human beings to be, by having redemption occur both by God and by humankind in the person of Jesus Christ. Both God and humankind, in Christ, "do enough" (*satisfactio*) to bring about the redemption of the human race in the sense of making the offer of redemption fully "done." Finally, because sin is essentially destructive and lethal, the process of reconciliation must do justice to (i.e., take into full account) suffering, death, and mortal threat to the human, but in a way that accomplishes the salvation of the human.

Therefore, the famous "satisfaction" theory of Anselm has nothing to do with satisfying a grievance in the Godhead by means of a bloody sacrifice that will finally appease the wrathful deity. On the contrary, it has everything to do with giving full scope to God and to humankind in the process of salvation. God is the initiator and the one who provides the "means" of redemption, but human freedom and graciousness are integral to those "means" because Christ dies freely and lovingly for our sakes and for the sake of God's desire to heal the division between the divine and the human. What is repaired, what is "satisfied," is God's good creation, which has been profoundly wounded by sin and is now decisively on the way to recovery.

The above summary of Anselm's satisfaction theology is the most favorable that a reading of the texts will allow. It shows that there are important biblical, particularly Pauline, motifs operative in his thinking. The priority of divine initiative in the reconcilation of creation to God (1 Cor 5:18); the free obedience of Christ, who did not have to die but freely did so (Phil 2); the decisive beginning of the restoration of creation in view of the damage wrought by sin to it (Rom 8:19-23): all these themes find important echoes in Anselm.

However, we cannot ignore the limitations of his theory. The primary analogue for Anselm's theology of redemption lies in the social bonds that link the people of his society and in the civil law that protects them, with the latter's concern for liability, compensation, satisfaction, honor, and payment. Thus a controlling image of *Cur Deus Homo?* is that of a feudal structure in which God is the lord and his creatures are the vassals. Just as harm done to the tight social fabric of feudal life affects the honor of the lord (not only his personal honor but the structural honor of the society as an integrated whole assuring its members place and meaning), so too with God and sin. Just as an act of reparation must do not only what is commanded but also something in excess of that to make things right, so it stands with what Christ did on behalf of sinners. One notion running through Anselm's theology is that of representation, the conviction that one can act representatively for others. In our own individualistic culture, such a relationship is hard to imagine, and it certainly cannot simply be a presumption of a present-day soteriological theory.

Anselm is deliberately employing analogous language when he compares God and creation to lord and vassals, the latter being debtors and God being the one to whom the debt must be paid. But the more important limitations of his theory have to do with the dimensions of the biblical witness to the redemption, which he fails to take into sufficient account. The foremost instance of this is the almost exclusive role he attributes to Christ's death. And even so he does not account for its violent character; he reflects only about Christ's death as an act or fate not required of the sinless one. The ministry of Christ on the one hand, and the resurrection on the other, receive inadequate attention; indeed, the ministry receives hardly any at all. The resurrection happens to Christ as a reward for the supererogatory act of dying rather than as an intrinsic part of the redemptive event. Other deficiencies can be mentioned as well. The role of the Holy Spirit as the divine mediating agent linking the Savior and the saved, and opening sinners to Christ's offer of salvation, does not enter the picture. The eschatological perspective of redemption, so important to the New Testament, does not receive its due, and the ecclesiological and sacramental moments in the New Testament are scarcely touched on.

We must conclude, therefore, that Anselm has produced a profound but narrow theological reflection on the mystery of redemption. In its key dimensions it shows fidelity to New Testament concerns, but it is too limited to do justice to the full range of truth expressed in the New Testament witness to our redemption. One of the consequences of Anselm's being the first theologian to devote a separate study to the redemption was that he initiated what would turn out to be a most unfortunate separation between Christology and the theology of redemption, a separation which many late-twentieth-century theologians have sought to overcome. Moreover, he began a line of thinking which reappeared during the Reformation in which Christ's sacrifice, his self-offering on the cross, is conceptualized in juridical terms as a form of legal restitution rather than in New Testament terms as a cultic sacrifice. The latter conceptualization, though also limited, relates more primordially to cosmic and personal dimensions of human life and less to the impersonal domains of legal system and law court.[41]

Peter Abelard. The twelfth-century philosopher and theologian Peter Abelard (d. 1142) adopted a very different approach from Anselm's. He was mainly concerned to accentuate the profound appeal that Christ's passion and death make to the affections of the human heart. He taught that God did for human beings what they could not do for themselves, namely, lift them out of their sinful predicament. Christ's saving influence on sinners was his supreme example of self-sacrificing love, in which they could experience an invitation and empowerment to conversion of heart that would issue in sound ethical living. It would be wrong, however, to reduce Abelard's theology to this single theological dimension. Abelard did not shy away from using the familiar terms of satisfaction, vicarious suffering, and so forth, but they were always in danger of turning into religious abstractions. As he wrote, "I think . . . that the purpose and cause of the incarnation was that He might illuminate the world by His wisdom and excite it to love of Himself."[42] F. W. Dillistone offers a helpful insight regarding this theologian of the medieval Augustinian school:

> The place of Abelard in atonement theology has been repeatedly discussed, and he is normally distinguished as the arch-exponent of what is called the subjective theory. But such a categorization tends to be confusing and unhelpful. In reality Abelard marks the transition from an outlook which saw God dealing with humanity *as a whole*, either through a legal transaction or through a mystical transfusion, to one in which the ethical and psychological qualities of *the individual within the community* began to receive fuller recognition.[43]

Thomas Aquinas. The Christology and soteriology of Thomas Aquinas (d. 1274) are in some respects united and in others separate. The basic structure of the *Summa Theologiae* expresses, in a way already traditional before Thomas, the fundamental structure of reality and the movement of all creation in relation to God: an *exitus a Deo*, or movement away from God (who is the first reality to be considered in the *Summa*), and

---

41. F. W. Dillistone, *The Christian Understanding of Atonement*, traces many of the connections between redemption-theories and culture.

42. Quoted in Dillistone, *Christian Understanding*, 325. Recently an important effort has been made to defend Abelard against the classic objections that he is Pelagian (i.e., the view that God's grace is not strictly necessary for salvation) and excessively exemplarist (i.e., the position that Christ is a model for us) in his soteriology. See R. E. Weingart, *The Logic of Divine Love: A Critical Analysis of the Soteriology of Peter Abelard* (London: Clarendon, 1970).

43. Dillistone, *The Christian Understanding*, 325.

a *reditus ad Deum*, or return to God in salvation. The *Tertia Pars* of the *Summa*, which the author did not live to complete, deals with the return of creation to God in and with Jesus Christ, the focus being mainly on Christ. After treating the incarnate Word, the grace of Christ, and the one mediator, he moves to the "mysteries" of Christ's life: his childhood, life, passion, and resurrection. Then he addresses questions dealing with the sacramental life of the Church and specifically with the sacrament of penance.

Regarding soteriology, Aquinas modifies Anselm's language about necessary reasons and prefers to say that Christ's saving of us by his passion was consonant (*conveniens*) with God's mercy and justice, but not necessitated by God's nature or any external force. The only kind of necessity that he admits is a necessity of end, i.e., if God freely chose to save us, then Christ's passion must have been for our sakes, for Christ's sake (i.e., for his exaltation), and for God's sake, for the fulfillment of all the things written of Christ in the Law and the Prophets.[44] When he turns to the question of the efficacy of Christ's passion, Aquinas seeks to demonstrate that it brought about our salvation by way of merit, satisfaction, sacrifice, and redemption. The type of causality involved was efficient causality. Then he analyzes the effects of the passion in terms of freedom from sin, liberation from the power of the Evil One, release from the debt of punishment, reconciliation to God, the opening of heaven's gate to us, and the exaltation of Christ. Finally, he considers the death of Jesus as a process of dying (during which Christ could merit) and as something distinct from the passion, referring to the separation of Christ's soul from his body, when no merit was possible.

Let us consider for a moment the basic notions in Aquinas' theology of Christ's passion. When he says that the passion saved us by way of merit, he designates a reward that has been earned and is therefore owed in justice to an individual. For Thomas, merit in the order of grace (which is what he is dealing with here) means merit as the fruit of cooperative grace, the performance by humans of free acts that are both completely dependent on grace and issuing entirely from the human freedom of the individual. Thus merit in the order of grace is grace crowning the grace that had previously brought about a free act in the order of salvation. There is no question of a human will on its own doing something that then puts a claim on God to deliver a reward, as Luther later took scholastic theology to be saying. Our salvation was merited by Christ, whose undergoing of the passion was, as a human "deed," thoroughly graced and completely free. But a second idea comes in here as well. Christ merited not only for himself (the glorification which was the resurrection) but as head of the Church; God all along intended Christ to be grace for others. Thus all who are members of Christ share in his merit, in the fruit (or reward) of his cooperative grace as head of the Church (*gratia capitis*: "grace of Christ's headship").

When Aquinas describes Christ's passion as satisfaction, he is, of course, taking up a favorite theme of Anselm:

> A man effectively atones for an offence when he offers to the one who has been offended something which he accepts as matching or outweighing the former offence. Christ, in his loving and obedient spirit, offered more to God than was demanded in recompense for all the sins of mankind, because first, the love which led him to suffer was all-embracing and his pain so great, as has been said above. Christ's passion, then, was not only sufficient but superabundant atonement for the sins of mankind. . . .[45]

Aquinas defines sacrifice in general terms to mean what people offer to God as a sign of the honor owed to God in order to please God. While Christ's passion was a crime on the part of those who caused it, on Christ's part it was the sacrifice that saved us. Because it was human, able to suffer, sinless, and belonged to the offerer who loved so tremendously, the flesh (*caro*) of Christ was a most efficacious sacrifice.[46]

The description of Christ's passion as redemptive involved several ideas for Aquinas. Sinners stand under obligation to the Devil and to God, to the Devil because they were bound in slavery to sin, to God because according to divine justice human beings were held to the debt of punishment. Since Christ offered the greatest satisfaction, namely his very self, we have been redeemed from both obligations. Aquinas then goes on to say that Christ in his humanity is the immediate redeemer because he was both the payment and the price paid for our ransom, and the whole Trinity is the ultimate redeemer because it was the Trinity that inspired the human Christ to suffer for us.

Regarding causality, Aquinas describes Christ's passion as the instrumental, efficient cause of our redemption because it is rooted in his humanity, which exercises that same causality on our behalf. The divinity is the principal efficient cause that brings about the effect of our salvation. When Aquinas turns to Christ's death, he asks whether it contributed to our salvation and, as mentioned above, distinguishes between Christ's dying, which is the same as his passion, and his being dead. Although as a deceased individual Christ no longer caused our salvation by way of

44. *Summa Theologiae*, 3a. 46, 1 (Blackfriars ed. vol. 54, trans. R. T. A. Murphy [New York: McGraw-Hill, 1965] 5–6).

45. Ibid., 3a, 48, 2 (Blackfriars ed., vol. 54, 79).

46. Ibid., 3a, 48, 2 (Blackfriars ed., vol. 54, 80–83).

merit, he continued to do so by instrumental causality as result of the union of his human nature with the divine nature.[47]

Aquinas's treatment of salvation does not focus narrowly on Christ's passion; he also gives considerable attention to Jesus' birth and public life. But the New Testament accent on Jesus' preaching, healing, and confrontation with the powers that be as activities anticipating and expressing the eschatological event of God's reign within an apocalyptic horizon of understanding is replaced by an incarnational Christology according to which Christ, in his baptism by John, his manner of life, his temptation, teaching, and miracles is the eternal Son of God living and acting through the instrumentality of his created human nature. In his discussion of Christ's exaltation, Aquinas asks whether Christ's resurrection and ascension are the cause of our salvation. These two events of Christ's exaltation, he responds, are strictly speaking the efficient and exemplary causes of our resurrection, not the meritorious cause. The principal efficient cause of our resurrection and of the salutary effects of Christ's ascension are the life-giving power of the divinity; Christ's humanity is the instrumental efficient cause because it is joined to the divinity.[48]

Aquinas's treatment of redemption, though not original, is a very balanced and tempered synthesis of many key contributions from biblical and patristic soteriology. Like Anselm's, Aquinas's approach has been called a theology of objective redemption, meaning that the emphasis falls on what God has done in Christ for sinners and on the offer of salvation that Christ's saving action constitutes for sinful humanity.

The Nominalists. In early and late Scholasticism, a movement both philosophical and theological developed that goes under the general name of nominalism. A principal representative of this mode of thinking was the Englishman William of Ockham (d. 1347). He denied the existence of universals (Platonism) and the objectivity of mental universals (critical realism). In theology, he rooted the existence of creatures and their natures and order exclusively in the divine will, fearing that the traditional rooting of them in the divine mind was a restriction of divine freedom. He distinguished between God's absolute will (*potentia absoluta*) and ordered will (*potentia ordinata*). In light of the former, all actual beings exist by virtue of pure contingency, one might almost say, arbitrarily. From the perspective of the latter, the actual order of things both natural and supernatural is necessary only to the extent that God's will is in fact willing them. Thus the actual moral order is rooted not in divine law as an aspect of God's nature, but in the totally free divine will. Redemption,

47. Ibid., 3a, 50, 6 (Blackfriars ed., vol. 54, 135).

48. Ibid., 3a q. 56, a. 1 and q. 57, a. 6 (Blackfriars ed., vol. 55, trans. C. T. Moore [New York: McGraw-Hill, 1976] 71, 97.)

therefore, is not the expression of an intrinsic order or suitability rooted in God's nature, but an event that happened the way it did because God, out of the divine transcendence, simply chose to do it this way: Christ's merits were imputed to sinners by a totally free (read: "disconnected") divine act. For the nominalists, it was attributing far too much ability to the human mind to seek intrinsic intelligibility in the suffering and death of Christ as the way of salvation.[49]

The Reformation and Soteriology

Martin Luther's (d. 1546) view of Christ's saving work on our behalf rests on his interpretation of the heart of the gospel. The only reliable way for us to come to saving knowledge of God is through the *theologia crucis* (theology of the Cross) rather than the *theologia gloriae* (theology of glory). The latter focuses on God as known by human reason from the beauty and goodness of creation. Such an approach misleads us into thinking that salvation comes about through the purported strength of our creatureliness. All of this is disastrous illusion, according to Luther. The *theologia crucis* reveals the truth about God and the truth about ourselves in the only reliable way. We are sinners, all of us; in and of ourselves we are always sinners as long as we are pilgrims here on earth. Everything we do or say or pray, insofar as we act on our own, is sinful. All our justice, all our goodness, all our good standing in God's eyes, all our salutary actions are Christ's imputed to us by God in such wise that we are made a new creation by them, but they never become our possession, something we can use or manipulate; they are constantly sent to us by the one who is other than ourselves, God's Christ. The assurance of justification, of being in a rightful relationship with God, fills us only to the degree that we own our constant sinfulness and throw ourselves on the mercy of God in Christ.

On the cross Christ lived out the abandonment by God that properly belongs to us sinners. The cry of dereliction, "My God, my God, why hast thou forsaken me?" (Mark 15:34) expresses the enormous, indeed inconceivable, distance between the Father and Jesus at that moment, as Jesus freely endured the experience of the chasm yawning between God's holiness and sinners' criminality. God's reality was revealed on the cross through its opposites: God's grandeur through Christ's misery, God's omnipotence through Christ's extreme vulnerablity, God's immortal life through Christ's agony unto death. This knowledge of God by way of the Cross is the only knowledge (*logos*) we sinners can rely on, because

49. H. A. Oberman, *The Harvest of Medieval Theology* (Cambridge, Mass: Harvard University Press, 1963).

it brings us back again and again to our real selves as absolutely in need of Christ's grace if we are to come to salvation.

John Calvin (d. 1564) was the initiator of the Reformed tradition of Protestantism, as distinguished from what the Germans call the Evangelical (*evangelisch*), or Lutheran, tradition (itself not to be confused with the movement of evangelicalism, which runs through a number of Protestant and Anglo-Catholic Churches in countries such as the United States). He taught that the full truth of Scripture must always be the core and norm of Christianity. He was well versed in the Fathers, especially the writing of Augustine. In addition, he was profoundly legal in his understanding of reality, having immersed himself in the legal system of sixteenth-century France. Like the authors of other soteriological theories, Calvin sought an analogy for the (ruptured) relationship between God and humankind among human relations, and found his primary analogy in the forensic arena, that is, the public law court as the center of the entire system of law by which a society is regulated and its life preserved. Unlike Anselm, however, Calvin typecast the sinner not as a debtor in civil court but as a felon in criminal court. For Calvin, the death of Christ was to be interpreted in terms of penal substitution. The justice of God has been radically offended by the sins of the human race, and it is necessary that the punishment commensurate with the collective crime of humanity be carried out so that justice is done. For their sins, human beings deserve the punishment of hell or eternal death. Yet God's love for fallen humanity is such that God has supplied one who will bear the full brunt of that punishment in fidelity to God and in love for humankind, a love in which he is totally united with the Father. Thus Christ's passion and death are a most profound experience of God's punishment, God's curse, and God's wrath, which Christ undergoes in place of us as the divinely chosen substitute for sinners. This substitutionary suffering and death culminates in the glorious exaltation of Easter, and spells the inauguration of a wholly new relationship between God and those who are predestined for salvation.

The criminal-law dimension of Calvin's understanding of Christ's death becomes apparent in this excerpt from his *Institutes of the Christian Religion*:

> To take away our condemnation, it was not enough for him to suffer any kind of death: to make satisfaction for our redemption, a form of death had to be chosen in which he might free us both by transferring our condemnation to himself and by taking our guilt upon himself. If he had been murdered by thieves or slain in an insurrection by a raging mob, in such a death there would have been no evidence of satisfaction. But when he was arraigned before the judgement seat as a criminal, ac-

cused and pressed by testimony, and condemned by the mouth of the judge to die—we know by these proofs that he took the role of a guilty man and an evildoer.[50]

The difficulty with this theory, as F. W. Dillistone points out, is twofold: (1) Neither sixteenth-century French criminal law nor Calvin's preoccupation with punishment, curse, wrath, substitution, and crime do justice to the Old and New Testament understandings of divine law in relation to Christ's suffering and death; and (2) Calvin's understanding of the social connections among people and of the nature and function of law is bound to his own cultural situation, and is not appropriate for the twentieth century.[51] The merits of his theory are his assertion that an adequate soteriology must take into full account the nature of sin in relation to God's justice and holiness, and that the kind of suffering and death undergone by Christ is linked to the nature of sin and the process of redemption, however that is conceived.

Both Luther and Calvin lived at a time when the medieval synthesis was coming apart, and the traditional structures that had connected people with God and each other and had also "protected" people from the all-holy God were no longer successfully performing their mediating function. Both Reformers turned people to the preached Word as the only reliable place of meeting between them and God. Compared with that Word, ecclesiastical customs, doctrines, and devotions were false supports, indeed fatal distractions. The horrendous Black Death of the fourteenth century had profoundly shaken the conviction that the living and the dead were connected in a stable system of relations of exchange, a conviction that had received popular expression in the exaggerated role given to indulgences, the practice of accruing merit on behalf of the holy souls in purgatory.[52] While the practice continued in the sixteenth century, the Reformers recognized that the living occupied an infinitely more vulnerable position with regard to death than many others were willing to admit. Only direct exposure to God in all one's sinfulness, and full dependence on the saving work of Christ offered in the Word, could give one the holy assurance of being justified in the sight of God.

Compared to Luther, Calvin was by far the more systematic thinker, with Luther remaining ever the preacher in the way he wrote and taught. For example, Luther did not shy away from classical mystical language

50. J. Calvin, *Institutes of the Christian Religion*, trans. H. Beveridge (Grand Rapids, Mich.: Eerdmans, 1983) vol. 2, ch. 16, no. 5, 99–100.

51. Dillistone, *Christian Understanding*, 196–200.

52. J. Dunne, *A Search for God in Time and Memory* (Notre Dame, Ind.: University of Notre Dame Press, 1977), ch. 3.

about the bridegroom and the bride when speaking of the relationship between Christ and the soul.[53]

Calvin's understanding of Christ's saving action in terms of law, condemnation, and the reconciliation of the guilty was dominant in Reformed Christianity for the next several centuries:

> It was essentially a simple structure which corresponded to the general experience of mankind. For Europe the sixteenth, seventeenth and eighteenth centuries constituted a time of ferment, wars, revolutionary tendencies, the struggle of minority groups for recognition and toleration. The one safeguard against complete anarchy was the existence of a system of law which was above individual caprice or even minority plots.[54]

But there were reactions to the Calvinist synthesis as well. Before the sixteenth century had passed, two Italians, Lelio Sozini (d. 1662; Socinus in Latin) and his nephew Fausto (d. 1604), developed a rationalistic version of Christianity from which would develop Unitarianism.[55] Their theology denied the doctrines of the Trinity, the divinity of Christ, the expiatory nature of redemption, and the resurrection of the body. According to Socinianism, God grants forgiveness freely as pure divine initiative, without Christ's paying satisfaction or playing the role of mediator. God freely relinquishes the divine right to satisfaction and payment, and reveals the divine justice in the very exercise of divine mercy. The Socinian contention that one death in time cannot, in any case, satisfy the demand for eternal death (as punishment for sin) for "the many" runs directly counter to the New Testament teaching that one has indeed died for all, and that in Christ's death God was engaged in reconciling the world to the divine life.

As so often happens in history, Socinianism provoked an antithesis in the ideas of Hugo Grotius (d. 1645), the famous international jurist. Grotius viewed God as a head of state who is concerned with the overall good of society rather than the exact punishment of each and every crime. This divine "Rector" seeks to deter crime by punishing some criminals as examples to all. If someone were willing to be punished as such an example, all the better. This was the case with Jesus of Nazareth, who served as a universal example and deterrent. Law, according to this paradigm, is conceived less absolutely and in a more "republican" fashion than by Calvin.[56]

---

53. M. Luther, "The Freedom of a Christian," in J. Dillenberger, ed., *Martin Luther: A Selection from His Writings* (Garden City, New York: Doubleday Anchor, 1961) 60.

54. Dillistone, *Christian Understanding*, 203.

55. *Encyclopedic Dictionary of Religion*, s. v. "Socinianism."

56. Dillistone, *Christian Understanding*, 204–5.

It is already clear how close the correlation is between the theology of salvation developed in a particular era and the operative theories of human relations, particularly regarding the rupture of relationship and its restoration. Law plays a very important role here, though, as we shall see, other analogues will be found in the modern period that are less universal. In his fascinating study of soteriology, to which I have already frequently referred, F. W. Dillistone makes the striking point that, as human knowledge of the world increased, the focus of soteriology narrowed more and more. Thus in primitive times redemption was a universal and cosmic happening involving human beings and natural processes. Later, human society alone became the focus of soteriologies, as we grew to understand natural processes through science and societal processes through legal theory. The penultimate focus shifted to interpersonal relationships within the family or in friendship, and the final focus to the psyche of the individual.[57] This does not mean that there are no cosmic redemption theologies at the present time (Pierre Teilhard de Chardin [d. 1955] comes immediately to mind) but that the characteristically contemporary soteriology is personalistic, with all the advantages and limitations of such an approach.

The Modern Period

In the post-Enlightenment period, the notion that one person's suffering and death could effect the liberation of others living at different times and places became inconceivable for many. As the image of the human person became that of the free individual who subjects all ties of tradition and authority to the scrutiny of critical reason, the world view that had provided the backdrop for the classical soteriologies disappeared. Theologies such as Anselm's were caricatured as primitive theories of a wrathful God seeking appeasement of the divine anger through the atrocious suffering of a son, who acted as a scapegoat for others who really deserved punishment. Immanuel Kant (d. 1804) is representative here. For him, all notions of representative atonement were outmoded. Christ was a moral example of self-giving love who fulfilled the categorical imperative to the limit.[58]

G. W. F. Hegel (d. 1831) has been described as the philosopher whose consciousness suffered more from the unreconciled condition of reality and of human society than did any other philosopher before his time.[59]

57. Ibid., 6.

58. I. Kant, *Religion Within the Limits of Religion Alone*, trans. T. M. Greene and H. H. Hudson, 2nd ed. (La Salle, Ill.: Open Court, 1960) 107.

59. H. Küng, *The Incarnation of God: An Introduction to Hegel's Theological Thought as Prolegomena to a Future Christology*, 221.

He introduced the word "alienation" as a general category of existence, into our language. For Hegel, alienation was not a partial aspect of life having to do only with individual sinners who had failed to observe the moral law. Rather, alienation was a moment of the very life of God, and a necessary dimension of the process by which God and the world become fully actual in a differentiated unity. As we have seen, in the universal process by which God comes to be fully conscious and actual as Being-in-and-for-itself, the other is posited by God as the divine self-expression, and the otherness of this expression is then overcome in a process of reconciliation whereby God becomes all in all. The othering and the reconciling are moments in the one life of God, and they are moments of the world process, which by divine necessity moves through phases of thesis, antithesis, and synthesis during which Absolute Spirit posits the other, cancels the otherness of the other, and then preserves the reality in the other by raising it to a new level of being (the threefold *Aufhebung*). As Hans Küng has shown in detail, Christ as a historical figure has a role to play at various points on Hegel's philosophical journey, but in the last analysis he becomes a symbol for the process that must go on in the eternal life of God and in the world-historical process: the thesis ("Incarnation"), the negation of the thesis in its limits ("Cross"), and the preservation and elevation of what is of enduring value in the thesis ("Resurrection"). The Good Friday of our salvation becomes a speculative Good Friday, an eternal process in the life of Absolute Spirit. For all the problems raised by Hegel's interpretation of Christology, he has challenged Christianity to continue to reflect on God's involvement in history and its suffering as revealed in Christ's suffering and death.

Karl Marx (d. 1883) took Hegel's philosophy of universal reality and "turned it on its head." Marx saw redemption not as a divine gift but as the fruit of an emancipatory struggle in which the oppressed of this world overcome their fatalism and, under the leadership of the vanguard of the proletariat, align themselves with the tendency of history. This is dialectical materialism, involving a class struggle by which the state takes over the means of production in order to move closer to the final goal of a classless society. Thus Marx, a secularized Jew, transformed the Old Testament prophetic faith into a fully immanent process that is bound to succeed as long as the oppressed recognize the need for a class struggle to wrest power from those who have allowed them to become creatures only worth what they are able to produce. Here reconciliation means the return of human beings to their inherent dignity as agents for whom labor is no longer alienating, and as persons who have ceased to be mere commodities. This reconciliation is a costly one, however. The price to be paid for it is all the suffering that accompanies the unavoidable conflicts marking the journey to the new future and the new humanity.

While enormously influential, non-Christian, indeed anti-Christian, thinkers of the nineteenth century were relating reconciliation of a totally immanent sort to the basic laws that they thought governed nature and human history, many Christian theologians were turning their attention away from objective systems of law, punishment, and reconciliation and toward the subjective experience of Christ and the Christian.

The German theologian Friedrich Schleiermacher (d. 1834) developed a theology that was thoroughly anthropological in its orientation. At the heart of human life and activity lies what Schleiermacher called *Gefühl* or feeling, that is to say, an immediate self-consciousness. This immediate self-consciousness, which in its most concrete form is "lived out" rather than the object of our introspection, reveals to us that we are bound to the world in a relationship involving both dependence or receptivity and activity or initiative. The reciprocal relationship revealed by consciousness is not the whole story, however. Schleiermacher found an immediate self-consciousness of absolute dependence, of unalloyed receptivity pervading all of our awareness. This receptive and active conscious feeling of absolute dependence is part of who we are, and it is impossible for any worldly reality or even the totality of worldly realities to cause it. The reality that causes this receptive and active conscious existence we call "God." But human weakness and sin can estrange us from our God-consciousness and turn it into idolatry.

Just as Schleiermacher spoke about God in terms of God's effect on human consciousness, so he referred to Christ in terms of his effect on the consciousness of the Christian community. From the experience of the Church as a community of faith, love, and hope, Schleiermacher moved "back" to Christ as the one person in history whose consciousness of God was perfectly clear and true. All that Christ said and did and suffered expressed his living out his consciousness of God in total fidelity. Christ's redemptive activity consisted in his assumption of believers into the power of his God-consciousness by including them in the new collective life (*Gesamtleben*) of love and grace, which stands in opposition to the collective life of sin. God's single intent has been to raise humanity to a high level of God-consciousness in community, and Christ is the agent who has done this.

A primary representative of Protestant liberalism in the nineteenth century was Albrecht Ritschl (d. 1889), a very influential Lutheran theologian who owed much to Immanuel Kant's moral approach to religion as exemplified in *The Critique of Practical Reason*. In a large study devoted to justification and reconciliation, Ritschl eschewed the metaphysical Christology of Chalcedon and the penal theories of redemption in favor of a more ethical theory stressing the notion of divine vocation. Jesus' death on the cross was the outcome of his lifelong dedication to his God-given vocation. Ritschl preferred Abelard's approach to that of Anselm. He viewed justification as a divine act of removing the consciousness of guilt as well as the sin and punishment involved in that consciousness. It was not a divine forgetting of sin but rather an act causing sinners to believe that God was no longer to be distrusted, as God would be if the divine wrath were directed toward them. Thus sinners were moved to trust, which is the heart of reconciliation.[60]

Adolf von Harnack (d. 1930) was another nineteenth-century Protestant liberal who rejected the penal notions of redemption, taking particular aim at Anselm.[61]

The nineteenth-century Scottish theologian J. McLeod Campbell (d. 1872), turning to a theme dear to the Letter to the Hebrews, used the analogy of intercessory prayer to help his fellow Christians understand *how* Christ's suffering and death had effected our salvation. If one person takes the burden of another's sins onto his or her heart and then bears that burden into the gracious presence of God, that is the best he or she can do for the other. Christ did this to the uttermost:

> He who responds to the divine wrath against sin, saying "Thou art righteous, O Lord, who judgest so," is necessarily receiving the full apprehension and realization of that wrath, as well as of that sin against which it comes forth into his soul and spirit, into the bosom of the Divine humanity, and, so receiving it, He responds to it with a perfect response—a response from the depths of that divine humanity—and *in that perfect response He absorbs it*. For that response has all the elements of a perfect repentance in humanity for all the sin of man—a perfect sorrow—a perfect contrition—all the elements of such a repentance, and that in absolute perfection, all—excepting the personal consciousness of sin; that by that perfect response in Amen to the mind of God in relation to sin is the wrath of God rightly met, and that is accorded to divine justice which is its due, and could alone satisfy it.[62]

Campbell understands Christ's action as a dying full of contrition and repentance for sin, yet not involving a personal consciousness of sin. But the New Testament is consistent in its portrayal of Jesus as never contrite or repentant; he is sympathetic with sinners, to be sure, but that represents a wholly different stance and attitude.

The American idealist philosopher of religion Josiah Royce (d. 1916) developed a view of Christianity that was profoundly and pervasively so-

---

60. A. Ritschl, *The Christian Doctrine of Justification and Reconciliation*, trans. H. R. MacIntosch and A. B. Macauley (Edinburgh: T. and T. Clark, 1900); see J. Richmond, *Ritschl: A Reappraisal. A Study in Systematic Theology* (London and N.Y.: Collins, 1978).

61. *History of Dogma*, vol. 6, trans. N. Buchanan (Boston: Little, Brown, 1889) 54-83.

62. J. McLeod Campbell, *The Nature of the Atonement*, 4th ed. (1856; reprint, London: Clarke, 1959) 136-37; cited in Dillistone, *Christian Understanding*, 289.

cial and communitarian. For him, self-consciousness was deeply social: We come to an awareness of ourselves by entering into relationship with other selves in the larger society. But as we move into the larger society, our self-consciousness and desire for self-assertion increase, putting us on a collision course with the law, which however is necessary for the well-ordered life of the society. This collision is inevitable and tragic. It brings about a divided consciousness, a state of affairs from which individuals cannot free themselves by their own efforts. What is then required is both repentance and forgiveness:

> To retain his status as a moral agent in this situation, Royce argued, a person must somehow *participate* in the divine judgment passed on man's sin and not find that it comes merely in the form of an alien condemnation by a divine despot. . . . Royce's solution to the problem is to have the agent acknowledge the need to judge himself consistently; in recognizing responsibility for the deed for which we cannot forgive ourselves, we at the same time condemn ourselves to what Royce called "the hell of the irrevocable." The disloyalty of disobedience to the law is a fact and, although our consciousness may come to alter, the disloyalty remains.[63]

For Royce, Christ the Suffering Servant founded what he calls the Beloved Community on the far side of human disloyalty. The sin of self-assertion is recognized as condemnable in justice by the sinner, because he or she has already condemned himself or herself, but God forgives it from beyond human consciousness. Thus the act of disloyalty receives a new meaning, indeed becomes a *felix culpa* (happy fault): "The world is now better than it would have been had the treasonable act never taken place."[64]

Soteriology in the Twentieth Century

In this century H. R. Macintosh (d. 1936) has interpreted the Christ-event in relation to the dynamics of forgiveness. Moving from the pattern of forgiveness as we experience it among ourselves, he seeks to approach what happened between God the Father, Jesus, and sinners while Jesus died on the cross:

> Jesus . . . could not convey the Father's pardon to the guilty in absolute fulness except by carrying His identification with them to the utter-

---

63. Thus J. E. Smith, "William James and Josiah Royce," N. Smart, J. Clayton, R. Sherry, and S. T. Katz, eds., *Nineteenth-Century Religious Thought in the West* (Cambridge and New York: Cambridge University Press, 1985), vol. 2, 340.

64. Ibid., 341.

most point: at that point He gave Himself in death. The Bearer of forgiveness perishes in giving complete expression to the mercy and judgment which in their unity constitute the pardon of God. It is tragedy, it is that inscrutable and catastrophic collison of good and evil of which in its measure human life is full. But, if the phrase be permissible, it is not pessimistic but optimistic tragedy; Jesus does not fall along with His cause, He falls that in Him the cause may live.[65]

During the first half of the twentieth century, some of the giants of Protestant theology have been Karl Barth, Rudolf Bultmann, Paul Tillich (d. 1965), and Reinhold Niebuhr (d. 1971). All of them shared a mortal opposition to nineteenth-century Liberal theology.

Barth regards the doctrine of penal substitution as still valid, but places primary emphasis on God's supreme initiative in the event of salvation. God is not bound by a system of law or pattern of compensation. God's justice is God's righteousness, God's utterly transcendent holiness. In the face of divine righteousness the sinner is nothing, indeed less than nothing, not simply lacking reality but in total revolt against Reality itself. God's mercy is an act of fidelity to the truth, which even sin cannot destroy, that humankind is created in and unto Christ. The situation that the sin of human beings has brought about, contradictory as it is, does not dictate terms to God. Out of infinite compassion and mercy and in full fidelity to the primordial divine desire that all be in and unto Christ, Christ died for sinners. The just and holy one died in place of sinners, suffering the infinite distance—*diastasis*—between God and sinners both for their sakes and for the sake of God's desire for humankind, which goes deeper than what sin can thwart. By assuming sinful nature, Christ in utter obedience to the Father suffered all that all might be saved. As Barth writes:

> . . . there is no reservation in respect of [Christ's] solidarity with us. He did become . . . the brother of man, threatened with man, harassed and assaulted with him, with him in the stream which hurries downwards to the abyss, hastening with him to death, to the cessation of being and nothingness. With him He cries—knowing far better than any other how much reason there is to cry: "My God, my God, why hast thou forsaken me?" (Mk 15:34). *Deus pro me* [God for me] means simply that God has not abandoned the world and man in the unlimited need of his situa-

65. H. R. Macintosh, *The Christian Experience of Forgiveness* (London: Nisbet, 1927) 205–6; cited in Dillistone, *Christian Understanding*, 302. In reaction to excessive attention in modern theology to forgiveness as the meaning of atonement, Gustaf Aulén, in a now classic work, insisted on the importance of the biblical and patristic understanding of redemption as an event involving warfare between God and demonic powers at work in history. *Christus Victor: An Historical Study of the Three Main Types of the Idea of the Atonement*, trans. A. G. Hebert (New York: Macmillan, 1969).

tion, but that He willed to bear this need as His own, that He took it upon Himself, and that He cries with man in that need.[66]

All human beings have sinned differently, says Barth, but in all their sinning there is the one fundamental sin of self-justification. Thus all have had a sentence hanging over them, and all have been condemned by the All-Holy One. However, God has fulfilled the sentence by becoming the one judged: "What took place is that the Son of God fulfilled the righteous judgment on us men by Himself taking our place as men and in our place undergoing the judgment under which we had passed."[67]

Christ was able to be judged because he was human; because he was the Son of God, he could accept this judgment and had the authority to carry out the divine judgment, which is really grace, thereby liberating us from punishment, accusation, and condemnation.[68]

In Rudolf Bultmann's view all theories of redemption fail because they objectify something that is alive and challenging for us only when we are confronted by it as a living Word. Words "about" salvation let us off the hook, so to speak, by causing the *pro me* (for me) character of Christ's saving deed to become lost from sight and hearing. Talk about something that went on between God and Jesus on the cross, or discourse about a universal theory, falls short of the good news. Jesus of Nazareth is a figure belonging to Jewish history. His death as a historical fact is important in that it did occur. But the only access to the true significance of that death as *saving event* comes from receiving the Word about it in the preaching of the Church, when the death and resurrection of Christ are full of eschatological life, challenging us to authentic existence as persons who in faith are freed from the power of sin, death, and the Law and thus opened up, again and again, to the eschatological future of God beyond all idols and beyond the securities of the Old Adam.[69]

Paul Tillich, in his *Systematic Theology*, regards Jesus as the Christ in whom the New Being has emerged in the context of our estranged history. "New Being" is his term for "the undistorted manifestation of essential being within and under the conditions of existence."[70] Christ is the new unity of essential being (God) and existence (creation) who works reconciliation by living through our estrangement as the authentic "God-Man." The doctrine of the atonement describes the influence exercised

---

66. *Church Dogmatics*, vol. 4: *The Doctrine of Reconciliation*, part one, eds. G. W. Bromiley and T. F. Torrance (Edinburgh: T. and T. Clark, 1956) 215.

67. Ibid., 222.

68. Ibid., 222–23.

69. R. Bultmann, "New Testament and Mythology," ed. J. W. Bartsch, trans. R. H. Fuller, *Kerygma and Myth: A Theological Debate* (New York: Harper and Row, 1961) 38.

70. P. Tillich, *Systematic Theology* (Chicago: Chicago University Press, 1957), vol. 2, 119.

by the New Being in Jesus as the Christ. The doctrine must have two basic aspects, as the tradition has recognized: an objective aspect, which considers (in Tillich's terms) the manifestation of the New Being with its atoning effects; and a subjective aspect, which treats what happens to us when we participate in those effects.[71] Paul and Origen were right to pay attention to the victory over the demonic that is a primary effect of the atonement, objectively considered. Despite his juridical and quantitative views of sin and satisfaction, Anselm's main achievement consisted in his recognition that any message from God that does not include justice cannot give people a good conscience. Abelard's soteriology is thus inadequate, according to Tillich, because it does not remove our anxiety about guilt or the deep feeling inside us that we should be undergoing punishment.[72] Depth psychology has taught us that healing follows the torment of existential insight into one's being: a certain kind of suffering (not every kind!) leads through brokenness to well-being. Tillich maintained that for Anselm "when [the believing Christian] prays that God may forgive his sins because of the innocent suffering and death of the Christ, he accepts both the demand that he himself suffer infinite punishment and the message that he is redeemed from guilt and punishment by the substitutional suffering of the Christ."[73]

Tillich himself does not like the term "substitution," and praises Thomas Aquinas for his teaching that Christians *participate* in the redemption won by Christ through being members of the one body of which he is the head.

Tillich's six principles for any doctrine of atonement are instructive:

1) God alone creates the process of atonement.

2) The divine reconciling love and the divine retributive justice are not in conflict in God.

3) God's removal of guilt and punishment does not overlook the reality of existential estrangement.

4) God's atoning activity must be understood as God's taking on our existential estrangement and its self-destructive consequences and transforming them in Jesus the Christ.

5) The Cross of Christ is the effective expression (manifestation by actualization) of the divine participation in our existential estrangement.

6) Human beings also share in the manifestation of the atoning act of God through participation in the New Being, which is the being of Jesus as the Christ.[74]

71. Ibid., 197.

72. Ibid., 199.

73. Ibid.

74. Ibid., 200–3.

Finally, for Tillich, salvation possesses three moments: regeneration, or participation in the New Being; justification, or acceptance of the New Being; and sanctification, or transformation by the New Being.

Reformed theology's predilection for theories of penal substitution appears in recent decades in the Christologies of Wolfhart Pannenberg and Jürgen Moltmann.[75] *The Crucified God*, by Moltmann, presents not an atonement theology but a *Kreuzestheologie*, a theology of or from the Cross. In this book he explores the relationship of God and Jesus to sin and sinners on the cross. For Moltmann, the scholastic analogy of being (like known through like) must be replaced by the Lutheran version of the *coincidentia oppositorum* (the "coincidence of opposites"), the view that in matters of faith and salvation we learn saving truths about God *sub contrario* (under their opposites), from what is totally unlike God. Thus God's love is revealed to us on the cross not by some obvious compassion and fidelity on Christ's part, but in and through Christ's experience of being abandoned by God. According to Moltmann, the cry of dereliction mentioned in Mark and Matthew is the most important and perhaps the only authentic "word" uttered on the cross. The painful division expressed by this cry does not stretch simply between human reality and God the Father; it exists within the Godhead itself, and affects both the Son of God and God the Father in a way proper to each. This insertion of the *diastasis* into the life of God is reminiscent of Hegel. Critics have protested that, rather than doing justice to the reality of suffering and death and the power of sin, Moltmann "sublates" them into God's eternity, where they lose their bite and character as real threats to God's reign. Moltmann, on the other hand, believes that the classical understanding of an immutable God and the failure to think out the Trinitarian implications of Jesus' death on the cross have prevented theologians from realizing just how profoundly God (Father, Son, and Spirit) was in solidarity with sinners in the suffering and death of Jesus.

A major frame of reference for contemporary reflection on redemption is our evolutionary view of the world. Recent Roman Catholic thinkers who have sought in varying degrees to develop Christology within this perspective have been Pierre Teilhard de Chardin and Karl Rahner.[76]

Teilhard was a Jesuit priest and a paleontologist. His lifelong effort was directed toward exploring the profound links that he recognized between science and Christianity. As science learned more and more about the patterns of evolution and the ascending trajectory that is inscribed

---

75. Pannenberg, *Jesus—God and Man*; J. Moltmann, *The Crucified God*.

76. Among Anglican works one can refer to C. E. Raven's *Natural Religion and Christian Theology*, vol. 2 (Cambridge: Cambridge University Press, 1953) and his *Teilhard de Chardin: Scientist and Seer* (London: Collins, 1962). For a modern development of Irenaeus' notion of recapitulation, see L. S. Thornton, *Revelation and the Modern World* (London: Dacre Press, 1950).

in them, as well as about the entropic tendencies of matter that evolution appears to overcome, it became apparent to Teilhard that the author of the Letters to the Colossians and the Ephesians, with his sense that all things are destined to come to full stature in Christ, possessed a vision of reality that was deeply congruent with the direction of nature revealed to the scientist.

For Teilhard, the process by which matter, considered as energy, becomes centered on itself is a process that arrives finally at hominization and at evolution's attaining consciousness of itself. Yet the road to the human, especially the road trod by humanity in its efforts to form a global community, bears always the marks of the Cross, of suffering, loss, and sin:

> . . . a universe which is involuted and interiorized, but at the same time and by the same token a universe which labors, which sins and which suffers. Arrangement and centration: a doubly conjugated operation which, like the scaling of a mountain or the conquest of the air, can only be effected objectively if it is vigorously paid for—for reasons and at charges which, if only we knew them, would enable us to penetrate the secret of the world around us.[77]

But is this arduous ascent leading somewhere, to a goal that provides an *issue* for human effort, which otherwise seems doomed to entropy? Teilhard found in Christianity a word of hope that could be directed to the question raised by science about *the resurrection of the body*. Although he did not develop a theory of atonement, Teilhard tried to convince Christians that they must see the primary words of Christianity (incarnation, Cross and Easter, sacrifice, suffering, and especially redemptive love) as requiring a cosmic context, as in fact the ultimately adequate way of interpreting the cosmos, this world of ours, which is not finally a testing place for our souls but the extended body of our humanity, called to attain full stature in the *resurrection of the body*.[78]

A major objection raised against Teilhard's view of the Cross has been that it seems to pivot around an understanding of suffering as meaningful and goal-oriented. But sin always and suffering sometimes have the character of the absurd, and while ultimately in the light of faith Christ's Cross is the most beneficial event that has happened in human history, there is a level on which it remains obscene and unintelligible, no matter how frequently such evil victimizing has occurred in the course of history. This is not a problem peculiar to Teilhard; it relates to any attempt to

77. P. Teilhard de Chardin, *The Phenomenon of Man*, trans. B. Wall (New York: Harper and Row, 1959) 313.

78. See R. L. Faricy, "Teilhard de Chardin's Theology of Redemption," *Theological Studies* 27 (1966) 553–79.

"fit" sin and suffering into a theoretical, interpretive framework. What such framework could make sense of the Holocaust?[79] Any "higher viewpoint" turned on the Holocaust would be blasphemous. How could the Holocaust be counted among the "growing pains" of humanity or the rigors of the ascent that humankind is called to make through history to greater consciousness and union? What benefit or good could possibly "justify" such an evil, beyond all reckoning? Christianity does not "answer" such questions, or does so at its peril. The story of Jesus tortured and abandoned on the cross of execration is no "answer" placing the Holocaust comfortably "in context." Nor, for faith, does telling the story of the crucified Jesus reduce to the dismal avowal, "Here is simply one more victim." The solidarity of Jesus with those young mothers carrying their infants, or with children holding up a starving grandparent, as they walked into the gas chamber, demands that Christians avoid every form of "explanation" and instead spend their energies on becoming free of racism and other lethal biases, and contributing to changing the structures that foster such attitudes.[80]

Karl Rahner's understanding of "Christology within an evolutionary view of world" is not explicitly soteriological. He approaches this topic in relation to the dynamism of the world toward self-transcendence, a dynamism that becomes conscious self-transcendence in human beings. For Rahner, all created reality participates in the infinite actuality of God; it manifests this participation by being dynamically oriented, in and through its finite actuality, toward "more being." A prime example of this is the emergence of human beings from lesser beings on the evolutionary scale. Rahner states that human beings have emerged in all that they are from the prehuman, while affirming that they are ontologically more actual than—"superior" to—the prehuman. But how can less beget more? Rahner answers that question by appealing to his understanding of divine creation and concursus, i.e., God's creative causality in effecting the being and activity of creatures. God is interior to all creaturely activity, not as a supplementary reality "next to" the finite agent, but as the innermost ground of the finite agent's ability to be self-transcending. Thus God is the transcendent ground for the emergence of the human from the prehuman, but the prehuman, at a certain stage of development and given the right genetic and other conditions, is the worldly ground for the emergence of what is greater than itself. (Rahner is countering the more traditional scholastic view that the matter of human be-

79. J. T. Pawlikowski, *The Challenge of the Holocaust for Christian Theology* (New York: Anti-Defamation League, 1982); A. J. Peck, ed., *Jews and Christians After the Holocaust* (Philadelphia: Fortress, 1982).

80. See J. T. Pawlikowski, "Christian Ethics and the Holocaust: A Dialogue with Post-Auschwitz Judaism," *Theological Studies* 49 (1988) 649–69.

ings may derive from evolution but the spiritual soul is infused directly by God.)

In any case, Rahner sees all creation ordered by God to Christ, so that the natural dynamism toward self-transcendence is understood by its infinitely higher analogue, namely, the God-initiated emergence of Jesus Christ as the one who in his humanity is God's own way of being human. In Jesus Christ human nature transcends itself utterly, into the very life of God, thereby achieving its own full substantiality as human life lived in freedom. This self-transcendence of human nature is not, however, an achievement of human nature by its own efforts. Not at all. From the moment of its conception, the human nature of Christ was creatively assumed by the divine Word as its own forever. And it is precisely because of God's creative assumption of Christ's human nature that humankind has undergone a self-transcendence in Christ's humanity which is the goal of all evolution and of the entire cosmos. In and through Christ's life, death, and resurrection, human beings through living faith become sharers in the divine nature; through Christ they transcend themselves into God's life, and thus acquire their full humanity.[81]

Rahner wrote an essay on the question of how Jesus' death (and dying) on the cross caused our salvation. To begin with, he points out that the causality could not have been efficient because then Christ's love and suffering would have changed God the Father's will into a *saving* will. Yet, as we have seen now many times, this view stands in complete contradiction to the whole burden of the New Testament. Our salvation was God the Father's plan and desire, and therefore the Son was sent to us in the flesh.

Rahner reasons that the causality proper to Christ's death is quasi-sacramental. Just as a sacrament causes grace precisely by signifying it, so too does Christ's death. A sacrament is ultimately brought about by God's grace; both the divine life offered by the sacrament and the human cooperation given in administering the sacrament are grace. The "efficient cause," if you will, of the sacrament is God's grace. The sacrament as sign is the expression of grace; it is how grace becomes present as a humanly accessible reality. According to Rahner, the effective saving will of God is given irreversible expression in the death (and resurrection) of Christ, and thus becomes present in history in a way that the power of sin can never undo.[82]

This quasi-sacramental understanding of Christ's death is brilliantly developed in the writings of Sebastian Moore. Making use of modern psy-

81. K. Rahner, "Christology Within An Evolutionary View of the World," in *Theological Investigations*, trans. K.-H. Kruger (Baltimore: Helicon, 1966) vol. 5, 157-92.

82. K. Rahner, "The One Christ and the Universality of Salvation," *Theological Investigations*, trans. D. Morland (New York: Seabury, 1979), vol. 16, 199-224.

chology as represented by Freud, Jung, and Ernest Becker, Moore explores the crucifixion of Jesus as a process that happened once historically to the man from Nazareth, but is now a living mystery into which Christians can be drawn. Put very succinctly, he describes how sinners can connect with Christ on the cross only if they have experienced God's love for human beings piercing the armor of their guilt-riddenness or apathy. If they have been touched by God's love "underneath" their sinning, they can be led to bring their sinning out in the open in all its colors (in meditation this would correspond to Jung's idea of "active imagining"). Then they perceive their sinning as an attempt to do in the beloved, that is, their own self-in-Christ, which before their experience of God's love was the hated or rejected self, so that the sinning had a feeling of lethal "appropriateness." Their sinning turns into contrition as they recognize that they are hurting Christ in the hurting of their own (now beloved) Christ-self. The lance that pierces Christ's side releases the blood and water of contrition and forgiveness.[83]

Salvation as Liberation. Another approach to the meaningfulness of the Church's message of salvation is found in contemporary political and liberation theologies. Writers such as Gustavo Gutiérrez, Jon Sobrino, and Juan Luis Segundo have criticized traditional understandings on a number of counts, one of them being that the exclusive attention given to the "big moments" of death and resurrection has taken a lot of the critical "bite" out of the Christian message. Believers in Christ may feel that they need only participate in the grace of the sacraments, particularly baptism, confirmation, and Eucharist, to become and be renewed as sharers in Christ's redemptive merits.

On the contrary, these theologians insist that the life and ministry of Jesus are required to interpret his death and resurrection. The pattern of his acting and speaking day by day bespeaks one faithful to God's reign of justice and peace and in deep solidarity with the the poor and outsiders who confronted, challenged, and provoked the "powers that be" when he discovered their oppressive ways, their hypocrisy, and their substitution of externals for interior and social righteousness. Conflict was not something that Jesus avoided for the sake of false peace. God's reign, he knew, involved the sword of side-taking and conflict (Matt 10:34: "Do not think that I have come to bring peace on earth; I have not come to bring peace, but a sword.") Whether these words are pre- or post-paschal, they indicate the provocative character of Jesus' ministry. The pattern of

83. S. Moore, *The Crucified Jesus Is No Stranger* (New York: Seabury, 1977). Additional contemporary studies of salvation in terms of psychology are D. S. Browning's *Atonement and Psychotherapy* (Philadelphia: Fortress, 1966) and M. Jarret-Kerr's *The Hope of Glory: The Atonement in Our Time* (London: S.C.M., 1952). See also B. Tyrrell's *Christotherapy II: The Fasting and Feasting Heart* (New York and Ramsey: Paulist, 1982).

annunciation and denunciation in his words and deeds expresses a mode of life that, in ways adapted to their circumstances and gifts and calling, Christians are called to follow. Liberation theologies give much attention to Jesus' ministry, because it reveals the life and nature of the person who was to be resurrected by God.

The life we live before dying is a life that counts. What we contribute to the society we live in is our unique contribution, and it will not happen if we do not make it happen. The provisional, limited, and ambiguous character of our day-to-day existence should not lead us to think—as many Christians have tended to—that this life is merely an entrance examination for heaven. The new heaven and new earth are beginning here and now. Eternal life is among us now in mystery and hiddenness, but truly. It does not wait until after death, as good theology has always recognized. The Second Vatican Council affirmed this truth in a famous passage in *Gaudium et spes*, the Pastoral Constitution on the Church in the Modern World:

> We do not know the time for the consummation of the earth and of humanity. Nor do we know how all things will be transformed. As deformed by sin, the shape of this world will pass away. But we are taught that God is preparing a new dwelling place and a new earth where justice will abide, and whose blessedness will answer and surpass all the longings for peace which spring up in the human heart.
>
> . . . while we are warned that it profits a man nothing if he gain the whole world and lose himself, the expectation of a new earth must not weaken but rather stimulate our concern for cultivating this one. For here grow the body of a new human family, a body which even now is able to give some kind of foreshadowing of the new age.
>
> Earthly progress must be carefully distinguished from the growth of Christ's kingdom. Nevertheless, to the extent that the former can contribute to the better ordering of human society, it is of vital concern to the kingdom of God.
>
> For after we have obeyed the Lord, and in His Spirit nurtured on earth the values of human dignity, brotherhood and freedom, and indeed all the good fruits of our nature and enterprise, we will find them again, but freed of stain, burnished and transfigured.[84]

Juan Luis Segundo has recently written a five-volume Christology[85] addressed to nonbelievers, people who wish to consider the significance of Jesus Christ for themselves in terms of the demands and challenges of

---

84. *Gaudium et spes*, no. 39 in W. M. Abbot, ed. *Documents of Vatican II*, 237.

85. *Jesus pf Nazareth Yesterday and Today*, trans. by J. Drury, 5 vols. (Maryknoll, New York: Orbis, 1984–88).

the present age. After an extensive treatment of faith and ideology, he finds in the Synoptic Gospels a political Christology and in Paul's Letters an anthropological one. He then evaluates Ignatius of Loyola's *Spiritual Exercises* as a classic of spiritual-practical inspiration embedded in the deficient Christology of his age. In the final volume, he presents his own point of view. His formulation there was anticipated by previous studies on grace, original sin, and evolution.[86]

Segundo treats faith not as a supernatural virtue, but as the human connection with ultimate values. An ideology means for him any set of instruments, or means, that can be employed for the realization of those values. He invites the reader to regard Jesus Christ and Christianity not as realities conveying ideologies that are perennially useful, but as realities offering hope that the values one seeks to incarnate in history through praxis will not be destroyed by death. The ideology that provides the means for the realization of ultimate values can be drawn from any quarter, as long as it genuinely serves the values in question. Segundo would maintain, for example, that any contrast between Christianity and Marxism that becomes a contrast between a faith on the one hand and an ideology (in the pejorative sense) on the other is erroneous. On a concrete level, Christianity and Marxism are each a mixture of faith and ideology; that is, of attachment to fundamental human values which cannot be proved speculatively but which show their truth in the very dynamism to incarnate them, and the particular means employed to incarnate them. Jesus himself employed ideologies, i.e, tactics, to implement the values of the kingdom. He focused on the Jews almost to the exclusion of Gentiles; he was partial to the poor and the oppressed, and denounced those whom he thought hypocritical and self-serving. In all of this Jesus had to deal with limited energy and resources, which meant that he had to love concretely, that is, with a partiality that could not escape ambiguity.

The Christian belief in Jesus' ministry, death, and resurrection offers something that all those engaged in liberative praxis in our world would do well to attend to, says Segundo. The eschatological promise in the Christian message cannot be theoretically proved, but it can be wagered on, and lived out in hope. Furthermore, that message invites greater involvement in the processes of history, and not a flight from history, because we will act as if the "body of our good works" has a future such as the one referred to above in the quotation from *Gaudium et spes*. Again, it is important to remember that Segundo is writing for nonbelievers. It is hard to avoid the impression, though, that he is also writing for those Christians who think that Christianity and Marxism are in every single

---

86. *Grace and the Human Condition*, trans. by J. Drury (Maryknoll, New York: Orbis, 1973); *Evolution and Guilt*, trans. J. Drury (Maryknoll, New York: Orbis, 1974); *The Liberation of Theology*, trans. J. Drury (Maryknoll, New York: Orbis, 1976).

respect irreconcilable because the former is true faith and the latter is nothing but false and distorting ideology.

The Feminist and "Post-Modern" Critiques. A fundamental and far-reaching critique has arisen in recent years on the part of feminist thinkers. Their criticism revolves around the concrete reality of Jesus Christ as male Savior, that is, as the Savior whose gender is male.

The feminist critique of Christology is part of a larger critique of patriarchy: the overarching social, political, economic, and religious pattern of male dominance that has existed for millennia and still structures most people's consciousness. Indeed, most people are so embedded in this way of perceiving the world that patriarchy is like a pair of spectacles rather than something we remember to take off and examine. Feminists ask whether a male Jesus is necessarily related to a male God (God the Father), and whether those persons who gradually become liberated from patriarchal structures will have to let go of or repudiate Jesus as they would let go of or repudiate a male God.

For these critics it is not enough to emphasize the point that God is neither male nor female, that God as infinite Spirit is without sex. God is not a sexual being, but God does have gender in that we habitually perceive and relate to God as male, as eternal Father and eternal Son.

Can the male Jesus do justice to women and to men? Can the male Jesus do justice to the concerns of feminists and their struggle to emancipate themselves from male domination?

This is a challenge to Christianity that cannot be ignored. Paradoxically, however, one must be healthily traditional in answering this challenge. I mean, one must be careful to preserve some of the critically most important achievements of past Christology. When the best of the tradition maintained that the divine Word assumed human nature as such and thereby saved it, it was saying in so many words that, while Jesus necessarily had individualizing characteristics, these were not principles of salvation. Jesus' human point of contact, his human ground of relatability to other human beings, was and is his humanity as such, not his being a Jew of the first century, a carpenter, of a certain height and weight—or of a specific sex and gender. This does not mean that sexuality is not an extremely important dimension of our humanity, but it does mean that, *soteriologically*, Jesus' sex was not important.

As F. J. van Beeck has well expressed it, the contemporary Church would be harmfully untraditional if it made the maleness of Jesus an issue that somehow presided over Jesus' relationship to women and their concerns rather than allowing Jesus, in living relationship to women, to do justice to them. Christian women are invited to risk experiential relationship with Jesus (something different from thinking the concept of male savior), in order to discover whether he is indeed able to do such justice to them. After all, this is what has had to happen again and again in the course of Christianity. Not that Christian leaders or members of the faithful have always shown Christ's patience and inclusiveness with regard to the concerns of an age. Christ does not transform human concerns without first offering them real hospitality. He never needed to enter into a self-defensive posture born of anxiety and lack of trust in God or in the redeemability of all creation. Is the Church able to imitate its Lord?

The issues raised by feminists are many, and feminism itself is not a single program of ideas. Some feminists who were formerly Christians have left the Church and given up their Christian identity. Some have turned to goddesses for their religious life. Others have chosen to remain Christians and to work for change from within the Church, recognizing that the transformation of consciousness they seek will take a long time for its realization. Feminism has been helpful in inviting Christians to be more careful and inclusive in their understanding of redemption. The classical tradition in theology has tended to consider pride the greatest sin, which some feminist authors have argued is a very male view. For many women, pride has not been the chief temptation, but rather flight from self and from responsibility. Many women need to be liberated from a deficient sense of selfhood and a situation of oppression in which they submit to, or conspire with, structures that do not permit them to trust their own experience and assert themselves.[87]

The feminist critique can also make us more careful about the use of such terms as "self-sacrifice" and "being a victim." We find forms of self-sacrifice in which a person's rights and dignity are denied, and instances of self-sacrifice in which the self has never had an opportunity to develop. Jesus knew his dignity, and he knew his rights; in freely offering himself, he possessed a self to offer. In a word, there is authentic and life-giving self-sacrifice, but also inauthentic and destructive self-sacrifice.

If one is a victim in the sense that one is simply the object of others' choices and actions, without exercising any freedom regarding the situation others have placed one in, that is evil. We are meant to be persons, not objects at the disposal of others. As we have seen, the best of the tradition on soteriology maintains that, even in relation to God who creates all that we are, we are called to be cooperators in our own redemption, not despite the fact that our redemption is by grace alone but because of it. God does not want human beings to be passive recipients of divine forgiveness; God does justice to our being persons by involving Christ's freedom and ours in the process of our salvation.

In the Eucharistic Liturgy, Christ is called a victim: "See the Victim whose death has reconciled us to yourself" (The third Eucharistic Prayer).

---

87. This is part of the thesis of J. Plaskow, *Sex, Sin and Grace: Women's Experience and the Theologies of Reinhold Niebuhr and Paul Tillich* (Lanham, Md.: University Press of America, 1980).

But Christ's manner of living and dying gave special content to the terms "victim" and "sacrifice." Jesus' person was never a passive object at the disposal of others. He became an object insofar as he was captured, tortured, and crucified. However, he was living out choices he had made, choices that involved his complete solidarity with sinners in their goodness as God's creatures, his resistance to or active noncooperation with their sinning, and his assumption of the destructive effects of their sin while remaining in relationship with sinners.

Liberationist (including feminist) and political theologies offer substantial critiques of much of the legacy of the Enlightenment in the West. In a number of ways their critiques converge with those "post-modern" philosophers and theologians who challenge several fundamental features of contemporary life in the West: the current understanding of human persons as individual subjects of consciousness; the idea of consciousness as a set of a priori structures which "dictate" terms to the world around; the rational man's (sic) hunger to control and dominate the environment, both human and natural, without regard to the cost exacted of the human race and our planet; the will to power that is hidden (or not so hidden) in the achievements of technological reason and planning. These fundamental elements of modern humanity are the objects searching and scathing criticism by the likes of Fredrich Nietzsche, Martin Heidegger, Jürgen Habermas, and Michel Foucault.[88]

The challenges posed by "post-modern" thinkers run wide and deep, and the scope of this present study precludes an extensive consideration of their strengths and weaknesses. Indeed, this confrontation of postmodernity and Christian theology consitutes a substantial portion of contemporary theological discouse, at least in North America and Europe. The critique of the modern notion of the human person as individual subject, as monadic source of power and truth, connects up with the Christological tradition, since the very notion of person has been constructed out of theological needs experienced by the early Church to formulate something of its understanding of God triune and Jesus Christ as thoroughly one, thoroughly divine and thoroughly human. In chapter 7 we shall examine the development of the idea of Jesus Christ's personal unity, and it would be useful to ask, as one observes the development of that idea, whether the "post-modern" critique of the "totalitarian self" applies to the idea of person as it has found expression at key moments in the history of Christology.

88. See, for example, F. Nietzsche, *The Portable Nietzsche*, trans. W. Kaufman (New York: Viking, 1954); M. Heidegger, "The Question Concerning Technology," in *The Question Concerning Technology and Other Essays*, trans. W. Lovitt (New York: Harper and Row, 1977) 3–35; J. Habermas, *Jürgen Habermas on Society and Politics: A Reader*, ed. S. Seidman (Boston: Beacon, 1989); M. Foucault, *The Archaeology of Knowledge and The Discourse on Language* (New York: Pantheon, 1972).

Christ and Liberative Representation. Walter Kasper and Dorothee Soelle have noted that the idea of representation lies at the heart of Christian theology. More recently, Frans Josef van Beeck has developed the conceptual content of this notion as a key Christological theme. It will serve us well to give some attention to this idea.

Representation refers to a certain kind of relationship between persons, which can be helpfully contrasted with substitution. In the relationship of substitution, one person can take the place of another because he or she can perform the function of the other. For example, if I am changing the oil in the family car and am called away to the telephone for an extended conversation, I can ask my brother to finish the job for me. My brother has substituted for me, because the only relevant feature of either of us, at this point, is our ability to perform a particular function. From a functional point of view, one of us can substitute for or replace the other.

Precisely as persons, however, one cannot replace or substitute for another. A person in his or her freedom is unique and irreplaceable. There is a possible relationship between human beings that neither makes one of them redundant nor attempts to reduce either of them to a function or other thing-like dimension. This is the representative relationship, and it has been admirably examined by Frans Jozef van Beeck.[89]

When A represents B, A offers acceptance to B without seeking to coerce B. If B is rejecting A and treating A like an object, there is one thing that A can do in response that is genuinely loving rather than retaliatory (giving like for like). A can rely on special resources (the love that others have and have had for A, God's love for A) to remain steadily in relationship with B, despite B's rejection of A. In choosing this response A is choosing an attitude and relationship toward B that is not a function of B's relationship and attitude toward A.

By staying in this (unilateral) relationship, A effectively represents B. That is to say, A represents B's authentic self, the possibility of B's becoming an authentic person. A also represents B's inauthentic self, which makes its mark on A's person: A bears the brunt of B's inauthentic self. There is a third representative relationship going on here as well. A represents all those who by their love and support make it possible for A to continue to remain open to B, even in the face of the latter's rejection.

This scheme, we must remember, does not teach us how to remain concretely in relationship with another. We may stay in a representative relationship or, over time, return to one, even if we have had to move away for the sake of our physical safety. There are many ways in which we can live out a representative relationship, in close proximity or at a distance; wise choices are called for here.

---

89. F. J. van Beeck, *Christ Proclaimed: Christology as Rhetoric*, 412–16.

It is clear that Jesus finally chose to be very near to those rejecting him. His whole journey to Jerusalem embodied that choice. "He turned his face toward Jerusalem." This decision indicated neither a masochistic nor a fatalistic mentality. All the evidence speaks in favor of its being a decision that found its strength in reliance on Abba's love, a love that made it possible for him to love those who were persecuting him.

Jesus' ministry and his suffering and death were representative relationships. He did not manipulate others' freedom in order to "convert" them, nor did he do something to make their freedom useless or insignificant. Love seeks the other's free response, the other's free prospering. Authentic love (and representation simply denotes an aspect of love's power in weakness) does not treat the recipient of the representation as a replaceable object or set of functions. Love involves the freedom to address another's freedom and give it room.

On Calvary, Jesus represented those who were executing him, not only the soldiers but anyone who had had a hand in his arrest, torture, and death. Those guilty of Jesus' death were contemporaneous with him and directly implicated in the tragedy. It is not correct to speak of people living at other times and places as guilty of his death. Some Jews and some Romans were involved, for a tangle of motives in each case; their intention was to protect systems of religious, political, and personal value that they considered supreme.

In this tangle the ultimate initiative was God's in all that happened to Jesus. For his part, Jesus chose to identify with sinners in a creative and transformative way, without becoming subjectively a sinner. He *freely* became a victim of sinners so that what they were doing to themselves could be made manifest, and at the same time he identified with the created goodness of sinners, which they were victimizing by their sinning. This is another way of talking about the representative relationship that Jesus undertook in solidarity with sinners.

God does three things that we cannot do ourselves, alone on our own. First, God takes the supreme initiative in identifying with sinners in their plight, and in moving toward sinners with infinite compassion. Second, in and through Jesus, God brings about the historical offer of God's love for sinners. Jesus in his graced human freedom fully receives the divine life that God offers, and in turn offers it to sinners. Third, God in the Holy Spirit unites the offer and its acceptance in an unbreakable bond, and extends to sinners the power to accept the divine gift in a way commensurate with the gift. Thus the divine basis of Jesus' representation of sinners is the Holy Trinity. The human basis is Jesus' graced human freedom, which remains faithful to God and faithful to sinners, a twofold representation reflecting the twofold fidelity of God to God's own nature as love, on the one hand, and to sinners, on the other.

Conclusion

In this chapter we have considered the integral humanity of Jesus Christ and the nature of the salvation effected by him as Lord and Savior. We have seen that the Church has not always found it easy to affirm the consubstantiality of Christ with us, because of what might be termed the "pressure" of divinity on his identity. We have also seen that it was not enough to teach that Jesus' human nature is like us in all things but sin; it was equally important to affirm that Christ in his (risen) humanity stands in relationship to all human beings, offering them hospitality, identifying with their gifts, needs, anxieties, and causes, and desiring to transform all that is human and bring it into a new future.

This active, relational consubstantiality led us to examine the development of soteriology down through the ages in order to learn how various theologians have treated Christ's redemptive work. We observed that Christ's saving work can be called "liberative representation" because of the solidarity he lived out in his ministry and continues to exercise as the Risen Lord active in and through his Church and through all who struggle for a more human world. The liberation he seeks for human beings is threefold: ultimately, liberation from sin and its power, and full participation in the divine life and in Christ's eschatological life, made possible by that liberation; second, liberation from passivity and the flight from responsibility for history and its outcomes: the process of conscientization; and third, liberation from degrading poverty and oppression, which stunts the development of true subjects of history and recipients of forgiveness and divine life.[90]

We have also noted that both God's mercy and God's justice are involved in the redemptive process. God's justice is the realism of God's mercy, and God's mercy is the heart of God's justice. Making the world right, with all its distortions, exploitations, and oppressions, involves painful solidarity with the world in its creaturely goodness as the recipient of the divine promise of an eschatological future. The death and resurrection of Jesus assure us that all initiatives to heal our broken world and our broken relationships, and all efforts to transform the oppressive structures of our world, if done in love, will last forever and will share in the coming-to-be of God's reign, which will mean a new heaven and a new earth.

Up to this point we have examined the development of the Church's understanding of Christ as one who belongs wholly to God and to us and as one engaged in the work of liberative representation. We shall now turn our attention to the *person* of Christ, because it is in his person that he is able to exercise this representational role.

90. G. Gutiérrez, *A Theology of Liberation: History, Politics and Salvation*, trans. and ed. C. Inda and J. Eagleson (Maryknoll, New York: Orbis, 1988) 36–37.

7

Jesus Christ as the Personal Mediator of Salvation and Liberation

We have seen how extraordinarily difficult it is to do justice to the full divinity and full humanity of Jesus Christ and to trace the depths of his relationship to the One he called "Father" and to those to whom he was sent. The exploration of Christ's identity cannot stop there, of course, because a whole other dimension remains which up until now has only been mentioned obliquely, namely, Christ's personal unity. In this chapter we shall explore that rich and elusive dimension, and do so under three topics. First, we shall look at the main lines of the early Church debates that culminated in the Council of Chalcedon (451) and at some key moments in the developing Christology of Jesus' unity with God since then. Next, we shall consider the contemporary issue of the relationship of Christ and Christianity to other world religions. Our final topic will be the role of the Holy Spirit as mediator between God and creation and the continuation of the Spirit's work in the Church.

The Personal Unity of Jesus and God

The question of Jesus' unity with God may appear to be, and sometimes ends up being, a matter of metaphysical dexterity, of proposing a more subtle philosophical solution than previous theologians managed to offer. This is very unfortunate, because the fundamental question is the question of our salvation and liberation. What difference to humanity does union with God make? What happens to humanity as a result of such a union? What kind of God is revealed by such a union? What does the union that Jesus possesses with God and all creation mean for our union with God and all creation? What are the differences and similarities between our union with God and Jesus Christ's? What importance does such a union have for the liberation of humanity, and indeed of the entire groaning creation?

The Way to Chalcedon

As we study the fifth-century debates on the personal unity of Jesus, we will find some features that are off-putting for those who prefer to interpret Jesus' meaning in the context of the Bible and with a predilection for narrative over theory. For one thing, the sweep of salvation history is lost from view as intelligent and believing people turn their minds to the problem of Christ's internal unity. Furthermore, the union of Jesus' humanity and divinity becomes the focus, whereas in the New Testament the focus is Jesus' relationship to the Father, a relationship revealed and rendered "confessable" by the persuasive power of the Holy Spirit. This relational, Trinitarian matrix will not count for much when the debate grows heated about the precise nature of the union *within* Christ. And finally, unless one is very careful in one's use of language, the discussion of the divine and human in Christ will unavoidably suggest that these are equivalent values which the human mind can "oversee" and adjudicate with respect to their mutual connection. As a result, the transcendence of God will not receive proper notice and allowance in the process of reflection and criticism.[1]

Having voiced these cautions, let us move on to the debates themselves.

Logos-Sarx and Logos-Anthropos

The two major schools in battle over Christ's personal unity were located at two major ecclesiastical and theological centers of the Eastern Church, Alexandria and Antioch: the Alexandrian Word-flesh (*logos-sarx*), or "monophysite" (used here in a neutral sense of "one concrete nature"), theologians on the one hand, and the Antiochene Word-human being (*logos-anthropos*), or "diphysite" ("two-natures") theologians on the other. As far as the shape and intensity of the controversies were concerned, the principal exponent of the former view was Cyril of Alexandria; the latter view was represented by Theodore of Mopsuestia (remembered for the quality of his thought) and Nestorius of Constantinople (distinguished by his ecclesiastical notoriety).

---

1. These objections of F. Schleiermacher to Chalcedon have been repeated by contemporary theologians such as W. Pannenberg, *Jesus—God and Man*, 285–87; see also P. Schoonenberg, *The Christ*, 51–66.

As we saw earlier, the Alexandrian theologians were principally concerned with the unity of Jesus Christ, the fact that he had one single, concrete existence (one single "nature," as they used the term *physis*). The sole governing principle of Jesus Christ was the divine Word; his human reality was an instrument of his divinity, completely subordinate to it. Moreover, the animating power that enlivened the humanity of Christ was the divine Logos. As Cyril liked to phrase it, Christ was "one incarnate nature of the divine Word." For these thinkers, our redemption demanded that there be but one principle of unity in Jesus Christ, if what Christ did for us was to be *God's* action on our behalf. A fundamental religious insight at work among them was the conviction that, when the divine and the human are properly related, the human yields to the divine, thereby finding its fulfillment and completion.

Although the Antiochene theologians had no intention of denying Christ's unity, they also wanted to do justice to those passages in the New Testament which indicated that Jesus was a genuine moral agent who made human choices, was authentically obedient to the Father while having his own will vis-à-vis "Abba" (expressed, for example, by his praying "Not my will but yours be done"), genuinely suffered, was ignorant about some things, and grew in grace before God and the people. The reality of our redemption demanded that Jesus be a free "someone" before God while at the same time in the most intimate union with God. The union between the Logos and Christ's human reality that the Antiochenes proposed sometimes sounded as though it existed between two moral agents, at least if one took literally some of the metaphors they favored. For example, they compared the relationship between the human and divine natures of Christ to an intimate marriage relationship. They also used less personal (or interpersonal) images, suggesting, with one such image, that the Word dwelled most intimately in the human being Jesus as in a tabernacle or temple.

We turn now to a closer examination of the views of the two Antiochene theologians mentioned above, followed by the position of the principal defender of Alexandrian Christology.

Theodore of Mopsuestia and Nestorius of Constantinople. Theodore of Mopsuestia is a significant figure of the Antiochene "persuasion" during the period before Ephesus and Chalcedon who tried to do justice to the fullness of Christ's humanity and divinity, to their distinction and unity. His formulation, according to Alois Grillmeier, fell short of the Chalcedonian solution but pointed in its direction.

Theodore insisted that Christ's created soul animated his body and was the principle of the acts that were redemptive for us.[2] His use of the phrase

---

2. A. Grillmeier, *Christ in Christian Tradition: From the Apostolic Age to Chalcedon (451)*, 427.

"the assumed human being" suggested to his critics that he conceived the union of the divine and human in Christ as an accidental or moral one. Indeed, he was accused of teaching what his mentor, Diodore of Tarsus, proposed, namely, that Jesus' two different kinds of activity lead one to affirm that he is "two sons." Yet Theodore wrote: "[Christ] became man, they (the 318 fathers) said. And it was not through a simple providence that he lowered himself, nor was it through the gift of powerful help, as he has so often and still (does). Rather did he take our very nature; he clothed himself with it and dwelt in it so as to make it perfect through sufferings; and he united himself with it."[3] This way of putting the matter attempts to distinguish between the union of the divine and human in Christ on the one hand and the spiritual and moral union of God and the prophets on the other. Theodore taught that the divine Logos and the human reality of Christ are both *hypostaseis*, each with its own *prosôpon*, i.e., each is a concretely existent individual nature with its own "countenance" or form of appearance. When Theodore considered the conjunction (*synapheia*) of the two *hypostaseis* in Christ, he affirmed Christ as one *prosôpon*. By virtue of this conjunction, Christ is one "common" *prosôpon* in two natures. Christ's *prosôpon* is produced by the Logos, who gives his own *prosôpon* to the "assumed human being." Grillmeier summarizes Theodore's view by explaining that "the one divine *prosôpon* permeates and at the same time shapes the humanity of the Lord."[4] The divine *hypostasis* of the Logos (with its proper *prosôpon*) takes on a human nature not in order to form a third, combined nature but to communicate an equality of honor, greatness, and worship to the human nature as conjoined with the Logos, so that the Logos and the human nature share that equality. Equality with the Logos does not belong to the human nature *per se*, but only as a result of its communication by the Logos to the creaturely reality.

The Second Council of Constantinople (553) declared Theodore a heretic because of statements that some sympathetic scholars think have been considered outside of their context in his overall thought and Christological project. When assessing him for his positive contribution, we may say that Theodore was Chalcedonian in seeking the distinctions in Christ on the level of nature and his unity on the level of *prosôpon*. But he fell short of that council in not doing full justice to Christ's personal unity; he had not come (nor had anyone at this point) to the understanding that Christ's unity arose from the self-giving of the Logos to Christ's human nature, which produced a union "in *hypostasis* and according to *hypostasis*."[5] One of the contributions for which he is remembered is the characteristi-

---

3. *Catechetical Homilies* 8.1; quoted in Grillmeier, *Christ in Christian Tradition*, 161.

4. Ibid., 432.

5. Ibid., 434.

cally Antiochene emphasis that he gave to the roles of grace and free obedience in Christ's life, roles that were not always happily formulated but nonetheless offered food for thought to later theologians who would attempt to complete a Logos Christology with a Spirit Christology.

A second major figure, one who learned much from Theodore of Mopsuestia, was Nestorius, who for a brief time before being deposed was patriarch of Constantinople. When he assumed the patriarchate, he learned that there was a dispute already under way in his church about the use of the term *theotokos* ("Mother of God"; literally, "Godbearer") as a name for Mary, with its traditional appeal to the *communicatio idiomatum*. The "communication of attributes," which had been given conciliar sanction in the language and structure of the Nicene Creed, affirmed both divine and human attributes (eternal generation, temporal birth, etc.) of the one Son of God, Jesus Christ, by virtue of the incarnation. Nestorius entered the fray and proclaimed that Mary was to be called neither *theotokos* nor (the other alternative argued for) *anthropotokos* ("Mother of the human one") but rather *Christotokos*, as a kind of *via media* or middle way. He did not say that *theotokos* was wrong, only that it should be avoided. He wrongly taught, however, that *theotokos* was not found in the teaching of the Fathers, and wrongly opposed the traditional *communicatio idiomatum* because he thought that it smacked of Arianism and Apollinarianism, i.e., that it implied that the sole active principle in Christ was the Logos and that his humanity consisted solely in a passive body devoid of soul. Grillmeier points out that Nestorius, while misguided in his position, was not a formal heretic in his objection to the "communication of attributes," because the doctrine was still being debated among theologians and had not yet received dogmatic definition, which would only occur at the Council of Ephesus.

In the ensuing debate Nestorius regarded Cyril of Alexandria and his followers as Apollinarians, and it did not help matters that Cyril had taken his key phrase "one incarnate nature of the divine Word" from Apollinarius. Such a manner of speaking signified to Nestorius that the transcendence of the Logos was in danger, for Cyril's view had turned the Logos into the immediate subject of Jesus' sufferings. He insisted that the two natures remained distinct and unchanged by their composition. The comparison with the union of body and soul, a favorite of the Alexandrians, meant for Nestorius a necessary, natural union, not a free and gracious one, such as exists between the divine Word and the human reality of Jesus. Furthermore, Nestorius anticipated Chalcedon in objecting to Cyril's reference to two natures "from which" an inexpressible union is achieved; in order to affirm their perduring distinction, Chalcedon chose the phrase "in two natures," which stands close to Nestorius' way of putting it.

Until this century Nestorius was considered an outright heretic for holding what was taken to be the extreme Antiochene position, which insisted so emphatically on the distinction between the human and divine in Christ that it asserted the presence in him of two persons, two sons. The so-called heresy of Nestorianism was not Nestorius's view, as contemporary scholarship has shown with the help of his autobiography, *The Bazaar of Heraclides*, discovered in 1895. Indeed he wrote, "We know not two Christs or two Sons or Only-begottens or Lords, not one and another Son, not a first and a second Christ, but one and the same, Who is seen in His created and His increate natures."[6] Moreover, he resolutely rejected any form of adoptionism. Nestorius sought a foundation for Christ's unity, all the while presupposing that he *was* one being. His favorite term for the unity was *synapheia* or *coniunctio*, a term that official Church teaching refused to adopt. The term in itself was not clear, and Nestorius had to qualify it at each turn with adjectives such as "perfect," "exact," or "permanent." Like Theodore, he spoke of a "common *prosôpon*" or a "*prosôpon* of union" in which the two natures are united, and meant by this that a third *prosôpon* emerges from the union of the two natures, so that the historical figure of the Gospels, the starting point for Nestorius's analysis, is one person, one *prosôpon*.

Nestorius allowed that both divine and human attributes and activities could be predicated not only of the respective natures, but also of Christ's one common *prosôpon*. However, he could not say outright, as the *logos-sarx* theologians could, that "the incarnate divine Word died on the cross."

He limited the distinction in Jesus Christ completely to the order of nature, one nature being distinct from the other; there was no distinction or division within the Son. Grillmeier describes the debate with Cyril of Alexandria as reflecting the opposition between Cyril's intuitive view, argued with immense force and a kind of fateful simplicity, with repeated appeals to John 1:14 and to the Nicene Creed, and Nestorius' conceptual position, which is bolstered by an abundance of analysis. Nestorius is the more modern, Cyril the more archaic thinker.[7] Each understood the statements of his opponent in terms of his own position, thus misunderstanding the opponent, and rejecting his statements as contrary to the faith. The two men never found a common ground from which to assess their own and each other's statements. With regard to the *theotokos* dispute, Grillmeier paints an intriguing scene of a strong, objective, and sharp-minded Church leader sitting Cyril and Nestorius down and forcing them to clarify their positions in terms the other could understand and to listen well to the other's views. From such an encounter it would have become

6. Cyril of Alexandria, *Contra Nest.* frag. 49, cited in J. N. D. Kelly, *Early Christian Doctrines*, 314.

7. Grillmeier, *Christ in Christian Tradition*, 444–45.

evident that they did not really disagree on substantive points. But Church history was not to take such a direct, irenic, and disciplined path.

Cyril arrived at the idea of the one ultimate subject in Christ, but did not show himself able to grasp the concept of person as such. Nestorius, by contrast, stressed the individuality of the natures in such a way that a solution to the problem of the unity of Christ's person could not emerge. Yet, as I mentioned earlier, the Antiochenes did recognize that the problem of unity had to be solved on the level of person and not of nature.

In striving to place the unity of Christ on a level other than *physis*, Nestorius had at his disposal the concept of *prosôpon*, which meant for him, as it did for Theodore, a concrete entity's appearance or countenance, the way a thing is seen, judged, and honored, and the way it exists and acts. Thus *prosôpon* had everything to do with individuality; it did not mean person as that notion later developed. Furthermore, lacking a metaphysics of the substantial unity of spiritual beings (a deficiency not restricted to him but general at the time), Nestorius was not able to account positively for the special character of the Christological union.

Cyril of Alexandria. Cyril, the patriach of Alexandria, came to appreciate Christ's human soul as the "natural principle of suffering." In the Nestorian disputes he recognized a real human psychology in Christ, and so clearly set himself off from the Apollinarians. Nonetheless, he still used "one nature" language as a way of contrasting himself with Nestorius. His primary contribution was expressed thus: "God the Logos did not come into a man, but he 'truly' became man, while remaining God."[8] He insisted that the union was substantial, not accidental, moral, voluntary, or by grace alone. This insistence left its mark on the Chalcedonian solution.

Cyril was of course certain about the distinction between the human and divine in Christ, but he was unremittingly opposed to the slightest suggestion that after the incarnation they were separate or separable. He was even willing to speak occasionally of two natures, provided that no separation was signified.

For the Alexandrian patriarch, *physis* and *hypostasis* were closely associated, the former meaning individual existent substance and the latter existence and reality; the latter was the "rounding off" of the former in actual existence. When Cyril in his most famous formula spoke of the one incarnate nature of the Word of God, he intended *physis* to denote the divine substance and Word of God to denote the subject or personal bearer of *physis*. The substance was incarnate insofar as the human nature of Christ had its ground of existence and being in the Word. But lack-

---

8. Cyril, *Or. ad Dominias* 31 (*PG* 76, 1228C); cited in Grillmeier, *Christ in Christian Tradition*, 477.

ing a way of adequately distinguishing between nature and person, Cyril was not fully able to develop Christ's unity as a unity of person.

> Cyril in fact transfers the unity in Christ into the "personal realm" while ascribing a duality to the *natures*. Here he has anticipated the distinction of the Council of Chalcedon and has helped to lay its theological foundations. He has a greater depth of idea, just as the Antiochenes have the greater clarity of formula. The synthesis of the Church will combine the two.[9]

The General Council of Ephesus (431). Although the Third General Council of Ephesus produced no new symbol of faith, it emphatically affirmed the Nicene Creed and used the Creed as its criterion of orthodoxy in dealing with the controversy between Cyril and Nestorius. At the council the Creed was read aloud, followed by Cyril's second letter to the patriarch of Constantinople. The assembly then affirmed by vote that this letter was in accord with Nicaea. When Nestorius's reply to Cyril was then read out, the assembly voted that it did not accord with Nicaea. Consequently, Nestorius was condemned and deposed as patriarch and later sent into exile. The council affirmed the traditional use of *theotokos* by asserting that one and the same is the eternal Son of the Father and Son of the Virgin Mary, born in time after the flesh; therefore she may rightly be called Mother of God.[10] In addition, Cyril's third letter with its twelve anathemas against Nestorius was read out, but it was not voted on and so cannot be considered part of this council's definition of faith. Finally, the council affirmed that Jesus Christ's humanity is worthy of adoration by virtue of its union with the divine Word. The living tradition of worshiping Christ in the Spirit, which was a source of the Nicene assertion of the first *homoousios*, was now explicitly affirmed in connection with the dispute over Christ's unity.[11]

In order to further agreement between the followers of Cyril and the Antiochenes, at the behest of Emperor Theodosius II, John of Antioch wrote a profession of faith that was agreeable to Cyril. It did better justice to Christ's distinct human nature than Cyril had done.

The text reads as follows:

> We confess therefore our Lord Jesus Christ, the only-begotten Son of God, perfect God and perfect man composed of rational soul and body, begotten before all ages from the Father as to His divinity, and the same in the latter days born of the Virgin Mary as to His humanity, for a union (*henôsis*) of two natures has taken place. Hence we confess one Christ,

---

9. Ibid., 482.

10. Neuner and Dupuis, *Christian Faith in the Doctrinal Documents*, 140–41.

11. Ibid., 147–51.

one Son, one Lord. In accordance with this union without confusion, we profess the holy Virgin to be Mother of God (*theotokos*), for God the Word became flesh and was made man and from the moment of conception united to Himself the temple He had taken from her. As for the words of the Gospels and of the apostles concerning the Lord, we know that theologians have considered some as common because they are said of the one person (*prosôpon*), while they have distinguished others as applying to the two natures (*physeis*), reserving those which befit God to Christ in His divinity while assigning those which are lowly to Christ in His humanity.[12]

In a letter to the Antiochenes, Cyril enthusiastically endorsed this formula for reconciliation, and in the process let two sacred phrases of his own, "one nature" and "hypostatic union" (*henôsis kath' hypostasin*), slip into the background. Instead, he accepted the favorite Antiochene language of "one *prosôpon*" and a "union of two natures." The *communicatio idiomatum* described in the Formula of Union was also less thoroughgoing than Cyril's. On the other side of the ledger, Nestorius's condemnation was secured and *theotokos* established as sound doctrine. Furthermore, Antiochene "conjunction" gave way to Alexandrian "union," and the subject in Jesus Christ was identified as the Logos.

In 448 the "aged and muddle-headed archimandrite"[13] Eutyches was condemned by the Standing Synod of Constantinople. At the gathering the patriarch Flavian read out a profession of faith that foreshadowed Chalcedon: "We confess that Christ is of two natures (*ek duo physeôn*) after the incarnation, confessing one Christ, one Son, one Lord, in one *hypostasis* and one *prosôpon*." This first identification of *hypostasis* and *prosôpon* was to become part of the conciliar formula of 451.[14]

Christological Developments in the West. During most of the time when considerable advances were being made in the East there was little of significance occurring in the West, which was less given to speculation. Tertullian had made an important contribution with his notion of the two "natures" (*substantiae*) and two "conditions" (*status*) in Christ. He maintained that the Word assumed a complete human nature, with body and soul, the latter being an intrinsic requirement for our redemption. The ultimate guiding principle was the Word, who took the humanity on himself. Tertullian chose to say that the Word clothed itself with human substance, the only other possibility for him being that the Logos was metamorphosed (*transfiguratus*) into flesh. Each substance preserved its own characteristic qualities and activities after the union. Both substances

---

12. Ibid., 151.
13. Thus Kelly, *Early Christian Doctrines*, 331.
14. Grillmeier, *Christ in Christian Tradition*, 523.

belonged to a single subject, *in una persona*. While certain that his weakness and suffering and death must be ascribed to Christ's human nature, Tertullian was quite able to speak of "the sufferings of God" and to make statements such as, "God was truly crucified, truly died."[15] In this capacity he anticipated the "communication of attributes" as well as the short-lived Theopaschite ("divine-sufferer") formula of sixth-century Eastern theology ("one of the Trinity has suffered"), which was approved by the Second Council of Constantinople in 553 but eventually condemned by the Western Church.

In the fifth century the only major contribution made by the West to the Christological discussion was that of Pope Leo the Great in his letter to Flavian, patriarch of Constantinople (449). The letter contained a noteworthy interpretation of the twofold activity in Christ: "The character proper to each of the two natures which come together in one person being therefore preserved, lowliness was taken on by majesty, weakness by strength, mortality by eternity." It affirmed as well that "the true God was born with the complete and perfect nature of a true man; he is complete in His nature and complete in ours." And finally: "For each of the two natures performs the functions proper to it in communion with the other: the Word does what pertains to the Word and the flesh what pertains to the flesh."[16] This balanced statement found acceptance with both Antiochenes and Alexandrians, even if it failed to settle some of the questions with which the East had been wrestling.

The General Council of Chalcedon (451)

Two years later the Council of Chalcedon met. In an effort to combat Nestorianism and Monophysitism, it approved a creedal formula that provided, as far as was possible, a much-needed resolution for the controversies of the century. The creedal formula reads as follows:

> [Prologue]
> [The Council] opposes those who attempt to divide the mystery of the incarnation into two sons. It excludes from the sacred assembly those who dare to declare subject to suffering the divinity of the only-begotten. It withstands those who imagine a mixture or confusion of Christ's two natures (*physis*). It rejects those who fancy that the form of servant assumed by Him among us is of a heavenly nature and foreign to ours in essence (*ousia*). It condemns those who invent the myth of two natures of the Lord before the union and of one nature after the union.

15. *De carn. Chr.* 5; cited in Kelly, *Early Christian Doctrines*, 152.
16. Neuner and Dupuis, *Christian Faith in the Doctrinal Documents*, 152–53 nn. 609–12.

[Definition]
Following therefore the holy Fathers, we unanimously teach to confess
one and the same Son, our Lord Jesus Christ, the same perfect in divinity
and perfect in humanity, the same truly God and truly man composed
of rational soul and body, the same one in being (*homoousion*) with the
Father as to the divinity and one in being with us as to the humanity,
like unto us in all things but sin (cf. Heb. 4.15). The same was begotten
from the Father before the ages as to the divinity and in the latter days
for us and our salvation was born as to His humanity from Mary the
Virgin Mother of God.

We confess that one and the same Lord Jesus Christ, the only-begotten
Son, must be acknowledged in two natures, without confusion or change,
without division or separation. The distinction between the natures was
never abolished by their union but rather the character proper to each
of the two natures was preserved as they came together in one person
(*prosôpon*) and one hypostasis. He is not split or divided into two persons, but He is one and the same only-begotten, God the Word, the Lord
Jesus Christ, as formerly the prophets and later Jesus Christ Himself
have taught us about Him and as has been handed down to us by the
Symbol of the Fathers.[17]

The formulators of the Chalcedon statement intended two things: to
be deeply traditional, and to address the contemporary difficulties. They
appealed to the Nicene Creed, in which two different sets of attributes
or activities are attributed to one subject, the eternal Logos of the Trinity.
Building on Constantinople I and Ephesus in addition to Nicaea, they made
use of Cyril's second letter, Cyril's letter to the Antiochenes containing
the formula of reunion, Leo's letter to Flavian, and Flavian's profession
of faith. All the significant phrases in the text of the statement can be
traced to sources antedating the council.

Grillmeier points out that the principal target of the formula was the
Monophysite threat, since it was considered the greater danger. Consequently, the formula's language does not favor the Alexandrian cast of
mind because of the Monophysite exaggeration of that viewpoint. As a
result, after the council many Alexandrian theologians considered the formula excessively "diphysite," i.e., Antiochene.

The council asserted that Jesus Christ is one *prosôpon* and *hypostasis*,
thus employing these terms as synonyms without, however, defining their
meaning. The distinction within Christ was placed squarely on the level
of nature (*physis*), while the unity resided fully in the sphere of person.
The one and the same Christ (a phrase, as we have seen, reaching back

---

17. Ibid., 154–55 nn. 613–15.

to Irenaeus) was acknowledged "in" (not "out of" or "from") two natures, without confusion (*asugchutôs*) or change (*atreptôs*), without division (*adiairetôs*) or separation (*achôristôs*). Thus the council established that by their union the two natures were not merged into a third kind of nature, so that each or one of them ceased to be itself (as the extreme Monophysites would have it), nor were they separate individual realities (à la Nestorianism). Furthermore, the council affirmed both *theotokos* as a title for Mary and the full humanity of Christ, body and rational soul.

The terms employed by the council fathers were not technically defined. Grillmeier suggests that none of the assembled bishops would have been able to offer definitions of them; their sense of the terms' appropriateness and content was more intuitive than speculative. In general their aim was to find a formula that would be faithful to Scripture, the previous councils, and the best of the emergent theological tradition.[18]

The Chalcedon formula gives the strongest expression to the Christian faith-conviction that in Jesus Christ we meet God's transcendence within immanence, that God's total involvement and self-commitment to the world and its history occurred and occurs in Jesus Christ (in the web of relationship fostered by the Holy Spirit). The union of the divine and non-divine comes to its unsurpassable and irrevocable height and depth in the living unity-in-distinction that is the life and person of Jesus Christ revealed in the Spirit. In having to do with Jesus Christ, we have to do with one who is completely with and among us, one who is in total solidarity with us, and one whose solidarity with us is thoroughly rooted in his total solidarity with God. As mentioned earlier, the focus of the formula, and of the Christological controversies it sought to resolve, was the internal constitution of Christ. There is something static about the formula's portrait of Christ, as well. The two natures are spoken of as united and distinguished, but there is no sense of the vital relationship with the Father, opened up and supported by the Holy Spirit, that is so much the interest of the New Testament, particularly the Gospels.

This creedal statement does not offer a Christology, but a pointed formula that confronts and seeks to settle critical disagreements within the Church. The ongoing life of the Church at that time—its preaching of the gospel, its liturgical celebrations, its catechesis, and its witness to the presence of the Risen Christ through the Spirit in the lives of countless faithful Christians as well as Christian communities—supplied the wider and richer "lived Christology" for the support and protection of which the council fathers made their solemn dogmatic definition.

Like the councils before it, Chalcedon is an instance of teaching that is *de fide definita*. In other words, its teaching expresses the revealed truth

---

18. Grillmeier, *Christ in Christian Tradition*, 545.

of Christianity in terms which, while not always found literally in Scripture, are recognized as faithful to the core of the New Testament witness and, in light of the disputes and heresies of the time, affirmed as necessary for the sake of the unity of the Catholic Church and its fidelity to the apostolic faith.

The Chalcedonian formula is a *via media*, drawing on values both Eastern and Western, Antiochene and Alexandrian. In the ensuing years such a formula, of its nature, will please many and yet manage to offend and leave many unsatisfied. And it will remain a *crux interpretum* (a test-case) for theologians up to our own day.

Post-Chalcedonian Developments in Church Teaching

The Chalcedonian "settlement" did not leave things settled for long. Because of the council's aversion to extreme Monophysitism, Cyril's insight into the role of the Logos in Jesus Christ as the fundamental, guiding principle of his life and action was not included in the council formula. Rather, the balanced, antithetical parallelism of natures in one person held center stage. This would lead to a permanent schism between the Eastern and the Western Churches centered around the values disputed at Chalcedon. To this day there are Nestorian (Chaldean) Christians in Iraq, Iran, Egypt, Syria, South India, and the United States. The Syrian Monophysite church continues an ancient tradition as well.

Neo-Chalcedonianism was a movement of the sixth century that sought to mediate between the two factions. Its efforts came into Church teaching at the Fifth General Council, Constantinople II (553), which declared that "the Word of God has been united to the flesh according to the *hypostasis* and that, therefore, there is but one *hypostasis* or person, and that this is the sense in which the holy Council of Chalcedon confessed one *hypostasis* of our Lord Jesus Christ. . . ."[19] In speaking of a union "according to the *hypostasis*" (*kath' hypostasin*), this council was the first to state its support for a "hypostatic union."

This declaration has been taken to mean that the one *hypostasis* in Jesus Christ is the *hypostasis* of the Logos, and that the Cyrillian concern for the hegemony of the Logos thus entered official Church teaching. The Chalcedonian formula had not identified the one *hypostasis* and *prosôpon* as that of the Logos. The implication of this is that the humanity is of itself "anhypostatic": Jesus' humanity is not a reality existing in itself, but receives its subsistence from the Logos.[20] As we shall see below, this

---

19. Neuner and Dupuis, *Christian Faith in the Doctrinal Documents*, 160 n. 620/5.

20. On the problems connected with *anhypostasia* see D. M. Baillie, *God Was in Christ*, 2nd ed. (New York: Charles Scribner's, 1955). Leontius of Byzantium has frequently been depicted as maintaining a doctrine of *enhypostasia*, i.e., the view that an "impersonal" human nature was

has been translated into the view that Jesus was not a human person, in the modern sense of the term.

Those who were continuing the *logos-sarx* tradition began to argue that the councils of Chalcedon and Constantinople II had not decided anything about the activities of Christ. Pope Leo in his letter to Flavian had spoken of each nature's performing the activities proper to it and operating in common with the other nature, but this view had not found its way into conciliar teaching. The Alexandrian-oriented theologians feared that Leo's parallel view of Christ's activities implied that Christ's human nature was a separate and independent source of operation. On the contrary, they contended that there was but one will (Monotheletism) and one activity (Monoenergism) in Christ. They seemed to interpret the New Testament's statements about the oneness of Jesus' will with God's as entailing an ontic identity or oneness in being of will and operation between the humanity and divinity *within* Jesus himself. Condemning these doctrines, the Lateran Synod of 649 affirmed that in Christ there are truly and properly two wills and two actions: "the divine and human, intimately united in the same Christ God, since it is one and the same who by each of His two natures has worked our salvation."[21] The Sixth General Council, Constantinople III (680–681), repeated the condemnation of Monotheletism and Monoenergism, giving it the binding force of a general council: "It was necessary that the will of the flesh move itself (*kinêthênai*), but also that it be submitted to the divine will. . . . For just as His most Holy and immaculate flesh, animated by His soul, has not been destroyed by being divinised but remained in its own state and kind, so also His human will has not been destroyed by being divinised. It has rather been preserved. . . ."[22]

In the eighth century an opposite error arose, one that looked in the direction of Nestorianism rather than Monophysitism: Spanish adoptionism, whose principal spokesman was Elipandus, archbishop of Toledo. According to him, Jesus Christ in his divinity was the natural Son of God but in his humanity was thoroughly like us in all things except sin so that he, like us, was the adopted Son of God, although to a unique degree. This position implied the presence of two sons in Christ, and so was a return to the position of which Nestorius had been accused in the fifth century. Pope Hadrian I condemned this adoptionist doctrine in a letter to the Spanish bishops entitled *Si tamen licet* (793): "The adoption of Jesus

"enhypostatized" into the person of the divine Logos, thus becoming personal. Brian Daley, an acknowledged authority on Leontius, has observed that "[this idea] has nothing to do with Leontius of Byzantium, and that the recent history of this theory, given out under Leontius' name, is a history of the kind of inherited misconception to which theologians seem peculiarly prone" ("The Christology of Leontius of Byzantium: Personalism or Dialectics?," 1, unpublished article).

21. Neuner and Dupuis, *Christian Faith in the Doctrinal Documents*, 167 nn. 627/10, 627/11.

22. Ibid., 172 n. 635.

Christ the Son of God according to the flesh . . . the Catholic Church
has never believed, never taught, never accepted when it was asserted by
a wrong belief. . . . But with one voice with Peter she proclaims that
Christ is the Son of God, because there is one Christ, Son of God and
of man, not by grace of adoption but by the dignity of natural sonship."[23]
The Council of Frankfurt condemmed a Gallic version of Spanish adoptionism in 794, but the clearest statement on it came from the Council
of Friuli in 796 or 797 under the leadership of Paulinus, patriarch of
Aquileia: "We confess Him to be in each of the two natures the real, not
the adoptive, Son of God, because, having assumed the human nature
(*assumpto homine*), one and the same is Son of God and son of man without confusion and without separation. He is naturally Son of the Father
as to His divinity, naturally son of His Mother as to His humanity, but
He is properly Son of the Father in both (natures)."[24]

In early Scholasticism there were three principal theories of the unity-
in-distinction of Jesus Christ. Peter Lombard summarizes them in his *Sentences*, a compilation of the sayings of the Fathers with commentary on
various theological topics that was profoundly influential in the Middle
Ages.

Advocates of the *assumptus homo* theory contended that the Logos assumed not merely a human nature, but a complete human being. Abelard
first developed this theory in the twelfth century. While not denying that
in Christ there is only one person, he also maintained that there are two
subsisting subjects or *hypostases* in him. Thomas Aquinas severely criticized this position because it seemed tantamount to asserting that there
are two persons in Christ, even if the term "person" is avoided; it sounded
very much like Nestorianism. The second, subsistence theory affirmed that
there is only one *hypostasis* and one person in Christ. For Aquinas, this
was the authentic teaching of the Church and not simply a theological
opinion. The third theory also derived from Abelard's school. Convinced
that the direct union of body and soul always issues in a human person,
proponents of this position argued that Christ's body and soul were united
separately with the divine Word, somewhat as a man or woman puts on
clothing. Thus the third theory was called the *habitus* (or "clothing") theory, as a result of this comparison. Aquinas ruled the "clothing" theory
out because such a separated joining of the body and soul to the Word
would mean that the relationship of Christ's humanity to the Word would
be an accidental one.

The subsistence theory has been dominant in Western theology since
its inception. As Thomas expressed it, "A human nature is united to the

23. Ibid., 174 n. 638.
24. Ibid., 175 n. 639.

Son of God hypostatically or personally, and not accidentally. Consequently, with his human nature he does not acquire a new personal existence (*novum esse personale*), but simply a new relation of his already existing personal existence to the human nature. Accordingly, this person is now said to subsist not only in divine nature but also in human nature.''[25]

For Thomas, a distinction had to be made between *that which* exists and that *by which* or *according to which* something exists. The former is the subsisting, or immediate, subject of existence, called a supposit, *hypostasis*, or (with reference to beings of a rational nature) person. The latter is that by which a supposit exists in a determined way. An individual woman, a squirrel, and a rose are each supposits, subjects of existence. The human nature of the woman is not itself the actually existing woman. Therefore, the human nature of Christ is the created way by which or according to which the divine Word or Son exists. The whole Jesus Christ, by virtue of the Logos, is one supposit, one subject of existence; but the human nature, considered by itself, is not a supposit or subject of existence.[26]

Some contemporary Catholic theologians have disputed this distinction of Thomas, believing that it does not do justice to Christ's human reality. Although they do not contend that Christ is two ontological subjects or two separate persons, they do argue that the human nature of Christ, in order to be fully actual and real, must have its own act of existence, which is not independent but fully derived from the divine Word. We shall consider some of these objections to Thomas's distinction later in this chapter.

The entire history of the debate about Christ's identity reveals a dialectical process of affirmation and correction in which at one point the divinity and at another the humanity receives the greater emphasis. Some of the discussions are extremely technical and philosophical, turning on various understandings of terms and various theories of person, nature, existence and relationship—the most fundamental structures of reality. But the best of the discussions are valuable and significant for more than theologians; the most pastoral questions concerning the meaning of the human, and the involvement of the transcendent and immanent God in our history, are at stake, as well as the relationship of Christianity to other world religions. The most fundamental question is, When God and the human fully unite, what happens to God and what happens to the human, and what good news does such a union reveal to us about each?

---

25. *Summa Theologiae*, 3a. 17, 2 *resp.*; (in the Blackfriars edition, vol. 50, trans. and ed. C. E. O'Neill [New York: McGraw-Hill, 1965] 59).

26. Ibid., 223–24.

The Development of the Notion of Person: Philosophy and Theology

In the history of ideas, the Trinitarian and Christological controversies have left their indelible mark on the development of the concept of person. The Church's need to find a faithful way of speaking about the Father, Son, and Spirit in one divine nature and the one Jesus Christ in two natures led to the formation of a concept of person that previously did not exist. It also fostered an ongoing history of tradition with regard to person, as theologians and philosophers sought to deepen and refine the concept in the service of Trinitarian and Christological doctrine. In the modern period the shift to Descartes's subject and the subsequent understandings of the human person as distinct from the natural world—even those theories that were antireligious and antitheistic—stand in profound debt to the earlier, religiously oriented quest.

In this section I want to sketch the history of the concept of person as a mainly Christological concept that serves the understanding of Jesus' unity with God.

Patristic and Medieval Contributions to the Notion of Person. We have already seen that the two most important Christological terms in the East were *prosôpon* and *hypostasis. Prosôpon* did not originally mean person but rather, as we noted, the "form of appearance" of a being, the mask that an actor wore or the role he assumed in a play. In recent years attention has been focused on a method of scriptural exegesis called the "prosopological" method.[27] Employing this interpretive approach, Tertullian began with the dialogue structure of certain passages in Isaiah and the Psalms, from which he derived a rule that "the one who speaks and the one about whom he speaks and the one to whom he speaks cannot be seen as one and the same."[28] The Spirit is the one who makes the statement, the Father is the one to whom the statement is made, and Jesus Christ is the one about whom the statement is made. Thus this early application of the prosopological method to tracing the presence of the Trinity in Scripture viewed the three divine *prosôpa* as dialogical realities in mutual relationship, an important contribution to later Trinitarian and Christological theology.

Of the two terms, the one that became the more significant, particularly after Chalcedon identified it with *prosôpon*, was *hypostasis.* This term had no distinctive meaning at the beginning of the controversies. As noted above, it was equivalent to *ousia* and *physis*; it denoted "actual being" or "a concretely existing being." Etymologically, *hypostasis* derived from two words meaning "under" (or "from below") and "to

27. For a discussion and references, see M. Slusser, "The Exegetical Roots of Trinitarian Theology," *Theological Studies* 49 (1988) 461–76.

28. *Contra Praxeas* 11; cited in Slusser, "Exegetical Roots," 464.

stand." Thus it designated the concrete being that supported accidents, i.e., modifications and qualities that could not exist of themselves. It also came to mean a reality existing of itself and not as a modification of another, whether it was itself modified by accidents or not. Stoics added a nuance by allowing the term to mean not only actuality but actualization. In Neoplatonism it referred to hierarchically lower levels of being emanating from the One.

Trinitarian disputes led to the distinction between *ousia* and *hypostasis* by Athanasius, according to which the first term meant what was one in God and the second what was threefold yet completely equal in being and honor: threefold actualization or manifestation of the one Godhead. Here *hypostasis* is a term for the concrete, the dynamic, and the relational, since the Three in the Godhead were recognized as able to be one nature by being mutually related. Thus, as noted earlier, *hypostases* in the Trinity referred to the three ways in which the one divine nature subsists (Basil of Caesarea). In this case the term is an analogous one; Father, Son, and Spirit are not univocally persons, and the term is predicated of each in a way that involves similarity and difference. Thus in each context the meaning of *hypostasis* must be determined by the opposed relations through which the persons of the Trinity differ from each other.

For the Cappadocians, the *hypostasis* consisted of a set of *idiômata*, or individual identifying characters of a substantial sort. Since *prosôpon* meant the form of appearance, *hypostasis* and *prosôpon* were on their way to becoming synonyms.

Boethius was a sixth-century lay philosopher and theologian who wrote the classic *Consolation of Philosophy* and is considered one of the founders of the Middle Ages. His definition of person is of prime importance for the history of the idea: *persona est naturae rationalis individua substantia* ("a person is an individual substance of a rational nature").[29] Boethius intended this to be a definition of the Greek term *hypostasis*. Person is viewed here as a certain kind of entity, namely, a concrete nature that is spiritual, distinct, and separate from others (incommunicable). Leontius of Byzantium wrote that to be a person is "to be for oneself" (*to kath' heauto einai*) or "to exist for oneself" (*to kath' heauto hyparchein*), a definition that connects up with our contemporary, ordinary-language understanding of the human person.[30]

In a treatise attacking Monophysitism, the sixth-century Roman deacon Rusticus, nephew of Pope Vigilius, criticized Boethius' definition of *hypostasis* for rendering the term inapplicable both to the Trinity, because

---

29. *Liber de persona et duabus naturis* 3 (*Patrologiae cursus completus*, ed. J. P. Migne, Series latina, Paris, 1844–55, 64, 1343; hereafter *PL*).

30. *Contra Nestorianos et Eutychianos* 1 (*PG* 86, 1280 A).

the Three are not each a substance, and to Christ, because his human *nature* can be described using Boethius' definition although he is not a human person. For Rusticus, person was a term denoting totality, and Christ's human reality is not a totality; whereas the total Christ, the divine Word with the human nature to which it is united, is a person. Two persons cannot form one person.[31] He also translated *hypostasis* as *subsistentia*.

In the twelfth century Richard of St. Victor also criticized Boethius' definition on the grounds that it can reasonably apply to the divine nature, which is not, however, a person. He defined person as "the incommunicable existence of an intellectual nature" (*intellectualis naturae incommunicabilis existentia*).[32] In book four of *De Trinitate* he stressed that the person is an existent reality, that is, it must be understood in terms of its origin (*ex*). The three persons in the Trinity differ from each other insofar as the Father is from himself and the origin of the other two, the Son is from the Father and the origin of the Spirit, and the Spirit is from the Father and the Son but not the origin of a divine person. Earlier Richard laid stress on the person as a relational being, when he eloquently described how the excellence of the person (whether divine or human) consists in love of the other, or self-transcending love (*caritas*).[33] In the Trinity there is not only mutual love, but a mutual love that is thoroughly shared with a third. Thus the person is ex-istent in a double sense for Richard: not only with respect to origin, but also unto or toward (*ad*) another in a relationship of loving dedication. This twelfth-century idea can be a fruitful source for twentieth-century personalist and social thought.[34]

Edward Schillebeeckx has pointed out that Boethius, Rusticus, and Richard of St. Victor all articulated essential aspects of the notion of person: (spiritual) individuality, totality, and interrelationality. In their manner of realizing these (ultimate) dimensions, the Three in the Godhead are perfect persons, while the human person-in-community, being finite, is ontologically deficient as person.[35]

The individually oriented concept of Boethius was favored by Thomas Aquinas in his treatment of the human person, while he gave attention to relationality in his Trinitarian reflections. The relational notion of Richard was developed by the Franciscan Duns Scotus. For the latter, the basic constitutive relationship of the human being is to God. Between person and nature there is no real distinction. Of itself "person" is a nega-

31. *Contra Acephalos disputatio* (PL 67, 1239 B).

32. *De Trinitate* 4 (PL 196, 944–45).

33. Book IV, chs. 22, 24 (*PL* 196, 945–47); Book III (*PL*, 196, 915 B–930 D).

34. See, for example, E. Cousins, "A Theology of Interpersonal Relations," *Thought* 45 (1970) 56–82.

35. E. Schillebeeckx, *Jesus: An Experiment in Christology*, 663–65.

tive term expressive of the fact that certain beings are actually independent (a negative value for Scotus) or are apt to become independent when given the opportunity ("aptitudinal independence"). In any case, being a person in this context is a kind of fall from grace! Positively, each human being has an obediential potency for union with God, that is, a potentiality that God can fulfill if God so desires. As a matter of fact, God's power has fulfilled that potentiality in the case of Christ's human nature by uniting it with the divine Word. Although he was acutely aware of the relational aspect of personhood, Scotus robbed the notion of person of all positive meaning, for "union with God" and "being a human person" (= false independence) stand mutually opposed in his thought.[36]

The Sixteenth Century. In the sixteenth century the Dominican theologian Bañez (d. 1604) developed a Thomistic theory positing a real distinction between person and nature. The person is a *modus subsistendi*, which is added to the nature to make it subsistent. In the case of Jesus Christ, the divine Word takes the place of the finite *modus* that normally actuates a concrete human nature; the divine Word supplies the human nature with divine subsistence. Everything that belongs to the order of nature is retained; the only thing that is "subtracted" is the finite *modus subsistendi*. The difficulty with this view is that, from the Thomistic perspective, existence and essence are proportionate and total dimensions of the reality in question. Does the Thomistic perspective, therefore, allow a human nature to be truly concrete and existent without its own proportionate human act of existence?

The Jesuit theologian Suarez (d. 1617) preferred to speak of person as a positive reality, a mode of existence of the nature of the substantial order (*modus per se existendi*). As summarized by Walter Kasper, Suarez's person is "an essentially necessary form in which the nature is manifested but not a new ontological reality."[37] Jesus lacks this mode, and in its place God has created a *modus unionis* that unites the divine and human natures. Suarez thus maintained that nothing positive has been taken from Jesus' humanity, and that the bond of unity is a positive ontological determination. The issue is, Can a created *modus unionis* unite the two natures? According to Kasper, if Suarez was trying to say that personality is realized not just accidentally but essentially in certain relations, this would have relevance for some modern efforts.[38]

The Modern Period. In the history of philosophy, one of the hallmarks of modernity is the so-called turn to the subject, which was initiated in

---

36. H. Mühlen, *Sein und Person nach Johannes Duns Scotus* (Werl: Dietrich-Coelde Verlag, 1954).

37. W. Kasper, *Jesus the Christ*, 242.

38. Ibid.

the Renaissance and received its first pivotal philosophical expression in René Descartes. Western thinkers—whether empiricists like John Locke or idealists like Schelling, Fichte, and Hegel—began to recognize the constitutive role of human consciousness in the emergence of the world around them, and the success of the new mathematical sciences intensified that recognition. At the same time, the enormous cultural changes that occurred with the breakdown of the medieval synthesis and the religious conflicts of the Reformation period led many to seek certainty not in traditions or structures but in the core of human self-consciousness. Person and self-consciousness became correlative notions, and the previous consideration of person as a category of ontology gave way to an increasingly psychological approach. Walter Kasper is no doubt correct in saying that ontology needs to be rethought in personal terms without surrendering the attempt to think of the person as an ontological as well as a psychological reality.[39]

This concern for the centrality of consciousness in the notion of the person entered into official Church teaching in 1951 when Pope Pius XII issued the encyclical *Sempiternus Rex*, commemorating the fifteenth centenary of the Council of Chalcedon. Taking note of a recent Christological study by the French Franciscan F. Déodat de Basly (d. 1937), who tried to retrieve the *homo assumptus* theory by positing two ontological subjects in Christ (the human one being assumed by the divine), the encyclical declared that there cannot be two ontological subjects in Christ:

> Though it is legitimate to study the humanity of Christ from the psychological view-point, yet in this difficult matter there are some who too rashly set up novel constructions which they wrongly place under the patronage of the Council of Chalcedon. These theologians describe the state and condition of Christ's human nature in such terms that it seems to be taken for an independent subject (*subiectum sui juris*), as though it did not subsist in the person of the Word. Yet, the Council of Chalcedon, in complete agreement with that of Ephesus, clearly asserts that the two natures of our Redeemer were united in one person, and it does not allow us to put in Christ two individuals, so that some *homo assumptus*, endowed with complete autonomy, is placed by the side of the Word (*penes Verbum collocetur*).[40]

Because *Sempiternus Rex* did not prohibit theologians from affirming a psychological, as distinct from an ontological, subject in Christ, Catholic theologians began to develop theories of the hypostatic union that took Christ's human consciousness into more account than previous theologians

---

39. Ibid., 243.
40. Neuner and Dupuis, *Christian Faith in the Doctrinal Documents*, 187 n. 663.

had. The principal names in this connection are Pietro Parente, Paul Galtier (d. 1961), Maurice de la Taille (d. 1933), Engelbert Gutwenger, and Karl Rahner.

Parente represents the Thomist position, which reflects the Alexandrian concern that there be only one ontological and psychological "I" in Jesus Christ.[41] The divine person exercises direct influence on Christ's human consciousness, and the latter is directly aware of the hypostatic union and of the "I" of the Logos as its own. The divine "I" of the Word is the single center and source of all operations. Thus consciousness pertains to person and not directly to nature.

Galtier, on the other hand, predicates consciousness first of the nature, not the person.[42] This allows him to ascribe a human consciousness to Christ as part of the fullness of his human nature: Christ has a substantial human "I" as well as a psychological "I." Galtier distinguishes between the ontic and the psychological levels in Christ, and does not affirm that Jesus' human consciousness is affected by the hypostatic union; indeed, the divine "I" is outside of Jesus' human consciousness. Gutwenger seeks to mediate between the two preceding positions.[43] For him, personhood and "I"-consciousness are indivisible, and there is no "I"-consciousness without the awareness of being hypostatically united to the Word. He affirms a human act-center in Christ, but its "I" is the "I" of the divine Word. This act-center is not conscious of itself.

De la Taille has formulated a position according to which God's self-communication to Christ's human nature is a creative actuation as well. In other words, when God gives uncreated being away, this results in the creation of a dependent actuality. Thus in God's self-communication to the human nature of Christ, there occurs by virtue of the self-donation a quasi-formal causality, a subordinate but real subsistence, which is the created term of the uncreated actuation of Christ's finite human nature. Felix Malmberg follows de la Taille in this view.[44]

In his treatment of the question, Karl Rahner takes as his starting point the conviction of perennial philosophy that being and truth are interchangeable, that is, that being is intelligible to itself and thus being is conscious to the degree of its actuality as being. To the degree that an entity is actual, that entity is self-present and, through that self-presence, present to other beings. Given this affinity or proportionality between being and consciousness, it is equally appropriate to think out one's Christology either onti-

41. P. Parente, *L'Io di Christo*, 2nd ed. (Brescia: Morcelliana, 1955).

42. P. Galtier, *L'Unité du Christ: Être, Personne, Conscience* (Paris: Beauchesne, 1939).

43. E. Gutwenger, *Bewusstsein und Wissen Christi* (Innsbruck: Felizian Rauch Verlag, 1960).

44. M. de la Taille, *The Hypostatic Union and Created Actuation by Uncreated Act*, trans. C. Vollert (West Baden, Ind.: West Baden College Press, 1952); F. Malmberg, *Über den Gottmenschen* (Basel, Freiburg, Vienna: Herder, 1960).

cally or ontologically. Within the framework of an ontic Christology, one considers Christ in terms of ultimate metaphysical structures such as subsistence, nature, and person. Considering Christ in ontological terms, on the other hand, means giving precedence to the "logos" or consciousness of Christ. For now we need only remember Rahner's reasoning that the personal oneness of Jesus Christ is maximally conscious because it is the highest actualization of a finite human nature that has ever occurred. Nevertheless, and without contradiction, the human reality of Jesus possesses a relatively autonomous human self-consiousness by virtue of which he is related to the holy mystery of God in wonder, praise, and thanksgiving. The human self-consciousness of Jesus is no less "autonomous" for being so thoroughly united with the divine Word. Rahner contends that the best of the Catholic tradition has always recognized that the more dependent a creaturely reality is on God the more that creaturely reality is "something in and of itself." Drawing on de la Taille's argument, Rahner proposes, as noted earlier, that healthy autonomy and healthy dependence are directly proportional because God's creative act truly makes created entities *real* beings. For Rahner, the Chalcedonian affirmation remains central: The divine Word has creatively and unceasingly assumed the human reality of Jesus as its own human way of being, and has done so from the first moment of that human reality's existence.[45] Rahner is careful never to refer to Christ as a human person.

Michael Schmaus suggests that the metaphysical and psychological dimensions of a person are capable of being separated and regarded as different levels in the person, without injury to the notion of person. In this view Christ could be affirmed a divine person with a human nature, with the latter possessing as part of its completeness a human psychological "I."[46]

Wolfhart Pannenberg made a significant contribution when he pointed out that the unity between the human and the divine in Christ cannot be addressed directly, but only indirectly. Along with Schleiermacher and others, he recognized that participation in the Christological controversies and the great councils tended to speak of the internal relation between the two natures and did not allow the Trinitarian framework to remain at the forefront, with the result that the New Testament's emphases on the relationships between Jesus and his Father and Jesus and the Spirit received insufficient attention in the controversies after Nicaea. Pannenberg warns against turning the relationship between the human nature of Christ and the Logos into a kind of "I-Thou" relationship (even Karl

---

45. K. Rahner, "Reflections on the Knowledge and Self-Consciousness of Christ," *Theological Investigations*, trans. K.-H. Kruger (Baltimore: Helicon, 1966), vol. 5, 193–215.

46. M. Schmaus, *Dogma*, vol. 3: *God and His Christ* (Kansas City, Mo.: Sheed and Ward, 1971) 248.

Rahner, at times, seems to do this). The divine Thou in Jesus' life was and is the Father, Abba, the ultimate divine "whither" of Jesus' prayer and devotion. Statements about the internal unity of Christ are arrived at by way of faithful reflection on the unity of Jesus with the Father, their mutual openness and intimacy being effected by the Holy Spirit.[47] Walter Kasper, Edward Schillebeeckx, and many others have followed Pannenberg in this regard.

Piet Schoonenberg begins his Christology with the conviction that, according to the New Testament, Christ is one person and a human person. His Christology develops biblically from the eschatological transcendence of Jesus realized in the resurrection. In the incarnation the eternal divine Word of God became personal. The Dutch theologian understands person to involve both a proper center of self-consciousness and relationality. The divine Word, in and of itself, is pure relationality and is not person in the modern sense of an autonomous center of consciousness, except by virtue of filling Jesus' human person. Schoonenberg speaks of the *enhypostasis* of the Word in the human person of Jesus. Thus he reverses the traditional, Chalcedonian view according to which Christ is a divine *hypostasis* in whom the "anhypostatic" human nature subsists and is "hypostatized." Later he shows himself willing to speak of the human reality of Jesus rooted in the *Logos*, writing: "Consequently we may speak of an enhypostasis of Jesus in the *Logos* . . . and conversely of an enhypostasis of the *Logos* in the man Jesus."[48] The Logos supplies the man Jesus with his ultimate ontological support (= *hypostasis* in one sense), while the man Jesus "personalizes" the divine Word by giving it an "autonomous" center of consciousness (= *hypostasis* in another sense) that it does not have apart from the incarnation.

Three Recent Roman Catholic Views of the Hypostatic Union. Modern theology has been very critical of the "two-natures" model of Chalcedon. Many Protestant theologians have abandoned it as not capable of expressing the religious significance of the biblical revelation of Christ. They tend to agree with the Reformer Philip Melanchthon (d. 1560) who protested that the important thing was not Christ's natures but his benefits.[49] Thus Christ's role in the justification of sinners should receive primary attention, with metaphysical discussions of his internal constitution seen as, at best, a distraction. Liberal Protestant theology rejected the two-natures model for this reason, taking to heart Friedrich Schleiermacher's criticisms of its shortcomings, which we saw earlier. In the twentieth century Karl

47. Pannenberg, *Jesus—God and Man*, 334-37.

48. P. Schoonenberg, "Trinity—The Consummated Covenant," *Studies in Religion/Sciences Religieuses* 5 (1975) 111-16.

49. P. Melanchthon, *Loci Communes* (1521), II/1.

Barth has dealt with the model, while Rudolf Bultmann, Paul Tillich, and others have largely ignored it.

A number of Roman Catholic authors have distanced themselves from the model as well. We saw above Piet Schoonenberg's proposal to reverse the neo-Chalcedonian concept, and to speak instead of the *enhypostasis* of the divine Word in the human person Jesus or the mutual *enhypostasis* of Word and human person. James Mackey views the Thomistic assertion that Christ's human nature does not have its own subsistence, but that the one person in him is the Word pure and simply, as "the least possible form of Apollinarianism, or the most tolerable, whichever expression is preferred."[50] William Thompson, while sympathetic to Walter Kasper's interpretation of Chalcedon (see below), finds it wanting in terms of praxis and in the light of psychosocial and deconstructive critiques.[51]

At this point I would like to present three preeminent contemporary Roman Catholic positions regarding the personal unity of Jesus Christ and then consider some of their differences and similarities.

WALTER KASPER. In his Christology Walter Kasper considers the person abstractly and concretely. Abstractly the human person shows a twofold aspect: On the one hand it is a unique and incommunicable "I," and on the other hand, to use Aristotle's phrase, it is "in a certain sense everything" by virtue of the human spirit's dynamic openness to being, truth, and goodness. Thus the human person is a tension-filled mixture of singularity and universality, of givenness and self-transcendence. The "all" comes to a point and a presence in each Tom or Dick, Marie or Joan, and in all their interactions. But interaction is crucial: Human persons come to be themselves only in and through relationships. Kasper invokes the oft-quoted Hegel text here:

> Ethical life, love, means precisely the giving up of particularity, of particular personality, and its extension to universality—so, too, with "friendship." In friendship and love I give up my abstract personality and thereby win it back as concrete. The truth of personality is found precisely in winning it back through this immersion, this being immersed in the other.[52]

Being a human person involves living out a radical question as well. As Kasper writes:

50. *Jesus, The Man and the Myth: A Contemporary Christology* (New York and Ramsey: Paulist, 1979) 246.

51. *The Jesus Debate: A Survey and Synthesis* (New York and Mahwah: Paulist, 1985) 324–38.

52. G. W. F. Hegel, *Lectures on the Philosophy of Religion* vol. 3, ed. P. C. Hodgson, trans. R. F. Brown, P. C. Hodgson, and J. M. Stewart (Berkeley, Los Angeles, and London: University of California Press, 1985) 285–86.

> Because he is a person, a human being is placed on both horizontal and vertical planes; he is the being in the centre. Yet this centre is not inherently static, but one that is dynamically drawn out beyond itself. In this movement man never comes to rest. He is open to everything, fitted for society yet constantly thrown back on himself, orientated towards the infinite mystery of God, yet mercilessly bound down into his finitude and the banality of his everyday concerns.[53]

According to Kasper, God's self-communicating love posits Jesus in his intrinsic human reality. That human reality is creatively assumed by the divine Word (Augustine's *ipsa assumptione creatur*: "in the very assuming of it, it was created") so that it is hypostatically united to the Logos. Precisely because Jesus is no one other than the Logos, in and through the Logos he is also a human person. Conversely, the person of the Logos is the human person. Kasper quotes Thomas Aquinas approvingly: "In Christ the human nature was assumed in order that it be the person of the Son of God." And again: "The Word became flesh, that is, a man; as though the Word itself is personally a man."[54] In the incarnation the aspect of the human person that is open and indeterminate (its being "in a certain sense everything") is filled or definitively determined by the union of Jesus' humanity with the Word, "so that through his unity of person with the *Logos* the human personality comes to its absolutely unique and underivable fulfillment."[55]

EDWARD SCHILLEBEECKX. Edward Schillebeeckx begins with the conviction of faith that every creature is both "of God" and a reality in itself. These are two total aspects of the creature. Every creature shares in God's being, and God as actual infinity is preeminently all the being that the creature is finitely. The distinction between the infinite God and the finite creature lies in the creature, not as being but as finite. The difference beween Christ and other persons is thus not to be sought in his being "of God" and their being "realities in themselves."[56] With regard to the notion of person, Schillebeeckx distinguishes the relational dimension ("to be a person is to be a being related to other persons") from the "center of consciousness" dimension ("to be a person is to be a being in and for oneself"). The former he describes as the perennial, "structural" aspect, and the latter as the modern, "conjunctural" aspect.[57]

---

53. Kasper, *Jesus the Christ*, 246.

54. *Summa Theologiae* III q. 2, a. 10; original reading; *Queastiones disputatae* 5: *De unione Verbi incarnati*, a. 1.

55. Kasper, *Jesus the Christ*, 248.

56. Schillebeeckx, *Jesus*, 628–33.

57. Ibid., 662–63.

It is important to note that we are concerned here not with a moral distinction between altruism and egocentricity, but with an ontological one between dimensions of personhood: being oriented to the other, on the one hand, and being a self who is an end and not a means, of "absolute" value and not simply a "bridge" to something else, on the other hand. To be sure, for human beings there exists an enormous ontological tension in being finite, embodied persons, a tension that is immeasurably exacerbated and darkened by the power of sin at work in human history. Accepting our being as from and unto God through a threefold process— receiving selfhood from the significant others in our childhood and beyond; fashioning selfhood through a history of fidelity to our own obscurely perceived truth in patient struggles with our self in the eyes of others; and, finally, most assuredly gaining selfhood through the "loss" of self in healthy forms of self-giving love as we contribute to the human community—this is a project that seems to require more than a lifetime! Yet we are invited to believe that becoming a human person is indeed a lifetime's "death in love" (T. S. Eliot).

Schillebeeckx continues:

> Deeper than [Jesus'] *Abba* experience, therefore, and its ground, is the Word of God, the self-communication of the Father. This signifies some such thing as a "hypostatic identification" without *anhypostasis*: this man, Jesus, within the human confines of a (psychologically and ontologically) person-cum-human mode of being, is identically the Son, that is, the "Second Person" of the Trinitarian plenitude of divine unity, "the Second Person" coming to human self-consciousness and shared humanity in Jesus. . . . Thanks to the hypostatic identification of that in God which because of Jesus we call "Son of God" with Jesus' personal-cum-human mode of being, the man Jesus is a constitutive (filial) relation to the Father, a relation that in the dynamic process of Jesus' life grows into a deepening, mutual *enhypostasis*, with the resurrection as its climactic point. . . . In him the one divine consciousness and absolute freedom, as "filially" experienced within the Godhead (in complete union with the Father), is in alienation rendered man, as a humanly conscious centre of action and human (situated) freedom. In that sense we are bound to say that Jesus' being-as-person in no way lies outside his being-as-man; yet in the end we cannot (without all sorts of qualifications) describe him as simply and solely a "human person," for then there would indeed appear an inconceivable "over against" between the man Jesus and the Son of God. . . . What we might well say is that the Word itself became a "human person" without there being any "opposite" between this man and the Son of God. But this seems to me im-

possible apart from what is falteringly expressed or signified by "hypostatic identification" (I prefer this term to *unio hypostatica).*[58]

FRANS JOZEF VAN BEECK. The Dutch-born F. J. van Beeck sets his consideration of person in a context that he believes must situate all Christological talk: the *actus directus* of faith, the community's and individual's full surrender to Christ in worship and witness.[59] This is the context in which Christological language makes its full point; apart from this context the language loses its instrumental character and becomes the object of scrutiny and reflection in a way that will never deliver full significance.

Progress in Christology, for van Beeck, involves participation in a threefold dynamic, which he analyzes as the rhetoric of inclusion, the rhetoric of obedience, and the rhetoric of hope: incarnation (the acceptance of everything human); the Cross (God and Christ's presiding over and reforming of everything human); and resurrection (the offer of a final future to all humanity after it has been accepted and reformed). The author locates his discussion of Christ as a human person first in relation to the rhetoric of inclusion. Being a person, human dignity, and human rights are profound and unifying contemporary concerns. Christ can be named human person, just as he can be named teacher, shepherd, judge, bread of life, or liberator. Each naming of Jesus brings a human concern to him. Today human person ordinarily means being a center of consciousness and freedom. We are invited to name Christ this way, not only in books and lectures but also in living relationship with him, by letting our naming of him include our contemporary concern that socially and economically oppressed people have the chance to become true centers of consciousness and freedom and therefore to escape from simply living life as it is named for them by others. Thus we are asking Christ to accept and do justice to our struggle and others' struggles to become persons.[60]

One of the starting points of van Beeck, then, is ordinary language and the human concerns it represents. In the process of presiding over our concern with personhood, beyond identifying with our concern and with us as human persons, Christ will reveal what being a personal "center" means when it becomes thoroughly obedient to God and Christ and lovingly exposed to all that concrete humanity in its sin and grace can bring to it. Being a center turns into being totally and healthily centered on God and on the needs of the neighbor, so that center does not mean a "storm-free zone" of impregnability; rather, it means having no false foothold in oneself but "standing" in total dependence on God, a "standing" that in turn is rooted in God's full turning to us. Thus being *enhypostatic* (=

---

58. Ibid., 666–67.

59. F. J. van Beeck, *Christ Proclaimed*, 232–51.

60. Ibid., 167–77.

being someone who stands in oneself) shifts from meaning that one possesses one's center guardedly in oneself to meaning that one continually receives one's center as total gift from the other and total gift for the other. One stands in oneself best when one stands in the gift of God's self-communicating love and grace.[61]

Van Beeck is asking theologians to consider how language in general functions and how technical terms in particular signify. He does not want theologians simply to add to their Christological discussions the admission that Christ is a human person. The kind of impasse that thinkers get into on points like this rests partly on the mysterious character of what is being talked about (the infinite mystery of God and the finite mystery of humankind oriented to God). It also rests on a forgetfulness of language and the way it is meant to comport healthily with life and relationships.

In speaking of the union of the divine and human in Christ, van Beeck defines the Logos as "that modus of Jesus' concrete humanity in virtue of which he is irreducible to his own nature, and totally related to the Father in the Holy Spirit."[62] He sees himself in continuity with the great Antiochene theologian Theodore of Mopsuestia, and with figures such as Suarez, in allowing for the relative autonomy of Jesus' humanity. The difference between him and them is that for them the union as a *relatio substantialis* or *modus realis essendi* is between the Logos and the concrete humanity, while for van Beeck the Logos *is* the *modus essendi*. This *modus essendi* is gracious "being-related" to the Father, which "embeds and enhances and totally carries Jesus' individual human person."[63] With Pannenberg, Kasper, and Schillebeeckx, van Beeck predicates the first *homoousion* of Jesus on the grounds of his relationship to the Father. The Logos is Jesus' being related to the Father.[64] We must be able to tell an authentic narrative of Jesus, and to recognize that his human life had significance for himself as well as others. Jesus' human person can be the subject of predication in this sense: It was the human source of a human life of action and passion, intention and frustration, that grew and developed and changed.

The Logos is thus regarded first and foremost as relational, as the Father's full self-communication to Jesus and Jesus' being related to the Father. The Logos is not primarily *hypostasis* in the sense of substance (= a reality that is "on its own" or that stands by itself):

61. Ibid., 457–58.
62. Ibid., 432.
63. Ibid., 457.
64. Ibid.

Jesus' being-receptive, his irreducibility to his own individual nature is unowed to—and thus of a different order from—his person, while yet informing his person completely. Jesus' relational identity—though in itself not of a substantial nature, but an utterly gracious *modus*—totally determines his human individuality. In Jesus, the supposedly self-reliant solidity of human individuality finds itself utterly confirmed and established and upheld by a seemingly unsubstantial relatedness in total trust and surrender to God. This man Jesus comes into his own on the strength of his surrender to God, whom no one has ever seen.[65]

The next question that van Beeck addresses is the divine nature and the *hypostasis* of the Logos. His concerns are to retrieve the Antiochene (and, more importantly, biblical) idea that God's nature is infinite grace, and not to make an easy and false distinction between what is "of nature" and what is "of grace" in the case of Jesus Christ.

Van Beeck has drawn on the Eastern Orthodox theologian Vladimir Lossky's interpretation of the *hypostasis* of the Logos in Jesus Christ for the statement given above that Jesus Christ, *in* his humanity, is absolutely irreducible *to* his humanity, i.e., to his own human person in the contemporary understanding of that word as concrete individuality. In Lossky's view, the human person is not something added to the human nature: "There can be no question here of 'something distinct,' of something 'of a different nature,' but [only] of *someone* who distinguishes himself from his own nature, of *someone* who goes beyond his nature while still containing it, who makes it exist as human nature by this overstepping, and who yet does not exist himself outside the nature which he '*enhypostatizes*' and which he constantly exceeds."[66]

Van Beeck identifies Schoonenberg's "human person" (meaning center of consciousness and freedom) with Lossky's "human nature." Jesus' absolute irreducibility to his own human person van Beeck identifies as his *modus* of "being related" to the Father. Furthermore, van Beeck prefers to interpret the tradition's *enhypostasis* by way of Jesus' absolute irreducibility to his own human nature.

We need to speak of "this man Jesus and more," the "more" (the Logos) designating not some separate additional entity but rather this man Jesus' total relatedness to the Father. Van Beeck favors a totally relational Christology, in which Jesus' consubstantiality with the Father emphasizes rather than neglects what he calls the "inner quality" of Jesus' total relationship with the Father.

What the tradition terms the "enhypostatic human nature" of Jesus, van Beeck refers to as "the human person of Jesus in its concrete individ-

---

65. Ibid., 437–38.

66. V. Lossky, *In the Image and Likeness of God* (Crestwood, New York: St. Vladimir Seminary Press, 1974) 120; cited in van Beeck, 394–95 n. 86.

ual nature"; what the tradition names "the *hypostasis* of the Logos," he calls "Jesus' absolute irreducibility to his concrete individual nature in virtue of his total surrender to the Father," which surrender *qua* relationship is the *modus essendi* permeating all of Jesus' life, action, and suffering.[67]

To consider the reality of the Logos correctly, we should keep three conditions in mind: (1) that the Logos be thought of as God's inclusive openness to all reality; (2) that the Logos have a positive, inner affinity with the human life of Jesus; and (3) that the Logos be considered in strictly relational terms.[68]

Van Beeck believes that the tradition has not thought of the Logos in thoroughly relational terms but rather as hypostatic and substantial, the final subject of all predications made of Jesus Christ. The author is seriously concerned about the "harsh" way in which Jesus' divinity is often described. To speak of the Logos as *hypostatic* is to speak out of the freedom of speech (*parrêsia*) made possible by the resurrection; it cannot be divorced from the worship and witness that convey resurrection faith. The hypostatizing tendency of human speech combines with our own need to justify and maintain ourselves, leading us to regard relationship as the least trustworthy ("substantial") of realities, and that which is centered on itself (the "person") as the most solid, reliable, and "substantial."

Van Beeck's discussion combines a sensitivity to the connotative power of language, to the relevant metaphysics, and to the struggles of human beings for authentic salvation. Thus, rhetoric, being, and attitude go hand in hand in his reflections.

He does not exclude talk about the Logos as *hypostasis*, but he prefers and argues for the use of Logos as a way of speaking of Jesus' total receptivity and responsiveness to the Father, which are absolutely irreducible to his concrete human person. If one employs the expression "*hypostasis of the Logos*," van Beeck cautions that two rules should be observed. First, the Logos should not be used to imply that the divine Word is autonomous or set over against creation; rather, the Logos is pure receptivity and response to the Father, and in profound affinity with creation, indeed, the "divine space" of its occurrence. And second, the Logos may not be spoken of as *hypostasis* in a way which would imply that its omnipotence has anything to do with overpowering, or impassibility or impassiveness; gentleness, sympathy, and meekness are the characteristics of the divine Word.[69]

67. Ibid., 422.

68. Ibid., 447–52.

69. Ibid., 459–63.

Van Beeck summarizes his argument thus: "*In* this active and totally gracious receptivity toward the Father, Jesus is himself as the Logos: God's living address to humanity. This constitutes the inner quality of what the tradition, in a bold gesture of hypostatization, has called the divine nature."[70]

It strikes me that van Beeck has made a number of substantial contributions to the ongoing Christological conversation. He provides a much-needed breath of fresh air in spelling out the functions of metaphor and terminological language. He situates Christological utterance (and, indeed, all theological speech) in its permanently significant and signifying venue, namely, faith-filled response in worship and witness to the presence of the Risen Christ, to the glory of God in the persuasive power of the Holy Spirit. Beyond these contextual and methodological considerations, he allows for the ordinary use of the term "person" in contemporary speech in addition to highlighting the concerns represented by the use of the phrase "human person." Finally, he shows a relational understanding of the Logos that is positively shaped by the story of Jesus' ministry, death, and resurrection and thoroughly Trinitarian. Trinitarian theology and Christology are here united. It could also be argued that, despite the technical language that he employs, his approach is thoroughly preachable, because the ontological and terminological do not stray far from the attitudinal and relational.

The proposals of Kasper, Schillebeeckx, and van Beeck differ from each other and share similarities as well. They differ regarding the question of Jesus' being a human person. For Kasper, Jesus is a human person through the incarnation of the Logos in himself; i.e., the Logos communicates personhood to Jesus' humanity so that by virtue of the incarnation the human nature is "personalized." Schillebeeckx cautiously avoids all expressions that would describe Jesus as a human person, preferring the traditional usage. At the same time, inspired by Piet Schoonenberg, he speaks of the mutual enhypostasis of divine sonship and Jesus' human reality. Van Beeck takes person to mean concrete self-conscious nature, and speaks of the Logos as a thoroughly relational *modus essendi* (reminiscent of Basil, Karl Barth, and Karl Rahner). He is not opposed to naming the Logos a divine person under certain conditions, but favors respecting the ordinary usage of our day.

The three theologians agree in some significant ways, too. They all seek to integrate the perspective of the New Testament into their Christologies, so that the transcendent, Trinitarian context of Jesus' life and identity, as well as his historical relationships with other human beings in service and self-giving love, are always kept at the forefront of consideration. All three further recognize that in becoming human the divine Logos be-

70. Ibid., 438.

comes an individual center of consciousness gifted with an immeasurable and permanent depth of relationality. The unity of Jesus Christ is preserved by their common rejection of any possibility of a duality on the ultimate level of the root of Christ's being. The divine Logos is the ultimate source and ground of Jesus' reality not just as creative ground but, to paraphrase Augustine's language, as the "assumptive ground" of his human reality. In other words, the Logos has assumed the human reality in such wise that that human reality is the Logos's way of being human personally.

We find a pluralism in Roman Catholic Christology at the present time, yet this is not peculiar to the late-twentieth century. What is striking is that, given the criticisms of the "two-natures" model over several centuries, it continues to be the subject of creative reinterpretations that take those criticisms into account while not being dissuaded by them from reformulating the model by stretching it or turning it around. "Two natures in one person" is not an adequate summary of the view of a Kasper, Schillebeeckx, or van Beeck, but the values connoted by that traditional phrase continue to guide their theological explorations of Jesus' personal unity.

The Universal Significance of Jesus Christ: Encounter with World Religions

The person of Jesus and his unity with God and with his fellow human beings involves far more than a subtle metaphysical discussion of his inner unity, as should be clear from the preceding. When the limits of the Chalcedonian perspective have been acknowledged, reformulations are called for that allow for the full relationality of Jesus in the Spirit both to God-Abba and to the whole world. Consideration of Jesus' person leads to a necessary examination of the claims of Christianity regarding Jesus and itself in the face of other world religions and the contemporary world's growing acceptance (at least in some quarters!) of pluralism.[71]

Throughout its history Christianity has made universal claims about Jesus as the Christ of God.[72] Reflecting the New Testament conviction that "there is salvation in no one else, for there is no other name under heaven" given to people by which they are to be saved (Acts 4:12), Christian missionaries saw themselves sent forth to the infidels to save them from the fires of hell. For Catholics, Saint Francis Xavier offers one of the most dramatic examples of this view in the Church's history. He labored mightily to baptize as many Indians and Japanese as possible in

71. See, for example, D. Tracy, *The Analogical Imagination: Christian Theology and the Culture of Pluralism* (New York: Crossroad, 1981); and his *Plurality and Ambiguity: Hermeneutics, Religion, Hope* (New York: Crossroad, 1987).

72. On contemporary questions arising from this universal claim, see L. Richard, *What Are They Saying About Christ and World Religions?* (New York and Ramsey: Paulist, 1981).

order to assure their salvation. The perceived line between light and darkness, truth and error, also divided Christianity from its own Jewish roots, for the Jews were regarded not only as those who did not believe in Christ but as those who had been offered salvation by Christ himself and had rejected it. In 1442 the General Council of Florence declared:

> (The Holy Roman Church) . . . firmly believes, professes and preaches that 'no one remaining outside the Catholic Church, not only pagans,' but also Jews, heretics or schismatics, can become partakers of eternal life; but they will go to the 'eternal fire prepared for the devil and his angels' (Matt 25:41), unless before the end of their life they are received into it.[73]

The Catholic Church's attitude toward other religions has changed profoundly since the fifteenth century, and has done so very recently. The Second Vatican Council gave expression to this new attitude in several of its documents. *Nostra aetate*, the "Declaration on the Relationship of the Church to non-Christian religions," affirmed the unity of the entire human race and the commonality of all people's basic question about the meaning of life.[74] Within that context it further affirmed that the Catholic Church "rejects nothing of what is true and holy in these religions. With sincere respect she looks on those ways of conduct and life, those precepts and teachings which, though differing on many points from what she herself holds and teaches, yet not rarely reflect a ray of the Truth which enlightens all men." Then it adds, "But she proclaims and must ever proclaim Christ, 'the way, the truth and the life' (John 14:6), in whom men find the fullness of religious life, and in whom God has reconciled all things to Himself (cf. 2 Cor 5:18f)."[75] In *Ad gentes*, the "Decree on the Church's Missionary Activity," the point is again made that Christ alone can purify other religions while at the same time fulfilling them.[76]

In the encounter between the major religions of the human race—Christianity, Judaism, Islam, Hinduism, and Buddhism—similarities and differences must both be given adequate attention. Christianity, Judaism, and Islam are religions of the Book, and all three are monotheistic faiths. Christianity interprets itself in relation to Judaism, and Islam interprets itself in relation to Judaism and Christianity, recognizing the Old Testament prophets and Jesus the prophet as holy figures who prepared the way for the revelation to Muhammad, Allah's greatest prophet. Hinduism is a religion of one God and many Gods, with a tolerance for other religions provided that they are incorporated into the larger pattern of

---

73. Neuner and Dupuis, *Christian Faith in the Doctrinal Documents*, 279 n. 1005.

74. Ibid., 288–89 nn. 1019–20.

75. Ibid., 289 n. 1021.

76. Ibid., 289–91 nn. 1023–26.

Hinduism. In its less "popular" forms, Buddhism is not a theistic religion, for a God distinct from the world would perpetuate the illusion of dualism. Nirvana is a condition of enlightenment in which one moves beyond all dualism, and even that is not a moving "beyond." Each of the world religions is a comprehensive world-view that is not regional but about *all* of reality. Thus each of these religions will interpret the other world religions (insofar as it has contact with them) with reference to itself.

Not long ago Peter Schineller offered a helpful map of the various ways in which Christian theologians interpret the Christ-event in universal terms. His focus is the different positions theologians have assumed regarding the indispensability of Christ for universal salvation.[77] He recognizes four major positions: exclusive ecclesiocentrism, inclusive and constitutive Christology, theocentric and normative Christology, and the view that Christ is one among many mediators of salvation. By a constitutive position he means one according to which salvation would not be a reality if the life, death, and resurrection of Christ had not occurred; Christ is necessary and sufficient as the one who brings about salvation. A normative Christology, on the other hand, sees Christ as the supreme God-given norm, pattern, or example of salvation, in the light of which other legitimate paths to salvation may be illuminated, evaluated, and purified. No Christology can be constitutive without also being normative, but a Christology can be normative without being constitutive. Vatican II clearly taught an inclusive, constitutive, and normative Christology, at least in outline, in *Nostra aetate* and *Ad gentes*.

Karl Rahner's Christology is inclusive, constitutive, and normative, and his theory of "the anonymous Christian" has become controversial as liberal views on the universality of grace and salvation have been challenged by more radical approaches. For Rahner, the term is not a label to pin on to non-Christians but a technical term to be used among Christian theologians in their reflection on the relationship between Christianity and non-Christians. The divinizing and forgiving grace of salvation is mediated to the entire human race throughout all of history through the unsurpassable event of Jesus' life, death, and resurrection. This grace is universal and pure gift; it affects and qualifies everyone's existential situation, whether they are explicitly aware of that fact or not. The grace that saves is the grace of Christ, and so all those who are open to the mystery of their lives and live out a fundamental yes to that mystery are themselves "Christian," in the sense that they live by Christ's grace.[78]

77. J. P. Schineller, "Christ and Church: A Spectrum of Views," *Theological Studies* 37 (1976) 545–66.

78. K. Rahner, "Anonymous Christians," *Theological Investigations*, trans. K.-H. and B. Kruger (New York: Seabury, 1974), vol. 6, 390–98; idem., "Observations on the Problem of the 'Anonymous Christian,'" *Theological Investigations*, trans. D. Bourke (New York: Seabury, 1976), vol. 14, 280–94.

This view has been criticized as another example of Christian imperialism in relation to non-Christians. The latter are being told that they do not really know who they are, and that Christians are the privileged ones who can name them in their truth. Rahner has countered that he can easily do without the term "anonymous Christian," but that his belief about Christ and salvation goes to the heart of Christian self-interpretation. Jesus Christ is constitutive and normative for all salvation throughout all of history, a point that is pithily expressed by his phrase. He recognizes that one or more Buddhists from their world-religious standpoint might want to call Rahner and other Christians "anonymous Buddhists," and he could understand their doing that.

Recently some theologians have pressed for an understanding of Christianity that would incorporate religious pluralism to a much greater degree, giving more latitude to the respective values of the various world religions.[79]

Hans Küng has criticized Rahner's notion of "anonymous Christian" as bringing in by the back door what may no longer be admitted through the front door, namely, the centrality of the Roman Catholic Church. For Küng, the notion entails the conviction that all that is good and valuable in other world religions is already somehow present in Christianity. He proposes that, when encountering other religions, Christian theology be theocentric rather than ecclesiocentric.[80] In his own work, *Christianity and the World Religions: Paths of Dialogue with Islam, Hinduism, and Buddhism*, he attempts such an encounter.[81]

John Hick, a Protestant theologian, goes further. He argues that Christianity must understand itself theocentrically, though in such a way that Jesus is interpreted as one of the most significant expressions of the divine, yet in no way exhaustive or definitive for any but Christians.[82] Indeed, Christians will be able to appreciate the value of other religions when they recognize the mythic character of their own incarnation language.[83] This does not mean that all religious traditions are equally good; they are capable of being "graded": "Is this complex of religious experience, belief, and behavior soteriologically effective? Does it make possible the

79. P. F. Knitter, *No Other Name? A Critical Survey of Christian Attitudes toward the World Religions* (Maryknoll, New York: Orbis, 1985); J. Hick, *God and the Universe of Faiths* (New York: St. Martin's, 1973); J. Hick and P. F. Knitter, eds., *The Myth of Christian Uniqueness* (Maryknoll, New York: Orbis, 1987).

80. H. Küng, *On Being a Christian*, trans. E. Quinn (Garden City, New York: Doubleday, 1976) 98.

81. Trans. P. Heinegg (Garden City, New York: Doubleday, 1987).

82. J. Hick, *God Has Many Names* (London: Macmillan, 1980).

83. J. Hick, ed., *The Myth of God Incarnate* (Philadelphia: Westminster, 1977).

transformation of human experience from self-centredness to Reality-centredness?"[84]

Raimundo Panikkar, an Indian Catholic theologian, distinguishes between the historical Jesus as an incarnation of the Christ, and the Christ as found in other world religions. While Jesus is the Christ, the Christ is not found in an exhaustive way in Jesus.[85]

Another Catholic theologian, the American Paul Knitter, is developing what he recognizes is still a minority view among Catholic and indeed all Christian theologians. According to him, full and genuine dialogue among the world religions will occur only if they approach each other as genuine *equals*. After a long study of current perspectives on the topic, he suggests

> . . . that Christians, in their approach to persons of other faiths, need not insist that Jesus brings God's definitive, normative revelation. A confessional approach is a possible and preferred alternative. In encountering other religions, Christians can confess and witness to what they have experienced and come to know in Christ, and how they believe this truth can make a difference in the lives of all peoples, without making any judgments whether this revelation surpasses or fulfills other religions. In other words, the question concerning Jesus' finality or normativity can remain an open question.[86]

The supreme difficulty facing any Christian theology wishing to assert that Christ is normative but not (inclusively) constitutive for salvation is the Church's confession of him as the incarnate Son of God. That central affirmation declares that Jesus' humanity was the real symbol of the divine Word, and was personally one with that Word. In and through the finitude of Jesus' humanity, God in the person of the Son entered fully into human history. Unlike prophets and saints before and after him, Jesus Christ is not simply a word *about* God, a word that no matter how saintly and full of grace it is, is in principle surpassable because it is a finite word about the infinite God. Rather, he is that Word become flesh in a real, historical event of salvation. It is significant that to make room for his view, Hick must treat the incarnation as a "myth" expressing a truth that can be posed in other, quite different terms. Once that is done, one must ask whether the very center has not been taken out of Christianity, and one is dealing with a religion of one's own invention.[87]

84. J. Hick, "On Grading Religions," *Religious Studies/Sciences Religieuses* 17 (1981) 451.

85. R. Panikkar, *The Unknown Christ of Hinduism*, rev. ed. (Maryknoll, New York: Orbis, 1981).

86. Knitter, *No Other Name?*, 205.

87. See J. Hick, ed., *The Myth of God Incarnate*.

The Universal Action of the Holy Spirit

As it is understood by Christians, the Christ-event involves the most singular of historical events—the birth, life and death of Jesus of Nazareth—and the most universal of movements—the incarnation of God's universal saving purpose (*mysterion*). What God all along, from "before the foundation of the world" (Eph 1:4), intended for creation, came to unsurpassable expression in the life, death and resurrection of Jesus, one member of creation, who is confessed the forerunner of the new creation, of the new humanity (Heb 7:20).

In order to do justice to this universal role of Jesus and as a fitting way to conclude this book, we need to become more explicit about the significance of the Holy Spirit of God in the Christological event. The Spirit is the revelatory medium of Jesus, the One who anoints Jesus to his task and role in salvation (Mark 1:10 par.) and leads him in his ministry (Luke 4:1-2). The Spirit opens up Jesus' humanity to the full self-communication of the Father, so that Jesus can know what the Father is doing and pattern his actions on the Father's. The Spirit is the connaturalizing "atmosphere" that Jesus breathes in and breathes out, as it were, that allows Jesus to savor his kinship with the Father, and lets that be the inner guidance of his life's choices. Jesus does not lord it over the Spirit, but is obedient to its promptings, learning over time how to discern and choose the Father's values, which are the values of the reign of God. From another perspective, the Spirit is the openness of the Father to Jesus, the full gift of the Father to Jesus, which infinitely respects the limitations of Jesus' humanity, while opening that humanity to the infinite riches of the Father, Source of all life and being. Because of the Spirit's role in the unity of Jesus and the Father, the Father is not "too much" for the humanity of Jesus, but rather that humanity can be the full expression of the Father (the divine Word incarnate). And thanks to the Spirit, the humanity of Jesus is not "too little" a reality for the adequate reception of the Father's infinity.

The Holy Spirit is the revelatory medium of Jesus in yet another sense, or in another direction. Not only does the Spirit open Jesus to the Father and the Father to Jesus, but the Spirit opens the world to Jesus, and Jesus to the world.

Throughout human history God has been striving to unite the world to the divine life, through the goodness of creation and in struggle against the sin and evil that rack creation. God has sought to achieve this liberating and unifying salvation through concrete, particular, external events, on the one hand, and through the interiority of persons (singly and collectively), on the other. For human history and all of creation is composed of the compenetration of "outside" and "inside," of the external, particular, datable, concretely encounterable, and focused, on the one hand,

and the interior, pervasive, time-binding, and "horizonal," on the other. For example, when an authentic Christian prophet speaks, we encounter an individual person uttering discrete human words, one after another. At the same time, we can experience an openness to the prophet, the truth of the words, and the God in whose name the prophet speaks. That man or woman is bearer of the Spirit, inspired by the Spirit, and the Spirit who moves him or her inspires us to hear the words as revelatory of God. The compenetration of external, spatio-temporal dimension (the "categorical") and the interior, unlimited, horizonal dimension (the "transcendental") of human life in the world corresponds, by virtue of God's creative and self-communicating activity vis-à-vis the world, to the compenetration of the distinct but inseparable events of the incarnation of the divine Word and the outpouring of the Holy Spirit. God dwells in and among us as the singular one and as the all-pervasive one, two distinct but mutually related ways in which God is among us as God. God is neighbor and the ultimate source of our openness to the neighbor; God is offer to us and in us as well as the full and adequate reception of the offer: Word and Spirit, Jesus and the Church-in-the-world.

Throughout human history the Spirit has sought to fashion an adequate historical expression of who God is and the adequate historical response to that expression of who God is. Christians believe that God sought it in Israel, then in a remnant of Israel, and finally, "in the last days," in Jesus, God's total self-expression (Word). It is as though salvation-history involved a cone which narrowed in the Christ-event, to open up again in the outpouring of the Spirit. The narrowing refers not to a restriction of the expansive presence and action of the Spirit, but to the particularization that the incarnation involved, one human being (in a particular, concrete community, of course) became the climactic place of divine self-disclosure and self-communication. In a most patriarchal age, he was a most non-patriarchal individual, in a most imperial age, he showed himself a most uncredentialed and "powerless" individual, in an age profoundly given to "ins" and "outs," he spoke and acted in a most inclusive way. The Spirit brings us to the particular, singular, and unique (Jesus and my neighbor), while Jesus invites us to the amplitude and encompassing mystery of the Spirit, that prevents us from making an idol of any person, event or cause, so that we allow God alone to be God, that we might be what we are called to be: truly human, together.

Conclusion

It is apparent that Christology is alive and well in the nineties, with new challenges facing it as Christianity seeks to learn what it is to be a world-

Church, a truly global community. Christians believe that Jesus Christ is able to do justice to the human and to do so out of the resources of God, who alone is the measureless measure of the authentically human. The effort to re-think Jesus' personhood, and the need to re-interpret his significance, even for Christians, in the light of Christianity's encounter with the other world-religions, are not separate enterprises, because the person is the place of meeting of God and the world, of the individual and the community, of self and "the other." Jesus' capacity to contain and do justice to the differences in our world will be tested in new ways in the coming years, as Christians learn to "pass over" to the viewpoint of other believers and then to return to their own place, deepened and otherwise altered. The framers of the Chalcedonian model did not have such challenges in mind in the fifth century, but the Christ they professed, the Christ who emptied himself for the flourishing of others and the glory of God, offers still the pattern for Christians today, as they find themselves invited to relinquish a customary sense of self, by turning to the other, whether the marginalized, the poor, the oppressed, or people of different faiths, in the trust that a deeper Christian identity and more profound paschal hope will be given them in that "passing-over."[88]

88. J. S. Dunne, *The Way of All the Earth: Experiments in Truth and Religion* (New York: Macmillan, 1972).

Recommended Readings

Chapter I: Introducing Christology

Van A. Harvey. *The Historian and the Believer: The Morality of Historical Knowledge and Christian Belief*. Philadelphia: Westminster, 1966. A perceptive study of the relationship between Christian commitment to, and secular knowledge about, Jesus Christ.

H. Richard Niebuhr. *Christ and Culture*. New York and San Francisco: Harper and Row, 1951. A classic study of five principal forms of Christology in relationship to their respective cultures.

Jaroslav Pelikan. *Jesus Through the Centuries: His Place in the History of Culture*. New Haven: Yale University Press, 1985. A sensitive exploration of the Christ's significance in art and culture over the centuries.

William M. Thompson. *The Jesus Debate: A Survey and Synthesis*. New York: Paulist, 1985. A very intelligent reflection on the contemporary situation of Christology and its prospects.

Chapter II: The Ministry of Jesus of Nazareth

James D. G. Dunn. *Jesus and the Spirit: A Study of the Religious and Charismatic Experience of Jesus and the First Christians as Reflected in the New Testament*. Philadelphia: Westminster, 1975. Offers a helpful perspective on Jesus' relation to *Abba* and to the Spirit.

John P. Meier, *A Marginal Jew: Rethinking the Historical Jesus* (New York: Doubleday, 1991). The first of several volumes about the historical Jesus.

E. P. Sanders. *Jesus and Judaism*. Philadelphia: Fortress, 1985. Sanders situates Jesus in the Judaism of his time showing the continuity and the differences between him and his contemporaries.

Edward Schillebeeckx. *Jesus: An Experiment in Christology*. New York: Seabury, 1983. A detailed study of the Jesus of the ministry as well as the early traditions of Jesus' death and resurrection.

Gerard S. Sloyan. *Jesus in Focus: A Life in Its Setting*. Mystic, Conn.: Twenty-Third Publications, 1983. A fine treatment of the Jewishness of Jesus.

Chapter III: The Death of Jesus of Nazareth

Martin Hengel. *Crucifixion in the Ancient World and the Folly of the Message of the Cross*. Philadelphia: Fortress, 1977. Gives a strong sense of the obscene character of death by crucifixion in the time of Jesus.

Gerard S. Sloyan. *Is Christ the End of the Law?* Philadelphia: Westminster, 1978. Treats the sensitive questions of Jesus' conflict with his own faith-tradition and of the Pauline understanding of the Law.

Sebastian Moore. *The Crucified Jesus is No Stranger*. New York: Seabury, 1977. A profound reflection on the process by which we can identify in a transforming way with the crucified Jesus.

Jürgen Moltmann. *The Crucified God: The Cross of Christ as the Foundation and Criticism of Christian Theology*. New York and San Francisco: Harper and Row, 1974. A contemporary Reformed theology of the Cross that has been ecumenically influential.

Chapter IV: The Resurrection of Jesus

Sebastian Moore. *The Fire and the Rose and One*. New York: Seabury, 1980. A speculative and helpful exploration of Jesus' resurrection in terms of the disciples' religious experience.

Jerome Neyrey. *The Resurrection Stories*. Wilmington, Del: Michael Glazier, 1988. A fine analysis of the New Testament resurrection narratives.

Pheme Perkins. *Resurrection: New Testament Witness and Contemporary Reflection*. Garden City, New York: Doubleday, 1984. Combines a detailed treatment of the New Testament material with an investigation of the meaning of death and afterlife in contemporary Western culture.

James D. G. Dunn. *Christology in the Making: A New Testament Inquiry into the Origins of the Doctrine of the Incarnation*. Philadelphia: Westminster, 1980. A thorough, balanced study of the development of the notion of incarnation in the New Testament.

Chapter V: Jesus Christ, God's Total Self-Gift

R. P. C. Hanson. *The Search for the Christian Doctrine of God: The Arian Controversy, 318-381*. Edinburgh: T and T Clark, 1988. A fine study of a crucial period in the history of the doctrine of the divine Word.

Monika Hellwig. *Jesus the Compassion of God: New Perspectives on the Tradition of Christianity*. Wilmington, Del: Michael Glazier, 1983. The author argues for a variety of ways of expressing the mystery of the divine Word in history.

J. N. D. Kelly. *Early Christian Doctrines*. 5th edition. New York and San Francisco: Harper and Row, 1978. A standard work on the early development of doctrine.

G. L. Prestige. *God in Patristic Thought*. London: S.P.C.K., 1964. Still a classic treatment.

Chapter VI: Jesus Christ, The First of the New Humanity

F. W. Dillistone. *The Christian Understanding of Atonement.* 2nd edition. Minneapolis: Fortress/Augsburg, 1988. A very interesting treatment of the relationship of theologies of the atonement to their cultural contexts.

Paul S. Fiddes. *Past Event and Present Salvation: The Christian Idea of Atonement.* London: Darton, Longman and Todd, 1989. A contemporary account of soteriology that seeks to do justice to both the event of two thousand years ago and the ongoing saving action of God.

Jaroslav Pelikan. *The Christian Tradition, A History of the Development of Doctrine I: The Emergence of the Catholic Tradition (100–600).* New Haven: Yale University Press, 1971. The author traces the main lines of early Christological development.

Edward Schillebeeckx. *Christ: The Experience of Jesus as Lord.* New York: Seabury, 1980. A detailed study of grace, sin, and salvation in the New Testament and in relation to our contemporary world.

Chapter VII: Jesus Christ as the Personal Mediator of Salvation and Liberation

Frans Jozef van Beeck. *Christ Proclaimed: Christology as Rhetoric.* New York: Paulist, 1979. A brilliant study of the relationship of Christological doctrine to Christian discipleship and worship.

Dermot A. Lane. *The Reality of Jesus: An Essay in Christology.* New York and Ramsey: Paulist, 1975. A brief, but clearly written and helpful overview of Christology.

Piet Schoonenberg. *The Christ: A Study of the God-Man Relationship in the Whole of Creation and in Jesus Christ.* New York: Herder and Herder, 1971. A landmark study of the personhood of Jesus in the context of all of God's activity in the world.

Karl Rahner. *Foundations of Christian Faith: An Introduction to the Idea of Christianity.* New York: Seabury, 1978. The sections on the human person, grace, revelation, and Christology lead the reader into the heart of this major theologian's lifework.

Index